D0198837

Walter Reid was educated at Oxford University, where he read history, and Edinburgh University. He is now based in the west of Scotland, but spends part of the year in France. His previous work includes *To Arras, 1917* (Tuckwell Press), and *Churchill 1940–1945: Under Friendly Fire*, also published by Birlinn.

Architect of Victory

Douglas Haig

WALTER REID

BIRLINN

In memory of
Ronald and Elsie Reid
and for
Janet, Julia and Bryony

This edition published in 2009 by
Birlinn Limited
West Newington House
10 Newington Road
Edinburgh
EH9 1QS

www.birlinn.co.uk

Copyright © Walter Reid 2006

The moral right of Walter Reid to be identified as the
author of this work has been asserted by him in accordance
with the Copyright, Designs and Patents Act 1988

All rights reserved. No part of this publication may
be reproduced, stored or transmitted in any form without
the express written permission of the publisher.

ISBN: 978 1 84341 045 4

British Library Cataloguing-in-Publication Data
A catalogue record for this book is available from the British Library

Designed and Typeset by Hewer Text UK Ltd, Edinburgh
Printed and bound by Cox & Wyman Ltd, Reading

CONTENTS

LIST OF ILLUSTRATIONS

Family group *circa* 1865
Douglas Haig about three years old
The Rt Revd John Percival
Haig's statue at Clifton
Haig's mother, Rachel Haig
Haig's sister Henrietta
'Daisy', Countess of Warwick
Doris Haig
Haig (left) with Haldane during their time at the War Office
Sir John French and Mrs Winifred Bennett, his 'little darling'
An unforgettable image from Richard Attenborough's film adaptation of *Oh! What a Lovely War*
The official image. Sir William Orpen's portrait of Haig for Brasenose College, Oxford
Reginald Brett, second Viscount Esher, the aesthete who was so closely involved in the preparation for war
Winston Churchill and 'Wully' Robertson
David Lloyd George
Statue of Haig in Le Square, Montreuil-sur-Mer
Haig's headquarters in the Chateau de Beaurepaire
Henry Wilson, 'Ugly Wilson', in a typically endearing pose
Colonel Maurice Hankey
John Charteris

Haig congratulating Canadian troops

Haig at work on his headquarters train with his secretary, Sir Philip
Sassoon

Haig with Joffre (left) and Foch

Foch bogged down on the Western Front

The Doullens Conference

The Doullens Conference chamber, untouched since 1918

The Great Victory March of 1919

Haig's body lies in state in St Columba's Church, Pont Street,
London before the funeral service in Westminster Abbey

Haig and his wife lie side by side in the grounds of the ruined
Dryburgh Abbey

ACKNOWLEDGEMENTS

The pleasure of writing this book has been greatly enhanced by the friendships formed with so many people who were prepared to share their time and knowledge with me.

My thanks are first of all due to the second Earl Haig. Despite experiences that might have disposed him otherwise, he remains ready to assist those who write about his father, and he made himself available for lengthy and productive interviews. He also read an early draft and responded with detailed observations. He and his family cannot fail to have been hurt by much that has been written in the past about his father, and it is all the more commendable that he remains accessible to researchers. I am most grateful to him.

The Field-Marshal's grandson, Douglas Scott, was most kind and hospitable, also reading and commenting on a draft typescript, and sharing with me insights from his grandfather's pre-war papers, which he is currently editing for publication.

In succession to the late John Terraine, John Hussey has done much to rehabilitate Haig's reputation, publishing a series of articles of precise scholarship whose scintillations illuminate aspects of his career. I must record my very great gratitude to him for devoting so much time to my typescript, supplying very extensive comments and directing me towards fruitful lines of further research.

Dr John Bourne not only allowed me to disturb him at the Centre of First World War Studies (of which he is the Director) at

Birmingham University, but also read and most helpfully and copiously annotated a late draft. I am very grateful for his time and trouble.

Major Gordon Corrigan commented extensively on a draft, at more or less the same time as his own television series *Great British Commanders* was broadcast. The inclusion of Haig in a short list of such men shows how far his standing has been reassessed.

As well as reading through the typescript, correcting points of fact and testing questions of judgement, Michael Orr kindly arranged some important copyright clearances.

I am delighted to have the opportunity of expressing my thanks to Dorothée Bigand of Montreuil-sur-Mer, Sir Martin Gilbert, Colonel Clive Fairweather, Dr Matt Houlbrook, Jean-Marie Monnet, Dr Gary Sheffield, Lieutenant-Colonel Dick Taylor, Frances Walsh and Derek Winterbottom.

I received expert and friendly assistance from the staffs of the National Library of Scotland (especially Colm McLaughlin, who knows the Haig papers as no one else does), the Liddell Hart Centre for Military Archives (particularly Kate O'Brien), Glasgow University Library, the Mitchell Library, Glasgow, and the Signet Library, Edinburgh.

Permission to quote from copyright materials was kindly given by the Earl Haig, copyright holder in respect of his father's papers, and the Trustees of the National Library of Scotland, the custodians of the papers, by the Trustees of the Liddell Hart Centre for Military Archives in respect of the Charteris, Edmonds, Gough, Kiggell and Robertson papers, by the Kiggell and Robertson families, and by Dr John Bourne, Professor Richard Holmes, Dr Correlli Barnett, Dr Gary Sheffield and the families of the late Ruth du Pree and John Terraine.

Doris Nisbet uncomplainingly faced up to my illegible manuscript, confused typescript and muttered dictation, as she has done for nearly thirty years (Haig was fortunate to have his Doris, and I have been fortunate to have mine), and produced something fit for my publishers, where Dr John Tuckwell was a model of patience and a source of good advice. Dr Lawrence Osborn detected and corrected innumerable instances of textual sloppiness, however well hidden, and Andrew Simmons moved the book through the production process with great skill and good humour.

Dr Daniel Scroop read a draft and made many helpful suggestions. He and David Hamill also provided me with unobtrusive and most welcome support, which meant much to me and for which I am grateful.

My daughters, Dr Julia Reid and Bryony Reid, read through the typescript, eliminated innumerable solecisms and suggested important editorial changes and clarifications. My wife, Janet, worked through many successive versions of the draft, and any discernible improvement is attributable to her judgement and diligence. She was also very tolerant of the invisible addititional member of our household. I dedicated a previous book to my family and had originally intended that this one would simply be inscribed to the memory of my parents. But such has been the love and very special support that I have received from Janet, Julia and Bryony that I should prefer to duplicate rather than omit a public acknowledgement: the book is therefore for them as well.

Abbreviations

ADC	Aide-de-camp
BEF	British Expeditionary Force
CIC CinC	Commander-in-Chief
CID	Committee of Imperial Defence
CGS	Chief of the General Staff
CIGS	Chief of the Imperial General Staff
CVO	Commander of the Victorian Order
DSD	Director of Staff Duties
GCB	Grand Cross of the Bath
GHQ	General Headquarters
GOC	General Officer Commanding
GSO	General Staff Officer
IG	Inspector General (of Cavalry)
KCVO	Knight Commander of the Victorian Order
MS	Military Secretary (in India)
QMG	Quartermaster General

MILITARY FORMATIONS

The smallest unit in the army, and the one that represented the ordinary soldier's immediate family, was the platoon, consisting of about fifty men. Platoons were grouped together in companies, and companies into battalions: sixteen platoons came to be the normal strength of a battalion. A regiment was composed of a number of battalions, the number varying throughout the course of the war, and if the platoon was the soldier's immediate family, the regiment was his extended family and the unit to which he owed his loyalty and which felt responsible for his well-being.

But at an operational level battalions were more significant, as they could be swopped around and used as the building bricks for the larger formations that fought the great battles of the war. Around four battalions formed a brigade, and perhaps three brigades composed a division. The divison was the largest autonomous unit in the army. It had its own field artillery, consisted of about 19,000 men, and was usually commanded by a major-general.

Above divisional level units were slightly abstract concepts. A corps was in essence the staff that administered two or more divisions (though the corps was real enough to have its own additional artillery), and an army was the staff (about 100 officers) that controlled two or more corps.

As the narrative reveals, at the end of 1917 there was an important reduction in the strength of the battalion and in the number of battalions forming a division.

PREFACE

Douglas Haig's only son died on 10 July 2009 at the age of ninety-one. I have recorded my gratitude for the help he gave me when I was researching and writing this book.

At the age of nine he found that he had inherited an earldom and the responsibility, as he saw it, for tending the memory and defending the reputation of the father he had loved and who, he increasingly felt, was unfairly treated by history.

At one level he was a conventional man, a product of a background whose values he did not greatly question; and for the rest of his life he unstintingly threw himself into the discharge of the duties that he regarded as his responsibility. He was still working for the British Legion in the year of his death.

His was a sensitive and artistic temperament. He was recognised as one of the foremost topographical artists of his generation, and his work is represented in many major collections. I suspect that he was too modest to recognise the extent of what he achieved in his own right.

The role he played in public life was neither the only one for which he was suited nor perhaps his natural one. When I told him at an early meeting that I sensed from his autobiography that for much of his life he had felt the burden of his father's memory to be a heavy one, he quickly replied that he still did. But it was not a burden that he wished to put down. It is wrong to say, as some obituaries did, that he spent his life trying to throw off his father's shadow. That was not at all how he saw things.

In Dawyck Haig's youth, as I try to show, Douglas Haig was a revered figure. It was a shock then to his family that thirty years after his death his achievements came increasingly to be challenged. To Dawyck and his sisters it was all the more hurtful when the attacks, some of which were directed against the values for which Haig stood, as much as against the man himself, were not only unfounded in fact, but also personal and spiteful.

Perhaps understandably, Dawyck Haig could be unduly sensitive to criticism of his father, but his considered wish, I think, would simply be for that criticism to be balanced and firmly based on the facts, rather than on myth and caricature.

The response to the hardback edition of this book, and some of the coverage of the ninetieth anniversary of the Hundred Days - that great, so often forgotten series of British victories in 1918 (on the eve of which Dawyck was born) which led to the end of the war, and over which his father presided – suggests that views of Douglas Haig, and, more generally, of the First World War, are undergoing revision. In one of the last letters I received from Dawyck Haig he said that the tide definitely seemed to be turning. It was good that he lived long enough to see that happen, and though he would have been too modest to say so, he must have known how much he had been involved in the process.

Walter Reid
Laroque-des-Albères
16 July 2009

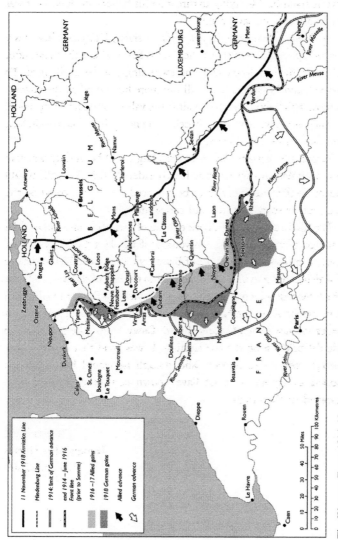

The Western Front 1914-18

1

BUTCHER AND BUNGLER
OR ARCHITECT OF VICTORY?

Douglas Haig died on 29 January 1928. In the years since the end of the Great War, almost ten years earlier, he had certainly not been at the centre of the national stage. On the other hand, his activities, particularly his work for the British Legion, continued to attract regular mention in the press. He was only sixty-six, and not known to be in ill health. His death was accordingly unexpected as well as sudden. It occurred late on a Sunday evening, and the news did not become generally known until the Tuesday morning: then for several days the newspapers were filled with memoirs and tributes. Even if Haig was never loved by the nation, like a Nelson, he was certainly respected, both by the millions of soldiers of whom very few indeed would ever have seen him and also by the great mass of the population, for whom he was the man who had brought victory to Britain and returned the world to peace. There was a profound sense of loss.[1]

Tributes poured in from around the world, from royalty, politicians and generals. From South Africa, Field-Marshal Smuts said: 'All honour to him. He left a record of qualities and work of which the British people may justly be proud.' When tributes came to be paid in Parliament, speakers sought to identify what for them had been special about Haig. In the House of Lords, the Marquis of Salisbury said:

In one respect the position of Lord Haig was different from and more difficult than that of any other Commander because of the vastness of the forces which it was his duty to control. This not only made the complexity of operations much greater, but it necessarily prevented him from having that personal contact with the soldiers in the field upon which great Commanders in the past have so much relied to inspire their armies to achieve their purpose.[2]

Lord Beauchamp said:

He was a man of a rare and single-minded devotion to duty – during these last few years we had, I think, specially learned to admire the reticence he has shown with regard to the great operations in which he was engaged. That is an example of dignity which has commended itself, I am sure, to every member of your Lordships' House.[3]

In the Commons, Major-General Sir Robert Hutchison said:

I loved Lord Haig. I have known Lord Haig all my life . . . I had the privilege of serving in two campaigns with him – in South Africa and in the Great War – and in the Great War for a time I was one of his Staff Officers. The memory of Haig will always remain with me, sweet, clean and just what I would like it to be.[4]

Brigadier-General Charteris, perhaps the closest of all his Staff Officers, quoted the verse that Kipling had written of Lord Roberts:

> Clean, simple, valiant, well-beloved,
> Flawless in faith and fame,
> Whom neither ease nor honours moved
> One hair's-breadth from his aim.[5]

He lay in state in St Columba's Church, Pont Street, London, for two days, while a constant stream of mourners, some 25,000 in all, passed by for more than twelve hours each day. Lady Haig came to the church twice. On the first occasion she left two wreaths of Flanders poppies on the coffin. Among those who came to pay their tributes were many sightless and handicapped ex-servicemen, who were helped through the crowds. A Scotsman laid a sprig of heather at the foot of the coffin.

The family had been offered a burial in St Paul's, the usual dignity for someone in Haig's position, but he had made it known that he wished to buried at home in Scotland. After a brief service in St Columba's, the official funeral took place at Westminster Abbey on 3 February. With all the pomp and ceremony appropriate to the obsequies of a famously victorious field-marshal, it was little less than a state funeral. The three eldest sons of the King, the Prince of Wales, the Duke of York and Prince Henry, walked behind the gun carriage that bore the coffin. With them walked two Marshals of France, Pétain, still the victorious defender of Verdun, not the peacemaker of 1940, and Foch, Supreme Allied Commander, defiant, magnificent, indomitable. Haig's charger followed his body, boots reversed in the stirrups. Ahead of the charger walked his servant of twenty-five years, Sergeant Secrett, who had carried his sick chief on his shoulders from his quarters in 1914. The huge crowds that attended the ceremonial were subdued, the atmosphere not that of a pageant, but intimate and moving to a degree that impressed itself on London and the Empire. Nothing remotely similar had taken place or would take place for any of the other First World War leaders. Indeed, of the Second World War leaders, only Churchill's funeral eclipsed Haig's. While the ceremony was taking place in Westminster Abbey, simultaneous services took place for Haig in cities throughout the United Kingdom, something that did not happen for Churchill.

After the ceremony, the coffin was taken by train to Edinburgh. It arrived at midnight. The ground was covered in snow. The coffin was carried on a gun carriage to St Giles' Cathedral on the ancient High

Street, through denser crowds than had ever attended a royal visit, in a silence broken only by sobs and by the pipe melody, *The Flowers of the Forest*, written to commemorate the Battle of Flodden in 1513. This haunting and historic lament, played so often in Scotland since 1914, was heard twice in the course of the journey from Lothian Road to St Giles'. The cathedral remained open until Haig's waiting countrymen had all passed by, some 70,000 in all. The minister of St Giles' and Dean of the Thistle, Dr Charles Warr, said that not since the burial of the Regent Moray in the sixteenth century had Edinburgh seen such a display of grief.

The mood of respect and admiration, perhaps even affection, to which the events in London and Edinburgh testified, remained undissipated until the outbreak of the next war, and even beyond that. Railway engines and streets were named after Haig. Children were given his names. Many statues were erected.

The most celebrated of these statues was unveiled on Whitehall on 10 November 1937 (though its design offended Lady Haig, who did not attend the ceremony, and technical solecisms disturbed cavalry traditionalists) in the presence of contingents of regular troops representing the navy, army and air force, and including Indian, Dominion and Colonial detachments: 2,000 serving personnel in all, together with 700 members of the Territorial Army.[6] The importance of the occasion and Haig's position in the national pantheon was reflected by the fact that the statue was unveiled by the Duke of Gloucester, a cavalryman himself. After the unveiling, the Duke laid a wreath and gave an address. On the following day, 11 November, after laying his wreath at the Cenotaph in commemoration of the Armistice, the King – against the advice of his home secretary – walked up Whitehall to the statue, inspected it and laid another wreath at its foot.

What prompts the writing of this book is the profundity of the change in the mood of the times, and in how the nation regarded Haig, which had taken place by the time that the same statue was the subject of press reports 61 years later, on the eightieth anniversary of the Armistice. The *Express* (as the *Daily Express* was known at the time) opened a campaign to have the Whitehall statue melted down, the metal to be used to strike medals for the families of those executed as deserters and mutineers.[7] Shortly afterwards A.N. Wilson wrote an article in the *Sunday Telegraph*, claiming that Haig had never deserved a statue in the first place.[8] And neither the *Daily Express* nor Wilson were maverick voices. The *Express* claimed that it spoke for 'the modern generation of military historians'. That is not the case, but it probably did speak, as did A.N. Wilson, for a body of generally well-informed and educated people with an interest in current affairs and twentieth-century history. What had happened to reverse Haig's fortunes in the two generations after his death? Haig's Oxford College was Brasenose. After the First World War the college was proud of its distinguished son, and enthusiastically celebrated his achievements. Two generations later the college's undergraduates defaced his portrait in the college hall with the inscription, 'Murderer of 1,000,000 Men'; and the war memorial at the college entrance was removed.

Little had changed in Haig's lifetime. The public's immediate reaction to the horrors of the war was to turn its back on them, and it was a full decade before the anti-war literature started to flow. C.E. Montague wrote *Disenchantment* in 1922, but it was only in the late 1920s that Rupert Brooke *began* to be displaced as the most popular war poet by Wilfred Owen, and that writers like Siegfried Sassoon, Robert Graves and R.C. Sherriff came to attention, and the process of displacement really only achieved full force in the 1960s. Interestingly, only Wilfred Owen, amongst these authors, was arguably anti-war: Graves and Sherriff were proud of their wars, and surprised to be thought anything else, and Sassoon was a brave officer who admired his men, even if he came to challenge the reasons for which the war was prosecuted.

As far as the history of the war generally was concerned, Churchill's magisterial account, *The World Crisis*, appeared in six volumes between 1923 and 1929. Haig's reaction to what he read of it is explored later, but Churchill's criticisms of Haig were qualified by a number of favourable comments, and he was kinder to Haig than to

Sir William Robertson, the Chief of the Imperial General Staff. Churchill worked closely with Edmonds, the Editor of the Official History, to whom he wrote, 'Please keep the proofs until we meet, and then we can run through them together. Of course the sarcasms and asperities can be pruned out or softened. I often put things down for the purpose of seeing what they look like in print. Haig comes out all right in the end because of the advance in 1918' . . .[9] That was in Haig's lifetime. After Haig's death, Churchill was more outspoken in his 1935 review of Duff Cooper's biography, a review which was later published in book form in 1937 in *Great Contemporaries*. His respect and even affection for Haig did not deter him from fairly critical judgements.

> Haig's mind . . . was thoroughly orthodox and conventional. He does not appear to have had any original ideas; no one can discern a spark of that mysterious, visionary, often sinister genius which has enabled the great captains of history to dominate foes with the triumph of novel apparitions. He was, we are told, quite friendly to the tanks, but the manoeuvre of making them would never have occurred to him [an understandable reminder to the reader of who *had* made them: Churchill himself.] He appeared at times quite unconscious of any theatre but the Western Front. There were the Germans in their trenches. Here he stood at the head of an army corps, then of an army, and finally of a group of mighty armies. Hurl them on and keep slogging at it, in the best possible way – that was war. It was undoubtedly one way of making war, and in the end there was certainly overwhelming victory.[10]

However, Churchill qualified these views with a critical proviso, whose time has come: 'But these truisms will not be accepted by history as exhaustive.'

Lloyd George's *Memoirs* were published in six volumes between 1933 and 1936, with a further two-volume edition in 1938. The tone of his view of the Commander-in-Chief was that 'Haig undoubtedly lacked those highest qualities which were essential in a great commander in the greatest war the world has even seen. It was far beyond his mental equipment.' More specific criticism was even more savage. The attacks contained in the *Memoirs* are amazingly vicious. An explanation for Lloyd George's bitterness is suggested later, but whether or not he wrote out of frustration at having failed to master Haig, the extravagance of his criticism was to provide Haig's enemies with the most volatile of ammunition. There was some controversy when the *Memoirs* appeared, but Lloyd George did not write as well as he spoke, and their significance was less in their immediate impact than in the material that they provided for subsequent generations of critics. Lloyd George himself later devalued his *Memoirs* when he said that he might have been wrong about Haig and Robertson. He admitted that he had no notes or diaries and for the 'Passchendaele' section of the book, which he dictated in moments of leisure during a golfing holiday in the Algarve, relied on a 'well-known military publicist' – almost certainly Liddell Hart.[11]

Lloyd George attempted to justify his attacks on Haig as being a response to the quotations from the Commander-in-Chief's diaries in the official biography, *Haig*, published by Alfred Duff Cooper in two volumes (1935–6). Duff Cooper's book, which enjoyed the benefit of access to Haig's diaries, is written well, if in a rather old-fashioned, orotund style. As an official biography it is favourable to its subject and deferential, even courtly, towards his memory, but it is written on the basis of solid information and its judgements are remarkably sound, even when viewed against the detailed scholarship amassed by subsequent generations of historians. Duff Cooper's two volumes were a substantial addition to two books by Brigadier-General John Charteris, a key member of Haig's staff: *Field-Marshal Earl Haig* (1929) and *At GHQ* (1931). The latter is intended to be an essentially contemporaneous account of events at Haig's headquarters; the former is a generally objective and accurate biography; generally objective despite the fact that Charteris was very much a protégé of his subject, and accurate despite the fact that it was written so soon after the war, when little documentation was available.

In the decade or so after Haig's death in 1928 a little criticism developed, but only a little. In 1930, instead of naming a street after him, Margery Allingham in *Mystery Mile* called Albert Campion's white mouse after him. This poor Haig was electrocuted, to demonstrate to Campion's client the horrible end that had been prepared for him. But as the peace of 1918 gave way to the war of 1939, Haig remained for the most part venerated by a deferential society, where substantial criticism of the nation's military leader would have been tantamount to questioning the worth of the sacrifice of so many of his fellow countrymen. It is true that military critics such as Basil Liddell Hart and Major-General J.F.C. Fuller – particularly the former – were critical of the generals who fought on the Western Front. Liddell Hart was carefully read by military historians, usually with respect. In books such as the *War in Outline, 1914–1918* (1936) and *Through the Fog of War* (1938) he did make serious criticisms of the conduct of the British High Command during the war. His views were, however, compromised by the extremes to which he sometimes went, and the occasionally unjustified asperity of his criticism. (Before reaching his chosen *métier* of military commentator, he had to mark time as the tennis correspondent for *American Lawn Tennis*, publishing a collection of his tennis writings in 1926 as *The Lawn Tennis Masters Unveiled,* and his objectiveness as an historian is sometimes diluted by the sensationalism of the journalist.) In any event, Liddell Hart, Fuller and Charles Cruttwell, who published *A History of the Great War 1914–1918* in 1936, were writing for a specialised readership, and Haig's reputation with the broad mass of intelligent observers was not substantially damaged.

But as the still deferential 1950s gave way to the iconoclasm of the 1960s an impenetrable critical barrage reinforced the scattered volleys of Liddell Hart and Fuller, and a much more dramatic assault on Haig's reputation took place: an assault so total and extreme that it remains to be seen whether further research and scholarship will ever be capable of provoking a fresh appreciation of Haig and his generals. The catalyst was the publication a few years earlier, in 1952, of *The Private Papers of Douglas Haig, 1914–1919*, edited by the future Lord Blake. That the book should have functioned in this way was ironic: Lord Blake had been asked to edit the papers by the second Earl Haig, then, as he has remained, devoted to an accurate and sympathetic representation of his father's role in the war. As is clear from his perceptive Introduction, Blake reviewed the documents and came to a judgement on Haig that was as positive about the Field-Marshal as any of his supporters could have wished. But the scale of the diaries and letters on which he drew was enormous. The only repository for Haig's confidences, his only means of letting off steam when he bore the huge responsibilities of command in France, was in the diaries and the letters which he wrote to his wife. The diaries alone have been estimated to contain at least three-quarters of a million words. Even drastically reduced to the 400 or so pages in Blake's edition, his words held many hostages to fortune. To his credit, Blake did not attempt to edit out material excised by Duff Cooper, who also had access to the diaries, when he wrote his biography. Readers in the 1950s were able to savour Haig's criticisms of the French, of Dominion and American troops, and social and political observations that were out of tune with contemporary thinking. There was material which could be used to argue that he promoted his career by intriguing with the Palace behind the backs of the politicians, disloyally weakening the position of Sir John French, his friend and his predecessor as Commander-in-Chief. The Blake edition of the Private Papers has been significantly supplemented by an important new edition.[12] Blake, as a political historian, had given prominence to the political aspects of the Papers; Gary Sheffield and John Bourne, the editors of the new edition, as military historians, give more prominence to the military aspects. In their Introduction they place the papers in the context of current research.

Elements of the diaries were useful to Alan Clark, when he published *The Donkeys* in 1961. The second Earl and Blake managed to delay publication of Clark's book for several months to obtain corrections of inaccurate statements in the draft, but, even if Haig was not the sole, or perhaps even the principal, target of the book, it presented a damaging picture of leonine ordinary soldiers led by

donkeys – stupid, stubborn generals, blinkered from the realities of
the war and comfortably billeted in luxurious châteaux, remote from
the fighting. The distinguished military historian, Professor Sir
Michael Howard, was entertained when he read the book, but said
it was a 'petulant caricature of a tragedy' and as a memorial to the
men who died in 1915 a 'pretty deplorable piece of work'.[13] But it
sold well and provided the inspiration for Joan Littlewood's Theatre
Workshop production, *Oh, What a Lovely War!* (Alan Clark claimed
that he sued Joan Littlewood for plagiarism and that they settled out
of court for 50 guineas.)[14] Joan Littlewood's production of 1963 and
Richard Attenborough's film adaptation of 1969 were each outstanding, though in different ways. Littlewood's was the more
inventive, an innovative piece of theatre, shaped as an entertainment
by pierrots. A fairly typical reaction, in this case by the highly
intelligent Bernard Levin, was that in a better regulated society Haig
'would have been employed, under the supervision of an intelligent
half-wit, to run the very simplest sort of public lavatory. Instead, he
ran a war: Battle of the Somme: British loss 65,000 in three hours.
Gain nil.'[15] Attenborough's film was glossier, but also profoundly
moving. Both were consciously didactic: Littlewood's particularly so.
Its historical adviser, Raymond Fletcher, described his input as 'one
part me, one part Liddell Hart, the rest Lenin!' The Theatre Workshop production was more in the spirit of the anti-authority mood of
the times exemplified by playwrights such as Wesker, than in the
more pacifist style of the film.

The effect of the work, in its two formats, was profound and its
mood was carried forward in much of the literature of the next twenty
years, including A.J.P. Taylor's *The First World War. An Illustrated
History* (1963), Leon Wolff's *In Flanders Fields* (1959), John Laffin's
British Butchers & Bunglers of World War 1 (1988) and Denis Winter's
Haig's Command (1991). Works of fiction, such as those by Sebastian
Faulks and Pat Barker, have generally adopted unquestioningly the
view that the struggle was, for ordinary soldiers, futile as well as
horrible, as have most of the cinema films and television films of the
period.

The assumptions created about the war since 1960, and about Haig in particular, have been so overwhelming that the generation that became young adults in the twenty-first century take it for granted that the war was one which Britain should probably not have fought and cannot really be said to have won; that it was waged by generals of blinding stupidity, whose outlook and military education had been formed by the middle of the nineteenth century, and who were callously indifferent to the fate of their men, from whom they are alienated to the point of psychosis by an implacable class hostility. Over all this, Haig presides, vain, technophobe, personally ambitious and uninterested in finding an alternative to fighting methods which slaughtered his men and the Germans in indiscriminate confusion. For many people Haig is identified with Stephen Fry's Lord Melchett in *Blackadder Goes Forth* (Haig himself was played by Geoffrey Palmer). When an attempt to reach an informed judgement on Haig was made by the BBC *Timewatch* programme (3 July 1996) four of the critics chose *Blackadder* as the accurate historical record of events against which to judge the programme.[16] Incredibly, *Blackadder* is a prescribed core material for the GCSE syllabus, and it is through such programmes, and the war poets, notably Wilfred Owen, rather than the history books, that children, and indeed their teachers, learn of the Great War.

The war poets to which teachers and pupils look for instruction are, as well as Wilfred Owen, people like Sassoon and Rosenberg. But these were not in fact the poets which were read – in huge numbers – during the war. Poets like the Reverend G.A. Studdert Kennedy, John Oxenham and Robert Service were immensely popular and their works applauded and validated the sacrifices that were being made in France and Flanders.[17] Just as the popular war poets outsold the more literary ones, so popular war fiction outsold the later anti-war output: 'It is often forgotten that this early wave of patriotic war books enjoyed far more acclaim than any of the later "disenchanted" British war novels . . . Book for book the British public over a 30 year period . . . seems to have preferred the patriotic to the disenchanted type of war book'.[18]

But Haig's critics have not been the only writers who have been active in the last forty years. Another band, usually known as 'the revisionists', have sought to create quite a different picture. The first of them was John Terraine, a revisionist *avant la lettre*, revising before there was anything to revise other than the roughly sketched caricature of Haig which was the conception of most of those with a nodding interest in the Great War. His starting point, bizarrely, was the same as those who were setting to work on Haig in a very different spirit: the publication of Blake's edition of the *Private Papers*. But his reading was a much closer one, and rather than looking for flaws of character or funny stories like Haig's concern that it should have been *his* horse which threw the King on a visit to France, he analysed in detail the evidence of what Haig had actually done during his time as Commander-in-Chief. His book, *Douglas Haig, The Educated Soldier* (sometimes described, even by Terraine's admirers, as 'Haigiography') was published in 1963, and was followed by many other studies of the Great War, including *The Road to Passchendaele* (1977), *To Win a War: 1918, The Year of Victory* (1978) and *White Heat: The New Warfare 1914–1918* (1982). Sometimes he was affectionately teased as 'Tommy' Terraine, and some of his judgements must be read with caution, particularly his acceptance of Haig's post-war argument that victory was won in 1918 directly out of the battles of the earlier years of the war and that they, for their part, were all designed to achieve the result that 1918 delivered. Terraine was well aware that when he set out to write his study of Haig 'my message will be running almost entirely against the mainstream of received opinion at that time',[19] and perhaps as a consequence his style was slightly overstated, sometimes intimidating and occasionally aggressive.

But he was persuasive, and inspired a generation of writers, who accepted his thesis even if they did not agree with every detail of his argument. The scholars who followed in his tracks included many, such as Correlli Barnett and Peter Simkins, who started off as adherents of Liddell Hart,[20] and it is to the credit of Terraine's pioneering scholarship that there are now very few serious military historians who, whatever the fine nuances of their judgement, would dispute that Haig was an intelligent, able and forward-looking commander. Indeed Terraine was chastised as far back as 1981 for banging on about what was now a settled issue, 'if we put aside the popular media'.[21] Terraine responded by saying that the proposition that the old myths about Haig and the First World War had been disposed of did not 'square with my own constant experience'. This dichotomy between what is a given amongst specialist historians and what is a given amongst the general body of educated readers frustrates the former, who despair of the possibility of a properly informed debate on the subject of the First World War in the way that other wars can be discussed and analysed.

The problem arises for two reasons. First, for most people knowledge of the First World War comes through school, novels, plays and films. All of these sources, particularly the educational one, are informed by the war poets more than by anything else. Richard Holmes has argued that the poets were atypically sensitive, and that their experience and their views of the war were not those of the ordinary soldier. It is too extreme to portray the poets as a gaggle of neurasthenic wimps. It would be crass to say that those ex-servicemen who survived the war unbroken in body or in mind, even those who looked back on their experience of comradeship in the trenches as the most intensely lived part of their lives, had not shut away in the reticent recesses of their brains experiences that would haunt them before their days were done, but which they could not articulate as the poets did. And all too many did not come back unbroken in mind or body, and all too many did not come back at all. But it is true that the poets were not typical. Even in the course of the war, the War Office recognised that the numbers of highly educated men who were coming into the army were proving more sensitive than peacetime volunteers. The poets tended to search for the pity of war, for what was personal, what was exquisite, what was poignant. They were not concerned to analyse tactics or strategy or the responsibilities of command.

The other element that has created a gap between the popular appreciation of the war (and Haig in particular), and the view of the professional historians is that for the last twenty or thirty years the thrust of scholarship has been to look not so much at individual generals, or even individual battles, but to analyse in painstaking detail what was actually happening on a day-to-day basis. By searching through archival material, particularly detailed records of individual units, it is increasingly possible to know what actually happened in the war rather than to rely on assumptions and speculations which served as history for many years. Haig's personal papers are so voluminous, and the wartime part was produced under such special circumstances, that it is always possible to find a surprising statement. They have been trawled over at very great length. Both in the emphasis of its extracts and in its Introduction, the new edition presents an image of Haig that is on the whole positive and is in line with contemporary scholarship. But the revisionists are climbing a huge mountain and may never reach its summit. When Gary Sheffield and John Bourne published an article in the BBC *History* magazine in March 2005,[22] in association with this new edition of the papers, of which they are the editors, it provoked a letter in response that pointed up the strength with which the traditional views are held and the way in which cultural views outweigh politico-historical research: '[W]holesale revisionism is very much in vogue . . . Wars are justified. Tarnished reputations are polished up. Haig has now been given the treatment by Gary Sheffield and John Bourne.'[23]

It has been recognised for some time that it is unlikely that much more will be learned about Haig by looking at the papers. What is more profitable is to learn from events, and to know what these events actually were, rather than what they had been assumed to be. This detailed micro-analysis has been the emphasis of most revisionists' work. It has demonstrated that a huge change took place in the nature of the British Army between 1915 and 1918, a 'learning curve' which fused a new all-arms approach that allowed the British Army to deliver victory in 1918: the *British* Army because at that stage in the war it was the British Army which was charged with the major role. The revisionists are frustrated by the fact that what they all share as a self-evident truth is not accepted by the general public. For them victory in 1918 was a British-led victory, won by the biggest British Army ever to take part in a continental war. To them it is perverse that instead of receiving recognition as the man who presided over the massive growth in the British Army from the six divisions of the British Expeditionary Force in 1914 to the reorganised, highly trained, multi-weapon army that delivered victory, Haig is vilified to the extent that a member of the Scottish Parliament, in a recent debate on the fate of the deserters during the First World War, argued that Haig, rather than the deserters, should have been shot.

In their frustration, the revisionists sometimes go too far. Some see Haig as a 'Great Captain', which he was not: he was rather a great administrator. Some attribute to him too intimate a part in the technical revolution of 1915–18. He was of course not involved in the detail. Similarly, it is illogical to say that, 'having been blamed for being a technophobe, Haig is surely entitled to credit for the changes that took place'. What Haig did do, and what he is not recognised as having done, was to invigorate and inspire the greatest application of science and technology to warfare that military history had known. Some revisionists exaggerate the scale and nature of Haig's achievement by investing the First World War with the moral quality of a contest between the liberal democracies and 'the first of three major challenges mounted by ideological enemies during the twentieth century'.[24] They go too far, but the idea of the First World War as an 'unnecessary war' – except perhaps for the Central Powers – has been exploded, and Britain could not have stood aside in 1914.

The revisionist writers who have published so much over the last twenty or thirty years, and the researchers who continue to reveal the detail of what actually happened on the Western Front, have revolutionised our view of Haig. In the autumn of 2005, Gordon Corrigan included Haig in a television series on Great British Commanders. Even in 2005 that inclusion provoked some surprise: twenty years earlier there would have been an explosion of bellylaughs. But the revisionists have been writing for a specialised, academic readership. Haig scholarship in the last thirty years has not consisted in a fresh biographical study of the man, but rather in a considerable number of sophisticated studies at archival level. Cumulatively this scholarship has meant that the army that fought the First World War can be seen to have gone through a revolutionary process of technological and administrative change. Haig's role has been touched on in nearly all these studies, aimed mainly at a specialist leadership, but his reputation in the round has not been revisited in their light. And their works are not biographies of Haig. There have been a few modern biographies, some better than others, but none has looked at the information now available in relation to the dramatic growth in the size of British forces in France during Haig's command, the embracing of science and boffinry, developments in infantry tactics and in artillery techniques, and Haig's adaptation of what was available and its application to his purposes. Even Terraine did not have access to this material when he wrote *Douglas Haig, The Educated Soldier*, and he specifically said that his book was not meant to be a biography, but an attempt to study Haig as a soldier, and particularly as Commander-in Chief.

Haig was a conservative man, who found it difficult to acknowledge change, but he did change in the light of changed circumstances. The reformer at the War Office was very different from the cavalry officer in India, Sudan and South Africa. He developed further in the context of the responsibilities placed on him as an army commander from 1914 to the end of 1915. Most of all, he demonstrated a flexibility and protean dynamism from the end of 1915 until the end of the war. Because of his unwillingness to admit that attitudes which he had long espoused were flawed, he rarely acknowledged that he had departed from his established principles. In his *Final Despatch* after the war, for instance, he manipulated what had happened to make it fit with the doctrines he had learned. A more imaginative man, a more perceptive man, would have acknowledged to himself and to the public what he had done. Had Haig made such an avowal, his reputation, as a man who had broken the military mould, would have been greater than it is. But ultimately his standing should depend not on what he said, or even thought, but on what he did. In this book I have attempted to reassess his early and middle career by looking at it free from the prejudice and hostility with which Haig studies have often been associated, and I have attempted to look at the final part of his career in the light of a synthesis of the results of modern research.

My position is not a straightforward endorsement of that of the revisionists. Although they are much better informed than Haig's detractors, they exaggerate his virtues (perhaps because they are aware of the burden of proof that has been imposed on them) almost as much as the critics exaggerate his failings. It does not follow that because Haig is not as bad as the critics represented him, he will be without fault in all military respects. He certainly had singular flaws, or at least quirks, of character. The most significant, from a military respect, was a capacity to be carried away by accesses of optimism which blinded him from time to time to reality.

This characteristic has not been understood or appreciated. His rigorous self-control, his repression of all emotion, has disguised the fact that Haig was, underneath everything, essentially a romantic, a cavalier who dreamed of victories wreathed in drama. I have attempted to bring out this element of his character, an element reflected in his devotion to the romantic border country from which his family hailed, his love of his family tradition, and Bemersyde, its seat, his idealised conception of country and Empire, the appeal for him of the dash and glitter of cavalry. Only by seeing what lay under the iron-cladding of his self-discipline can one understand the whole man. To do so does not excuse, for example, the prolongation of the Somme and Third Ypres, but it is essential to understanding what caused their prolongation.

That he presided over the greatest victory that has been won essentially by a British feat of arms does not make him the greatest general that Britain has produced. And the war that the Entente Powers fought was not what some of the revisionists assert it to be. France fought to defend her soil, and Britain fought because it was not in her interest that the Continental landmass should be dominated by any one power. From the point of view of humanity and democracy it was well that the Entente and not the Central Powers were the victors, but it should be remembered, in view of what Haig, and indeed most of his countrymen, said and believed, that Britain did not go to war essentially to defend liberal values. German democratic institutions, certainly, were insubstantial compared to those of Britain and France, but it is not easy to see that the Kaiser's Germany can be equated with that of Hitler or the Russia of Stalin. Insubstantial though her democratic and liberal values may have been, Germany's credentials in these respects were much better than those of the third Entente nation, Russia, where the secret police, the Okhrana, still regretted the disappearance of their favoured instrument of torture, the knout.

My conclusions will, I think, be clear, but not, I hope, obtrusive. It is for readers to make their own assessment of Haig's stature. He himself always said that he did not care what people said about him, as long as it was based on the facts.

2

FAMILY AND YOUTH

The Border country, an area of about 1,800 square miles straddling the Cheviot Hills and lying on what is now the Scottish side of the line that separates Scotland and England, has seen more blood spilled than perhaps any other part of the British Isles. The families that lived here till late medieval times were fierce and independent and stood in awe neither of each other nor of the crowns of either England or Scotland. The Borders lay largely beyond the laws of both countries. The way of life of the lawless clans who dominated the area – 'the Border Reivers' – was one of raiding and marauding. They lived in defensive castles, peels and keeps, so solid that many of them still stand, largely intact. Haig's family came from this anarchic, warlike background, its roots as deeply planted as any.

The legends and poetry of the Borders were an essential part in the early nineteenth-century image of romantic Scotland, largely created by the inspiration of Sir Walter Scott (though he was far from the only man of his time to be fascinated by the folk tales and songs of the region), as he collected the ballads of the Borders into his *Minstrelsy of the Scottish Border*. The history of the Haig family, like much of the history of the region, is cloaked in myth and legend, and the author of the family history in 1881 found himself bound to reject much of the tradition as 'unverifiable'.[1] Even the family's famous motto:

Tyde what may, what e'er betide,
Haigs will be Haigs of Bemersyde

is in part myth. The lines are said to have been composed by the locally famous poet, Thomas the Rhymer, but the name 'Haig' did not replace the family's Norman name, 'de Haga', until at least 100 years after the time of Thomas the Rhymer.

But the de Hagas, and then the Haigs, did play a central part in the bloodthirsty history of the Borders. In the fifteenth century, in dispute with the Abbot of Melrose, the whole family, 'and others, their advisers and abettors', were excommunicated for a full three years.

The political history of the region was hugely fluid: Scottish families frequently fought alongside English families against the Scottish Crown, and the allegiance of English families was equally unpredictable; but ultimately, as something approaching the modern nation state evolved, a firmer commitment was required. Although the de Hagas had crossed the Channel specifically to support the Norman succession, their allegiance was transferred to the Scottish Crown, and they fought on the Scottish side at Stirling Bridge, Halidon Hill, Otterburn and Flodden. Douglas Haig's cultural background was firmly founded in a consciousness of a distinct Scottish identity, and this background was reinforced by a substantially Scottish upbringing, at least until he went to Oxford.

Bemersyde, the square border keep of which Thomas the Rhymer spoke, was the headquarters of the senior branch of the family. But Bemersyde was something of a problem for Douglas Haig. He was very far from being part of that senior branch: John Haig, Douglas's father, was sixth in descent from the second son of the seventeenth Laird. Douglas Haig aspired to the distinction of being Haig of Bemersyde: he took the name as part of the title which he received at the end of the war, but even before then, during the war, when a peerage was first offered to him, correspondence reveals that he had been testing out the Bemersyde connection, rather as Kitchener practised the signature 'Kitchener of Khartoum' before the title was

his. He was proud of the fact that the Haigs were said to be the oldest
family in Scotland, a distinction that for this essentially romantic
man eclipsed anything that the King could confer on him. It
mattered to him that he should be installed at Bemersyde as head
of the family. Even after he became the Earl Haig of Bemersyde, the
house and estate were not his until they were purchased by subscription and given to him. The gift was made after the war, but had
been canvassed as early as October 1916, when Haig wrote to his
wife:

It was nice [of F. S. Oliver of Edgerston] to think of the country
presenting me with Bemersyde, that old place on the Tweed
that has never belonged to anyone but Haig. We must finish
the war first before we think of any such things. Besides it is
sufficient reward for me to have taken part in this Great
Struggle, and to have occupied no inconsiderable position
among those who have helped our country to weather the storm.

It was his son, and not he, who was finally recognised by the Lyon
Court, which regulates such arcane matters in Scotland, as head of the
Haig family.

The Borders, with their history and romance, were Haig's spiritual
home, but his immediate surroundings were the more tranquil,
arable flatlands of Fife; and the family background was not in land,
but in whisky. His father, John Haig, started out in life at a fairly
modest level, but proved to be a very successful whisky distiller. His
income in the 1840s of £10,000 a year equates to considerably more
than £600,000 per annum today, and this substantial income was
capitalised in 1876 when the business was sold to Distillers Limited.
John Haig, Master of the Fife Hounds, and the proprietor of Cameron
House, near Markinch, had therefore become a very substantial local
personage: but it is crucial to remember that his background was that
of trade. In the nineteenth century, and indeed throughout Douglas
Haig's time in the army, such a fact was of great significance. Even in
1963, when John Terraine published *Douglas Haig, The Educated*

Soldier, he felt constrained to say, 'Douglas Haig's father was a distinguished whisky distiller, *a calling which requires no apology . . .*'

Haig was never an aristocrat or even a substantial landowner (because the farms that are now part of the Bemersyde inheritance were not acquired until after his death), and this was an important factor in determining certain of his attitudes. He was never the *arrant* snob that some of his critics have suggested. He had an endearing interest in quite ordinary people with whom he came into contact, and would remember, for instance, private soldiers and NCOs who crossed his path in the course of the war. All the same, in a snobbish age he was not immune from snobbery, with an inclination to write off people, whether French generals or the Chief of the Imperial General Staff, as not being gentlemen. He was not wholly at ease with many people outside his close family, and his excessive formality may have derived from a certain insecurity. At any rate, in the hierarchical world in which he grew up, and indeed spent all of his life, since he could not be pre-eminent by reason of his birth, success would depend on distinction in his profession.

John, Haig's father, married well. Rachel Veitch, who was eighteen when she married the 37-year-old Haig, was as it happens from another Border family, the Veitches of Eliot and Dawyck. They had all the social distinction that John Haig could wish, but none of his money: the Veitches had fallen on bad times and Rachel came to the marriage without a dowry. But she was much more than a suitable social match: she was very beautiful, she was devoted to her husband, and she had inexhaustible love for Douglas and her other children.

John needed her support. He suffered from asthma, which Douglas was to inherit, gout and the effects of alcoholism. He spent every winter at continental spas. On one of these cures Rachel wrote from Vichy to Douglas: 'Your father is looking so well;' he had, for 'the first time . . . done without Brandy, Whisky or Kirsche before breakfast.'

Despite his indispositions, John continued to work hard in his business, his fortunes continued to advance and his employees were well treated. He became a Justice of the Peace and a captain in the

Leven Artillery Corps. He hastened to employ the latest technology and involved himself in coordinating pricing among different producers and as a spokesman for the industry. He had no less than eleven children, of whom nine survived, but his interests and his benevolence centred much more on his business than on them. He had a prodigious temper and his children's response was to avoid him as far as possible. He seems to have had little lasting influence on them.

Of the eleven children, Douglas, born on 19 June 1861, was the youngest. He was born at No. 24 Charlotte Square, Edinburgh, which the Haig family took in connection with the children's education. He was his mother's favourite, and she lavished attention on him. Although Haig did not enjoy female company, the three greatest influences on him were feminine: his mother, and after her death his sister, Henrietta, and after his marriage, his wife, Doris. Each of them in turn devoted their lives, for a period, to supporting him and promoting his interests in every way they could. His mother's portrait hung above his bed at Bemersyde at the end of his life.

Little Douglas had a shock of yellow hair. His older brothers and sisters cut off his curls and made him carry them to his mother in his pinafore. They were amongst her papers at her death, and those who wish to can still see them today in the Museum of Edinburgh. He was a headstrong little boy, a fact acknowledged on the drum which his mother gave him, inscribed: 'Douglas Haig – sometimes a good boy'. When he was to have his photograph taken, tantrums were only brought to an end and rebellion subdued by allowing him to pose with a toy pistol in his hand. Amateur psychologists can make something of this, but the resulting photograph is bizarre: with full cheeks and a decadent expression, Douglas wears skirts, not unusual for a little boy in these days, carries his pistol, and looks like an infant Oscar Wilde *en travestie.* Photographed a year or two later in his first kilt, he has already the uncompromising stare that is reproduced on so many statues. Descriptions of Haig in these early years refer to prominent teeth and suggest that he was not particularly good looking. The photographs that I have seen of him in his youth do not particularly support this view: at any rate by the time that he was in his teens he was an exceptionally good-looking young man and he maintained his stern good looks for the rest of his life. Haig took great pains to keep fit; his bearing was erect and soldierly until the very last stages of the war, when the stress of events gave him a slight stoop. His face was expressionless, a fact which was regarded by some as indicative of strength of character and imperturbability. In photographs he appears to lead with his moustache, and his appearance is strikingly similar to that of Lord Olivier, whom Kenneth Tynan described as looking like a retired major from Sunningdale. The eyes are penetrating, and the moustache thick but well clipped, at least until the later years of the War: at that stage, perhaps as a result of the time he had spent with French generals, it becomes much more bushy and more wayward. He would not have liked the thought that he was going native and imitating the *poilus*.

Though it is difficult to imagine the First World War generals without their moustaches, it is something of a surprise to this generation to be reminded that in Haig's time an army officer was obliged to have a growth on his upper lip. Sir William Robertson records in his autobiography that when he was Commandant of the Staff College, he had to have one officer discharged from the college because of his refusal to wear a moustache. 'No one would be so idiotic as to think that an officer is any better for wearing a moustache than he is for shaving or clipping it off, and the regulation has since been abolished, but staff officers are expected to set an example of obeying the King's Regulations.'[2] The young man in question was embarrassed by a rather weedy growth, but he did not lack courage: in the war, by which time he was not required to wear a moustache for his country, he gave his life.

A contemporary referred to 'that great, Fife chin'. When he wished to make a point strongly, his head would be tilted back, and the chin thrust forward. He had an iron control of his temper, and generally spoke with courtesy, with a quiet voice. But when occasionally he *did* lose his temper, he could be excoriating, and a savage rebuke from someone of his bearing was not easily forgotten.

Rachel's influence on Douglas was largely the expression of her very strong religious faith, and her belief that her life was to be devoted to the care and upbringing of her children. As John's influence was minimal – he was to die in 1878 of an abscess of the liver (providing in his will that his workforce could drink as much as they wanted on the date of his funeral; they subsequently tried to claim this as an annual entitlement) – there was great scope for Rachel to seek to influence her children as she thought right, and to impart to them her strong moral convictions. Douglas's sister, Janet, wrote to him that: 'Her devotion to us shortened her life by many years.' Her health was never strong, but she took no account of that in the care and attention that she lavished on her children, particularly her three youngest sons, John, George and Douglas. She rose at four every morning and from them on supervised the family until she attended their prayers at bedtime. She believed that every individual was able – and was under a duty – to form the shape of his or her life; at the same time checks or setbacks were not of concern because everything was the expression of God's will. She wrote in 1859 to a tutor of her son, Willie:

Our object is not to make Willie a distiller or anything in particular. We desire to develop in him to the utmost such gifts as he has received from God – to improve those intellectual qualities in which he may be deficient and to cultivate his moral powers: – to see him grow up a humble and earnest Christian – an accomplished, well-informed and liberal-minded *gentleman* – with these qualifications be his lot in life what may, he will command respect and be in a position to derive happiness in whatever position of life God may place him . . . As for myself I attach so much importance to scholarship – especially as an antidote to the vulgarity and narrowness of mind which active commercial pursuits are apt to engender in the best . . .

There is no evidence that Rachel's religious views played any great part in Haig's own beliefs until well into the war. At that time however as we shall see later, his interest in religion was to grow significantly, and a confident, Christian fatalism undoubtedly supported him in his years as Commander-in-Chief.

Haig's education consisted in a series of ad hoc arrangements. He first went to school as a boarder at Mr Bateson's school at Clifton Bank, in St Andrews, in 1869 when his father had to go abroad to take the cure. Later in the same year he and his brother John went to the Edinburgh Collegiate School, which was in Charlotte Square. The family's Edinburgh house had been given up by now, and the two brothers lodged with a Miss Hepburn in Castle Terrace. A master there recalled him as a 'clean, well turned out boy' who was intellectually backward.[3] His brother, John, acknowledged that Douglas had educational problems, and thought that they originated in his experience at the Edinburgh Collegiate School: a disappointing start to an academic career that was never to be distinguished.

In 1871 Douglas went, like John, as a boarder at Orwell House, a preparatory school at Clifton-on-Dunsmoor, Warwickshire. The headmaster was David Hanbury, a former Rugby pupil. The school was only two and a half miles from Rugby, and it was intended that Douglas should go on to that school. Hanbury refused to recommend for Rugby any pupils who did not, in his view, meet that school's requirements, and Douglas's time at Orwell House was a difficult one, as it became more and more apparent that Rugby would be beyond his abilities. His Latin was poor, as was his spelling and writing. 'As he is backward he ought to be more attentive.' There was something of a duel between Hanbury ('It would not do Douglas any harm if he worked a little harder') and Rachel ('My own darling boy take the hint and try and work a little harder . . . Tell me all about it, as there is no one, as you know, whose thoughts centre so much on you my darling Douglas . . . Your advancement into Big School is my great desire, as you know so well').

By the time he went to Orwell House, Haig was in poor health, suffering from acute attacks of asthma. A relative described him in one these attacks when he stayed with her in his holidays: 'The boy was sitting up in bed with a shawl round his shoulders fighting for breath and smoking *datura tatula* cigarettes, which seems to do him good . . . He continued to suffer from asthma for many years, but undoubtedly cured himself by his determination always to avoid anything that might bring on a fresh attack.'[4] Throughout his early life he was at pains to take steps to avoid provoking recurrences of his asthma. There is a view amongst some doctors that asthma is associated with high achievers and with a determination to succeed.

His school reports from Orwell House make fairly dismal reading, and cannot entirely be attributed to his ill health: 'Very backward in Latin'; 'spelling very poor and writing careless'; 'rather tiresome at times'.[5] Hanbury advised that 'It is hardly worthwhile his going up to Rugby as he will be chucked out in a year or so.' Rachel: Rugby was 'not so particular as Mr. H. would lead one to suppose'.

Ultimately, however, and in typical fashion, Rachel accepted Mr Hanbury's advice:

I had a letter last Saturday from Mr. Hanbury writing to know where we thought of placing you, as he could not advise you to go up for Rugby as your knowledge of Greek was so deficient you would never pass . . . Of course, as you know, I was very sorry to get Mr. H's letter, but then I felt satisfied it was for your good as I had so completely cast it upon God to do for you exactly what He knew was to be for your good, and now I have no more regrets about it if it be for your good.

The school to which Douglas was sent, in lieu of Rugby, was Clifton College. Clifton had been founded in 1862, in fairly clear imitation of the values and tradition of Rugby. The school was owned by 400 shareholders and each shareholder had the right to nominate a boy for a place in the school.[6] But I can trace no evidence that Haig entered the school in this way, and even if he was not up to the standard of Rugby, he probably deserved to be admitted to Clifton on his own merits. Moreover Clifton came a pretty good second, after Rugby, in the matter of formation of character; and Haig's brother, John 'Bee', had already gone there. In any event, perhaps Haig could never have escaped from going to Clifton. Studious readers will have noted that his first school had been Clifton Bank, and that his preparatory school was at Clifton-on-Dunsmoor.

Clifton was good for Haig. Its headmaster, who had in fact been a master at Rugby under Dr Arnold, was John Percival. He was one of the towering figures of Victorian education: he was successively headmaster of Clifton, President of Trinity College, Oxford, headmaster of Rugby, and finally Bishop of Hereford. He was associated with the establishment of innumerable educational institutions: he seems rarely to have visited a provincial city without establishing a school or university. He was involved in the foundation of University College, Bristol, of Clifton itself, of Redland High School, and of Somerville College, Oxford. 'A son of the humblest of parents he nevertheless proved himself to be a Prince of Nature, arrestingly handsome, outstandingly intelligent, morally incorruptible, tirelessly hardworking'.[7] His father had been a farmer and part-time wrestler. Despite this unlikely background, by sheer determination, hard work and brilliance of intellect he gained a double first at Oxford. When Percival came to Clifton, Archbishop Temple promised that he would do for the school what Arnold had done for Rugby. Sir Henry Newbolt, a contemporary of Haig at Clifton and, according to Lawrence Binyon, one of his few close friends, said that Percival had 'the grace of a marble statue'. When G.F. Watts saw Percival enter a crowded room, he immediately exclaimed: 'Who is that man? I must paint his portrait.' For Percival, as for the other great Victorian educators, education was not, as it perhaps is for us, merely a process to qualify children for material advancement: it was a vitally important means by which *moral* advancement might be achieved. Men and women would be made better people, and would be inspired to work for a better world. Percival was above all energetic, seized of the urgent desire that boys should work hard, play hard and pray hard.

Later in life, in almost every aspect of his behaviour and in the demands he made of others, Haig seems to have absorbed in full measure the culture of the Victorian public school, and it is tempting to see behind this the influence of Clifton, modelled on Rugby, and presided over by Percival. Many who know nothing else of Clifton College will be aware of the poem that Haig's friend, Sir Henry Newbolt, wrote and that is so closely associated with the school, *Vitaï Lampada*, with its famous couplet:

> But the voice of a schoolboy rallies the ranks,
> 'Play up! play up! and play the game!'

The poem was written in 1897. Newbolt came to dislike it: 'It's a kind of Frankenstein's monster that I created', he was to complain. But it was well received both by the critics and the general public and, significantly, it enjoyed a revival of popularity at the outbreak of the War. It is interesting that when that war broke out, Newbolt was recruited to the War Propaganda Bureau to help to shape public opinion. His expression of a distinctive ethos is unmistakable, and that the ethos is that of Clifton is underlined by the fact that a collection of his poems is called *Clifton Chapel*, and one poem indeed carries that name. It contains the lines:

> To set the cause above renown
> To love the game beyond the prize,
> To honour, while you strike him down
> The foe that comes with fearless eyes.

Even a recent Clifton appeal to its old boys contains many quotations from Newbolt. Of the school itself he wrote:

> For though the dust that's part of us
> To dust again be gone,
> Yet here shall be the heart of us,
> The school be handed on.[8]

The atmosphere that Newbolt created is powerful, and the epitome of the nineteenth-century public school spirit. Haig was unable to escape its influence and, in later life, he repeatedly falls back on the code and values that were taught at Clifton, a code and values that, of course, could be relied upon to reinforce and hold together the army and the Empire. But although he may have been unable to escape every nuance of its influence, Clifton had a limited immediate impact on Haig's maturing mind. Even if Sir George Arthur exaggerates when he describes Clifton as 'where [Haig] worked with little distinction and played games with even less',[9] Haig never really integrated into the apparatus of the school. Charteris suggests that the most permanent influence that Clifton left on Haig was provided by the school motto, *Spiritus intus alit,* 'The Spirit that quickeneth,' was a phrase that was repeatedly on Haig's lips throughout his life, reflecting his strong personal convictions.

Having interviewed Haig, Percival concluded that he was not capable of entering the Fourth Form and was therefore ineligible to reside in the School House, and instead he was boarded out for about fifteen months with one of the masters, Mr Marks, from whom he received private coaching. It was not until January 1877 that he was admitted into the Fourth Form and was able to enter School House.

His school progress was described later by N. Whatley, headmaster in 1929:

> He was placed in the Lower Fourth on the classical side. At the end of his first term he was promoted to the Upper Fourth. After two terms he was promoted to the Lower Fifth. Up to that time he had made quite rapid progress. In the Lower Fifth he seems to have slowed down, and remained there for four terms, during which he slowly made his way up the form. He was seventh in the form when he left in April 1879.

By his final term, Haig was able to pass first in Latin. His mother responded:

> Oh! Such pleasure it has given me! Your report! So satisfactory and delightful and to me *so true* . . . This 'decided improvement'

is to me the more satisfactory since your time at Clifton *is so short*. I should like you to leave the best of characters behind you – and so would you, yourself my darling.

Even if he achieved this distinction in Latin (which he hated), he showed neither ability nor enthusiasm for sport. His brother John was to say that Douglas was 'never very good at games' and Rachel was concerned that he might become a 'weakly Cad'. Cricket would 'make you strong and manly'. He did manage to play rugby for his House and was awarded a school cap, and Lady Haig was to find a Clifton contemporary who described him as 'full of guts and by no means lacking in fun . . . a dour fighter, active as a cat and as brave as a lion'.[10]

As to whether he was to 'leave the best of characters behind' him, when he left the school, the fact is that he seems to have made very little impression at all on his contemporaries. The description of the 'dour fighter, active as a cat and as brave as a lion', may require to be viewed with some caution. It is extracted from some notes explicitly provided to Lady Haig for the purpose of her biography from the one school fellow who recalled anything of Haig at Clifton. As she herself acknowledged, 'few seem to have known him intimately, for he was of a very reserved nature.' Throughout his time in School House he shared a study with Richard Threlfall, who as Sir Richard Threlfall, FRS, was to be much involved in the application of scientific research and inventions to the war effort. Despite the fact that his old study mate was by this time the Commander-in-Chief of the British Armies in France, Threlfall never, ever spoke of him.[11] Similarly, the man who as a boy had sat next to Haig in the Lower Fifth said in a letter to Charteris in 1929 that Haig had made no close friendships at the School – perhaps because he never reached the Sixth Form.

His minimal impact at Clifton is confirmed by Major-General Sir Francis Younghusband in a contribution in the Memorial issue of British Legion *Journal*, a contribution which is all the more interesting for its departure from the extravagant tone of most of the other contributions:

Haig as a boy at Clifton was inclined to keep himself to himself,
and I do not remember that he had any particular friends – nor,
as far as that goes, any particular enemies. He was, perhaps,
rather a proud boy, good-looking, and more careful about his
appearance than were the generality of boys and one of those
boys who like to go their own way, neither troubling other boys
nor letting other boys trouble them.

We were in the same house together, and this is the
impression left upon me. And I must remember him fairly
well, for I was able more than forty years later to identify the
study he had in the School House, and his identification of it
and my own were the same. But as a boy he made no mark in
the school. He did not rise to the sixth form and his only
distinction at games was his 'cap' at football. He was an
undistinguished, aloof boy – a hero of neither boys nor masters.
No one who knew him as a boy at Clifton would have been fool
enough to prophesy that he would become the greatest national
hero of his day. Nor, I should imagine, would even Haig
himself. For he was composed and self-contained rather than
ambitious and imaginative. At school he was always the gentleman, but never the hero.[12]

Equally, he made little mark academically. His career through the
forms stalled, and he had been stuck in the Lower Fifth for four terms,
when he left Clifton in April 1879.

Haig might have stayed on longer at Clifton but for the fact that,
contrary to his wishes and those of both his form master and Percival,
Rachel had decided that it was time for him to move on to Oxford.

[B]y going *early* you will be finished *early* and ready to begin
your Profession or Trade at once when you pass . . . *You are not
too young* and the time would be lost don't you think, were you
to delay . . . going to College.

[D]o as I have always done in such cases *seek to be directed* – and
you may rest assured *God will shew you* and my dear boy isn't it

delightful to feel that you will be *wisely* directed and you may rest passive in the matter . . . I trust that you will *ask for guidance as the matter concerns much* of your future happiness in life and we know nothing can prosper without God.

In the event, Haig's passage from his youthful education to the more mature world of university was tragically marked by Rachel's death on 21 March 1879 at the age of fifty-nine. She had been in poor health for some time. In the autumn of 1878 Haig had had to return to Clifton leaving her seriously ill. On the following day Percival wrote to Haig's sister, Henrietta, and mentioned the family's 'prolonged anxiety. I hope that the doctors are now giving better hopes of her recovery and that her life may be spared to you . . . I feel that she will be glad to know from me that yr brother though he does not make much progress with his classics, and is not naturally fond of learning, is I am sure vy anxious to do his duty and live an honourable and manly life.'[13]

Haig was heartbroken by her death. She had doted on her favourite son, and he, unlike some of his siblings, never rejected her values. During his holidays he had spent days talking to her on her sickbed, but he was all the more affected by her death because he had been unable to return home to be with her when she died. As a consequence of her death, he postponed his entry to Oxford, and, with his brother Hugo, visited the United States. Little is recorded about the trip, but it afforded him an opportunity to mature and see himself as an independent individual. From now on his plans and objectives are his own. Though he might rely heavily on Henrietta, and later Doris, for support, no one directed his path.

His move to Oxford at the age of nineteen also effectively broke his close connection with Scotland, at least until he moved to Bemersyde after the war. He had been brought up till this age in a thoroughly Scottish environment, had some experience of the Scottish education system, and had worshipped as a member of the Church of Scotland, with its strong sense of purpose, uncompromising morality and intellectual vigour. It is not surprising that throughout his life he saw

himself as a Scotsman and that others continually remarked on his
Scottish character. What is a *little* surprising is that despite the
worlds in which he was subsequently to move – an aristocratic
Oxford, Sandhurst, fashionable regiments and the upper échelons of
society – he retained a marked Scottish accent, which became even
more pronounced in times of crisis. '[I]n his more emphatic moments
[he] tended to lapse into broad Doric'.[14] The second Earl recalls only
a standard English accent, but, whatever his accent, Haig was in
temperament essentially Scots, and he always regarded himself as a
Scot, albeit of a Unionist disposition: when he came to live at
Bemersyde towards the end of his life, he gave his address, in the style
of the times as Melrose, *North Britain*.

From his schooldays onward he took with him the formality of
bearing that Younghusband hints at when he refers to Haig's care
about his appearance. He was scrupulously correct in his behaviour
and etiquette, and was a perfect and thoughtful host. Harold
Nicolson, a very well-qualified judge, described him as having
exquisite, but rather over-formal, manners. Others referred to his
style of *Grand Seigneur*, distinctly *de haut en bas*.

3

IN TOP BOOTS AMONGST THE INTELLECTUALS: HAIG AT OXFORD. SANDHURST AT LAST

The Oxford to which Haig went in October 1880 was *far* closer to the picture painted by Max Beerbohm in *Zuleika Dobson* than we can readily imagine.

There were some scholars who entered the university by way of competitive examination. The rest of the undergraduates (all male) were 'gentlemen Commoners', distinguished by their 'tofts', the silk tassels worn on their caps; and providing they had sufficient means, they faced no entrance requirement. All that was necessary was that once in residence they should pass a simple, and very crammable, examination known as 'Responsions' or, colloquially, 'Smalls'. Responsions were no more than the re-examination of work done at school. Haig did not require to face even this modest hurdle as, despite his lack of enthusiasm in the classics, he had already obtained a certificate of proficiency conferring exemption while at school.

Most Commoners sought only a Pass, rather than an Honours, degree, and many did not trouble to take a degree at all. For such people Oxford was a place for expanding one's social rather than intellectual horizons, and for making the transition from the world of public school to the wider world of London clubs, gentlemanly pursuits and, perhaps, a suitable profession. The gulf between 'Passmen' and 'Classmen' widened after reforms of 1872: 'By its character and the methods of teaching which it called into being, the Pass School was in danger of becoming a joke.' There was little choice in the questions to be answered, which consisted of not much more than interrogation on set texts and points of grammar. The degree for which Haig read was simply a Pass. No stigma was attached to failure, as it was no great problem to resit just those parts of the exam that had been failed.[1]

Haig might have been expected to have some difficulty, after his fragmented schooling, in adapting to this rarefied existence, but he settled down into it very easily. He came with an income of about £500 a year, about £25,000 in today's terms, and was therefore able to live in some style.

As recently as 1871, as a member of the Church of Scotland, he could not have gone to Oxford at all. The Test Acts, passed in 1672, precluded anyone who was not a practising member of the Church of England from holding public office, and between 1689 and 1702 the legislation had been extended to apply to members of the universities of Oxford and Cambridge. Although the Test Acts were generally repealed in 1828, they continued to apply to students and dons at Oxford and Cambridge until the passing of the University Tests Act in 1871. The purpose of a university education changed greatly, if not overnight. In the period to 1850 the majority of undergraduates entered holy orders, but by 1882–91 the percentage had reduced to approximately thirty-nine per cent.

Haig's choice of a college, Brasenose, was slightly surprising. Brasenose was not one of the smart colleges for which he might have been expected to opt. Christ Church, Oriel, Balliol and University were the colleges for the sons of the great landed magnates. But if Brasenose was not one of the richer and more prestigious colleges, it was all the same thoroughly respectable: nearly a third of those admitted to the college between 1815 and 1820 became country gentlemen and its Phoenix common room was reputed to be the oldest social club in Oxford. It had a 'marked but not exclusive predilection for the exercises and amusements of outdoor life'.[2] Rowing was only the sport for which it was best known. The Principal was Dr Craddock. At his first meeting with Haig he told him, 'Ride, sir, ride – I like to see the gentlemen of Brasenose in top

boots.' One of Haig's contemporaries at Brasenose was the later Lord
Justice Askwith, who supplied much of the information about Haig's
time there. Craddock's advice to Askwith was: 'Drink plenty of port,
sir, you want plenty of port in this damp climate.'

Throughout most of his life, Haig kept a most extensive diary. He
began it at Oxford in 1883:

> Having often times heard of the advantages to be derived from
> keeping a diary, I determined to keep one. The difficulty is to
> have a good day to begin upon.
>
> I think it is well to start on the 19th day of last June upon
> which day I was 21 and put down as many events as I can
> remember with accuracy which happened from then until this
> day [in February 1883].

At this time the diary is not continuous, but it does give an
indication of the sort of life Haig lived at Oxford.

He studied a number of required courses: Greek, Latin and
Rudiments of Religion. In addition he chose to read French literature, elements of political economy and ancient history. There is no
indication that he took any of this very seriously. Lord Askwith said
that: 'No dinner and no club . . . deterred Haig if he was not
prepared for a particular lecture or essay', but in fact his régime was a
very relaxed one. Mornings might be spent 'drawing and reading in
my rooms' and the afternoons were given over to sport. Brasenose's
favourite activity, rowing, was quickly abandoned: ('He could not
bear the monotony of tubbings or the upbraidings of coaches'), but
not before he had won two cups. In his second year he took up polo,
which was to become his great enthusiasm. Polo had been introduced
to England by the 11th Hussars as recently as 1870, but had already
come to be an essential skill, almost a route to promotion, in the
Victorian army. Legend has it that Haig wrote to the university
authorities for permission to play the game in the University Parks,
claiming that it was of great antiquity and had been brought to
Europe by Marco Polo. The first game against Cambridge took place

in his time, Haig scoring the only Oxford goal. He played for the
university in 1882 and 1883, frequently later represented his
regiment, and indeed played for England at the sport. In the spirit
and dash of polo can be seen the seed of Haig's later devotion to the
cavalry.

He lived a privileged time at Oxford, though not exceptional
amongst those of his background. He maintained horses, so that he
could ride with the Bicester Hunt, as well as his string of polo ponies.
A full-time groom was employed. He ate and drank well, and ordered
expensive wines and good food, dining out or in his rooms rather
than in Hall.

He was a member of the socially acceptable university clubs of the
day: the Bullingdon, the Vampyres, the Phoenix and Vincent's. The
first and last of these were, and remain, élite establishments, the
Bullingdon for aristocratic, hunting undergraduates, Vincent's for
sportsmen.

Although Haig mixed with people such as Sir Edward Grey and
Lord Robert Cecil, he did not greatly warm to those of exceptional
ability. Askwith, admittedly writing long afterwards, and with
benevolent intent, recorded that:

> Haig spent much of his time working in his rooms but attended
> the big college lunches which were occasionally held. He knew
> and was pleasant to everyone, not minding with whom he sat
> but by no means courting popularity. He liked to talk quietly to
> his neighbour about a subject interesting to his neighbour or
> affecting the life or athletics of the college rather than his own
> interests. He loved a quiet joke but I never heard him make one.
> To Hall he seldom went but dined out, always returning early,
> and hating to sit up at night.

Askwith's recollection here was certainly partisan. He mentions
elsewhere that at a dinner for old Brasenose members in London
in 1909, Haig recalled his delight at having nothing to do for two
years after passing Smalls. But his vignette of Haig sitting slightly

aside from the centre of things, thinking his own thoughts, a detached observer, not only fits with what his schoolmates remembered of him, but is true of how he was to live his life: never clubbable, capable of deploying learned social skills, but always self-contained and apart.

Oxford conformed to the episodic nature of Haig's education: he missed a whole summer term as a result of influenza (an early indication of his less than robust constitution), and the consequent failure to comply with the university's residence requirements meant that he could not take his Pass degree without spending another eight weeks in Oxford. It is a reflection on his attitude to the university that he chose not to delay his future career by returning to complete that eight weeks' residence, and he never did take a degree, though the age limit for entry to Sandhurst may also have been a constraint. In 1889 he wrote to the Bursar of Brasenose, asking whether he could obtain an MA if he completed his residence for his BA. He explains that he had missed one term of residence because 'I was seedy':

Up to date I have not been able to keep this term, owing to my having joined the Army, but I hope some day to make the term good, and take my MA. Having been to Oxford for three years it is just as well to have a degree, to show one went thro' the place fairly creditably, for it seems that a fair proportion of those who go through the university now return without one. I shall probably be able to keep the term in two or three years' time, but probably the College authorities have other views on the subject.

But he did not keep the term.

Haig never regarded Oxford as a major formative experience, and the university remembered him better than he remembered it. He was made an honorary fellow of his college even before he went to the Western Front (when he asked the college if he had passed enough exams for such a distinction), and in June 1919 his college gave a

dinner in Oxford Town Hall for him: the college hall was not big
enough. Responding to the principal toast, Haig replied:

> It is here in Oxford that is found the main stronghold of the
> opinion that the highest and most important object of educa-
> tion is the formation of character. Believing as I do that our
> national character is chiefly due to our success in battle, and
> being aware of the criticisms that from time to time have been
> levelled against university education, it is only natural that I
> should seek to turn an occasion such as this to profit, by telling
> you how convinced I am you are right.

The college magazine, *The Brazen Nose*, reported:

> At conclusion of the dinner the guests returned to the college
> where a bonfire had been lit and many of the vice-principals of
> the past must have turned in their graves as Brasenose men,
> unchecked and unreported, fed the fire with various assortments
> of fuel, not unassisted, so scandal reports, by an old member of
> the college whose name is world famous.

Seventy years later, the successors of these Brasenose men defaced that
old member's portrait in the college hall. But Oxford had done more
for Haig than perhaps he realised. In his time there he had matured
from a schoolboy who had fallen in with all his mother's wishes, to an
independent and very assured young man who knew where he was
going. His diary entries at Oxford show considerable self-satisfaction,
and an undisguised pride in his achievements.

During the war he said that what he had gained from Oxford was
the ability to form his own judgements: '[B]y the time I went to
Sandhurst I had learned to think for myself: I didn't, like so many of
the other fellows, take everything I was taught for Gospel.' This he
said was a lesson that remained with him all his life.[3]

One of Haig's tutors at Oxford was Walter Pater. The congruence
of the athlete and the aesthete, of the bluff, outdoor Haig and the

fastidious author of *Marius the Epicurean*, is delicious. 'Faint, pale, embarrassed, exquisite Pater', tiptoed through life, said Thomas Hardy, like 'one carrying weighty ideas without spilling them.' He was a well-known Oxford figure, in his swallow-tailed coat, striped trousers, top hat, kid gloves and, always, a silk, apple-green tie. On one occasion Haig by contrast arrived for his tutorial wearing hunting clothes under his gown, and his mind was not on Homer. 'Next week,' Pater murmured, 'I suggest you read Thackeray or Dickens.' Thackeray and Dickens were far from Pater's idea of serious reading-matter, and the rebuke would have been damaging to a thinner-skinned man than Haig. Later Haig admitted that 'Pater would discourse to me about Plato, when my own desire many a time was to be out hunting.' 'But,' he claimed

> there was one thing I did learn from Pater, and I have never forgotten it. He used to impress on us that, if we were to express our ideas fully and clearly in writing, we would need first of all to think out clearly what it was we wanted to say; then we would need to be equally careful to find the right words in which to say it, for it might well be that there was only one word, or one form of words, that would be quite right for the matter in hand. And he told us too that we would never acquire that except by long discipline and practice . . . What a pity some of my army friends hadn't learned that lesson better! They issue an order one day; but it is so badly worded that they have to issue another next day to explain or correct it.[4]

He did learn to express himself on paper with outstanding clarity, but Oxford did not do for him what it might have been thought to exist to do: his intellectual development had not advanced in any way. Haig was far from dim, but he certainly was a late starter. It may be that he simply did not bother to work until he felt that something was worth working for. He was always against scholarship without a purpose and disparaged the 'pundits' or 'scribes'. Although intelligent, he was not remotely an intellectual. Abstract ideas did not interest him. He rarely read books that did not bear on his profession. His information on other subjects was taken from magazine articles, and it was taken unquestioningly. If he thought for himself more than 'the other fellows' at Sandhurst, that tells us less about him than about them. If he read that something was the case then that was the end of the matter. This uncritical acceptance of what he was told fed that propensity to be misled by over-optimistic intelligence which was to prolong some of the battles in the war.

It is not obvious why or when Haig decided to make his career in the army. There was no military tradition in the family. The idea may have been planted by Henrietta, who had originally wanted her brother John to go into the army. Certainly she was to take the closest of interests in Haig's career. The notion that he had decided on the army before he left Clifton is contradicted by the Reverend George Duncan, his chaplain in France from 1916, who talked to Haig about his Oxford days at length during the war: he says that Haig had no idea of his future career when he left school to travel across America 'as far as California and then spent three years of glorious irresponsibility' at Oxford.[5] As early as his first evening at Brasenose he told Askwith that he intended to be soldier, though he briefly and bizarrely thought of a career in the Diplomatic Service, a wonderfully inappropriate dream.

Haig told Askwith that he was too old to go into the army 'in the usual way'; but going to Sandhurst direct from school, which was the usual way, would in any case have posed problems for Haig. Although not intellectually demanding (indeed there had not been any entrance examination for Sandhurst until 1877), getting in to the Royal College required a huge amount of learning by rote. Sir Henry Wilson, Chief of the Imperial General Staff by the end of the war, was proud of the fact that he failed no less than three times to get into Sandhurst, and Haig would have had to work hard to go direct from Clifton. There was, however, an easier route: someone who had passed the purely formal 'Responsions' examination at Oxford (or the Cambridge equivalent, 'Previous') could go direct to Sandhurst without sitting an examination at all. Some have taken the view that this was Haig's intention all along, and that it was only for this reason that he went to Oxford. I find no evidence to support that theory, intriguing though it is, and I suspect that he went to Oxford simply in obedience to his mother's wishes.

At any rate, having gone to Oxford without an examination and having left it without a degree examination, Haig was able to go to Sandhurst on 12 February 1884 without sitting an entrance examination. All the same, he attempted to bring himself up to the same level as the other competitors, by spending six months at a crammer near Hampton Court.

When he entered Sandhurst, Haig was three or four years older than the other entrants, and there must have been a certain coolness on the part of his juniors, who despite their youthfulness had passed examinations that he had bypassed. If they were cool, Haig was never the man to display warmth, and he formed no lasting friendships at the college.

What he did do, for the first time in his life, was to work very hard. The work at Sandhurst was largely theoretical and involved much learning by rote. Haig displayed the discipline that was to mark the rest of his career, and slogged through the work doggedly. He started the habit, which was to endure, of planning out his day according to a strict timetable. Time off-duty was similarly planned, and allocated to pursuits which would tend to promote his career. The two sports to which he was dedicated, hunting and polo, can both be seen as such. There are few memories of Haig's time at Sandhurst, but the impression is that he was regarded by his colleagues, from whom he was separated by age and by his unblinking ambition, with awe. This would not have disconcerted Haig: he was never to understand a desire for popularity. When he was cramming for Sandhurst he was invited by a friend, George Drummond, to join some of his future fellow-students in a game of roulette. His response was pretty intolerable and not calculated to endear him to his colleagues: 'It's all very well for you fellows. You are going into the army to play at soldiering. I am going into it as a profession, and I am going to do well in it.' His room-mate at Sandhurst, General Sir Walter Congreve, VC, as he would become (who had been sent down from Oxford for shooting at a don with an air-gun), recalled that: 'After a lecture he would sit down and write out his notes, which few RMC cadets have done before or since.' One would have gone some distance to steer clear of Haig at this stage in his career, and indeed for quite a time afterwards. His room-mate at school never mentioned his name, and his room-mate at Sandhurst described him as 'taciturn and rough'.[6]

His developing ambition is illustrated well by a story from one of Haig's Oxford contemporaries: 'I said I thought that the Army did not shew much of an opening. His chin went out squarer and more determined than ever as he replied: "It all depends on the man himself how he gets on in any profession. If I went into the church I'd be a bishop".'

He had been transformed from an underachieving and unendurable schoolboy into a highly ambitious and motivated young man. The ability was no doubt there all along, but something had activated it. Haig was now a man with a keen sense of his own destiny. The affable but unremarkable Oxford undergraduate had become an abrasive careerist. During the following years he did what was not then done, and particularly not in the polo and cavalry circles in which he moved: he displayed his desire to advance his career, and set out to acquire precisely the skills which he thought would be required in the type of conflict which he foresaw.

What was the catalyst which precipitated this change? Some have thought it was his mother's death. He certainly was devoted to her. The second Earl thinks it was because he so venerated her that Haig married late. All that can be said is that in the period between her death and the end of his time at Oxford, Haig had found a vision that was never to leave him: a sense of his ability and of his duty to fulfil his potential. It does not greatly matter whether he was trying to achieve what his mother had wanted for him or whether, on the contrary, as no one was now directing his footsteps, he had for the first time to mark out his career for himself. His sense of his own worth never thereafter deserted him.

At Sandhurst he was appointed a senior under-officer in his company. Senior under-officers often became bullies or tyrants. Haig was neither, but he was a perfectionist and required strict discipline from the fellow cadets who were under his authority. His time at Sandhurst reinforced his capacity for existing at a distance from those around him, but Haig received from the Military College (not yet an Academy) what he wanted: in less than a year he passed out first, winning the Anson Memorial Sword as senior under-officer. One of the instructors, when asked who was the most promising cadet, replied: 'A Scottish lad, Douglas Haig, is top in almost everything – books, drill, riding, and sports; he is to go into the Cavalry, and, before he is finished, he will be top of the Army.'[7]

4

REGIMENTAL LIFE. INDIA.
JOHNNIE FRENCH

Haig left Sandhurst and entered the army at one of what John Terraine identified as 'three outstandingly poor spells in the British Army's history', the final decade of the nineteenth century, the years that lead up to the South African War. The important Cardwell Reforms had taken place, bringing the War Office together in one building and one entity, abolishing purchase of commissions, grounding regiments in the counties, and basing them on 'linked' battalions, one abroad and one at home. But despite, or even because of, the Reforms, the army was not a unified and systematised body: it was a disparate series of units, scattered over the vast span of the British Empire. In Whitehall, Lord Wolsley and Sir Evelyn Wood, whose protégé Haig was to become, tried to improve the effectiveness of the military machine, and in India, Lord Roberts concentrated on the garrison army. But there was little coordination between these few significant and conscientious officers; and over the whole military edifice presided its Commander-in-Chief, Queen Victoria's cousin, the Duke of Cambridge, who was to hold his office for thirty-nine years. His blinkered conservatism is encapsulated in the famous story of his introducing an Aldershot lecture on foreign cavalry: 'Why should we want to know anything about foreign cavalry? We've better cavalry of our own. I fear, gentlemen, that the Army is in danger of becoming a mere debating society.' On another occasion: 'The British officer should be a gentleman first and an officer second.'

In view of his prowess on the hunting field and at polo, it is not surprising that Haig chose to go into the cavalry. Appropriately he decided on a regiment that had been raised in Scotland, the 7th (Queen's Own) Hussars. The 7th Hussars was a proud regiment, distinguished as much for its long and splendid fighting history as for its social renown and reputation for dandyism: 'The Saucy Seventh'. Haig was to spend no less than nine years with the regiment. He gave it good service, but he never developed the intense, familial affection that very frequently existed in those days between regimental officers and the regiment in which they often spent their whole careers. Equally, after he left the regiment he was not linked to it by emotional ties. For him, the 7th Hussars was a vehicle for advancement.

For its part, the regimental history has few records of Haig except in relation to his polo activities. As early as 1886 he was part of the English polo team that went to America. Later, playing polo with the regiment in India, he is said to have reduced the art of 'dribbling' at full speed to a mechanical certainty.[1] There was plenty of time for polo. The cavalry claimed they existed to die for their country in time of war and to give tone to the army in time of peace, and in these times of peace, the day's duties for an officer in the 7th Hussars would be finished by mid-morning.

Almost immediately on his return from polo in America, the regiment was ordered to India, and in July 1886 Haig embarked on the troopship *Euphrates*. Haig's observation of the activities of the officers' wives on board was that: 'Women are at the bottom of all quarrels.' The rich, good-looking and eligible bachelor remained always remote from scandal.

When he reached India, Haig's initial months in the subcontinent were marked by the ill health that was to recur frequently throughout his life. In March 1887 he went down with enteric fever and was ill for a month. The frequency of his illnesses was such that at one point he wrote: 'If I get any more fevers I shall probably leave India at once.' His interest in his health may have flowed from the fact that he wished to keep it in such order that it would not obstruct his

ambitions, and some of his illnesses were certainly real enough, but at
other points his concern for his health, and the pains that he took to
protect it clearly amount to valid valetudinarianism, if not to actual
hypochondria.

By drawing not just on Haig's diaries, but also on the account of
Sergeant-Major H.J. Harrison, who served under Haig in India, one
biographer gives an unattractive picture of a humourless, ambitious
officer, five years older than his peers, striving to make up for lost
time.[2] The relevant chapter is entitled 'A Martinet'. Harrison had
reason to dislike Haig, but his account in fact balances criticism and
praise:

> On the drill ground, in the riding school, on the field, and in
> Camp or barracks, Haig was the same brilliant worker. At all
> times and in all weathers, Haig went about 'Soldiering', and
> Haig's soldiering was admitted by all who mattered to be
> unrelated to ordinary drills and tactics, but was embellished
> with a kind of finishing off process exclusively Haig.

When Harrison first arrived in India:

> Lt. Haig in plain soldierly language made it clear to every
> member of the draft that every soldier in that famous regiment
> must be a man, and that effeminate or sentimental qualities
> would prove a menace, and a detriment to promotion . . .
> Exactitude, Promptitude, Smartness and strict veracity were a
> few of the virtues our adjutant strictly adhered to, and sympathy
> for a technical error was unknown . . . Procrastination, Slowness
> of Perception, untidiness and Nerves, were items calculated to
> make Lt. Haig spit fire . . . A dull-witted man was Haig's pet
> aversion.[3]

Haig told the men that he had sacrificed the pleasures of family life
and social contact and he expected his men, similarly, to be 'blindly
devoted to their duties . . . with . . . human sentiments totally

eradicated.' It is relevant to Haig's long period of celibacy that for practical reasons he was opposed to soldiers, even other ranks, being married: 'And a man who approached him with an application to [marry] did so with fear and trembling.' The efficiency of the army was not to be compromised.

Harrison recalled an incident when an unfortunate signaller lost control of a temperamental horse. He was accused of being an idiot and then ordered by Haig to the infirmary to be checked for mental disorder. He was then, on Haig's instructions, given a dose of powerful laxative before being returned and confined to barracks for twenty-eight days. If Haig had really done this he would have been guilty of a grotesquely excessive reaction to a minor and inadvertent offence.

Harrison himself was the victim of Haig's prejudices: in this case a prejudice against those whose special duties sometimes excused them from what Haig regarded as the real business of training, drills and parades. When Harrison was examined for promotion to sergeant, the other two examining officers sanctioned the promotion. Haig vetoed it on the grounds that signallers, such as Harrison was, should not be given positions of responsibility. On appeal his decision was overturned.

Harrison is not corroborated, but it is consistent with other glimpses we have of Haig at this time and his motive in compiling his narrative was not malign: his account is made in a letter to Lady Haig as a tribute to his former officer, who had impressed him with his decision 'to renounce sentimentality, human inspirations, and affectionate feelings, to embrace a real, hard, irrevocable task of producing soldiers for his country and Queen.'

All the same, and despite its reassuringly balanced style, Harrison's account must be read with great caution. It has been analysed in depth by John Hussey, and set against the evidence of other veterans who wrote to Lady Haig after her husband's death.[4] Harrison's account proves to be full of inconsistencies and must be regarded as most unreliable. He attributes to Haig a prejudice against married soldiers, but it was not Haig but regulations that laid down that only twelve per cent of other ranks could marry, and amongst them no man beneath the rank of sergeant could marry without at least seven years' service, two good conduct badges and a small amount of money in the bank. If soldiers contracted unauthorised marriages, as they sometimes did, their wives had no right to quarters, food or education for their children, and it was therefore often a kindness to encourage soldiers to remain single. The individual testimony of soldiers who happened to write to Lady Haig is of limited value: in general they would only contact her if they were well disposed, and their recollection of events thirty-five years in the past may not be particularly accurate, but some of the memories to which John Hussey refers are quite touching, particularly those of Sergeant Griffiths, 'an old man well over seventy years and my memory not the best':

I had a breakdown in health and was in Hospital with Interic [*sic*] fever off and on for 12 months around the time Haig was made Adjutant in mid 1888 . . . He would come down to the hospital and talk to the serious cases, ask if he could do anything for you, he would write to your friends in England if you was not well enough, he was most kind to me.

While he could be benevolent to private soldiers, Haig's diaries show him to be, even at this early stage in his military career, remarkably critical of his superior officers. The speed with which he had adopted not only a passion for the cavalry branch in general, but also very strong ideas on how cavalry could be improved and best deployed is surprising, as is the confidence of the views which he urged on all who would listen.

Far from the frontier areas in which regular action could be expected, Haig had been posted to the part of India known as the 'Sloth Belt'; but he was far from slothful and his hard work and commitment to his profession were recognised at an early point by his appointment as adjutant. In this post he was left with much authority by his colonel, who was far less engaged in his profession than Haig. Haig, by contrast, not only sought to advance his own professional knowledge, but encouraged younger officers to read French and German training books which he lent them. Typically, as well as spending leaves in Europe and Australia, he also devoted time to studying conditions in the North-West Frontier in Khelat and Baluchistan and in Ceylon.

His commitment to his profession was not unremarked: in 1891 he was appointed brigade major at a cavalry camp and in 1892 he was attached to the Headquarters Staff of the Bombay Army. Major-General Gatacre was so impressed with Haig's report on a cavalry manoeuvre that he had it printed for general circulation. Gatacre was one of many remarkable Victorian warriors. He began in the unreformed army, and his promotions to lieutenant and captain were by purchase. His later promotions, which led to the rank of major-general, were achieved as the result of bravery, a capacity for remarkable physical endurance, and by dedication to his profession. His reputation was at its highest in the Sudan, where he commanded a division of two brigades at the Battle of Omdurman, and at its lowest in South Africa, where he lost Stormberg in 'Black Week'. In India in the early 1890s, in the course of hunting with the Bombay Jackal Club, he was bitten by a jackal. Temporarily deranged, he had his bungalow windows barred, to deter jackals from jumping in.

Haig's capacity for paperwork was recognised: his secondment to the Bombay Army was to reduce a jam of paper. Recognition did not happen by chance. Haig was always ready to establish links with superior officers who could assist his career. In India he wrote a commentary on a new scheme for the instruction of cavalry reconnaissance which he sent to General Bengough. The General's response was just what Haig had wanted: 'If all or most cavalry officers took as much practical interest in instructing their men, we should have our Cavalry . . . equal to any in Europe.'

Even more significantly, Haig made contact in India with Colonel John French, whom he met in November 1891. Haig had little in common with French. What French had, however, was a high profile and an enthusiasm for cavalry no less ardent and outspoken than

Haig's. He was a rising star in the cavalry branch of the army and Haig was to take very great pains to secure his support.

Johnnie French, as he was still known even after he became Field-Marshal Lord French of Ypres, was so crucially involved with Haig at various stages that his own character and career must be briefly looked at. French was loved by his men as Haig never was, and like Roberts and Kitchener, but again not Haig, was idolised by the public at large at a time when the photographs of successful generals circulated like those of footballers in a later age. Appalling verses celebrated their achievements, like this one which followed French's success at Colesberg in South Africa:

> 'E's so tough and terse,
> 'E don't want no bloomin' nurse,
> And 'e ain't 'ad one reverse,
> 'Ave yer, French?

When one reads lines such as these one is grateful for Kipling.

But French was not cast in an obviously heroic mould. He had been intended for the navy and not the army, but sea-sickness brought him ashore. He was short, and wore an unusually long tunic that emphasised his lack of height. He was stout, and had the legs of a cavalryman. In civilian formal dress he resembled a walrus. But his appearance impeded neither his military career nor his extensive amorous activities. Throughout his life he was involved in a series of romantic entanglements. As a young man he entered into an ill-advised marriage which lasted for only three years. Divorce at that time could well have meant the end of his career, but his wife appeared, perhaps for a consideration, as the guilty party, and news did not leak out: neither his second wife nor his daughter, who died in 1979, were ever aware of that first marriage. Affairs followed, both before and after his second marriage to Elenora Selby-Lowndes, one of eight sisters known as the Belles of Bletchley. His wife tolerated his infidelities. He had affairs even with the wives of brother officers. As commanding officer of the 19th Hussars he went off to the Indian hills with the wife of a senior officer during his leave, quickly described by his juniors as 'French leave'. As a result he was cited for adultery: he was lucky this scandal did not cost him his career.

His final affair occurred in the war, when he formed a long-lasting relationship with Mrs Winifred Bennett. She was a tall, elegant lady, and photographs of her beside her short, portly, elderly lover are sad and absurd. But each needed the other, and in the difficult days of 1915 French found strength in Winifred's support and in their astonishingly ardent romantic love. They were said by French to Winifred to be 'Two shipwrecked souls who have found one another.'[5]

If French's romantic life was impulsive and imprudent, it was matched by the mismanagement of his financial affairs. He was constantly short of money, constantly investing unwisely when he had money, and constantly borrowing to avert disaster. His urgent financial requirements were satisfied at one stage by assistance from Haig in an episode which will be noted later in this narrative. In 1893, French was on half-pay, perhaps as a result of the Indian divorce scandal. It turned out that the setback was temporary, but if he had remained on half-pay for more than two years, compulsory retirement would have followed. He occupied his time on long walks, and as he could afford no horses he took up cycling. There is an exquisite little cameo of French in his straitened circumstances, on his bicycle: 'He was too self-conscious to be seen practising on a road, so he would march his sons to a secluded spot and then enlist their aid. He never mastered the process of mounting, and would disappear into the distance hopping wildly alongside his machine, but failing to get astride it.'[6]

He could be short-tempered, but on the whole had a gregarious, outgoing temperament, full of boyish enthusiasm. Friends were addressed as 'dear old boy' and his letters to them were full of easy-going affection. His letters to Winifred are unrestrained in their revelation of his innermost emotions. He was deeply moved by the carnage of the war. He gave full and bitter expression to his reactions to his dismissal as Commander-in-Chief.

Views differed and continue to differ on his military ability. Richard Holmes reviews the range of opinions that have been expressed. Sir James Edmonds described him as 'only *un beau sabreur* of the old-fashioned sort . . . a vain, ignorant and vindictive old man with an unsavoury society backing.' For General Sir Hubert Gough he was 'an ignorant little fool'. Esher and Churchill thought well of him. Haldane, despite his respect for Haig, described French as having 'been a great Commander-in-Chief, a soldier of the first order, who held the army as no other could.'[7]

French obtained a commission by the back door route of the militia. If a militia officer were nominated by his commanding officer and passed an examination, he could go into the regular army without the academic challenge of the Sandhurst examination; it was a route of which others, such as Henry Wilson, made use. It was in this way that French moved from the navy to the 8th Hussars, though it took him two shots at the examination before he made it. He gravitated soon to the 19th Hussars, and there he seems to have devoted some time, but not a lot, to studying the military classics. Edmonds says that French made no serious study of his profession. Holmes says that he was much influenced by Sir Edward Hamley's *Operations of War.* Laffin says that he borrowed the book from the War Office Library but could not understand it and though he read 'a few' military books, he did not follow them. He was certainly a good regimental commander. As a cavalry leader he had the necessary qualities of dash and élan. He was an efficient commander with some insights: he could see, for instance, the value of combined military and naval operations. He was not without imagination, but as Commander-in-Chief in France he was too lightweight to hold the army together in the face of the scale of the problem that existed. He was perhaps also, to his credit, too sensitive to preside over the suffering that he saw.

Haig's career would cross and recross with that of French from now on, but for the moment General Bengough was able to supply more immediate assistance. Haig had now been in India for several years, but it was not ideal habitat for him. He had not seen action. He was getting older. The Commander-in-Chief, Lord Roberts, did not share the cavalry views of Haig and French. Roberts was a supporter of the mounted infantry concept, to which Haig was opposed, and Haig was in no position to elaborate his own views on the use of cavalry in the subcontinent. His route of escape from the cul-de-sac, geographical and professional, in which he was now placed was by passing the Staff College and acquiring the letters 'psc' after his name.

The helpful General Bengough recommended him for the College. 'As the exam for the Staff College is very hard, I think the sooner I come home the better,' Haig wrote to Henrietta, and on 9 September 1892 he left India.

> Find regimental Sergeant Major Humphries waiting at launch for me. We all go aboard *Peninsular* – quite melancholy parting. Humphries wrung my hand and said I was the 'best sort he had ever had to deal with . . .' I feel quite sorry at leaving them all.

'Quite melancholy parting . . . I feel quite sorry at leaving them all': he was less than broken-hearted on leaving the regimental family (presumably, though in fact wrongly, he thought, for good) and moving on in his career.

Repulsed and then Victorious. Staff College

On his return to London from India, Haig went on leave until June 1893, and was able to prepare for the Staff College entrance examination. He spent all day at a crammer and stayed at his sister's flat. Henrietta was on holiday with her husband: she had married Willie Jameson, the rich scion of another whisky family, Irish this time. As result of her marriage she was able to offer Haig material assistance throughout his life and through her he now had access to the very top levels of society. Willie Jameson was a keen yachtsman and a friend of Edward VII: Haig came to know Edward VII, both as Prince of Wales and then as King, and thus forged a friendship with the royal family, later strengthened by his wife's connections, which critically advanced his career. Henrietta had other friendships that were important for Haig, not least her acquaintanceship with the Duke of Cambridge. She had no children, and she took an intense interest in the welfare of her young brother, to whom, until his marriage, she was the closest of confidantes. In a sense she took over the role that his mother had filled, but with the significant difference that she was there to aid and abet Haig's wishes, and not to impose her own. In addition to the companionship and moral support which she supplied, her wealth was much greater than her brother's, which became progressively inadequate to support the (not excessive) demands required of his position; and she was able to make Haig's life more comfortable than it would otherwise have been.[1]

She was worried about his Indian illnesses and insisted, probably without having to press very hard, that he undergo a medical examination.

> In order to set *your* mind at rest regarding *my* health, I went and saw a dr. after leaving James's [the crammer] tonight at 5pm. One Hamilton Brown of a certain fame and certainly a most careful and painstaking Physician. He looked at me all over! My tongue of course, chalked with a pencil the size of my liver on my skin, put things in his ears and listened to my lungs and heart and so forth. He said he would pass me as a 'thoroughly sound man' *but* a *little* below par. So I hope you will be satisfied now. All I want is plain food and a certain amount of exercise.

Henrietta had left her cook behind, who provided 'just what my *digestion* requires'; but to assuage further concerns about his health, Haig went on to take a cure, an exercise he was to perform repeatedly, at Schwalbach:

> I am getting on nicely here, thank you, and am feeling all the better for the waters. My times are somewhat earlier than the ones you followed. I am out by 7 am and get 2 half glasses drunk in time to have breakfast at 8o.c. I then go out again about 10.30 take glass and bath at 11o.c. Walking about between drink and bath of course. Then another glass and a bit of walk and back here at 12. Then lunch at 1.15. At about 4 I have some chocolate as I have grand hunger here! . . . I get back about 7.30 and have dinner. I have omitted the afternoon drink which we take on the way for the walk.

One of the papers for the Staff College examination was German, and Haig spent time with a German family in Düsseldorf; he had worked on his French at Fontainebleau during Oxford vacations.

The Staff College existed, under that name, only after 1857. Its first professor of military history was Colonel (later Lieutenant-

General Sir Edward) Hamley (Edward Hamley, 'the strategic ped-
agogue', is thought to have been the model for W.S. Gilbert's Major-
General Stanley:

> For my military knowledge, though I'm plucky and
>   adventuring
> Has only been brought down to the beginning of the century.

The intake was quite small: fifteen in 1858 and twenty-three to thirty-
four each year thereafter. The cavalry, but not only the cavalry, tended
to look down on it as an irrelevant talking shop. 'You can teach them to
be soldiers, but you can't teach them to be gentlemen.' Ian Hamilton
said that: 'It was a proud boast of the Gordons, that none of their officers
had ever entered the Staff College or ever would.'[2] Very few cavalry
officers did: only thirty-eight between 1856 and 1881.

> Regiments were likely to shunt the idle, overtly ambitious, or
> otherwise unwanted officer to Camberley – or at least not stand
> in his way – until the Staff College attained such a high
> reputation that it became an honour to have an officer ac-
> cepted.[3]

Over the years this suspicion of the Staff College reduced, but even in
Haig's time a qualified regard for Camberley is reflected in the fairly
low standard of the entrance examination.

The examination that Haig sat was held from 29 May to 12 June,
over a total of forty-two hours. The outcome was painful. Overall he
had finished amongst the twenty-eight who would have been
selected, but he had failed mathematics, where he scored 182 out
of 400. Two hundred points were the qualifying hurdle, and
mathematics was a compulsory subject. The shock of failure in
the Staff College examination and the blow to his pride is reflected
in the fact that he kept that failure in mathematics secret from most
of his colleagues all his life. Much later he felt secure enough to write
to his friend General Kiggell:

> Both Braithwaite and myself failed to pass the examination in mathematics for the Staff College, and neither of us have found any need for a more thorough knowledge of mathematics than we already possess![4]

He had been unlucky: the new director-general of military education had been concerned that the entrance examination was based too much on rote, and that the questions could be predicted in advance. He wrote in his report on the 1893 examinations that 'A gentleman, recently deceased, had examined in Mathematics for many years;' the choice of questions had 'followed rather closely on fixed lines, so that candidates working out thoroughly the old papers could tell pretty nearly what sort of questions would be set.' The director-general introduced what he called 'a little variety' in the 1893 papers and Haig was not the only one to be caught out. The failure rates in the three preceding years had been 5.1%, 9.2% and 15.8%; in 1893 the failure rate was 31.3% for a paper which has been judged as being more or less in line with modern A-level standard.[5] The matter was raised in Parliament and the Secretary of State for War, Campbell-Bannerman, acknowledged that there had been a problem which he said had been addressed by reducing the qualifying mark to achieve comparability with earlier years: Haig does not appear to have enjoyed the benefit of that concession.

The reason may be that by the time the concession was being made, another obstacle had fallen in Haig's way: on the basis of the college's medical examination, he was diagnosed as being colour blind and not qualified for nomination to the college. He had undergone a preliminary medical examination in January 1893 when he failed to satisfy the doctors that he could 'match certain pale green and pale pink wools'. A month later, however, he was told by the War Office that, despite his problem with the wool, 'the medical report was satisfactory and consequently [he] was allowed to compete' in the examination. He took the precaution, all the same, when he was back in Düsseldorf for a cure, to consult a very eminent German ophthalmologist, Professor Alfred Mooren, who was able to reassure

him on the question of his eyesight. Why the Adjutant-General, Sir
Redvers Buller, subsequently announced to Haig, after the examinations, on 10 August 1893, that the medical board's report on his
colour blindness debarred him from staff employment is not clear.
There are suspicions that Henrietta's lobbying may have been
counterproductive – or that Buller may have wanted to promote a
candidate from his own regiment. At any rate, Haig was irritated. ('Is
it not rather late to fall back on the medical report now?' after he had
gone to the trouble of sitting all the examinations.) He asked Mooren
for a written report to supplement his earlier, oral opinion. Mooren
reported that 'Captain Douglas was capable to distinguish all sorts of
colours may they have been fundamental or compliemental [*sic*].'
Mooren was an ophthalmologist of very considerable reputation in
Germany and elsewhere, and the idea that his opinion was bought, as
some of Haig's critics have suggested,[6] is fanciful. Haig was also
examined by Professor Edmond Landolt, a distinguished ophthalmologist of Paris and Zurich. His only criticism of Haig's colour
judgement was that the perception of colours was slightly defective,
to the extent that the tones of red and green did not give a distinctly
clear coloured impression; and that when they were saturated, Haig
confused them with grey. Apart from this slight degree of what is
known as Daltonism, 'the eyes are perfectly healthy and are not
threatened by any disease.'

There is no doubt that Haig did suffer from a degree of colour
blindness throughout his life, although it never affected the discharge of his professional responsibilities. It was a subject never to be
mentioned in Haig's presence and jokes about it were strictly
forbidden, but he was demonstrably incapable of distinguishing
brown from pink or red. His niece, Ruth du Pree, in a charming
recollection of her uncle: 'One night I had on a green dress and when
I asked him the colour of it he said it was yellow. Next night I tried
him with another colour, but he was not pleased.'[7]

Haig returned to India and his regiment. The return was all the
more humiliating in that he did not resume his former position:
another officer was in that post, and Haig dutifully accepted a

subordinate post as second in command of a squadron. He displayed no bitterness at the blow that fortune had dealt him: he threw himself uncomplainingly back into regimental duties. He had many attributes which were unappealing, but one of his more attractive qualities was a steadiness, almost nobility, in the face of reverses. His determination to advance in his career was unchecked. Indeed, even before returning to India, he chose to attend French cavalry manoeuvres at Touraine, a decision which reflected not only his interest in cavalry, but also, more unusually, a readiness to study this arm in other armies. The manoeuvres involved two divisions and Haig was seeing something on a scale unknown in Britain. His report was a full one and it is interesting, in view of his criticisms of the French during the Great War, that he found the French staff 'practical men . . . not a mere body of theorists' who 'go about their work with method and common sense'. This report was significant in that it brought Haig to the attention of Sir Evelyn Wood. Sir Evelyn was Quartermaster General, then effectively Chief of the General Staff. He was also a member of the reforming 'Wolseley Ring'.

Sir Evelyn Wood was one of the key figures in the evolution of the late nineteenth-century British Army. He started out, like Johnnie French, not as a soldier but a sailor, but in his case it was not sea-sickness that stopped him going to sea, but vertigo that stopped him going aloft. As a sixteen-year-old midshipman in the Naval Brigade he was sent to the Crimea in 1854, where he received his first recommendation for a Victoria Cross. When he was severely wounded at Sebastopol, and almost lost his arm, he was invalided home and, while there, decided to join the cavalry: he reported to the depot of the 13th Light Dragoons with his arm still in a sling. In the following year he was back in the Crimea, now in the army, and within the month was again in hospital, this time with pneumonia and typhoid fever. His parents were told that he was dying and his mother, Lady Wood, arrived at Scutari to find one of Miss Nightingale's young ladies, exasperated by her duties, striking her son as he lay in bed. Against medical advice he was taken home to England,

and he recovered, despite the fact that in Scutari he had been so emaciated that the bones of both hips had come through his skin. He was in India at the Mutiny and his second recommendation for the Victoria Cross was approved: for courage in rescuing a landowner from a large band of robbers. Thereafter he was in the thick of colonial warfare in the Ashanti War, the Zulu War and the Indian expeditions. He was involved in the peace negotiations at the end of the first Boer War and, despite the fact that Wolseley referred to the treaty as ignominious, was much in favour with politicians and the Queen. As Quartermaster General in 1893 and Adjutant General in 1895 he was at the centre of the practical improvement of the army as a fighting force. As a clergyman's son, he had entered the cavalry with limited means: he was not there as a playboy, but as a career soldier, and his commitment and professionalism made him a ready ally for Haig, who developed a close relationship with him.

Haig did not lie back and supinely accept the Staff College reverse. He was still a fairly lowly officer, older than most of those of his rank, but he was working on finding an alternative route to the Staff College. He left his regiment again in 1894, his departure marked by a remarkably personal letter from his commanding officer addressed, most informally, to 'My Dear Douglas':

> I cannot let you go without saying that I appreciate what you have done for the Regiment. You came back to a position that a great many people would have disliked extremely . . . Instead of making a grievance at all, I know what a lot of pains you have taken and how much improvement in [your] squadron has been owing to you . . . I cannot say how much you will be missed by all of us, officers, NCOs and men. Your example to the Regiment has been worth everything to the boys. You know I wish you luck. You are, I think, bound to succeed because you mean to. I hate saying 'Goodbye' as I am sadly afraid I shall never soldier with you again, but only hope I may. Yours very sincerely Hamish Reid.[8]

After his rejection by the Staff College and before departing for India, Haig had immediately appealed: the mathematics questions

> *were different* to those set in previous years – Now in every *official* report on examinations for entrance to the Staff College the attention of the intending candidates is called to the papers previously set, and they are directed to them as guides as to what is required of them. This year's candidates have been misled in the Mathematical Papers.

When this appeal failed, the usual reaction followed: Henrietta wrote to both Sir Evelyn Wood and to the Inspector General of Cavalry, Sir Keith Fraser. Fraser replied sympathetically, saying that Henrietta's brother 'is the very man the Cavalry requires as Staff Officer'. He wrote to the Acting Military Secretary, but did not hold out any hopes of success. But the approach to Fraser had not been a waste of time: he responded to a request from Sir Evelyn Wood and appointed Haig as his ADC, when the latter returned to Britain from India. Fraser was, like Haig, a strong defender of the cavalry, but not unaware of the need for improvement in that wing. Throughout the autumn manoeuvres of 1894, Haig worked closely with him. He and Fraser and others of the 'progressive' element in the cavalry recognised that to come to terms with technical advances and adopt truly effective training, the British Army had a huge task on its hands. Fraser was appreciative of the work that Haig did, during his brief secondment: 'I have the smartest soldier in the army as my ADC.'[9]

Haig's thoughts on cavalry will emerge later, but in view of the fact that he is frequently represented as conservative, narrow-minded and chauvinist, it is worth stressing that he was in fact particularly open to the study of cavalry abroad. In 1894, as in 1893, he observed French manoeuvres, preparing a report that was full, even if not quite as full as that of 1893. In 1895 he made a long visit to Germany. The facilities that were made available to him were impressive despite some obstruction by the British military attaché, Colonel Swaine, who appears to have been resentful of the young intruder. Typically,

Haig had taken the precaution of obtaining a letter of introduction from Fraser to the Governor of Berlin, and the Governor treated Haig with great hospitality and opened doors that would otherwise have been closed, even to the extent of having Haig invited to a dinner at which he was seated opposite the Kaiser:

> I find myself not among the foreign officers but at the end of the table opposite the Emperor . . . After we had been a certain time at dinner the Emperor drank the health [of the officer on my right], then signalled to him that he wished to drink my health. So I stood up and emptied my glass to the Kaiser in the usual style – 'nae heil taps' [*sic*: 'No heel taps' was a nineteenth-century injunction that sometimes formed part of a toast, meaning 'no holding back'.]. He did the same . . .
>
> After dinner we went into the picture gallery and the Emperor came and asked about my regiment, about Keith Fraser and what I was anxious to do and the length of the leave which I had. Altogether he was most friendly.

These expeditions had a purpose, and Haig's report on the German cavalry manoeuvres, *Notes on German Cavalry,* was an important document in which he argued that the German model of devolving authority to junior officers made a valuable reduction in staff work and paper.

He was recalled from Germany by an order from Johnnie French. French was commanding the cavalry in one of Sir Evelyn's Wood's 'staff rides', manoeuvres without troops, and wanted Haig as his staff officer. This afforded him the opportunity of consolidating his connection with both these influential senior officers. In the aftermath of the staff rides, Sir Evelyn Wood wrote: 'It gave me great pleasure to meet you . . . I think I may honestly say of you, what we cannot always say, that the expectation, though great, was even less than the pleasure you gave me by your conversation.' Those who found such pleasure in Haig's conversation composed a very limited group. Haig noted: 'Sir EW is a capital fellow to have upon one's side as he always gets his own way!' He could not have said less. Later, taking the waters in Germany, Haig wrote, not quite sycophantically, to Wood:

> Dear Sir Evelyn, I was greatly delighted to receive your kind letter and thank you very much for what you say about me. I shall always remember with more than pleasure the kindly way you spoke to me during the staff tour.

Apart from getting to know Sir Evelyn Wood, with whom he had only corresponded until now, he met also the old Duke of Cambridge, about to retire after his thirty-nine years as Commander-in-Chief, but not before he had assisted Haig to reach Staff College. The report on his German visit was delivered to Wood later in the year. During the First World War, Wood referred to this paper in his memoirs: 'Haig knows more about the German Army than any officer in England.'[10] There was nothing improper about the way in which Haig had managed his contacts, but his skill was consummate. The Duke had the power to allow a candidate who had obtained 3/8 of the necessary marks to go to the College without further examination, written or medical. Wood and Fraser both appealed to the Duke to exercise this discretion in favour of Haig, who had achieved 182 out of 400. The Duke, Henrietta's friend, agreed.

Haig arrived at Camberley on 15 January 1896, and the date of his arrival, along with his mark in mathematics and his colour blindness, represents the third little controversy about his route to the college. In terms of the Staff College regulations, amended by Army Order 72 of 1896, the Duke's nomination allowed Haig to go up to college in 1894 or 1895, but not thereafter. He was not, however, the only officer for whom the regulations were not strictly enforced.[11]

Haig was not idle in the period before he went to the College: he participated in cavalry manoeuvres as a brigade major. He completed a new cavalry drill book, started by French, and it was a mark of his prestige that as a mere captain, and without experience of command in the field, he should have been invited to take over from his distinguished predecessor.

Sir Keith Fraser went off to the South of France in the course of 1895, and Haig spent the winter hunting, having taking a small house in Warwickshire. He was not obsessed by hunting and if the sport were poor, he was happy to return to his study of military books. Some of his friends thought he was doing what he thought a cavalry officer should do, rather than what he particularly wanted.

It has been suggested that, even by the time he left Staff College, Haig's career was in the doldrums: at thirty-five he was still only a captain, and there was no discernible evidence that significant promotion would follow. On the contrary, it can be seen, without the use of a lot of hindsight, that even *before* he went to Staff College, far from having stalled, the Haig phenomenon was underway. He had established a network of important connections, and the personages who viewed him benevolently did so not on the basis of his charm, but because of his dedication to his profession and his mastery of its technical aspects, expressed in his many reports and the new cavalry drill book. By the time he arrived at Camberley, Haig was an important cavalry moderniser, whose views were listened to.

He entered the Staff College as the Duke of Cambridge was succeeded by Wolseley as Commander-in-Chief. The army was now embarked on a period of reform and modernisation. The Staff College itself was in a period of change. There was not yet a *General* Staff, and the purpose of the College was not so much to teach strategy or even grand tactics as to provide able officers who would be the staff of senior commanding officers. What was stressed was logistics and administration, although not to the total exclusion of the inculcation of the development of more elevated, strategical skills. The two years he spent at Camberley were critical for Haig, not least in the sense that what he learnt there was the last that he was to learn of the theory of military art: by the time he left, his mind had matured and largely closed, and he was unreceptive to new theories of warfare (which is not to say that he was unreceptive to technological refinements in relation to existing theories).

The intake in 1896 was a remarkable one: Allenby, Edmonds,

Thomson, Capper and Haking were Haig's contemporaries. General Sir George Barrow described Haig at the Staff College:

> Haig did not stand out among his fellows at the College because of any intellectual superiority. It was not brains that got him forward; there were several who were bigger and better-stored brains than he. Neither was tact, of which he had little; nor imagination of which he had none. It was not hard work, for others worked as hard, some harder. It was his personality and his power of concentration . . . His was the dominant personality that made itself felt in every company, in every place, in the office, on the polo ground, in the mess, in the field.

Barrow contrasted Allenby and Haig. Allenby had wide interests in nature and in the arts. He was a fellow of the Zoological Society and had his own aviary: 'It was a pleasure to go for a walk with him, when he would point out a name and discuss the tendencies and peculiarities of all the birds, trees and flowers we passed on our way.' Haig, by contrast, had no interests outside the army, other than polo.[12] (At the age of seventy-four Allenby went to Patagonia on his last fishing trip to see if the salmon there were really as big as those in the Tay.)

Another comparison of Haig and Allenby was made by a sensitive observer, Field-Marshal Lord Wavell:

> In spirit and in body they were fellows – strong, enduring, and upright; but in mind there was a wide difference between them. Allenby had the finer perception and the greater knowledge; his intelligence had, as already shown, a wide range and many interests outside soldiering; he took every opportunity to visit new places and to acquire fresh learning. He was earnest and thorough in his profession, but it was by no means his only, probably not even his first, interest. Haig on the other hand, had a single-track mind, intensely and narrowly concentrated, like a telescope, on the one object. Except his profession of soldiering, and later his family, he had no real interests of any

kind, and little knowledge; nor had he any desire for knowledge, unless it bore on his own special subject. Very quick of temper in his youth, he had so disciplined his mind and body to serve his fixed purpose that he seldom showed anger or impatience. Allenby, by nature of a more tolerant humour, indulged as the years went on infrequent outbursts of violent temper. Haig, secure in his own self-confidence, seldom listened to the opinion of others; Allenby, equally strong-willed, would always pay heed to those who had knowledge. Haig recorded all events in a carefully kept diary; Allenby made no note whatever of his acts or thoughts, and destroyed practically every letter or paper he received. Haig had a deeply religious strain, and was a regular churchgoer; Allenby, though a constant student of the Bible, made little observance of the outward forms of religion.

To sum up, Allenby was the more broad-minded and the more human; Haig by virtue of concentration, the more technically efficient. Their differences in character can be attributed to their respective nationalities. Haig was Scottish to the bone, Allenby was English to the core. The two men never understood each other well, nor were easy in each other's company.[13]

Edmonds later described the class of 1896:

Of the batch of 31, 4 (2 generals) were killed in action or died of wounds . . . Of the remainder, 2 cavalrymen [Haig and Allenby] became Field Marshals and peers. 15 became generals (of whom 8 where knighted); 1 (the youngest) got no further than a colonel; 3 retired for reasons of health before 1914; one resigned as he had come into a fortune; and one 'the bravest of the brave' shot himself, his mother-in-law and her lawyer in *une drama passionelle*. [*sic*][14]

Edmonds recorded that Allenby was very popular but 'looked a typical young English foxhunting squire; he had little to say for himself and 'was obviously out of his depth'. Edmonds was later told that the staff thought Allenby dull and stupid and were surprised by an excellent speech he had made at the Farmers' Dinner: in fact it was Edmonds and another who had written the speech.[15] Haig and Allenby were candidates for the Mastership of the Staff College drag hounds. The gregarious and affable Allenby defeated his aloof and unappealing rival.

The new spirit of reform was to provide the college with greater staff resources, but for the moment there were only six officers and two civilian instructors, one described as 'bone idle', and only one had ever served on a staff. The commandant, Colonel Hildyard, sought to resist the army tendency to learn by rote: 'We do not want any cramming here. We want officers to absorb, not to cram.'[16] It is not clear that this stricture was acted on, even if it was wholly understood.

The most influential teacher was 'the Professor' (as he was then known), Colonel G.F.R. Henderson, the author of an outstanding study of Stonewall Jackson. Henderson was an inspiring teacher. Sir William Robertson, who was a contemporary but not a direct one, at Camberley recorded that 'of the different causes which are alleged to have given us the victory over Germany, not one should be assigned a more prominent place than the influence and teaching of Henderson at the Staff College.' But 'the Professor' was severely pedagogic. Every village in the Shenandoah Valley had to be memorised and listed in order.[17] Haig lost marks on one paper because he omitted reference to one bridge amongst the strategic points in the Valley of the Shenandoah. The emphasis on an historical approach to military science was overdone. A study of Jackson's campaigns was of value, based as they were on large armies fighting with modern weapons and sustained by largely industrial economies; it is less obvious that a detailed study of Napoleon's campaigns had huge relevance to the kind of fighting that would take place in the upcoming century. Haig was not alone, however, in seeing many principles of war as being unchangeable, and during the War would frequently sneer at those who appeared to have lost sight of Napoleon's *dicta*.

He was not uninfluenced by what he learned about Jackson. There had been no systematised study of strategy in the United States before the Civil War, but Jackson, along with Lee and Johnston, had made it his business nonetheless to follow the advice of Napoleon: 'Read and *re-read* the 88 campaigns of Alexander, Hannibal, Caesar, Gustavus, Turenne, Eugène, and Frederick. Take them as your models, for it is the only means of becoming a great leader, and of mastering the secrets of the art of war. Your intelligence, enlightened by such study, will then reject methods contrary to those adopted by these great men.' Jackson, and Haig, assiduously studied the models to whom Napoleon had pointed, and no less assiduously studied the campaigns and pronouncements of the Emperor himself.

Throughout the War, Haig remained totally committed to the Staff College view of a 'structured war', and he never departed from the conviction that war consisted of a series of separate episodes: importantly, the notion of preparation and wearing out of enemy reserves, followed by a decisive offensive stage, involving exploitation of the 'wearing down phase,' provided him with an intellectual justification for some of the most terrible months in the Great War.

Haig's intellectual capacities were observed by some of his contemporaries at Camberley. One of the 1897 intake, George Barrow, said he could always tell what military text Haig had read last. Edmonds said his mind was like a faulty telephone: it had to be shaken to make it work. Edmonds, again, reported Haig as being terribly slow on the uptake and on one occasion refused to accompany him on a ride, saying that 'I could not afford to be handicapped by you any longer . . .'

Edmonds' attitude to Haig is complicated, and his role in establishing Haig's position in history was – or could have been – critical. In 1919 he was appointed not to write but to direct the writing of the Official History. He soon took over the writing of the most important part, the history of the Western Front. He was in a position to make or break reputations, and he might have been expected to do enormous damage. He had been a brilliant young officer: he passed first into the Royal Military Academy, Woolwich, and effortlessly passed out first, with the sword for the best gentleman cadet. Until the war, his career was marked out by achievement. He was the most outstanding officer in his year at Camberley. His ability was widely recognised, and his stimulating conversation impressed his interlocutors. He revelled in the nickname 'Archimedes', even using it to sign letters to the press.

But the war was not a good one for him. On the retreat from Mons he broke down as the result of physical and mental strain. He was recalled to GHQ, and remained there for the rest of the war, ending as he had begun in the rank of colonel. It is easy to see that he might have been embittered, and some have thought he was hostile to Haig and Allenby in the Official History because he had formed a dislike of them when they were all three together at Staff College,[18] but in reality he got on well with Haig, to whom he was always 'Archimedes' in correspondence, even if he, as an engineer, thought the army too dominated by cavalrymen, who did not see the war as the series of siege operations which an engineer could negotiate.

Thus Edmonds criticised tactics in 1915 (the criticism would have been valid in 1916, but was increasingly wide of the mark in 1917 and 1918):

[T]he old lessons of siege-warfare were not applied . . . instead of the gun and mine preparing a way for the infantry, it was the infantry which was expected to open a door for an inroad of horsemen against the enemy's rear.[19]

The problem is that there were two Edmonds. He was not embittered by his low-profile war; in fact he was an outstandingly happy man. He did say on one occasion, as he wrote the History: 'I have just sacked three lieutenant-generals in swift succession,' but on the whole he was far from censorious – some would say too tolerant – about the generals who passed through his hands. But the other Edmonds, who became increasingly dominant as the years passed, was savage and excoriating. He concocted anecdotes and expressed judgements that were entertaining, malicious and unfounded in truth. He entertained himself and those with whom he shared his witty confections, in what was for him an elaborate game. In the process he departed from the views he expressed in the History and which were those he truly held.

It was the unreliable Edmonds who wrote in a letter regarding an article on 'British Generalship' in the January 1950 *Army Quarterly*:

> Unfortunately in 1914, French secured the command and kept it, and exercised patronage in favour of cavalrymen . . . To secure the succession of Haig, French, most unjustly, made the excuse to send home Smith-Dorrien, a really good soldier . . . [Then Haig found Gough an army]. Four cavalrymen commanded armies – Allenby, Gough, Byng and Birdwood, all in my opinion – I was in the same year as Allenby at Camberley – below the standard of intelligence and they provided themselves with Staff Officers of their own calibre.[20]

The Official History is of such length and detail that it is not easy to know precisely what Edmonds thought of Haig. In conversation with Liddell Hart, Edmonds said: 'I have to write of Haig with my tongue in my cheek. One can't tell the truth. He really was above the – or rather, below – the average in stupidity.'[21] Edmonds certainly exercised a self-restraint that was not usually his dominant characteristic when he wrote, and edited, the Official History. He admitted to not 'crabbing my contemporaries, who were my friends and splendid fellows in tight places'. Tim Travers also holds that Edmonds tended to water down his criticism of Haig and put 'awkward evidence' into the footnotes.[22] But Edmonds should certainly not be thought of as essentially hostile to Haig, either in his recollections of Staff College or in the Official History. He tells us that Haig never

> made the slightest attempt to 'play up to' the instructors. If a scheme interested him he took tremendous pains with it; if he

thought there was no profit in working it out, he sent in a perfunctory minimum. I remember a road reconnaissance sketch on which most of us had lavished extreme care, marking all the letter-boxes, pumps, gateways and fields and such-like. Haig handed in a sheet with a single brown chalk line down the centre, the crossroads shown and the endorsement '20 miles long, good surface, wide enough for two columns with orderlies both ways'.

When he arrived at Staff College, Haig never said anything to his fellow students about the hurdles he had had to overcome. His story was that he had qualified in 1894, but for private reasons chose to delay his arrival. He seems to have made no particular effort to fit in with his colleagues, or make himself agreeable. Arthur describes him as shy and detached, a flaw that is all the more remarkable in that it might have been thought to inhibit the professional advancement for which he sought. It would have been advantageous to enjoy the goodwill of fellow officers, many of whom could be expected to hold senior appointments. Edmonds recalled:

> My fellow students were a cheery, sociable lot, with the exception of Captain Douglas Haig . . . who worked harder than anybody else, was seldom seen in the mess except for meals, [and] kept himself to himself.

On another occasion, in the Memorial Issue of the British Legion *Journal*, although he was choosing his words more circumspectly, Edmonds still revealed criticism of Haig's manner at Camberley.

> Haig almost at once came into prominence by winning the Light Weight Point to Point race. Having made a speech at the dinner afterwards, he won the approval of his fellow-students by saying very briefly that to do good rein-exercises one must hunt and play polo, and keep fit. He did not, however, become 'popular' in the year. As a captain he had a briskness of manner,

an abruptness, almost ruthlessness in speech which cut all conversations short. He managed to rile even the amiable giant of the class, an officer subsequently justly described in Lord Kitchener's final despatch from South Africa as 'imperturbable'. This roughness of manner, due largely to shyness, gradually left him.[23]

The story is well known of his request for leave, soon after his arrival at Staff College. The leave book was on public display and, with crass insensitivity, Haig inserted as the reason for the request: 'to shoot and to meet the Prince of Wales.'

It was a flaw in Haig's character that he simply did not, for most of his life, see that he should try to be *nice* to people. In later life, his achievements secured, he became more relaxed, and he was always a very thoughtful host. But except within his immediate family circle, he was far too driven in the pursuit of his career and his commitment to his profession to deviate into jovial bonhomie. Indeed he would have regarded it as wrong, if not dishonourable, to do so, a compromise. The author, as a fellow Scot, may be allowed to say that this attitude is not unknown among his countrymen. Haig's shop-talk and devotion to his *métier* may have impressed his superiors, like Sir Evelyn Wood and the Prince of Wales, but would not make him an agreeable dinner companion in the mess.

At Staff College Haig's health, and particularly his digestion, seems to have been far from robust. While the other students enjoyed substantial but simple lunches of cheese, pickles and new bread at the local pubs, Haig found this fare too challenging.

Charteris says that most of Haig's humorous stories, a 'somewhat slender repertoire', were obtained while he was at the Staff College.[24] No biographer of Haig should avoid a judgement on whether he had or had not a sense of humour.

His early letters and diaries, written before he took himself too seriously, have a lighter touch than he displayed later, and a sense of humour of a dry, understated, Scottish kind can occasionally be observed. But there are very, very few examples of Haig jokes, except some unconscious ones, of which the best is worth recalling. At the end of a regimental sports day before the war, Haig spoke to the assembled participants: 'I congratulate you on your running. You have run well. I am sure that you will run even faster when you see the enemy'. The truth seems to be that Haig had little, if any, sense of humour. Like many humourless men he *learned* that certain situations were regarded as humorous, without really understanding why. He was capable of heavy-handed practical jokes. When Haig was in command at Aldershot and the Governor's House was partially destroyed by fire, he and Lady Haig were standing in a gutted room, able to see through the charred floorboards Charteris standing in the floor below. Haig thought it was amusing to seize a bucket of water and empty it on Charteris. General Sir James Marshall-Cornwall said flatly that Haig had no sense of humour. His children disagreed. Haig was a devoted father and his relationship with his children was remarkably informal. His son described the domestic atmosphere as 'cosy'.[25] Fun, within certain limits, was permitted, and it may be that a sense of fun can exist without a sense of humour. His daughter, Lady Victoria Scott, said that Marshal-Cornwall may have reached his conclusion because Haig did not like dirty stories.[26] He certainly did not like smut. On one occasion during the war a column of troops passed singing a bawdy song, in which their colonel was enthusiastically participating. Haig stopped them and told them that although he enjoyed the tune, he did not like the words: the words in question are not now known, but it is difficult to think that, whatever they were, they were not permissible in such circumstances.

The subtitle to John Terraine's biography, *The Educated Soldier*, is misleading for those who do not know the technical meaning of the word 'educated' in the context of the late nineteenth-century army. The 'educated' soldier was one who did not regard the army simply as a social pastime, but as a professional career, important enough to require the study of the theory, as well as the practice, of war, and in particular the study of the technical developments which were so rapidly occurring at that time. Haig was 'educated' in that sense, which is better conveyed by the title of Terraine's book in its French translation: *Douglas Haig, Soldat de Métier*. His education, in a broader sense, at school had been patchy and at Oxford negligible. He learnt much at Staff College but how far it was of value to him, rather than tending to close his mind and make him unreceptive to new ideas, is questionable.

In his written examinations he did well, although Henderson said that he spent 'more time than you can properly spare to my problems'. Brian Bond records that Henderson said to some of Haig's contemporaries: 'There is a fellow in your batch who is going to be Commander in Chief one of these days. No, not any of you, Captain Haig'. Plumer, who examined Haig in his final exercise, reported that his concluding performance at the Staff College was mediocre. He had, however, learned some things that were worthwhile, along with others which were probably not. Perhaps most importantly, he absorbed the advice, reinforcing that of Pater, that an officer had to be capable of communicating in a language that was unequivocally comprehensible – which in practice meant using simple and straightforward language. In his written communications Haig had this ability, in sharp contrast to his inability to express himself orally, which will be noted later. His written orders, reports and letters were models of succinct clarity. He avoided jargon, and expressed himself clearly, with strength, and not without a certain elegance.

6

ACTIVE SERVICE IN THE SUDAN WAR

If Haig, as he finished at the Staff College, had reason to feel that his career might at last be about to take off, he must also have been conscious of the fact that, at thirty-five, he lacked any experience at all of active service. For all that he had written about the need for training war-ready armies full of the offensive spirit, he had not yet heard a shot fired in anger. This lack of active service was now effectively repaired: for most of the next five years Haig saw action in one continent or another, even if largely as a staff officer.

The first instalment of this new phase in his training was in the Sudan. Partly because of the intense interest that arose in connection with the death of Gordon, this chapter in British imperial history has attracted a great deal of attention. In 1880 a young Muslim leader, the Mahdi, inaugurated an uprising, in the course of which he not only defeated Egyptian troops sent out to tackle him, but also destroyed a British expeditionary force. Gordon, who had already been in the Sudan investigating the slave trade, was sent out again, but his force was defeated and he was killed, an incident which impressed itself memorably on the minds of the British public. There were numerous illustrations of Gordon calmly meeting his fate at the top of a flight of stairs as the Mahdi's warriors attacked him. Despite much criticism, Gladstone declined to take retaliatory action. The Mahdi died shortly after Gordon, and it was some time before the

British government took the view that his successor, the Khalifa, was at least as undesirable as the Mahdi himself.

Haig's career now crossed for the first time with that of Kitchener. Kitchener, unlike many senior officers, was neither strongly pro- nor anti-Haig, but from now on their professional paths intertwined intimately until Kitchener's death in 1916. Kitchener was an ambitious and conscientious officer, a bachelor, wedded to his career. Initially an engineer, he mastered the skills of cavalry, if not the skills of administration. In 1882 he had chosen to take secondment to the Egyptian army, then controlled jointly by Egypt and Britain, and within ten years he was its commander-in-chief, the Sirdar. Later he said that as Sirdar his greatest problem was that because his thick shock of fair hair refused to go grey he feared that he would not be taken seriously. He was tall, and very lean, which made him appear taller still, with legs that seemed too long for his body. His chest was narrow and his shoulders bottle-shaped. His moustache was bleached almost white by the sun, in contrast to his face, which was bronzed. His rise from being an unknown sapper without money, connections or remarkable intellect, was based on a combination of judicious silence and careful self-advertisement, sustained by perfect health and intermittent hard work. He was a slow thinker, though quick to act when his mind was made up. Even his friends considered him muddle-headed – not that there were many friends: he always stood a little apart from the world, which he may not have much understood. He had a distinct cast in his eye which made people feel he was looking right through them, and his deployment of this characteristic intimidated others, and contributed to the impression that the popular press promoted of a stern, silent leader.

At this stage in his career he cultivated the press. In Cairo he made great friends of all the correspondents. G.W. Steevens of the *Daily Mail* was particularly important. His book, *With Kitchener to Khartoum,* created the image of Kitchener as the 'Sudan Machine', the 'Man of Destiny'. Unusually, Kitchener had acquired a useful knowledge of colloquial Arabic, and he fostered the idea that he was also knowledgeable about the intricacies of local politics. Stories spread about travels in the desert in Arab disguise. The mystique grew. Later he could afford to jettison the press (on one occasion he pushed through a crowd of would-be interviewers, bellowing: 'Get out of my way, you drunken swabs') but by then, after Egypt, his career was unstoppable, and by the time of the outbreak of the Great War the public regarded him with both awe and affection.

After the Sudan he developed bizarre acquisitive habits. When he was offered a gift, as he frequently was in the approbation that was showered on him, he confidently asked for gold plate. When staying with friends, he asked his hosts for any of their possessions that took his fancy and sometimes simply took them without asking. He built up an extensive collection of pottery and porcelain. He never married, although there were many flirtations, a possible engagement and a wooing of Helen, Lord Londonderry's daughter. He was friendly, in his old age, with Catherine Walters, 'Skittles', a celebrated serial mistress and (when she lived in France) *grande cocotte.*

In 1896 he was ordered to retake the province of Dongola, and subsequently his instructions were extended to defeating the Khalifa in Khartoum. He planned his campaign with care, building railways as an alternative to transport on the Nile, with its dangerous cataracts. Ultimately the battle would be lost or won as a cavalry action. The Dervish cavalry was strong, and the warriors were fanatically brave and, for native forces, reasonably well armed.

In preparation for the final part of the campaign, Kitchener telegraphed Staff College for some special service officers: Haig, Blair and Capper were those who were chosen. The choice of Haig was neither the result of luck nor solely of ability. (But his abilities may have helped: one of the exercises given to Haig at Staff College had been to draw up detailed proposals for an expedition to the Sudan – at a time when Kitchener was already on his campaign – and it was highly regarded both by Henderson and by the other marker, Colonel Fleming.)[1] Huge numbers of young officers were pulling every string they could find to be seconded to the Egyptian Army in order to advance their careers. Indeed, when Haig arrived in Egypt he said: 'The longer I stay here the more lucky I seem to have been in having got to this Egyptian Army. The crowd of fellows that have asked to be taken and been refused is very great . . . Kitchener will only take the best now and picks and chooses from the hundreds who are anxious to come.' This observation is not free from the disingenuousness which frequently marks his reflections. His benefactor, Sir Evelyn Wood, was now Adjutant General and on 4 January 1898 he had sent a telegram to Haig: 'Will be selected for Egyptian Army.' Haig's departure for Egypt was marked not just by Sir Evelyn's benevolence, but also by an invitation to spend a weekend at Sandringham with the Prince of Wales. Despite an inauspicious start – he went to the wrong station and arrived late so that he could not join the royal party until after dinner – the weekend went well and before he left, 'HRH desire[d] me to "write regularly" to him from Egypt.' Significantly, perhaps, one of his fellow guests was Sir Evelyn Wood.

Like the Prince of Wales, Wood also asked Haig to write to him, and to express frankly his views on his senior officers and their ability. One biographer puts forward an ingenious but unconvincing defence of Haig's readiness throughout his career to report on his seniors behind their backs, by suggesting, though without citing any evidence, that Percival, at Clifton, would have wanted to know exactly what was going on in his school and that there would not have been the tradition of disapproval of sneaking that existed in other public schools. Thus, 'Haig would not have found himself in a dilemma' when asked 'to write letters full of frank opinions of his seniors and their operational skills. His more traditionally educated brother officers might not have approved if they had known.'[2].

When he arrived in the Sudan Haig wrote to Wood: 'I am half doubtful whether I should give you my opinion of the Native Army without being asked for it first of all. So I won't give you my opinion but will state what I have seen and you can judge for yourself as to whether the Brigades are trained to fight.'[3] Wood would not have been displeased by such a letter: he was critical of Kitchener's abilities and Haig was supplying exactly the sort of information he wanted.

Haig undertook his campaign well provisioned. He had asked Henrietta to send out 'Two or three boxes of supplies, each box not to exceed 150lbs in weight and to be about *3ft long x 1 broad and 1 deep.*' What he wanted in the boxes were 'jams, tinned fruits, cocoa, vegetables, haddock in tins, tongue, biscuits, some hock and a bottle of two of brandy or any sort of drink.' In addition, he wanted soap, toiletries, blankets, sun shades, hats and silk underwear. There were three camels to carry the boxes, plus four horses, a donkey and a goat. One camel was reserved exclusively for Haig's claret. He had 'a cook . . . the black fellow "Suleiman" as a body servant . . . a syce for every two horses and a camel boy.'

Initially he was disappointed by the lack of action: 'British officers [are] not here for this kind of patrol! A native might well have been sent!' Haig had been sent out to command a squadron, but to his annoyance the Sirdar did not want a change of squadron leaders made while he expected a Dervish advance. Haig noted and reported to Henrietta the confusion that surrounded the Sirdar, who had two ADCs but no staff, properly speaking. Kitchener attempted to control everything himself, with the result that many minor tasks that should have been delegated were never attended to at all. This was typical of Kitchener's way of working throughout his career. The title he received after the Sudan, Kitchener of Khartoum or K of K, was parodied as 'K of Chaos' by those who had an opportunity of observing his methods of work. Haig reported what he found to Wood, who replied that he had 'pointed out to [Kitchener] that however well he may be able to command large bodies of troops without any intermediate links . . . he is not immortal, should a bullet or sickness strike him down, it would be hard on his successor.' Eventually Haig had his first experience of action. On 21 March, the Cavalry Brigade, in a reconnaissance exercise at Atbara, was successfully ambushed by a small Dervish force. He reported to Wood:

1. The outpost service, tho' theoretically right, was carelessly done. When I passed the picket in question, many were lying down, apparently asleep.

2. The eyesight of the Egyptian vedette can't be relied on. For the Dervishes passed the front line of vedettes.
3. The pluck of the Egyptian cavalry man is right enough in my opinion.
4. The Horse Artillery against enemy of this sort is no use. We felt the want of machineguns when working alongside of scrub for searching some of the tracks.

The fourth point is interesting, in the light of the frequently expressed view that Haig did not understand the importance of the machine-gun: indeed, just before going to the Sudan, he had visited Enfield to study the Maxim gun, on which he frequently commented favourably during his time in the Sudan.

A little drama occurred at about this time, which shows Haig in an unusually human and heroic role. An Egyptian soldier had been wounded in the shoulder and was lying on the ground expecting to be run through by the Dervishes, when Haig galloped up to him, picked him up, put him on the front of his saddle and took him off to safety. This cameo, so redolent of skirmishes on the borders of the Empire, was recorded in a painting of the event which Haig's brother officers presented to him before he left the Sudan.

Shortly after this episode, Haig was appointed brigade major on the staff of Colonel Broadwood, the Commander of the Egyptian Cavalry: his abilities, rather than, necessarily, his wishes, were taking him to the staff role that was to be his *milieu*. The cavalry, consisting of ten squadrons, each under the command of a major, of whom six were British, was acting as an escort to Generals Hunter and Maxwell, who were testing out the main Dervish position on the Atbara. As the force started to withdraw, it was attacked unexpectedly by both Dervish infantry and cavalry. Haig seems to have been acting as the Colonel's galloper. 'The situation was a difficult one, and to add to it a strongish north wind prevented our seeing clearly the moment a squadron moved.'

When the Dervish cavalry attempted to capture the Horse

Artillery, Haig brought them out to safety. As he did so, he came on Captain Mahon, with the main body of the cavalry:

> He could not see anything for dust . . . Mahon is a sound fellow and said 'I can't see what happened, what do you suggest?' I said at once, 'Place one squadron on flank . . . of guns and support Le Gallais with your other two on *his* left. I will then bring Baring and the remaining three squadrons on your left rear as a third line.' Mahon advanced. I gave Baring his orders, putting all three squadrons under him. I then galloped on to find Broadwood (who I knew must be with Le Gallais' squadrons) in order to know his wishes as to the action of the guns. On my way I found the two squadrons coming back at full gallop. We were able to stop them, the horses were pretty well beat, and they advanced a little way. I thought there was no time to lose to ask for orders, so I went direct to their Maxims and told them they must come into action against the most threatening of the enemy (which I indicated) as soon as the cavalry cleared their field of fire. I then went off to Broadwood . . .

The tone of initiative and confidence is already noticeable.

Broadwood (in advance, and relying on Haig for information) personally led a flank charge which brought the action to a conclusion. The casualties, at about thirty, were better than might have been expected, and the cavalry considered that they had done well: 'This I hear is the *first time* the Gyppe [*sic*] Cavalry has ever had anything in the way of fighting to do. This accounts for the delight at headquarters at discovering that they don't run away.' Haig certainly presents himself in a favourable light, but his account is probably perfectly fair. What emerges is a good example of Haig's spectacular composure under pressure. The reliability of his account is confirmed by the fact that he was rewarded by Kitchener with a Brevet Majority.

Haig was certainly pleased with his performance: 'Broadwood was much obliged to me for my assistance and told the Sirdar so.' He allowed himself a flourish of courageous insouciance to his sister: 'You say that you are anxious. That is all nonsense, because neither the Dervish Horsemen nor the bullets of their infantry worry me in the least.'

He was not as impressed by the Egyptian cavalrymen as he had been at the earlier skirmish:

> The Gyppie Cavalry acted *steadily* on the whole, but there was no glorious charging home, as some of the tales I have heard would have us believe. Moreover, if the Dervish horsemen had *really* come on, I feel sure that few of the Brigade would have escaped. Indeed General Hunter gave us his opinion just before the maxims opened fire, he thought 'Sauve Qui Peut' must be the only ending. However all's well that ends well and the Gyppie Cavalry are considered heroes.

Haig would not have been Haig if some criticism of Broadwood had not followed. It is true that Broadwood had reconnoitred exhaustively, to the point of compromising the quality of his horses. He wanted to meet the Dervish horsemen from a position of strength, and Haig was able to reinforce his views by referring to Napoleon's policy at Jena. Following the most recent action, Haig said of Broadwood: 'He . . . was wrong to charge as he did with the first line, for the whole Brigade then passed from his control. But he is a very sound fellow, and is excellent at running this show.'

Haig's criticism of Broadwood for leading a charge and thus not being in a position to control the men under his command is interesting. Although a passionate advocate of cavalry, for him the arm had a defined tactical purpose and was not simply there to gallop around the battlefield.

This action, like the earlier skirmish, was no more than a preliminary for the Battle of the Atbara, which took place two days later, on 8 April 1898. It was essentially an infantry action, and the cavalry was not much involved. Churchill described it memorably:

At 20 minutes to 8 the Sirdar ordered his bugles to sound the general advance, the call was repeated by all the Brigades, and the clear notes rang out above the noise of the artillery. The superior officers . . . dismounted and placed themselves at the head of their commands. The whole mass of the infantry, numbering nearly 11,000 men, immediately began to move forward upon the *Zeriba*. The scene as this great force crested the ridge and advanced down the slope was magnificent and tremendous. Large solid columns of men, preceded by a long double line, with the sunlight flashing on their bayonets and displaying their ensigns, marched to the assault in regular and precise array. The pipes of the highlanders, the bands of Sudanese, and the drums and fifes of the English regiments added a wild and thrilling accompaniment.

The appeal to Churchill's romanticism was irresistible. Haig was less sure: 'We have just received the London papers of 9 April with accounts of the Atbara. What rubbish the British public delights to read. The exaggeration of some of the reports almost makes a good day's work appear ridiculous. The headings of the *DT* are so over-drawn that instinctively one says "Waterloo eclipsed".'

To Sir Evelyn Wood, Haig wrote:

Why was the attack frontal? It seemed to me, from the very first day that we reconnoitred the place, that an attack on the enemy's right offered great advantages . . . Next, what about the use made of the artillery? Distant fire was not required; in fact the 1st and only range was some 700 yards. Our side says the guns did tremendous damage. Mahmud and over 300 questioned by Fitton (who is a sort of intelligence officer here) say, 'We did not mind the guns, they only hurt camels and donkeys. The infantry fire was what destroyed us' . . . Another point is the formation of the force for the attack . . . This may have accounted for our severe losses . . . Briefly, my plan of attack would have been to establish as many infantry as the front

admitted, in a fire position as quickly as possible . . . Moreover, it was possible for more than one place to enfilade the front
trench with machine guns. Two brigades would have more than
sufficed for this. A third brigade, guns and cavalry to have
destroyed the fugitives *in* the river bed (600 yards wide or more)
in the scrub beyond and in the desert. The fourth brigade as a
reserve. The weak point in my plan is that I calculated as if I had
troops that can shoot and manoeuvre. It would be unwise to rely
upon the Blacks doing either *well*. So all the more credit is due
to the Sirdar for limiting himself to a moderate victory instead
of going for annihilating Mahmud's army.

Sir Evelyn replied:

You gave me an excellent description of the reconnaissance and
your little rough diagrams made it all so clear I could almost
fancy I was there . . . What you write about the effects of the
artillery fire is borne out by all the officers I have seen . . . Your
observations on the tactical teaching are I think worthy of all
consideration. It is rather sad to me to think I am getting too
old to think how I might better your tactics of Good Friday.[4]

Despite Haig's barbed approval of Kitchener in his final sentence, the
vehemence of the criticism of his Commander-in-Chief by a young
and still very inexperienced officer is remarkable.

The final and most famous battle of the campaign, Omdurman,
took place on 2 September. This engagement, celebrated from the
fact that it contained the last major cavalry charge in British military
history, was also famously described by Churchill, who was at the
heart of the charge with the 21st Lancers. The engagement was
dramatically simple and successful from the point of view of the
British, and was a massacre so far as the enemy was concerned:
Kitchener's forces formed a hollow square, into which the Dervishes
were drawn. 'They hurled themselves in successive masses at the
British and Egyptian lines; smitten by shrapnel, by machine gun fire

and by rifle fire which the Grenadier Guards opened at 2,700 yards, the extreme range of the Lee-Metford rifle, they fell in thousands.'[5]

In a letter to Wood, Haig was, inevitably, disparaging about this great charge. Sixty-five men and 109 horses were killed or wounded in an attack on a position of no significance. His letter, as so often, disagreeably and vehemently critical of a senior officer, and perhaps not untainted by sour grapes, deserves consideration as evidence that Haig, contrary to what is often asserted, never saw the cavalry as a meretricious, do-or-die galloping machine.

You will hear a lot of the charge made by the 21st Lancers . . . We onlookers in the Egyptian cavalry have feared this all along, for the regiment was keen to do something and meant to charge something before the show was over. They got their charge but at what cost? I trust for the sake of the British Cavalry that more tactical knowledge exists in the ranks of the *average* regiment than we have seen displayed in this one. Yet the commanding officer has had his command extended . . . I wonder why? Is he a tactician? No. Is he a good disciplinarian? No. Is he a stud groom? I cannot think that the Promotion Board fully appreciates the responsibility that rest [*sic*] with them [*sic*] when they put duffers in command of regiments.

The tangents of Haig's career and that of Churchill were repeatedly to cross.[6] Soon afterwards 'young Churchill' who was going north by steamer was kind enough to take a letter for Haig to Sir Evelyn Wood, again critical of Kitchener:

The Officer in Chief Command (be he the Sirdar or Hunter) insisted on doing every detail himself in place of trusting a Staff Officer to allot the camping areas to units. I had occasion to see this, for on 24th August I covered the advance of the Egyptian Army with my squadron, 2 maxims and 1 company Camel Corps . . . The plan of having two bodies of cavalry (the 21st Lancers and ourselves) under independent commanders, but employed in advance of the army with one objective, cannot be too strongly condemned. It led to much waste of horseflesh, to say the least; and had the enemy possessed even 500 horses, might have resulted in disaster.[7]

The role of the Egyptian cavalry at Omdurman was limited but important in concentrating the attention of a section of the Dervish army. Their orders to withdraw were taken to them by Kitchener's ADC, Henry Rawlinson, later one of Haig's army commanders, who described the event after the battle:

At length we could see our contact squadrons under Douglas Haig gradually withdrawing as the Dervishes advanced . . . I rode out to him over the ground which an hour later was heaped with dead and wounded Dervishes. When I reached him he was within about 600 yards of the enemy's long line, and I noticed that his confident bearing seemed to have inspired his fellaheen, who were watching the Dervish advance quite calmly.[8]

Rawlinson went on to say that as a result of Haig's bearing he engendered a confidence amongst the fellaheen to the extent that, 'for the first time in history, they were able to stand and attack the warlike Dervishes.'[9]

Haig's criticism of Kitchener to Wood after the battle was characteristically forthright: 'He seems to have no plan, or tactical idea, for beating the enemy beyond allowing the latter to attack the camp'. He allows himself an allusion to his own role: 'To me it seems truly fortunate that the *flower* of the Dervish Army exhausted itself first in an attack and pursuit of the cavalry. Indeed the prisoners say, "You would never have defeated us had you not *deceived* us" '.

After Omdurman, there was not much left to do. On 4 September a service was held for Gordon in Khartoum. That was an appropriate gesture for a man who had been abandoned by his country. Less acceptable was Kitchener's decision two days later to destroy the Mahdi's tomb. The body was burned and thrown in the Nile, and the skull presented as a trophy to the Sirdar. This grotesque act of triumphalism was criticised – as well as applauded – and eventually Kitchener secretly had the skull buried.

Wood offered Haig a transfer to Whitehall and the Horse Guards. Haig's reply is interesting, and typical of many statements he was to make later, particularly in India and during the war. To modern eyes his disavowal is unconvincing, but it is important to remember that in Haig's time, and for someone from his background, the idea of selfless submission to duty was a very real one, and a concept that did animate men in those less individualistic days. But despite that, and taking every extenuating circumstance into account, Haig was extremely ambitious and the tone of his remarks is difficult to take at face value:

I think that in spite of the feeling in this army against new arrivals that they will give one credit for training my squadron and doing my best *always* for the show, *not for myself*. I don't want credit for it because it pleased me and kept me well during the trying heat at Berber all summer. Now I think this show is pretty well over and though I am ready to remain if the Sirdar requires a Squadron Leader, I think your kindly advice about slackness in hot countries very much to the point and I am ready to come home in any minor capacity.

THE SOUTH AFRICAN WAR.
REGIMENTAL COMMAND.
THE DEBATE OVER CAVALRY. INDIA

The job Haig had expected at Whitehall did not materialise, and the immediate sequel to Omdurman was anti-climax. He returned to his regiment at Norwich for six months, after which he was appointed brigade major to French, and moved to the 1st Cavalry Brigade at Aldershot.

Charteris records that Haig was at a low point at this stage:

Neither the brevet rank nor the new appointment satisfied him. He felt the Egyptian campaign had been a failure as far as he was concerned. He was 38 years of age and still a regimental captain. There was no prospect of swift promotion. The goal of his ambition was still dim and distant. The war in Egypt was definitely over, and there seemed little probability of any further active service in the near future. His work at Aldershot was not absorbing, and the amusements of London entirely failed to attract him. He fell a victim to discontented ambition. Even his studies were in arrears as he became morose and brusque in manner. This was perhaps the least satisfactory year of Haig's military life: but it proved only a brief interval.[1]

Further active service was to become available much sooner than Haig expected. In the meantime he consolidated his relationship with Johnnie French, who had bounced back into his life.

At this time French's finances – never in good shape – were in particular disarray, following a typically ill-advised investment in South African gold-mining shares: there was a real risk that he might have to leave the army and might even be declared bankrupt. It was against this background that Haig made him a celebrated, and for his critics notorious, loan of £2,000. Haig's father's fortune had been divided amongst his many children. All of them received a worthwhile share, but the bulk was reserved for those sons who went into the family business. Although Haig started off in life with an income that was more than sufficient for a young officer's needs, the demands imposed by senior rank meant that his disposable income became increasingly slender. For most of his professional career Haig ran an overdraft. By the time he and his young wife went to India it was as high as £16,000 (perhaps £800,000 today) and in 1915 it was still £6,000 (£300,000). In 1917 he cited financial constraints as the reason for declining a peerage when it was first offered to him. He never became a rich man. Even after a parliamentary grant of £100,000 and the gift to him, by subscription, of Bemersyde, his estate at his death consisted of only £17,599. 3s. 6d. The loan of what is in today's money something like £100,000 is therefore fairly remarkable, and does raise the question of whether he was taking pains to put the influential French in his debt in more than one sense. Some of his supporters have simply dismissed the suggestion as *ex facie* absurd; others, notably John Hussey have argued against this view in more detail.[2] Hussey has shown that the initiative for the loan was a request from French, and not an offer from Haig, that French was within about twenty-four hours of bankruptcy, and that Haig's initial reaction to the situation was to offer a guarantee, rather than a loan which he could scarcely afford. His own man of business, Charles Boxall, persuaded him that nothing less than a loan would save French. Boxall told his client that in 'my own experience I have always found it far better to provide them money [as opposed to guaranteeing a debt] when helping a friend.' He warned Haig clearly of the risks he was taking: 'You must understand quite precisely from me that altho' I will shew with pleasure how the money you send is

applied I have absolutely nothing whatever to do with it as a matter
of business for of course there is nothing practical to rely on but the
General's word and in short nothing of "business" in the transaction
so far as you are concerned.'

Haig and French were profoundly different, and Haig must have
found much to disapprove of in his Chief's lifestyle. He told his sister
why he was helping French: 'It would be a terrible thing if French
were made a Bankrupt – such a loss to the army as well as to me
personally. For of course we can do a lot here together towards
improving things.'

What were Haig's true motives? Hussey suggests a test for the
modern reader:

> Haig was a man of surprising impulse . . . and he saved his
> friend. Had he refused help, French would have been bank-
> rupted. Should he have refused? Until the reader has squarely
> faced and answered that question I believe that he cannot pass
> judgement on Haig.

Perhaps not, but another question is whether Haig was not far too
intelligent not to apprehend that as a result of the transaction French
would be a valuable protector for the indefinite future. In reality the
matter cannot be resolved by either approach on its own. Haig was
not a complicated man, but he was complicated enough to be
animated by a mixture of motives.

The loan was not repaid for many years (probably not until 1909),
although French did pay interest. In 1903, when Haig was in India,
he left instructions that French should not be pressed for repayment.
When at one point repayment was not being made and his trustees
were for taking action, Haig wrote to his sister: 'I would prefer to lose
the money rather than that General French be pressed for it . . . With
my present pay I can live in luxury out here. I cannot stand the
"bunya" class. You know the bunya of course. How he sits round his
bags of grain, flour and foodstuffs and ghee and, fat and greasy, gloats
over every pice, and grinds the wretched tiller of the soil down by

usury and close dealings.' He wrote to Henrietta a few months later, asking her to thank an American friend for his 'kindly wishes "to make a pile for me", but I believe I have as much money as is good for me. I have some good ponies and horses and enjoy myself pretty well without feeling the want of money. Too much luxury is ruining the country (I mean England), and also the Yankees!'

Richard Holmes gives a good appraisal of the transaction, as well as describing Haig on his frequent visits to Anglesey House, French's residence at Aldershot:

> He talked freely enough to French on military topics, particularly on the situation in South Africa, which both men thought would lead to war. He was less than forthcoming to French's daughter Essex: she remembered him as being 'desperately dull'. Sometimes he would break a painful silence by saying, 'Very nice tea today, Essex', while on other occasions he would gaze at the mongrel Daphne and mutter, 'Daphne, poor old dog'. Whatever Haig's failings as a conversationalist, he was certainly far more astute than his Brigade Commander in the management of money. Haig was more likely to ride naked down the Mall than to get into debt: his letters and diaries reveal a pronounced pre-occupation with money, and in the spring of 1899 Haig had disposable cash at the very moment when French urgently required it. He borrowed the sum of £2000 from Haig and although this appeared to be a loan, it seems that it was never repaid [probably not the case]: it was certainly outstanding four years later . . .
>
> Some might suggest that it was hardly ethical for a junior officer to make what was in fact, if not in theory, a substantial gift . . . to a senior, knowing that the senior was responsible for initiating the reports which would determine his immediate military future.[3]

At any rate, for the immediate future French's financial concerns were resolved. Very soon, too, Haig's concern that he would not see active service again also disappeared. As the crisis in South Africa deepened, French was selected to command the cavalry there – despite the fact that at this stage he had seen no active service at all – and Haig was appointed as assistant adjutant-general, his chief staff officer. Haig prepared for his new role with typical conscientiousness, examining past campaigns in South Africa and preparing a paper on tactics. He was seen off at Southampton on 23 September 1899 by Henrietta and another officer from the 7th Hussars, his friend John Vaughan. Once embarked on the Union Castle liner *Norman,* Haig found that no accommodation had been provided for him. When French discovered this he invited Haig to share his cabin on the top deck, and both of them had access to the Captain's bathroom. They arrived at Cape Town on 10 October, the day before the outbreak of war. Immediately they re-embarked for Durban and then entrained for Ladysmith. Once arrived, French was directed to occupy Elandslaagte. This was a successful operation, in which the British infantry was imaginatively commanded by Sir Ian Hamilton, with the support of the cavalry, dismounted at one point. It was a small enough action, with British casualties of 263 and Boer casualties of 363, but it was the first British victory in South Africa. Caricatures of French appeared in the *Illustrated London News*, and he began to appear as a popular hero. Haig was involved significantly both before and after the action: before in drafting the orders, and afterwards in examining the prisoners, of whom there were 188. French's force remained in and around Ladysmith for a little longer, but the Boers were beginning to concentrate their strength on the position, and Buller, the Commander-in-Chief, just arrived in South Africa, sent a telegram requesting that French and Haig should report to Cape Town immediately, so that French could take charge of the new Cavalry division shortly to arrive from England.

The train on which French and Haig left Ladysmith was the last to get out for four months. Haig described the journey to Henrietta:

A train was starting at 12.30pm. We got our kit and ten horses put in. The Railway Manager did not think we could get past

the Boers as they had fired on a morning passenger train.
However, we insisted on going . . . All were enjoined to keep
out of sight for the first two hours. Twenty minutes went by
without any untoward event. We then got near a place called
Pieter's Station. Several bullets, in fact a regular volley, rattled
along the side of the vehicles, and we heard several shells
explode. We did not see anything for we had a wooden shutter
up and we all four lay on the seats and floor of the carriage. The
train went on and then suddenly stopped. The door opened and
we expected to see some Boer inviting us to descend! We had
got into one of our own posts left to protect the line and the
individual who opened the door was a British officer. On we
went again with the same precautions, before we were told we
should be shot at again three miles down. Sure enough there
was a very loud report and other shots. When we got to Colenso
we examined our train and found a two and a half or three inch
shell had got through the second truck. If this shell had hit a
wheel, not to mention the engine boiler, we would certainly
have been now on our way to Pretoria instead of in Durban. Or
indeed if the Boers had torn up a rail, the engine driver would
not have seen it because the moment the Boers began shooting
he lay down amongst the coal.

Particularly in view of the fierce enmity which was to develop
between Haig and French during the war, the picture of the two
future field-marshals huddled together on the floor of the compart-
ment is even more appealing than their sharing the captain's bath.

The British commander in South Africa was initially Buller with
Kitchener as Chief of Staff. The position of chief of staff at that time
meant effectively that Kitchener was second in command. Sir Redvers Buller, VC, was sixty-six, a veteran of the China War of 1860,
the Red River expedition in Canada, the Ashanti Wars, the Zulu
War, the 1881 Boer War, the Egyptian Campaign of 1882 and the
expedition which failed to rescue General Gordon. His command did
not survive Black Week, in December 1889, when Gatacre was

defeated at Stormberg, Methuen at Magersfontein, and Buller himself at Colenso. In contrast to events such as these, Johnnie French's (relatively minor) cavalry operations relieved the gloom at home. The blow to British self-confidence that Black Week represented is difficult for us now to understand: the most powerful empire in the history of the world was in very real danger of being defeated by a handful of farmers. The government's reaction was to move Buller sideways, to take charge of the relief of Ladysmith, and to replace him with an even older man, 'Bobs', Lord Roberts.

French was summoned on 29 January 1900 to Cape Town to confer with Roberts, taking him away at first temporarily, and two days later permanently, from his command in the Colesburg area. His operations there were of critical importance, not only in establishing his reputation (and therefore indirectly benefiting Haig) but also in validating the claims of the cavalry enthusiasts. He had

> checked the invasion of Cape Colony, safeguarded the Midland line of communication . . . His thrusts attracted Boer reinforcements which might have been used, with damaging effect, elsewhere. Even the *Times History,* generally critical of British Commanders, spoke of an 'enormous unbroken series of successes'. It went on to commend the moral ascendancy established by French at this critical time, his quick and practical grasp of tactics, and his readiness to throw every available man into the firing line at the vital moment.[4]

The new role which Roberts had for French was to push through to the north-west towards Kimberley and then east to Bloemfontein. Unfortunately for Haig, Roberts and the War Office decided that French required for this a staff officer who was more than a substantive captain, and appointed in his place Colonel the Earl of Erroll. Erroll had four years of command under his belt (although he had not attended Staff College). French reacted with a telegram to Kitchener:

May I point out the appointment of the Assistant Adjutant
General to the Cavalry Division was promised by Sir Redvers
Buller to Major Haig with the local rank of Lt.Col. I was
officially asked to recommend an officer to fill his place as
Deputy Assistant Adjutant General. I honestly beg that the
Field-Marshal will be pleased to confirm this. Major Haig has
performed the duty of Chief Staff Officer to a division since
landing in Natal. He has acted in this capacity under my
command in three general engagements and many smaller
fights. I have several times mentioned him in despatches.[5]

The reply was that: 'The Field-Marshal Commander in Chief fully
realises the very excellent services rendered by Major Haig and much
regrets not being able to meet your views as regards his taking
position of AAG of the Cavalry Division. That position however the
Field-Marshal thinks must be filled by the appointment of a senior
officer and he feels sure you will find in Colonel the Earl of Erroll an
efficient officer.'

In the event, and very quickly, Erroll was found not to be up to the
requirements of the position and after a personal interview between
French's ADC, Sir John Laycock, and Kitchener, he was removed and
Haig returned to his former position.

Roberts' object of relieving Kimberley was achieved, substantially
by French, on 15 February. The relief of Kimberley was a crucial
justification of all the claims made for the use of cavalry. On 10
February Kitchener had emphasised to French the importance of the
relief of the town. French said that if he were still alive on 15
February he would be there. Roberts' address to cavalry officers on 10
February is well worth quoting:

I am going to give you some very hard work to do but at the
same time you are going to get the greatest chance cavalry has
ever had. I am certain you will do well. I have received news
from Kimberley from which I know that it is of importance that
the town should be relieved in the course of the next five days,

and you and your men are to do this. The enemy have placed a big gun in position and are shelling the town, killing women and children, in consequence of which the civilian population are urging Colonel Kekewich to capitulate. You will remember what you are going to do all your lives and when you have grown to be old men you will tell the story of the relief of Kimberley . . .

French's advance on the town was carried out at a speed that took the Boers by surprise, and on the morning of 15 February he was just outside the town, at Klip Drift, facing a small enemy force of 900 men on a fortified ridge. French had no less than 8,000 cavalry and 6,000 mounted infantry. Instead of reducing the ridge with his substantial force of fifty-six guns, French threw the 16th and 9th Lancers at it. Despite intense fire, only seven men were killed in the charge. French and the rest of the cavalry pushed through, to find the ridge now deserted by the Boers, who had fled in the face of the Lancers' attack. This was the army's last dramatic cavalry charge. As Roberts had foreseen, it was indeed recalled by veterans who gathered each year for the rest of their lives on 15 February. It was also, for Haig and the other cavalry enthusiasts, just the evidence they required to support their argument. Haig wrote at the time to his friend Lonsdale Hale:

You will I think agree with me that the Cavalry – the despised *Cavalry* I should say – has saved the Empire . . . You must rub this fact into those wretched individuals who pretend to rule the Empire! And in any case, before they decide on reorganising the Army, let them get the experience of those who have seen the effect of modern firearms and have learnt to realise that the old story is true, viz: that "moral [a word often used at this time in preference to 'morale'] is everything", and not merely guns but men who can use them is what is wanted to defend the Empire.

Klip Drift was acknowledged as a major achievement for French, and for the cavalry. *The Times History* recorded that

The charge at Klip Drift marks an epoch in the history of cavalry. With other cavalry charges of former wars it has little in common, save the 'cavalry spirit' . . . the quick insight that prompted it, the instantaneous decision that launched it against the enemy, the reckless, dare-devil confidence that carried it through. In its form it was something wholly new . . . The thin line of unseen riflemen, with its wide gaps covered by converging fire, which had proved so unapproachable to the slow, short-winded foot soldier, availed nothing against the rushing speed and sustained impetus of the wave of horsemen . . . This was the secret French had divined.[6]

The Official History was equally unrestrained in its approval: 'the most brilliant stroke of the whole war'. But Klip Drift and the relief of Kimberley were not what they seemed: this was not an *arme blanche* charge against a well-established enemy. The speed of French's advance on the Boer position, the artillery support he enjoyed, and the fact that the enemy were only lightly disposed were all significant factors; as *The Times History* said, it had little in common with cavalry charges of earlier wars. Only some twenty Boers were killed, and French and Haig and others who subsequently pointed to the Klip Drift cavalry charge as a vindication of the argument for the moral ascendancy of mounted troops armed with cold steel misled themselves and those whom they addressed. Kimberley was tremendous for Haig and other cavalry enthusiasts, but a spurious success. For the army and the public it was a dashing victory in the best cavalry tradition and the achievement of traditional cavalry was emphasised at the cost of the mounted infantry. The comparison was an unfair one, because the latter were deprived of resources, training and good mounts.[7]

After Klip Drift, Haig was very briefly put in command of a brigade. But French must have found himself lost without his principal staff officer, because after only a day or two Haig returned to that role. In it, he was partly responsible for uncharacteristically poor staff work, which resulted, as a consequence of bad timings in

orders, in the failure at the Battle of Poplar Grove. Roberts at the
time was of the view that an opportunity of ending the war had been
lost.[8]

The war was not in fact to end for another two years. From Haig's
personal point of view, this was perhaps as well, because his valuable
work as French's staff officer was now to be complemented by
command in the field. His old friend, Sir Evelyn Wood, was pressing
from London for command of a cavalry regiment for him. Haig's
comments to Henrietta do not lack their frequent disingenuousness
and he may have had his own suspicions that French was selfishly
hanging on to him:

> French is only too anxious to help me on but I think that in
> remaining on as his Chief Staff Officer I did the best for the
> Cavalry Division, for him and for myself. One did not foresee
> this war lasting so long, otherwise I might have taken command
> of some scallywag corps or other. So don't make a fuss about my
> being now in the position I started in. Recollect many have
> gone lower down, and as to rewards, if you only know what
> duffers will get and do get HM's decorations and are promoted
> you would realise how little I value them. Everything comes in
> time, and decorations come in abundance with declining years
> and imbecility. No one yet on the Staff, fortunately, has a
> decoration of any kind, otherwise we might have achieved
> disaster like the other *decorés*!

Henrietta was not the only one who had suspicions about French's
motives for retaining Haig on his staff, in defiance of Evelyn Wood's
direction that he be found a regiment. Kitchener wondered: 'Is
French really trying to help Haig, or is he tired of Haig and does he
want to shunt him to make room for some young protégé of his
own?'[9]

Henrietta's letters to Haig were rarely critical, and her parcels were
as welcome as her letters. She was asked to supply, for example, silk
drawers, the only underwear that was comfortable in the heat during

the long days in the saddle. She did, however, take Haig aback by warning him that the Prince of Wales ('Tum' behind his back) was concerned that he was 'too fond of criticising . . . senior officers'. [He] 'may be correct, but it does not do.' Haig retorted:

> I never criticise people except privately, and what a stupid letter it would be if I did not express an opinion. Besides, I think we would have better generals in higher ranks and the country would not have passed through such a period of anxiety had honest criticism, based on sound reasoning, been more general in reference to military affairs during the last twenty years.

It was difficult for Haig: whatever his motives, he very much wanted to criticise senior officers. Anyway, as he had told Henrietta at the time of Omdurman: 'What Tum likes is gossip'. Tum may have liked gossip, but he was very touchy about any hint of lack of respect, and if the letter had come into his hands, that would have been the end of Haig's career.

Later in November 1902, Haig wrote to Henrietta again, regarding his role on French's staff:

> By the way the General [French] mentioned to me that you had written to him some time ago and apparently conveyed the impression given you by old Evelyn that he (General French) had not done all he could and might have done to push me on. Now as I have told you often, the General wrote to Evelyn several times about me, and to others recommending me for all sorts of things, so you are quite under a misapprehension.

Old Evelyn was almost certainly correct. French was exerting himself less than he might have done to see that Haig got a command of his own. That is hardly surprising: although French had a number of excellent and promising officers with him – Allenby, Horne, de Lisle and Hunter-Weston – Haig was much the most valuable, described in *The Times History* as 'an invaluable Staff Officer, one of the few in

the whole army capable of doing real general staff work.' Haig's staff
diaries as Column Commander in Cape Colony were on loan to the
Staff College for very many years as models of such documents.[10] *The
Times History* was not necessarily favourable towards staff officers. It
was written by Leo Amery, who saw part of his role as promoting
army reform: 'Englishmen who would not dream of sending a crew to
Henley Regatta whose members had never rowed together before
were quite content that a general's staff should be hastily improvised
at the last moment from officers scraped together from every
corner.'[11]

It was a delicate situation for Haig. He could not afford to sever the
valuable link with French, whose stock had risen dramatically in the
course of the war. He was gaining experience of staff work at a senior
level and putting himself into a situation in which he had few rivals.
In any event Henrietta was doing everything that could be done to
find him an independent command and was not forbidden to
continue doing so.

By the end of 1900 the government was concerned about the
Boers' guerrilla tactics. It was decided that the response should lie in
an emphasis on mobile columns. The Boers were to be restricted by
Kitchener's 'blockhouse' system, with its barbed-wire fences. Boer
families, including women and children, were moved into camps.
The name given to these camps is one which would come to chill the
blood through the new century: 'concentration camps'.

The independent role Haig was eventually given was command of
initially three columns, 2,700 men; and in April 1901 he was
promoted to command all the mobile columns in the Midland
district of Cape Colony.

Already, in July 1900, Haig had written to Henrietta: 'The policy
of treating the Boers with leniency has not paid so far. They surrender
their arms and take an oath of allegiance, but on the first available
chance they go out on commando again.' The operations in which
Haig was taking part involved destroying homesteads, executing
farmers and placing women and children behind barbed wired fences.
Haig saw a practical argument against burning farm buildings,

'when [the Boers] have such a vast area from which they can draw supplies.' But he did not have moral objections. He was not allowed to hang two rebels whom he had caught. His reaction was: 'there is too much "*law*" and not enough rough and ready justice in this land.' In August:

> The authorities are all for blood now, I hear! This will have a good effect. There were three men shot at Colesberg when I was there. I did not care to go and see the spectacle but all the local Dutch magnates had to attend and a roll was called to see that they were present. I am told the sight was most impressive and everything went off well.

Haig's views would be typical of those of his brother officers. In their eyes, the Boers did not deserve the protection of the rules of war, since they chose not to adhere to these rules. They often dressed in khaki uniforms and were able to come within range of British forces before their identity was discovered. Controversially, they made use of explosive bullets.

Haig's command was an unorthodox one and the experience he gained in control of mobile columns was not part of the normal command structure. It is not what Sir Evelyn Wood had wanted: his intention was that, in charge of a regiment, Haig would be able to train new cavalry leaders. But eventually – and in addition to his columns – Haig was appointed to command of the 17th Lancers. The transfer of command did not go smoothly: Herbert Lawrence, who had been in charge of Intelligence while Haig was with French, was a 17th Lancer, and within the regiment it was thought that he, rather than an outsider, had earned its command. He was disappointed, and retired from the army for several years, (returning in the War and working well with Haig as his chief of staff in 1918). His colleagues were also disappointed, and Haig had to make an effort to win acceptance. That took some time: he was regarded by officers and men as lacking in sympathy and understanding.[12]

Although he worked hard and conscientiously in command of his mobile columns, it was not work for which Haig was ideally suited. Counter-guerrilla operations of this sort require an intuitive skill; and a conventional approach, no matter how systematic and painstaking, was never going to hunt down Smuts and his colleagues. The intelligence officer, Colonel Wools-Sampson, said, when he heard that Haig had been given independent command: '[He] would be so fixed on not giving the Boers a chance, he'll never give himself one.'[13] All the same, during his command he wore down two-thirds of the Boer commanders.

Peace was signed on 31 May 1902. Haig returned to England from South Africa in September of that year, after some months in command of a military sub-district of Cape Colony. One of his final duties was to escort Smuts, who would have Haig's career in his hands sixteen years later, to the Peace Conference. Fortunately, he concluded that as Smuts had been to Cambridge he could be regarded as a gentleman.

During the war Henrietta had become very concerned about her brother's lack of rewards and decorations. Haig's response, typically, was that he did not want to be one of 'these self-advertising people like [Baden Powell] and family.' With peace, things changed, and Haig's uniform was never the same. He was made Brevet Colonel and was awarded the CB. He was appointed ADC to King Edward VII, as the Prince of Wales now was. He had been mentioned in despatches no less than four times, and he had the medals and clasps of the campaigns in which he had fought. These honours were deserved. He had worked very hard for them, both as a column commander, when he combined a huge amount of administrative work with much time in the saddle, and also in long, diligent hours of staff work. Interstices that others might have devoted to social activities he used to advance his professional career. At Cape Town, at the beginning of his South African period, for example, Haig, awaiting orders for ten days in the Mount Nelson Hotel, where he shared a bedroom with French, made use of the time to draw up a memorandum on *Tactical Notes*, setting out the lessons of the fighting in which he had already taken part.[14] 'These operations have shown clearly the increased power of action possessed by cavalry, now that it is armed with a good carbine.' Interestingly, for someone who was profoundly opposed to mounted infantry, he provided details of four occasions when the cavalry, *dismounted,* had performed outstandingly well. Indeed, at the time of his service in Sudan, he himself had used dismounted cavalry. He was thinking of the value of dismounted cavalry, rather than that of mounted infantry, but he does go on to 'question whether the Dragoon-Lancer is not a mistake! His lance hampers him . . .' He forgot this view after the South African War had ended, when he was giving formal evidence on his views on the lance.

Men are animated by a complicated mixture of motives, and can certainly be high minded and honourable as well as ambitious. It is important not to allow some of Haig's transparently disingenuous abjurations of ambition to blind us to the fact that he *did* have high ideals, and that his attitude to duty and the Empire, though not easily comprehended today, was entirely genuine. At the end of the South African War, his nephew, Hugo, debated leaving the army in order to farm his estate in Fife. He decided not to do so, and Haig responded approvingly in a letter which is important in setting out his views on ambition and duty – and which reveals his romantic commitment to the imperial dream:

It would be absurd for a lad of your years and without any real experience of the Empire and its inhabitants to settle down into a turnip grower in Fife. Leave these pursuits until you get into the doddering age! Meantime do your best to become a worthy citizen of the Empire . . . It has been your *good fortune* [Haig's emphasis] not only to become a soldier, but to have served and risked your life for the Empire – you must continue to do so, and consider that it is a privilege . . . The gist of the whole thing is that I am anxious not only that you should realise your duty to your family, your Country and to Scotland, but also to the whole Empire – 'Aim High' as the Book says, 'perchance you may attain.' Aim at being worthy of the British Empire and possibly in the evening of your life you may be able to own to yourself that you are fit to settle down in Fife. At present you are not, so be active and busy . . .

Don't let . . . mediocrities about you deflect you from your determination to belong to the few who can command or guide or benefit our great Empire. Believe me, the reservoir of such men is not boundless. As our Empire grows, so is there a greater demand for them, and it behoves everyone to do his little and try and qualify for as high a position as possible. It is not ambition. *This is duty* [again Haig's emphasis].

On Haig's return to England after his second experience of active service, there was none of the feeling of a stalled career which had, according to Charteris, concerned him after his return from Omdurman. He now commanded a regiment, and his views were sought after and listened to by those who counted, even if that was more on the basis of his writings than his experience in the field. That experience remained limited, and he would not command fighting troops again until after the outbreak of war.

He was in demand for not just one, but two, employments. Both were attractive. Kitchener wished to appoint him as Inspector General of the Mounted Forces in India, and French wanted him as Commander of the Aldershot Cavalry Brigade. Haig recognised the attractions of both positions, but preferred Aldershot. In the event, Roberts, whose decision it was, appointed Haig to India. The appointment of the officer whom he was to replace did not expire until October 1903, and Haig spent the time until then with the 17th Lancers. Regimental life appealed to Haig no more as a colonel than it had done as a subaltern, but he filled his time with the regiment with characteristic energy, and in the end felt closer links to the 17th Lancers than to any other regiment with which he had been associated.

The regiment was stationed in Edinburgh, 'a bad place for cavalry – no drill ground and half the regiment on detachment – so', he wrote to his sister, 'I wired General French and asked him to try and get the station altered to York, or Aldershot. Indeed, any place is better as a cavalry station than Edinburgh.'

His request was not granted, but he was able to devote time once again to polo, and during his brief spell with the regiment led it to victory in the Inter-Regimental Tournament, a victory which he celebrated with unusual enthusiasm. After an uninspiring dinner with the defeated Blues at the Regent's Park barracks, the 17th Lancers felt that something livelier was called for, and at their colonel's invitation and expense they moved on to the Savoy for supper. The latter part of the evening was a jovial one, and Haig entered much more into the spirit of things than was his custom, protesting noisily when the lights were lowered, and the barman called: 'Time, please, gentlemen, time.'

As well as returning to polo, he took up golf, which was to be the sporting exercise of his middle age. Golf was played on Sundays. Accompanied by one or two of his younger officers, he walked four miles to and from the course, carrying his clubs, and played two rounds. He was a benevolent colonel, insisting on paying for the expenses of his junior officers whenever he was with them, even though many of them were far richer than he, but generally avoiding the Mess, in case his presence there inhibited his officers.

In the spring of 1903 Haig gave evidence to the Elgin Commission appointed to look at the lessons of the South African War. He argued for the provision of light transport for the cavalry, so that the amount of kit carried by cavalrymen could be reduced:

Equipped as he was with an unnecessarily heavy saddle and wallets, a nosebag of horse food, rifle, sword, lance, great coat, blanket and other paraphernalia, the cavalryman looked more like a travelling showman than a death-dealing soldier. No one knows more than the cavalryman himself how all these goods and chattels retarded his progress in pursuit of the wily Boer and to what extent they were responsible for knocked-up horses.

He also put in a plea, as he no doubt felt a Lancer had to, for the retention by certain regiments of the lance, which was currently under attack.

The lance was not the only apparently antiquated weapon that was being advocated at this time. Major-General J.P. Brabazon gave evidence to the Commission on the Imperial Yeomanry: 'For the Latin races the sword or the lance, for it is natural to them to always give the point. The Anglo-Saxon race invariably chop or strike, and I believe the lightest, most handy, effective, and demoralising (to your enemy) weapon would be a light battle-axe or tomahawk. It would be light, easily carried, and a desperate arm in a mêlée.'[15]

In October Haig was invited to stay with the royal family at Balmoral. There he was presented with the CVO. The Order was, as it still is, in the personal gift of the monarch, and represented an intimate and very special mark of approval from the Crown. Haig recognised it as such, and saw it as distinct from the other military awards which he received. He reported that the honour was given to him 'in recognition of the services which I had rendered in the past and would render in the future as IG of cavalry in India, and also as "a mark of HM's personal esteem".' The King renewed his request that Haig should write to him, despite the rebuke for criticising senior officers.

When Haig arrived in India, Kitchener, the new Commander-in-Chief, had just submitted to Curzon, the Viceroy, a scheme for reform of the Indian Army entitled *The Reorganisation & Redistribution of the Army in India*. The nub of the plan was to substitute two armies for the existing commands, with the objectives of reducing the garrison troops to a necessary minimum, of putting in place a war organisation and of making that war organisation correspond with peace formations, so that the passage from peace to war could be effected seamlessly. The two armies were to be commanded by generals with names that combine splendidly: Blood and Luck.

Kitchener's task was part of a wider programme initiated by the Viceroy, a programme of extensive reform and modernisation. Curzon had written to Kitchener before his appointment as Commander in Chief: 'I look forward with much confidence to the benefit of your vast energy and great experience. I see absurd and uncontrolled expenditure; I observe a lack of method and system; I detect slackness and jobbery; and in some respects I lament a want of fibre and tone'.[16]

Kitchener's task was to bring together the scattered series of garrisons that was the army in India. It was the result of his work, if not his intention, that the Indian army was able to contribute as it did to Britain's efforts in the war. Haig's role in this was to modernise the training of the cavalry. He was an ideal choice. He had delayed his departure to India in order to work on a new edition of *Cavalry Training,* which was being revised in the light of the experiences gained in South Africa. Preparation of this edition involved facing the debate which was being fiercely argued between supporters of the cavalry in its traditional form on the one hand and the reformers on the other. Sometimes the debate was carried on at a juvenile level, in a spirit of simple rivalry. Haig gave an example of this approach in a letter to Henrietta, describing the march on Pretoria: 'The infantry are quite jealous of the successes of the Cavalry. The poor creatures merely carry their guns without loosing off! In fact they simply wear out their boots to no purpose!!' But the divisions were deeper and more serious than that. Both sides found evidence to support their respective cases in the experience of the South African war. The flat-trajectory bullet and the range of modern rifles which made firearms much more effective weapons than swords and lances, the fact that firearms could not be used effectively from the saddle, the skill of the Boer riders, who used their horses to make rapid advances, but then dismounted to fire: all these tended to erode the traditionalists' case. They, on the other hand, pointed to the victories at Elandslaagte and, in particular, Kimberley, as vindicating all that was epitomised by cavalry, the *arme blanche*, the phenomenon of men galloping, knee to knee, using bare steel at close quarters.

The lessons which the traditionalists took away from South Africa were flawed to the extent that cavalry there had *not* truly performed as they claimed. At Kimberley, as has been noted, the success lay not in the cavalry charge, but in Roberts' skill in bringing huge numbers to bear on a relatively small defensive force, and in the phenomenal speed of French's march. But for the traditionalists the argument was one of almost spiritual intensity. There was much reference to morale (or more usually 'moral'). Giving evidence to the Elgin Commission in 1903, French said that: 'If the Cavalryman is taught to rely mainly on his rifle, his moral is taken away from him, and if that is done his power is destroyed.' Haig had given evidence to the Commission that half the cavalry should have swords and the other half lances, on the basis that in a clash with enemy cavalry, the only weapon that would be of use would be the lance: a reasonable view if cavalry clashes took place, and there was no reason then to suppose they would not. Roberts attacked him a little unkindly: 'Haig . . . inclines to the lance though he can have had no experience of its use in war.' With hindsight, Haig's views at this time can be and have been attacked on the basis that they did not second-guess developments of warfare in the 20th century. For instance:

Foresight was not Haig's strongest point. For him, studying war meant prostrating himself at the Temple of Napoleon, Wellington and Blücher. His head stuck in the sands of time, he could not see the future that lay ahead. Like French, who claimed that 'nothing can make me alter the views that I hold on the subject of cavalry', Haig refused to accept that long-range rifles, deadly machine-guns and powerful artillery would annihilate lancers before they could even attempt to prove the worth of their cherished weapons.[17]

Similarly, Haig has been ridiculed for saying that the rifle bullet had 'little stopping power against the horse'. He did not of course mean that a horse could not be killed by a rifle bullet; he was not a fool. But while noting the effect of modern, small-bore bullets, he failed to take into account the significance of their velocity. He was arguing always that the effect on morale of a mass of trained cavalry, approaching at full gallop with swords drawn, would cause the dissolution of ranks of infantrymen. He was not a seer, and did not envisage the mass use of machine-guns or the barbed wire of the Western Front. When such conditions did exist, he quickly enough modified his views on cavalry. What he said was reasonable enough at the time he said it:

It must be borne in mind that the days of small armies are past and it is a simple fact that *large armies entail large numbers of cavalry* [Haig's emphasis]. The Army, then, which assumes the strategical offensive, has, as a general rule, the best chance on employing the most effective manoeuvres but much depends on the quality and handling of the cavalry. Cavalry, then, sharing enormous power conferred by the low trajectory rifle and rapidity of fire, plays a role in grand tactics of which the importance can hardly be over-estimated . . .

The role of the cavalry on the battlefield will always go on increasing because:

1. The extended nature of the modern battlefield means that there will be a greater choice of cover to provide the concealed approach of cavalry.
2. The increased range and killing power of modern guns, and the greater length of time during which the battle will last, will augment the moral exhaustion, will affect men's nerves more and produce greater demoralisation amongst the troops. These factors contribute to provoke panic, and to render troops, short service soldiers nowadays, ripe for attacks by cavalry.
3. The longer range and killing power of modern arms, the more important will rapidity of movement become, because it lessens the relative time of exposure to danger in favour of the cavalry.
4. The introduction of the small-bore rifle, the bullet from which has little stopping power against the horse.
5. The role of cavalry, far from being diminished, has increased in importance. It extends to both strategy and tactics; it alone is of use in the service of exploration and it is of capital importance in a general action.[18]

In the conditions of 1906, when he wrote these words, these views were fairly sound. Fairly sound, but another observer had a more perceptive view of the significance of the small-bore rifle: 'The flat trajectory of the small-bore rifle together with the invisibility of the man who uses it' revolutionised the art of fighting for G.R.F. Henderson.[19] Haig was with almost all of his contemporaries, whether reformers or traditionalists, in failing to foresee the effect of modern weapons on traditional cavalry tactics.

One specific proposal that flowed from the South African experience, and which Haig particularly opposed, was the proposal for 'mounted infantry'. During the war some units were drawn up from scratch for this role, and others were created from infantry battalions and in particular from Dominion troops. They proved to be very effective. Haig, as a professional cavalryman, regarded such hybrid creations with disdain, and scorned the Dominion troops as 'Colonial Scallywags'. It is not easy to justify Haig's dislike for mounted infantry. His position was that he expected a cavalryman to be able to dismount and use his rifle like the mounted infantryman, but *also* to be able to provide the shock attacks and pursuits of which the mounted infantryman would be incapable. Sir Evelyn Wood was the man who conceived the idea of mounted infantry. He had served with both the infantry and the cavalry and he proposed that each infantry battalion should train one mounted company. Haig had to be circumspect in attacking the concept for which his benefactor was responsible: he had written to Henrietta from South Africa: 'The Mounted Infantry craze is now I trust exploded. So far they have proved useless, and are not likely to be of use until *they learn to ride.* But you had better not give these views to Sir Evelyn, for both he and Lord Wolseley are the parents of the Mounted Infantry.' One of his notable opponents, as a proponent of mounted infantry, was the remarkable Erskine Childers, cousin of Gladstone's First Lord of the Admiralty and Minister of War, clerk in the House of Commons, believer in the British imperial purpose, author of *The Riddle of the Sands* and ultimately shot by firing squad in Dublin, a traitor in the eyes of both the British government and the Irish Free State. Childers volunteered for South Africa and joined the Honourable Artillery Company. As a result of his experience in the Boer War he became critical of the traditional training methods of the British army and published two important books, *War and the Arme Blanche* (1910) and *German Influence on British Cavalry* (1911). In India, Haig established a permanent cavalry school and on his first inspection was not pleased to see in it a road called 'Childers Road'. Where did it lead? The commandant of the school had a beautiful explanation: 'Ah, Sir, that road is a cul-de-sac, and leads to the cemetery.'

Haig was not a blind traditionalist, as many cavalry officers were, who simply wanted to preserve unchanged the institution to which they belonged. On the contrary, he considered that there was huge room for improvement and a necessity to train the cavalry far more effectively than in the past, so that, for instance, cavalrymen were able to make best use of modern firearms. His time in India proves this point dramatically. It was spent in a whirlwind of activity. Inspector's drills were carried out at the gallop. He had three changes of horses (mostly steeplechasers or pigstickers, and faster than ordinary chargers).[20] He pushed his men and was a hard master, particularly on senior officers who had been slumbering in the eastern sun. Promotion now took place on merit and not automatically as in the past. He introduced economies to make it possible for young officers to survive on their army salaries.[21] He was severe towards more senior officers: 'The subaltern and junior captain of the Indian Cavalry are the best of their rank in the army. There is a sad falling off in the rank of major, and the commanding officers are almost all past their work.' He added to the process of inspection and occasional exercises an injection of innovative thinking by introducing staff rides, tactical exercises without Troops, 'Tewts' as they would later be known. Five staff rides were carried out during his three years in India, and each lasted a week. The experience from the rides was distilled in his book *Cavalry Studies*, which contained, amongst other important lessons, the observation that

Certainly a knowledge of military history is all-important to an officer. In studying it we see the great masters at work. We learn from their experience and become acquainted with the difficulties to be encountered in applying principles. But such work contributes little to developing our powers of decision. On the other hand 'war games', 'staff rides' should be framed chiefly with the latter object.

Perhaps the sentence in *Cavalry Studies* that most accurately epitomises the real nub of Haig's military philosophy is this: 'Success in battle depends mainly on moral and a determination to conquer.' The dash of the cavalier always appealed.

As well as establishing the cavalry school, he toyed with the idea of sending Indian army officers to Camberley, but then instead developed the Indian Staff College at Quetta, a sort of Indian Camberley which had been established by Kitchener. Quetta is now the Pakistan Staff College, and a huge portrait of Kitchener hangs in the entrance hall.

General Arthur alludes to a problem which Haig addressed in India, and does so with such delicacy that it is far from clear what he is talking about:

There is a point one might like to shirk but which has its place in any review of Haig's stewardship in India. It is not to peer too intrusively into the arcana of a man's life to allude to its austere purity, to suggest that in this respect there are men of high courage who shrink back with something like horror from certain forms of evil, to whom it would be shame 'even to speak of those things done in secret'. For such a man, whatever his experience, and however constantly he may rub shoulders with the world, vice is vice, and can neither be laughed at nor licensed. On his arrival in India Haig heard quickly and with something like dismay of the ravages made by disease among the British troops serving in the country. Formerly, the existence of vice had been recognised and regularised, with the result that the temptation to be impure had stared every young soldier in the face. Public opinion had put a term to such a system, and it could only remain for those in authority not to rely on the publication of cantonment laws but to appeal by every means to every man's sense of self respect and regard for his real welfare and the honour of his regiment . . . [Haig] looked, of course, for no moral Utopia, but no name, nor effort, was subscribed more heartily than his to the famous Memorandum in which officers were urged to encourage in their men a belief in leading a good and healthy life, and in every way – not least by themselves setting an example of self restraint – to protect them from a grave and devastating evil.[22]

In his time in India, then, Haig had been able to improve the quality of the cavalry hugely, and had put in place institutions and training regimes which would maintain its improved standard. But in the battle over the future of cavalry, he had initial reverses. Roberts had not been pleased with Haig's contribution to *Cavalry Training*:

Haig, I am surprised to find, still clings to the *arme blanche* system, and in the chapter for the Revised Edition of the Drill Book, which was entrusted to him to write, on Collective Training, there is not one word about Artillery or Dismounted Fire. Haig, supported by French and Scobell, insists on Cavalry soldiers being taught to consider the sword the chief weapon and the rifle as a kind of auxiliary one . . . I am all in favour of cavalry soldiers being bold riders, and endeavouring to overthrow their enemy's mounted men, but I am convinced that in 99 cases out of 100 this will be done more effectively by Artillery and Dismounted Fire in the first instance.

Later, with Haig safely in India, Roberts was able to get his way, writing to Kitchener: 'The revised *Cavalry Training* is getting on and I hope it will be published next month. A good deal of it was started by Haig . . . and consequently much of his work has had to be rewritten'.[23] Again, despite Haig, Roberts abolished the lance in 1904.

But, in broad terms, the cavalry argument was tending to be won by Haig and the traditionalists.

In India, Haig observed at first hand the problems of what was known as the system of 'Dual Control': the Commander-in-Chief, Kitchener, had the responsibility of training the army, but other military matters were the responsibility of the Viceroy. Curzon was no friend of the army. On one occasion he annotated a document: 'I rise from the perusal of these papers filled with the sense of the ineptitude of my military advisers.' He could be difficult in petty matters as well as grand ones. His title was Curzon of Kedleston, but he signed himself simply 'Curzon'. Kitchener on his arrival in India signed himself 'Kitchener of Khartoum'. Astonishingly, Curzon took the time and trouble to write to him to say that using the full signature would occupy unnecessary time and space. Kitchener agreed, but not without noting that a colleague who could be difficult in regard to such a minor matter could be difficult in more serious ones. Interestingly, a few years later, Curzon was signing himself 'Curzon of Kedleston' despite the space that the signature took up.[24] Curzon was no cipher, and in his Vice-Regal Council he took advice from a major-general before issuing directives which were, so far as Kitchener was concerned, orders. The arrangement was productive of considerable heat, and Haig described it well in a letter to Henrietta:

> The C-in-C India really has very little power. All the Supply, Transport and Finance are under an individual called the 'Military Member of the Council'. That is to say that Lord K may order men to Thibet [*sic*] but he does not know whether they will starve or not because he has nothing to do with the supply arrangements. Such a system is obviously ridiculous. It is like a pair of horses in double harness without a coachman. The latter ought to be the Viceroy, but he has too many things to attend to already even if he were capable of discharging such duties, which the majority of Viceroys are not.

Haig returned to England on leave in 1905. Before he left India, he had a two-hour meeting with Kitchener, when the latter put to him the difficulties inherent in the system of Dual Control, with the intention that Haig would be able to make useful representations in London.

8

EMERGES INTO SOCIETY. MARRIES

During the summer of 1905, which he spent on leave in England, Haig started to sell himself and raise his profile in society. He made a determined effort to become less *farouche* and to cultivate the genial aspects of his disposition, such as they were. For the first time he was regularly seen at race meetings and at important social gatherings. He was promoted at this time to major-general. Having been the oldest captain in the army, he was now in fact the youngest major-general. The activities of this good-looking young general, with a reputation for dash in the Sudan and South Africa, were recorded in the gossip columns.

Predictably, a discreet veil obscures his *tendresses* and *amours* in these years – except for one remarkable affair. Frances ('Daisy') Maynard was just six months younger than Haig. Her father and her grandfather, the third Viscount Maynard, both died when she was four, leaving her most of the family estates, which produced an income in 1869 of £20,000 a year. She was not only very rich indeed, but also very beautiful. Queen Victoria considered her as a bride for her youngest son, the Duke of Albany, but it was his ADC that she married, Lord Brooke, the eldest son of the Earl of Warwick. As Daisy Warwick she was in the inner ring of the glittering social circle that revolved round the Prince of Wales. She entertained widely at Easton Lodge and in London. She met the dashing young general, and they became lovers.[1]

It challenges the picture of Haig as ultra-conservative, inarticulate and awkward that Daisy should have chosen him for a dalliance. Despite her impeccably aristocratic background, she was a most unconventional woman. From an early point she had an interest in philanthropy that went far beyond the usual good works. She felt that something more was needed, and she established a variety of institutions that were intended to address social problems structurally. One of them existed until 1969 as the Studley Agricultural College for Women. By 1904 she had joined the Social Democratic Federation, and later she stood for Parliament as a Labour Party candidate (against her son's brother-in-law, Anthony Eden).

She had no shortage of admirers, and it says something for the breadth of Haig's political views that she found time for him, and he for someone who would dismiss the Great War as the product of the capitalist system, and welcome the Russian Revolution. As a Countess who proclaimed the class war, Daisy was something of a sport, in the botanical sense.

She was something of a sport in other senses too. Five years after her marriage she began an affair with Lord Charles Beresford. The peculiar code of her circle is reflected in the fact that when she discovered that his wife had become pregnant she was furious, and she wrote him an irate letter which was opened by Lady Beresford. Scandal threatened, but Daisy skilfully defused the situation by telling all to the Prince of Wales, an acknowledged expert on the protocol of adultery. He not only saved her from ostracism, but adopted her as his mistress. She came after Lily Langtry and before Alice Keppel, to whom the Prince escaped from Daisy's increasingly serious social theorising. She was not present at the Tranby Croft baccarat scandal, but (as Lady Brooke) was 'the Babbling Brooke' who was thought to have leaked the story. Again it was Edward who saved her from the consequences of this social *gaffe,* and in the following year he supported her again, when the Beresford affair threatened to revive, with a real risk of a divorce.

Haig's detractors have never explicitly alleged homosexuality, but he worked and often lived in an exclusively male world. As a senior officer he was inevitably surrounded by young ADCs and others who became part of his household, and some of them could not help being good-looking. That is enough to have prompted one or two insinuations or hints. They are quite without support or substantiation, but it is useful to be able to set against them not only a long, happy and very close marriage, but also the evidence, which has not before been mentioned, of this affair with one of the most desirable women of the day.

To complete his emergence from chrysalis into something a little short of social butterfly required the acquisition of a wife. When, two years earlier, Haig had taken part in the Inter-Regimental Polo Tournament and defeated the Blues in the final at Hurlingham, in the Royal Box with Queen Alexandra was the honourable Dorothy Vivian, the Queen's lady-in-waiting and Haig's future wife. After his death, in her biography of Haig, she described the game:

> To the surprise of all, the game did not progress as expected. The Blues did not seem to be getting on well. Their play became wild, while the team of the 17th Lancers continued a steady, combined game. Everyone noted that the strong player who never missed or sent a crooked shot, and who kept the whole team together, was *Colonel Douglas Haig*, playing back. Many comments were made in the Royal Box about the Colonel's remarkable play and his alert, smart appearance.

Dorothy Vivian did not speak to Douglas Haig; she would have liked to have done so and asked her brother George, a member of the regiment, to introduce her to Haig after the match. George did not play the part of Cupid, explaining that Haig was known to be a 'woman-hater'.

There had been an earlier, but even less substantial, contact between Haig and the Vivian family. In the South African War Dorothy's brother, Lord Vivian, had been seriously wounded. An unofficial telegram arrived saying that he had died, and the officer responsible for a corrective telegram that gave the true facts to the delighted family was none other than Colonel Haig.

Dorothy's great-grandfather, the first Lord Vivian, commanded a cavalry brigade at Waterloo and her father was a diplomat, serving as Minister in Brussels and in Rome. Her mother was a keen gambler and appropriately died at Monte Carlo. Dorothy and her twin sister Violet spent their childhood at the Embassies in Brussels and Rome. Violet, the first-born of the twins, had outstanding looks and charm. Dorothy at first was quieter and her father thought she suffered from an inferiority complex which he helped her overcome. His sensitive efforts were very successful. Life in the embassies – particularly in Rome – brought Dorothy into contact with the socially élite of the day. There was a strong artistic presence. Busoni, Augustus Hare and Tennyson were among those who drew and wrote poems in her album. By the time the family left Rome, Dorothy was shy no longer.

When her father died young, just as he had been appointed ambassador in Paris, Queen Victoria, as a mark of sympathy, decided to appoint one of his daughters as a maid of honour, and the choice of Dorothy, always attractively impulsive, was made when she proved the livelier of the two at an interview with the Queen. After Victoria's death Dorothy *and* Violet were appointed as two of Queen Alexandra's maids of honour.[2]

Now, on his 1905 leave, Haig was invited to stay with the royal family at Windsor Castle for Ascot Week. Dorothy was one of the party and found herself playing golf with Haig in a foursome. One of the other players, the Duke of Devonshire, was outstandingly incompetent, and Haig and Dorothy had ample opportunity to talk together while the Duke hacked his way around the course. Haig kept pulling a gold watch from his pocket, which Dorothy interpreted as a sign of boredom or irritation: in fact the watch had been given to Haig by his mother to be given to his future wife. Dorothy, not knowing how Haig's mind was working, thought he had not particularly enjoyed the afternoon and was surprised when he asked her to play again the following morning. The afternoon of that day was spent together at Ascot; they talked together after dinner and

Haig invited her for a third game of golf the following morning.
When the morning arrived Haig, to her surprise, told her that he did
not wish to play. He paid off the caddies and then, unable to find a
bench, and as the grass was wet, announced: 'I must propose to you
standing.' Dorothy had thought that Haig might be moving towards
a proposal, and despite its unexpected precipitateness she had no
hesitation in accepting. When Haig was asked about the speed of his
decision, he said that he had often taken much more important
decisions much more rapidly.

Marriage at Haig's age and to a much younger wife was not unusual
in these days and his circles. Many of his contemporaries in the Great
War had been of mature years when they married, and their brides were
younger than they. But in view of the speed of Haig's assault on
Dorothy, it is impossible not to conclude that his proposal, at the age of
almost forty-five, was a career move. When, in 1903, Haig had been
hoping for the Aldershot command, rather than India, he had said, 'I
fancy the excellent house at Aldershot . . . will oblige Lord Roberts to
select the husband of "dear Mrs. so and so" because the nursery rooms
will exactly suit the family!' Again, when Roberts, as Haig had
predicted, sent him to India rather than Aldershot, he remarked,
'So no doubt Roberts' pals (or ? Lady R's pals) have been chosen . . . [for
Aldershot].' There was a saying in the Indian army to the effect that
lieutenants must not marry, captains might marry, majors should
marry and colonels must marry. As an up-and-coming general, with
hospitality to give and receive, and in order to take part in the social life
which would assist professional advancement, Haig should be married.
Some senior generals did remain bachelors – Kitchener was an outstanding example – but they handicapped themselves.

And Dorothy, or Doris, as she preferred to be known and as Haig
always called her, was eminently suitable. Charteris knew her well
(although she did not think much of him, describing him as dirty
and untidy) and recorded that:

Lady Haig fulfilled to perfection the difficult role that falls to
the lot of the wife of great man. She never interfered in official

business, yet she was always there to help her husband. Her tact and intuition never failed. She was a discreet and sympathetic confidante and she strengthened his faith in his own power to overcome difficulties. She devoted every moment of her married life to her husband; and in the midst of all the responsibilities which he was called upon to face she was never absent from his mind . . . Marriage brought to Haig completeness. While it did not reduce his ambition for high office, it gave it a different perspective.

Whatever Haig's initial feelings were towards Doris, he certainly came to love her, to trust her and to rely on her. John Terraine even suggests that 'the very successful marriage worked to some extent against him', because he tended to withdraw into the warmth of his family relationship which 'became more and more the exclusive focus of his emotional life'.[3]

Despite a background of some sophistication, Doris was a straightforward, wholly loving person. She found complete fulfilment in devoting herself to the welfare of her husband. Indeed she came almost to love him too much; for Haig she was the central part of a support system and Doris had a demanding concept to live up to. She subordinated every other interest to his. Her loyalty, devotion and uncritical support was total. She never truly recovered from the shock of his death. He found full personal happiness in his marriage. In a domesticity that for its time was unusually cosy, he found support and solace from an external world with which he was never quite comfortable.

Doris was an ideal consort in other ways. As one of the Queen's maids of honour, she had close links with the royal family, even closer than those which Haig had been careful to develop. The immediate consequence of the engagement was that the Queen had to be advised at once. She was in her bath, so Doris had to shout through the door to tell her the news that General Haig had proposed to her.[4] The King's response to the news was to tease Haig: 'What do you mean coming to my house and trying to take away one of the Queen's best

Maids of Honour?' The permission of Doris' mother, Lady Vivian, was also required. Lady Vivian did not welcome visitors, and on his arrival Haig was told that he would not be seen. He replied that he would not leave until he had been seen and duly obtained the permission he required. When she heard what was proposed, Lady Vivian said: 'My daughter cannot possibly be ready in three weeks.' According to his niece, Haig gave her a fairly offensive ultimatum in reply: 'It will be then or not at all.'[5]

The engagement took place within thirty-six hours of the couple's first meeting, and the wedding only a little more than a month later. It was in the private chapel at Buckingham Palace, the first time the chapel had been used for a ceremony not immediately connected with a member of the Royal Family. The wedding breakfast was given by the King and Queen. Haig's career could scarcely have been urged on more propitiously.

Lady Haig quotes one of the letters of congratulation which she received when the engagement had been announced. It was from St John Broderick, who was Secretary of State for War from 1900 to 1903:

Dear Miss Vivian

Will you think me intrusive if I write you a line of very warm congratulations on your engagement? When we were labouring in 1901-2 I used to hear from returning officers one chorus of panegyric of the ideal staff officer, who from the first had made the reputation of his chiefs, and I always knew whose name would follow the preamble. I do not suppose there is a more appreciated or successful officer in the Army, and I wish you joy with all my heart.

Yours v. truly

St. John Broderick[6]

The honeymoon was spent at Willie and Henrietta Jameson's country home in Warwickshire, Radway Grange. The arrival of the happy couple at the house was unusual. They had planned to travel by train, and Lady Haig was dressed for that, in white coat, dress and hat. In the event the reception lasted so long that they decided instead to motor. Lady Haig's dress was unsuitable for the dirt and dust of a motor car journey in these days, so they stopped at Henrietta's town house and she was supplied with an old ulster and cap. By the time they reached their destination Haig decided it would be quicker if they abandoned the car, took a short cut through the woods and the fields and then climbed over a high fence. They arrived, by this strange route and with Lady Haig in strange garb, to find that the whole village had been decorated in their honour and all the villagers were waiting to receive them. The empty car had driven under an archway of flowers and the villagers had rushed to the front of the house, waving flags, to meet Lady Haig coming over the fence in her husband's old clothes. Henrietta was there with them for part of the time and travelled on with them to Paris, where they embarked for their return to India. Doris was aware that it must have been a difficult situation for Henrietta, who was no longer the only woman, or even the more important woman, in Haig's life, and characteristically she felt sympathy for her sister-in-law.

Haig remained close to his sister, and there was no estrangement, though Henrietta now took a much less active, less promotional role in relation to Haig's career. Doris was infinitely supportive, but a far simpler, less worldly person, and her role was never what Henrietta's had been.

Haig had hoped that he might not return to India after the wedding: he was anxious to continue his process of military reform in London, rather than the subcontinent, and indicated that he would welcome an appointment at the War Office. The King therefore asked French to request the Secretary of State for War to appoint Haig Director of Staff Duties. Despite, or possibly because of, the royal intervention, the Secretary of State, Arnold-Forster, declined:

> AF thinks that the King is trying to push you into that appointment simply on personal grounds and because you and your wife are friends of his. Like all political intriguers

he is always suspicious, and thinks people are acting as he would probably act in similar circumstances.[7]

The directness of the King's intervention is, however, interesting. King Edward told Doris, before she and Haig left for India, and he was not joking, that she must not let marriage interfere with the work of one of his best generals.

Back in India, Haig presented his bride to the Commander-in-Chief. Kitchener, a bachelor, though not without some experience of women, became totally inarticulate.

When 1905 came to an end Haig set off on inspection of outlying stations leaving Doris in Delhi. He suffered a number of serious attacks of malaria, and both of them were pleased when orders were received for Haig to come to London as Director of Training.

AT THE WAR OFFICE WITH HALDANE.
ARMY REFORMS. INDIA AGAIN

In the next phase of his life, Haig was at the centre of the military machine. On the basis alone of what he achieved during his years at the War Office he would be entitled to more than a footnote in the military history of Britain in the twentieth century. He came to his new responsibilities conscious this was a role that he was qualified to play, and he had the backing of an unassailable array of supporters. It was at this time that it was said of him that, 'I would rather have Haig's luck than a licence to steal horses.'[1]

It was Lord Esher who had been impressed by Haig's evidence to the Elgin Commission and who had tried, through the King, to have him appointed as Director of Staff Duties. Esher even proposed that Haig should be made Chief of the General Staff at this time, an appointment for which he was far too junior. His initial appointment was as Director of Military Training, but after only a year he was promoted to the staff duties appointment that Esher had earmarked for him.

The history of Britain's preparations for the First World War cannot be told without reference to the extraordinary career of Reginald Baliol Brett, Second Viscount Esher. No one in recent history, and few in the whole of Britain's history, has had so much influence on affairs without any public position or authority. A year or two in Parliament had been enough to satisfy Esher (initially a Conservative but soon to become a Liberal) that he much preferred to

be an unpaid puppet-master, controlling events from the shadows.
During the War, when he was de facto head of British Intelligence in
France, and a point of contact for the Cabinet, the military and the
King, he was asked by his son whether he was going to hold a formal
appointment from Kitchener or the Prime Minister. 'It will open
doors much more easily in this country [France], where the first
question is always: "What position does he hold?"' Esher's response
set out his approach throughout his life:

> I am not going to put myself out. I never do. Nor am I going to
> *regularize* my position which means that someone can give me
> orders. I never have . . . It is such a new idea to the French and
> it makes them sit up.[2]

He declined offers of Cabinet positions on several occasions. The
Dictionary of National Biography described Esher as 'possessing all the
attributes of success except the conviction that it was worthwhile.'

He was partly French and could recall sitting on the lap of a
wizened old man who had played the violin for Marie Antoinette. He
moved from Eton to Cambridge, where he spent a long time without
deciding very clearly what he was going to do. He became Parliamentary Private Secretary to Lord Hartington and, it is surely safe to
assume, the only PPS to have driven his chief by sleigh through the
snow to a Cabinet meeting.

Esher was a strange mixture of serious concern for his country and
of precious sensibilities, of veneration for the institutions of the state
and the privileges of the monarchy, combined with a capacity for
original thought and sympathy for new social doctrines. Somehow or
other he made an instantaneous transition from gilded youth to elder
statesman, so that at a remarkably early age he was perceived by
heavyweight politicians, considerably his seniors, as a repository of
wise advice and far-seeing judgement. That he was so regarded is all
the more surprising in that his financial management, not assisted by
his love for the turf, was very poor, and his personal life was marked
by a series of intense romantic friendships with good-looking teenage

boys. These attachments were consummated by no more than passionate kisses and an extravagance of emotions, and they seem to have been regarded by those who knew of them with tolerant amusement. The strangest of these relationships was that between him and one of his own sons.

After his brief parliamentary career he took an appointment in the civil service as Secretary of the Office of Works. In this capacity he saw much of the old Queen Victoria. On her death, Edward VII, who had observed Esher's devotion to his mother and his utility to the monarchy, came to rely increasingly on him for all sorts of advice. By the end of 1903 he met or corresponded with the King every day, and for the rest of his life he was in fact, although entirely unofficially, the royal family's most trusted adviser. When Edward VII died, George V, who had some common sense though little intellect or appreciation of intellect in others, quickly depended on Esher much as his father had done. The King had an embarrassment of advice. He inherited from his father Francis Knollys, who had been in the Royal Household since 1862 (and his appointment was almost a dynastic one, succeeding *his* father, who had been treasurer and Comptroller to the then Prince of Wales). Knollys was a devoted adviser to Edward (though regarded as suspiciously Whiggish by the Tories) and became a close friend of Esher. George's *own* adviser was Arthur Bigge (who became Lord Stamfordham in 1911). Bigge lacked political prejudice as much as a sense of humour, but Esher was almost as friendly with him as with Knollys. It would have been unthinkable for Esher to have dreamt of intriguing against either, or fomenting any rivalries between them, and when the King did feel that Knollys, who was now seventy-five and had lost some royal confidence as a result of his handling of negotiations relating to the Parliament Bill, ought to be making way for Stamfordham, Esher did all he could to ensure that he was moved out painlessly.

Esher's particular interest, apart from the monarchy, was defence. It is difficult to see this exquisite creature, smoking his rose-scented aromatic cigarettes, as essentially martial. Immediately after Cambridge, it is true, he obtained a militia commission. He certainly loved uniforms and observers were amused, and sometimes irritated, by the excuses he found for wearing them. In the course of his life he was very frequently described as an *éminence grise*. He was certainly eminent, but such an elaborate dandy could never be really *gris*. At an early stage in his time at the Office of Works, he was responsible for a marquee that was erected in the garden of Buckingham Palace for the reception of visiting heads of State, in London for Queen Victoria's Diamond Jubilee celebrations. No ventilation had been provided; the heat became overpowering and one after another fainted. Esher, in full court dress, including a rapier, rose to the occasion. He drew the sword and deftly sliced the canvas flaps to make windows, stabbing a housemaid who was on the other side.

All the same, he was correctly identified as being capable of making a crucial importance to Britain's preparedness for the sort of war that was expected. Esher was a member of the Elgin South Africa War Commission and in the course of its sittings he wrote daily to the King with a detailed account of the witnesses' evidence. He also advised Edward of the views of the party leaders, and did not hesitate to pass on his own opinions, even when they were at odds with those of other members of the Commission. Having worked at the War Office during his time with Hartington, he was still in touch with many of his associates there. His contacts with the palace involved three or four meetings a day with Knollys at this time. St John Broderick, the Minister for War – and many others – resented Esher's influence and activities and the fact that so often, before a matter even reached the Cabinet, 'the issue had been largely pre-judged on the incomplete premises of an observer who had no official status.' However valid a constitutional objection, Broderick's comment was slightly unfair to Esher's judgement, which was generally very sound, and the King was so appreciative of this fact that he wanted Esher as Secretary of State for War. That did not happen, but Esher was appointed to chair the War Office Reconstruction Committee ('the Esher Committee') to advise on the creation of an army board. It recommended the establishment of the Army Council, and a result of the Committee's report was the re-establishment of the Committee of

Imperial Defence, at last on a proper basis. A year later, in 1905, Esher joined the CID as a permanent member. From 1904, all appointments to the War Office were agreed, and often suggested, by Esher.

In the years running up to the war, he and Haldane, the Secretary of State, worked closely together: their views were similar and Esher was particularly committed to the establishment of the Territorial Force, though for him it was essentially as a precursor to comprehensive military service.

Esher, Haig and Haldane were thus closely involved in the enterprise of reforming the army and preparing it for a modern war. In September 1906 Esher accompanied Haig on army manoeuvres. Haig disturbed Esher's sleep by snoring on the palliasse next to him. Haig and Esher were very different and Esher came to find that Haig was unreceptive to ideas with which he hoped to inspire him, such as the concept of comprehensive military service: the youth of the country must be expected to serve in the Army in the same way as earlier legislation required them to attend school. All the same, Esher admired Haig's single-mindedness and reliability and in time came to see the solidity of his judgements as a strength as well as a weakness.

Even before the general election of 1906, Edward VII had urged Balfour to bring Haig back from India to the War Office. He was an officer 'whose experience of staff work in the field and whose high abilities should be utilised in this particular branch where initiative and organising power are at the moment much wanted, however great the loss to India may be of that officer's services.'[3] After the Liberal landslide of 1906 it was Haldane who sent for Haig. In his speech in the House of Lords on the occasion of Haig's death, Haldane said:

We had no doubt that the Germans could not, in face of our magnificent and superior Fleet, invade this country directly: we knew them too well to think that they were likely to try. But they had other means. If they could get possession of the northern parts of France, Calais, Dunkirk and Boulogne, then, with long-range guns and submarines, and with air fleets, they might make the position of this country a very precarious one in point of safety. That problem had to be thought out, and after surveying the whole Army, I took it upon myself to ask Lord Haig, who was then in India, to come over to this country and to think for us. From all I could discover, even then, he seemed to be the most highly equipped thinker in the British Army.

It is important to note that people of the calibre of Haldane, and certainly not only in posthumous tributes, regarded him as an innovative and penetrating thinker. What was perhaps a more surprising element of Haldane's speech was that he went on to say: 'In conception of the objects of a battle, in clear ideas of how to use his troops, I doubt whether there has been anybody since the great Marlborough who was his equal.' That was a remarkable tribute from someone who knew Haig well, who knew all the other military leaders of the time, and who had come to know much of military theory and military history. Many of even Haig's most enthusiastic supporters specifically concede that he did not have the innovative genius of a Marlborough or a Wellington. Indeed, it may be that there is little place for such flashes of imagination in the context of modern warfare – or at least, in the context of the First World War by the time Haig became Commander-in-Chief.

Haldane, described on his death by *The Times* as 'one of the most powerful, subtle and encyclopaedic intellects ever devoted to the public service of his country', is a fascinating figure, and not an obvious soulmate for Haig. A Scot who had chosen to practise at the English Bar, a Bar bachelor, married to the law, politics, the study of philosophy and a sybaritic social life, he had little in common with the practical and ascetic Haig.

Yet he and Haig worked very well together and each man respected the other, even if Haig would rather have escaped to the family hearth in the evenings than share Haldane's extended, almost Churchillian, post-prandial disquisitions in the billiard room.

Haldane was portly (a 'fat, big man', Haig recorded after their first meeting), resembling somewhat Stanley Baldwin, with a heavy face that disguised the acuity of his mind. He was described by Osbert Sitwell as 'entering a room with the air of a whole procession'. He held cigars in a silver cigar fork. When he was elected Lord Rector of Edinburgh University in 1905 Bernard Shaw wrote to him about his Rectorial Address:

> I read your address to those unfortunate students very carefully; and I must say that it is like your Right Honourable cheek to talk to them like that. Why will people not tell the truth? Here are you, the most conspicuous living example in this kingdom of the realisation of all these students' ambitions – a Scotch philosopher who has beaten all the practical men and the statesmen at their own game. This you have achieved by doing exactly what you liked; smoking a great deal too many cigars; eating in a manner that shocked Mrs. Sydney Webb; and, generally, making the greatest possible success of the world, the flesh, and the devil. And yet you go down and tell those unhappy young people, in lofty and inspiring periods, that you do it all by a life of contemplation, aloof from the world at Weimar.[4]

Haldane had the capacity to get the best out of those who worked for him. J.A. Spender described him with an officer who could well have been Haig:

> I have a memory of Haldane in respectful talk with a tongue-tied, verbally incoherent, but extremely able soldier. How patiently he worked at him, how skilfully he brought up the buried treasure, without breaking any of it, with what goodwill they parted, and what mutual desire to meet again!
>   Haldane was in all these respects an extraordinarily modest man, and entirely free from that worst vice of politicians of putting the dialectically unaccomplished in the wrong when

they are essentially in the right. He knew the value of the able inarticulate and could never be imposed upon by voluble superficiality.[5]

Haldane was probably the most successful and important Secretary of State for War that Britain has ever had. Certainly, without the initiatives he took, Britain could scarcely have taken part in the First World War. It was a cruel reward that when the War came, for narrow political reasons he was caricatured, particularly by the *Daily Express,* and harried by the press until he dropped out of office when Asquith formed his coalition government in May 1915. Professor Oncken of Heidelberg made the claim that Haldane had referred to Germany as 'his spiritual home'. That was to take the notorious phrase out of context: all that he had said, at a dinner party held by Mrs Humphrey Ward in April 1913 to allow him to meet some German professors, was that Professor Lötze's *classroom* in Göttingen, where he had studied after Edinburgh University, was his spiritual home.[6]

Haldane started by considering the requirements of India, a question that had received some preliminary exploration by Balfour in the Committee of Imperial Defence. From that he moved on to consider the requirements of the Empire as a whole. By 1908 the army was in the course of being reorganised into a force which after providing foreign garrisons would have an expeditionary force of six infantry divisions plus one cavalry division, and a home defence force consisting of fourteen territorial infantry divisions and fourteen mounted yeomanry brigades.

What united Haig and Haldane, apart from the fact that they were both born in Charlotte Square, Edinburgh, Haldane at No.17 and Haig at No.24, was that they were both seized of the urgent necessity of transforming Britain's defences into something that could carry her through a major war. Haig's seriousness was self-evident; Haldane's was disguised by his urbanity, but he, no less than Haig, saw a clash with Germany as a self-evident likelihood, if not a certainty. They were not of course alone: Hankey is another example of the cadre that realised that there was only a very limited period left in which to transform Britain's ramshackle military machine into something capable of meeting the organised might of Germany. The 1902 report of the Committee on Military Education, one of the inquests into the South African War, revealed serious deficiencies:

> The Committee are compelled to report that the evidence laid before them has brought out in the strongest possible light the grave fact that the Military Education of the junior officers in the army is in a most unsatisfactory condition . . . The witnesses are unanimous in stating that the junior officers are lamentably wanting in Military knowledge, and what is perhaps even worse, in the desire to acquire knowledge . . . The Committee have been informed on the highest authority that the majority of young officers will not work unless compelled; that 'keenness is out of fashion'; that 'it is not the correct form'; the spirit and fashion is 'rather not to show keenness'; and that 'the idea is, to put it in a few words, to do as little as they possibly can'.

Amongst the key witnesses were Sir Evelyn Wood, Sir Ian Hamilton and Lord Roberts.

> By no part of the evidence laid before them had the Committee been more impressed than by that which shows in the clearest manner the prevalence among the junior command ranks of a lack of technical knowledge and skill and of any wish to study the science and master the art of their profession.[7]

The Liberal Party had swept to power in 1906 committed to peace, retrenchment and reform. There are two stories about how Haldane became Secretary of State for War. He was not an obvious candidate for the field of Mars, with his almost spherical figure and the appearance, as L.S. Amery said, 'of the old-fashioned family butler'. On one account Haldane looked in on Campbell-Bannerman to see how cabinet-making was proceeding. 'What about the War Office?' he asked. 'Nobody,' said C-B, 'will touch it with a pole.' 'Then give it to *me*.[8] The more likely history is that he was first offered the post of Attorney General and then the Home Office, both of which he declined, and then the War Office which he accepted.[9] The appointment cost Haldane a lot of money: he had earned over £20,000 a year in his last year at the Bar. He had already published a variety of works on (largely Hegelian) philosophy, including *The Pathway to Reality*, the Gifford Lectures that he had given in the University of St Andrews. Campbell-Bannerman's comment on his appointment was: 'We shall now see how Schopenhauer gets on in the Kailyard.' Immediately Haldane reached the War Office, he was asked by General the Hon. Sir Neville Lyttelton what reforms he proposed to introduce. He had an excellent reply: 'As a young and blushing virgin just united to a bronzed warrior, it is not expected by the public that any result of the union will appear until at least nine months have passed.' He was later to say that he spent half his time apologising to the government for the existence of the army and the other half apologising to the army for the existence of the government. After a period of gestation that was considerably shorter than the conventional nine months, Haldane concluded, very much following Esher, that what he had to do was first, to organise the army as an expeditionary force and not simply for the defence of the British Isles, secondly to reorganise the voluntary forces as a second line of defence, and thirdly, to develop a general staff and ensure that it had a strategy on the German model. His success in achieving these objectives was important and will be examined in detail. In passing, it is worth recording that his historic successes were achieved in a context that was acceptable to the radical liberal tradition: in his first Estimates, he reduced the army's strength by 16,600 men and its budget by £2.6 million.

These budgetary constraints are crucial to an understanding of the military preparations for the Great War. The intellectual rigour of Haldane and his team went hand in hand with a parsimony that flawed their achievements. By 1914 Britain spent just 3.4 per cent of national income on defence, little more than half of Austria-Hungary's commitment (6.1 per cent). In 1900 the part of the British

Defence Estimates relating to the army amounted to £86.8 million and by 1914 £29.4 million. 1900 was of course a special year, in the middle of the South African War, but 1914 was only just ahead of 1910's £27.6 million.[10]

After the Liberal victory of 1906, the emphasis of the government's policy, quite apart from its traditional distaste for military expenditure, was on social issues, and the Chancellors of the Exchequer, Asquith followed by Lloyd George, first actually cut army expenditure, both in global terms and as a percentage of gross public expenditure, for four years and then carefully contained increases in the last years before the war. They were assisted by adhering right up till the outbreak of war to the formula for army expenditure devised by the Mowatt Committee, which had been set up in 1899 as a result of the problems thrown up by the South African war.

Thus, when Seely, the Secretary of State for War, published the Army Estimates in March 1914, he could say:

> When allowance has been made for the automatic growth of the pension charges and the million [pounds] now provided for Aviation, the effective cost of the Army is actually less than in the year 1907-08; it is nearly 2 millions less than it was in 1905-06, and only a quarter of a million more than it was at the lowest point since the [South African] war . . . If it be further remembered that since 1905-06 the general level of prices has risen by some 20 per cent, it will be realised that, though the total of the Estimates shows an increase, the interests of economy have by no means been neglected.[11]

Thus also Kitchener could say of the Cabinet: 'Did they remember, when they went headlong into a war like this, that they were without an army, and without any preparation to equip one?'[12]

Many faults had been revealed by the South African War. In particular, it had strengthened the argument for a General Staff in London, to act as a coordinating and directing authority and to support the Commander-in-Chief in the field. This was not the first time that the need for a General Staff had been apprehended, but there had always been considerable opposition to something which was seen as redolent of the militarism of France, and particularly that of Prussia. In both these countries powerful General Staffs had existed for some time. Campbell-Bannerman, who was Secretary of State for War from 1892 to 1895, wrote: 'In this country there is in truth no room for a general military policy . . . we have no designs against our European neighbours.'[13] The nearest things to a General Staff that existed prior to Haldane were the Defence Committee of the Cabinet and the Colonial Defence Committee, but the former never met except in times of emergency and the latter had no power to do more than make recommendations. The Esher Committee had made important recommendations, but only some of them were implemented. An Army Council was set up, and the post of Commander-in-Chief of the Army (the position that the Duke of Cambridge had so long enjoyed) was abolished. By Order in Council of 22 November 1909, the first military member of the army council was styled Chief of the General Staff.[14]) But by the time the Conservatives lost office in 1906, very few of Esher's other extensive recommendations had been implemented.

Haig became a member of the Army Council, on the staff of the Chief of the General Staff. As Director of Military Training, he was responsible for preparing the British Expeditionary Force and the Territorial Force which Haldane was to establish for war duties. When he became Director of Staff Duties in 1907 his responsibility was for reforming the staff training programme and the employment of staff officers, in the course of which he deployed Camberley products. He was thus intimately associated with all that Haldane was attempting to do, and he was working to address the threat to which Haldane was referring in the tribute in the Lords that is quoted above. Haig wrote to Major (later Major-General Sir) Frederick Maurice:

We may well be fighting Germany in the next few years . . . if we do, the right place for us to fight is where we can use our naval and our military power together with the greatest effect. In battle with troops as brave and efficient as the Germans, we shall have to fight long and hard before we can hope for a decision. It will be dangerous to attempt a decisive blow until we have worn down the enemy's power of resistance.[15]

This expressed Haig's views well in advance of the war and is interesting in three respects: first, his assumption that there would soon *be* war with Germany; secondly, his view that Britain's military and naval capacities should be brought together, something which was to recur in his thinking repeatedly during the war; and thirdly, he is already talking about a wearing-down process, which some think he tended to emphasise *later* to justify a war of attrition.

Haldane's successes were not achieved without difficulty. For him the need for an Expeditionary Force was self-evident: it was to consist of six infantry divisions, and one of cavalry. To provide for the defence of the British Isles, and also to provide reserves for the expeditionary force, he wanted to use the yeomanry and militia. The militia tended to consist of county grandees, who proved very resistant to his proposals. In the face of their intransigence, Haldane boldly abolished the force and replaced it with a special reserve. He established a new territorial force, in which the yeomanry and volunteer forces were incorporated, and which proved invaluable in the war. Haldane initially wanted twenty-eight divisions for the territorial force. This had to be cut by half, a cut which Haig, looking for the military ideal rather than the politically possible, unsuccessfully opposed. As Director of Military Training, Haig had a huge workload in establishing a training programme for these new units, in addition to the seven divisions of the Expeditionary Force. Haldane and Haig were adamant that the Territorial Force should not be a second-rate imitation of the Expeditionary Force itself, and training and equipment were standardised. The value of this approach was well demonstrated during the war. Haig's duties as Director of Training were not narrowly interpreted. 'Although called "Training" the department also deals with "war organisation" and "home defence" so that now it is the most important directorate in the General Staff at the present time.'

Of the Expeditionary Force that Haldane and Haig created, Edmonds said: 'In every respect the Expeditionary Force of 1914 was incomparably the best trained, best organised and best equipped British Army which ever went forth to war.' Every aspect of its deployment was thought through. Haig noted that even the mobilisation telegrams were written and only awaited signature.

A General Staff had been created, but not yet an *Imperial* General Staff. Haig argued for extension of the staff to embrace the Empire, and Haldane was in agreement. At an Imperial Conference of Dominion Premiers, Haig promoted the adoption of the British model for their forces, a proposal which was agreed. This enabled the Dominion divisions to liaise easily with British units during the war. When war was declared in 1914, Canada, South Africa, Australia, New Zealand and all the smaller countries of the Empire not yet formally independent were automatically at war with Germany in the same way as Britain was. The coordinated staff work of the Imperial General Staff which snapped into effect was dramatically efficient, and at least as good as forward planning in the Second World War.

Alongside this intensely busy period in his professional life, Haig's domestic life moved forward too, although in a strictly separate orbit. Doris records that on one occasion she was allowed to attend manoeuvres:

My husband had purposely taken a horse for me to ride, but when I met him out with the troops and dared to go and speak to him, he just looked at me as if he had never seen me before. His blue eyes, which were usually so kind, took on a steady hard look which quite alarmed me. He was altogether too military. The other highly placed officers, however, were most kind when I went and talked to them.

Within the domestic circle he was not nearly so fearsome. He successfully tricked Lady Haig with an imitation egg-yolk from Hamleys.

Their first child, Alexandra, was born on 9 March 1907. The family lived in a rented house near Aldershot. Haig rode there every morning before catching a train to London, returning late at night. Another daughter, Victoria, was born on 7 November 1908, and in 1909 Haig was knighted. The order he received was the KCVO, like the CVO a distinction within the Royal Victorian Order awarded on the personal initiative of the monarch as a mark of esteem.

Duff Cooper describes Haldane's love of working on into the small hours after a substantial dinner:

> To Haldane such work was the breath of life, such hours were habitual and the discussion of difficult problems to the accompaniment of continual cigars was the pleasantest way of passing the time. But Haig did not talk easily and did not smoke at all. He was accustomed to early hours, fresh air and much exercise. It is not surprising therefore, that after a year and a half of such strenuous labour his health gave way and during April and May 1908 he was seriously ill.

This serious illness was not the only indisposition from which Haig suffered in these London years. Soon after his return from India he was found to have developed an enlarged liver as a result of his bouts of malaria, and with Doris he took the waters at Tarasp in Switzerland. He had recourse to a 'magnetic health giver' who was seen every day for a month. It was when he was at Tarasp that he met Leopold de Rothschild, later simply 'Leo Rothschild', a member of the banking family and a noted racehorse owner, who became a lasting friend, and a generous one. Throughout the war he made many gifts of fine wines and spirits which ensured at least a moderate degree of conviviality at GHQ. Haig's ailments were as remarkable as the remedies. He suffered from what he recorded as an attack of ague. 'Ague', meaning a fever and its symptoms, was a word which first appears in the English language in the fourteenth century. It was occasionally used until the nineteenth century, but its heyday was in the seventeenth century, and by the time Haig used the word it was splendidly

archaic, almost Shakespearean. One wonders if he had been listening
to the chimes too much with Sir Andrew and Toby Belch. His
interest in his health extended to an obsession with avoiding the
effects of old age and infirmity. His rigorous regime of exercise
(during the war he ran and later walked in the grounds of his
headquarters) was supplemented by a series of faddish diets. Sour
milk, wholemeal bread, 'Sanatogen' and oranges were all tried. (But
he was not sympathetic to other people whose diets were finicky. He
came across the Prince of Wales in October 1918: 'He seems a good
sporting lad, natural and sincere, but rather faddy over his diet. Eats
no breakfast, but has jam in large quantities with "morning tea". His
small stature makes me think he was starved as a baby.'

During these days, Haig dabbled slightly, and Henrietta rather
more, in the world of spiritualism. Posthumously, he has suffered
from some consequent teasing and it has also been suggested, usually
in conjunction with a discussion of his religious views, which will be
noted later, that a belief in spiritualism affected his military decisions. There is really nothing to support this argument. He never
seems to have consulted a spiritualist except when keeping Henrietta
company. This episode took place just after the death of a brother
who had himself been a medium, and his motive was simply that of
supporting Henrietta, who believed that their brother could be
contacted through the medium of spiritualism.[16] He did ask a
medium whether the 'company basis' or 'battalion basis' was more
suitable for the expansion of the Territorial Army, but everything
about Haig and his career says that he was far too much of a practical
bent to have put the question entirely seriously.

On 20 September 1906:

[a]t 3pm went with Henrietta to see a medium, Miss
McCreadie . . . [she said that] I had come recently from abroad
and was now settling down. Seemed to be drawing a great force
around me which would be of assistance in the new Scheme . . .
She thought a 'company basis' better than a 'battalion basis' for
expansion of Territorial Army. Then I gave her a letter from Mr.

Haldane (the S of S). She said he was a 'very clever man'. Honest
and far seeing and would fight to bring people around to his
opinions. Asked by Henrietta about me (before she went under
control) she said she felt I wanted magnetism and had been
unwell but was getting better. It seems as if I would go abroad
for some special object of a wide and important nature. Much
would depend on me. Then when under control by a little
native girl 'Sunshine' she said that I was influenced by several
spirits: notably a small man named Napoleon aided me. That it
was in my power to be helped by him for good affairs but I
might repel him if his influence was for bad, tho' he had become
changed for the better in the spirit world. I was destined to do
much good and to benefit my country. Asked by me how to
ensure the Territorial Army Scheme being a success, she said
thought governed the world.

On another occasion, the spirit of Hector MacDonald, a hero of
Omdurman, was raised and 'a guitar was played in mid air'.

Much fun can of course be made of all this. But spiritualism was in
the air in these days and was taken more seriously than it is today.
Henrietta believed in it and their deceased brother had himself been a
medium, so Haig was unlikely to have been severely sceptical, even if
he was not a convinced believer. De Groot says that the visits that
Haig made to Miss McCreadie 'were too frequent to be explained as
idle curiosity' but to me they seem to be no more than curiosity and
pretty well idle, at that. One medium he dismissed as 'a great fraud',
and even if he was interested to know if there might be something
more to others, such as Miss McCreadie, his interest seems to have
been no more than a passing one at this phase in his life. Spiritualism
is not mentioned in his later diaries, nor is there any suggestion that
any aspect of his conduct was influenced by it.

Charteris records that Haig was not clubbable in these years. He
did not attend political dinner parties, and although he sometimes
took colleagues home for dinner, after the meal they adjourned to a
study to continue their work. 'Strictly formal in his dealings with his

own superiors, he demanded the same rigid observance of rank from those serving with or under him.' He was courteous, 'but his courtesy had in it something of the frigid. There was ever an intangible barrier that effectively prevented any approach to intimacy or even cordiality.'[17] Charteris knew Haig primarily in a professional connection, and his observation was mostly limited to that milieu. Elsewhere he says that: 'Friendship in the ordinarily accepted sense of the term was almost unknown to Haig. He gained, but rarely reciprocated, the friendship of others.'[18] That is a little too sweeping. Outside strict professional confines, Haig did have some friends and sometimes slightly unusual ones. But it is fair to say that his friendships were few and were very often with men who could advance his career.

Haig worked on some important publications at this time. *Field Service Regulations* was a manual designed to standardise the procedure of staff officers in any situation which they might find themselves. It was not his creation, but he pressed hard to have it accepted, partly by using staff tours to demonstrate that its principles did work.[19] He was also working on the completion of *Cavalry Studies*.

In 1907 a new edition of that work was published. The previous edition (Haig's one, which had been watered down with a reforming preface written by Roberts), was only three years old, but the 1907 edition showed that Haig and his school of cavalrymen had won the argument. It did concede, and Haig would not have disagreed with this, that 'thorough efficiency in the use of the rifle in dismounted tactics is an absolute necessity', but it also contained the ringing affirmation: 'It must be accepted as a principle that the rifle, effective as it is, cannot replace the effect produced by the speed of the horse, the magnetism of the charge, and the terror of cold steel.' The victory was emphasised in June 1909, when the lance was reinstated as an official weapon (French had never taken any notice of its abolition, and his 1st Cavalry Brigade, composed of lancer regiments, carried their lances on field training). In 1906 the first edition of *The Cavalry Journal* appeared, designed to encourage professionalism within the cavalry.

In April 1909 Haig was offered the post of Chief of the General

Staff in India. He accepted, but delayed taking up the post until October, in order to finish his work at the War Office. He was not without faults as an office worker and even more imperfect as a politician. He did not welcome the give and take of critical debate. He upset some of his colleagues who felt that the militia should be handled gently, and it needed Haldane's sensitivity to allow the displaced militia to migrate to the special reserve. When he left the War Office, Haldane recorded that 'Haig always infuriated [the Director of Organisation & Recruiting] by his manner, and it may be easier now'.[20] It has been suggested that as a reformer Haig was conservative and could have gone further in promoting a more open discussion of tactics and strategy within the general staff. But Haldane, distinguished as he was in philosophy and in science, a future Lord Chancellor, a founder of London University, described him as nothing less than 'a military thinker of a very high order'. From a man of Haldane's fastidious intellect, that was high praise. After Haig left the War Office, Haldane said to him:

> It gives me the sense of comfort which comes from seeing that there are in our Army those who are thinking out military science with a closeness which is not surpassed in the great military schools of thought on the Continent. You have cause to look back on three memorable years' work with satisfaction, and to say to yourself *'quorum pars magna fui'*.[21]

Immediately after Haig and Lady Haig arrived back in London in 1906 they were invited to stay with the King and Queen at Windsor. Haig was delighted that the Queen complimented him on how well his wife was looking and how well turned out her hair was.[22] A press report recorded the presence at a shooting party at Sandringham in January 1908 of 'General Douglas Haig and his pretty but very delicate-looking wife . . . [I]n a cosy marquee . . . the fare, although not so elaborate as at some of the shoots given by ambitious millionaires, is by no means Spartan, and is always piping hot, while the Royal servants laid a table and wait with as much ceremony as at a meal indoors.' Lady Haig was reappointed as a maid of honour although the King thought it an inappropriate post for a married lady and when the baby was brought to see the Queen he remarked that it was 'most improper'. Before they departed for India in 1909 Lady Haig and the children stayed at Balmoral for a full fortnight. There the Queen insisted on seeing the baby bathed and took the older child out with her for a drive every day. 'The Queen felt very sorry for me having to leave the children, and Princess Victoria wanted to adopt the small baby, who was a very lovely child even at that age.'[23]

Haig went out to India for the third and final time without great enthusiasm, leaving Alexandra at the age of two and a half and Victoria at the age of eleven months with Henrietta in Suffolk. When he was originally offered the post of CGS by the Commander-in-Chief, Sir O'Moore Creagh, he declined, saying that he was too occupied on the Imperial General Staff '– besides the Simla people were such a crooked lot I could not work with them! [Creagh] replied that he would like to join with me in ousting the rascals! and I could think the matter over for a week.' Going abroad, further, would mean leaving his children at home, 'and my wife coming out with me and visiting them each winter etc.' Ultimately, although he would have preferred to complete his work in Whitehall, he decided it was his duty to go. He explained the position to his assistant at the Department of Staff Duties, Brigadier-General Launcelot Kiggell: 'On thinking the matter over, and looking at the importance of starting a General Staff in India, weeding out Simla, and developing the Imperial General Staff, I thought it best I should go.'[24] The words 'weeding out Simla' were inserted as an afterthought after the letter had been written. Before departing, he planned to insinuate Kiggell into his position as DSD: 'If I can only arrange to get you [in my position] here, while I'm C of S in India, we might do much towards creating the beginnings of an Imperial General Staff.' Kiggell, who lacked confidence but was manoeuverable, was diffident about his suitability for the post, but Haig pressed him to accept the appointment:

I . . . don't agree with your views on Brigadier Kiggell! Nor do you correctly value the importance of 'continuity' in the directorate and for the success of the Imperial General Staff. H. Wilson should go to a brigade: his being senior to you must not be allowed to interfere with the relationship of the DSD to Commandant S. Coll – if it does that latter must be unfit for his position.

I agree that it would be well that DSD should be a major-general but then the officer who is selected should be promoted – not a less well equipped man selected because of his rank![25]

When, two months later, Kiggell did indeed succeed Haig as DSD: 'This is a triumph for ability and honesty, over incapacity and intrigue.'[26]

Thereafter there is a fortnightly correspondence between Kiggell in London and Haig in India. Its tone is fascinating. Although a brigadier and now in the very position that Haig had just vacated, the former is treated very much as a junior and as a means of exercising control over the Whitehall apparatus and indeed many other aspects of army organisation. When Kiggell looked like escaping to become commandant of the Staff College, Haig put a quick end to the proposal: 'On no account should you go to the Staff College. The development of the General Staff will be thrown back for many years if you leave your present job now.' Kiggell did ultimately go to the Staff College, but not for a further four years.

Kiggell's rival had been Henry Wilson, always associated with plots in Haig's mind. Another Wilson was the object of Haig's vicarious intriguing through the agency of Kiggell some two years later when Matthew ('Scatters') Wilson was mentioned as a potential commandant of the Staff College:

Delhi

5.iv.11

My Dear Old Kigge . . .

I hear Sir J. French has promised Wilson (the C-in-C's Mil Sec) a nomination for Camberley next winter! I think 'Scatters'

has done his work as MS well, because he has no axe to grind –
But as his name implies ('Scatters') he is not very reliable – the
one quality which in my opinion, a Staff Officer cannot do
without. He is however merry and bright, and is first rate on the
personal Staff, of course. But if the question is put to you, you
should ask J. Vaughan about him as a regimental officer – V
was his last C.O. – I mention this as I understand Mrs. Scatters
is working French and the Powers that be, and I feel that the
Staff College is the place of all others from which female
influence should be excluded.[27]

In India, the Commander-in-Chief was no longer Kitchener, but
Creagh, and the Viceroy no longer Curzon, but Lord Minto, and soon
afterwards Lord Hardinge. In London the Secretary of State was Lord
Morley. The Dual Control issue had been addressed, but not resolved.
Kitchener had achieved the combination of the roles of Commander-
in-Chief and military member of the Council. While this sounds the
neatest of solutions, it created anomalies of Gilbertian complexity,
which Charteris described:

As Principal Staff Officers they had direct access to the Commander in Chief and could act in his name; as Heads of divisions in
the Army Department they could only approach the Army
Member through the Secretary, and receive the Army Member's
orders through him. As the Commander in Chief and the Army
Member were one and the same person, and as the Army Secretary
was Secretary to the Government of India, with direct access to the
Viceroy, it is easy to realise the confusion and friction that
inevitably resulted . . . Cases were not unknown of a Commander
in Chief disagreeing with himself as Army Member.[28]

Haig, in an unusually donnish turn of phrase, described the system as
the 'canonization of duality'.

Part of Haig's purpose in going to India had been explained in a
letter to Kiggell:

[I]t is of vital importance to have the machinery available in India trained as soon as possible to turn out Staff Officers who may be of use when the time comes, and the resources of that country organised for Imperial needs instead of only for India's at present.[29]

This purpose was frustrated. News of a study which he ordered on the feasibility of sending an Indian expeditionary force to Europe in time of war reached London, where Morley, no militarist, at once vetoed the project. Hardinge was told that the scheme should be ended and all the work already done destroyed. Haig relayed this order to the officer involved, Hamilton Gordon, but, the latter said: 'There was a look in Haig's eye which made me realise that he would not regard any deviation from rigid adherence . . . with undue severity,' and copies of the plan were preserved and the scheme implemented in the course of the first months of the war.[30]

Haig's second objective lay in an improvement in the army training, in particular that of staff officers. How successful Haig was in this objective is a matter of debate. There is certainly evidence in the diaries and letters which indicates frustration. He did not have the strong support from O'Moore Creagh that he had enjoyed from Kitchener. These Indian generals had some splendid names. O'Moore Creagh's was corrupted into 'No More K'. He was an Indian Army veteran of forty years' service, who never quite understood what Kitchener's concerns had been, and he did not wish to disturb a genial relationship with Hardinge: 'The C-in-C wishes to oblige the Viceroy because the latter is so agreeable to him, and says that he (the Chief) should not pay house rent but that his residence should be furnished and kept up like that of a Lord Governor of a Province!' When he left India Haig predicted that 'The Viceroy and the C-in-C will be glad when I cease to be CGS here. The Viceroy is not at all pleased with the lines taken in the G.S. memo . . . and the poor C-in-C is under the influence of us both, and has consequently given contrary opinions from time to time!' The frustrated plans must not be exaggerated; much was done by the medium of the staff tours which Haig again favoured, and which were planned in minute detail. Significantly, they concentrated not on Indian requirements, but on war in Europe and, *ex facie* strangely, given the geographical circumstances, involved a close study of German Army organisation. In these tours Haig again stressed the distinct phases which war would follow:

1. the manoeuvre for position;
2. the first clash of battle;
3. the wearing-out fight of varying duration;
4. the eventual decisive blow.

His degree of success in India is perhaps not of huge materiality. It is true that he did not have the general support for his efforts which he had enjoyed in London. Equally, the outcome of his efforts in London was much more important than his success or otherwise in India.

His views on the future for India were probably not untypical of people of his background at this time. He wrote to Kiggell on 20 July 1911:

Personally, I feel that there are only two ways of treating India; either we must look forward to the time when India will be in the same position as one of the Dominions, and we must prepare for it gradually, looking forward, say, another 100 years; or the other way is to treat India entirely as a vassal state and keep it entirely under control. For this we shall want a very much larger army than we have now, and it seems scarcely possible, having started to give people a voice in the government, to change our steps.

There is thus, in my opinion, no other course than to give the sons of the fighting class an opportunity of becoming officers; only those, however, who show that they are morally and intellectually fit for such appointments. We want to begin very slowly, looking ahead for say 50 or 75 years, and beginning with 5 or 6 a year according as suitable candidates come forward.[31]

Even when he was contemplating India and the Indian army, however, he was thinking of the storm, inevitable as it seemed to him, that would break out in Europe, and it is interesting to see that, again, he thinks in terms of a 'wearing down' process. He wrote to Kiggell on 27 April 1909: 'As regards meeting "the storm" which we all foresee, it seems to me that it will last a long time, and we'll win by wearing the enemy out, if we are only allowed three more years to prepare.'[32]

When the Haigs first arrived in India, they were involved in a round of dinners, dances and late nights. Lady Haig loved it but 'in the early hours of one morning, when I saw him sitting in his red uniform and looking so handsome – and hiding so well his boredom – it occurred to me what I was doing, and I remembered King Edward's kind warning about his military career. From that day onwards, I feel rather proud that I avoided staying late again, pretending that I was sick of meeting the same people night after night'.[33]

Haig was a vigorous Inspector and disappeared on extensive tours, after which his junior officers were too saddle-sore to sit. His absence on the tours allowed Lady Haig the opportunity to let her hair down. In her biography, she tells of a dance she organised. An inexperienced ADC bought far too much wine ('enough for an army' said Haig on his return) and the evening ended with Apache dances and then a game of 'pig sticking', the women riding on the men's backs and using billiard cues as spears.

Lady Haig presents an intriguing picture of dressing for dinner parties in the subcontinent. Dresses were very tight and ayahs had difficulty in dealing with the patent hooks. One lady, 'rather a gaunt female', said that she had no problems: 'I pull my dress to the front, fasten the hooks, turn it round and push my arms in.' Lady Haig and her fuller-bodied friends could think of no suitable response. She was lucky: '[Douglas] would allow time, after dressing himself, to fasten the devilish hooks. At first he was rather clumsy and fumbled a bit, but after a few days he soon mastered the job'.[34]

But she was far from being an irretrievably frivolous person. She joined a first aid class and arranged that it should be allowed some practice at a hospital in Simla. There she gained experience in bed-making and bandaging, and even attended the amputation of a finger. Encouraged by Haig, who felt that the existing medical and nursing arrangements were unsatisfactory for wartime conditions, she experienced something of the hard work and sadness entailed in nursing patients, and came across cases of kalazar plague, cholera and many types of malaria and leprosy. Eventually she was responsible for the formation of Voluntary Aid Detachments in India. In the course of her nursing duties she was told that a patient under an anaesthetic could be awakened if tickled under the fifth rib. She relayed the story to the German Crown Prince when he was staying with them in 1911. He insisted on a practical demonstration and lay down on top of a billiard table while Lady Haig tickled him.[35]

Haig was an even less frivolous person, but his rigidly timetabled day in India was far from onerous:

> He was in his office at Army Headquarters by 10 am, worked – generally at a standing desk – from then until lunchtime. After lunch he would work for two hours in his study in his own home, then followed exercise, polo, tennis and riding – until dinnertime, and after dinner work again until 10 pm, when with clockwork regularity he sought his rest.[36]

Haig rarely let his own hair down, and never very far. Charteris, who was with him in India, says that 'he entertained largely', but then adds tellingly 'if not lavishly'. He does, however, give a tantalising glimpse at a fancy dress ball of the 'somewhat unbending Chief of the General Staff arrayed as Henry VIII'.[37]

Towards the end of 1911, Haig was disturbed at night when a decoded telegram was brought to him from Haldane, asking if he would be prepared to take over the Aldershot Command. His immediate response was typical: 'That could have waited until the morning.' He had of course no hesitation in accepting what was in reality the senior active command in the Empire, and one that automatically carried with it command of I Corps of the British Expeditionary Force (which, he told his staff before he left India, he expected to be deployed within three or four years).

At the age of forty-nine and despite his slow start, he had leapfrogged many of his seniors. He was being given what he regarded as the best command in the army, while most of his contemporaries still awaited command of a battalion or a regiment. Moreover, he had been appointed to the command in preference to senior officers such as Sir Hubert Plumer, Sir James Grierson and Sir J. Wolfe-Murray. There were domestic considerations involved:

> Smith-Dorrien wrote to me privately about taking on his furniture and carpets etc. at Aldershot. Rather a big order! I have written to him but my sister will go and have a look at the things, with someone to act as my agent, when she returns from Canada – but I have a good deal of furniture stored in England so in any case I don't want to take all S.-D.'s things. Personally I think Government House ought to be kept furnished by government just as the lieutenant-governors' houses in India are state property – It is difficult for General Officers to collect a mass of furniture for three or four years without losing money over the sale of things when their time is up.[38]

He delayed his departure in order to be present in India when George V, who had succeeded Edward VII in May 1910, came to the Imperial Durbar at Delhi to review his Imperial Troops and be acknowledged by the Indian Princes in the most extravagant and exotic of ceremonies.

Lady Haig's description of the Durbar is worth reading:

> The 12th of December was the most important day, the real ceremony of the Durbar. All the Princes of India made obei-

sance to their Emperor. We left early, in order to reach the arena in good time. The sight that burst upon us was one difficult to describe . . . The arena was in the shape of a horse-shoe. It was simply crammed with Indians of all descriptions and, with their coloured turbans, they looked exactly like a huge mass of flowers. The jewels worn by the Indians flashed in the brilliant sunshine. It is of course, well known that an Indian always wears the best that he possesses when he wishes to do honour to his friends or guests.

Their Majesties' arrival was heralded by a salute of 100 guns. We all rose to our feet whilst the procession passed and the Indians salaamed to Their Majesties. As they alighted from the carriage, the pages met them and took charge of their purple trains and they walked up to their golden thrones on the dais, bowing to right and left. The Viceroy and Lady Hardinge and the members of the household then seated themselves near Their Majesties. The Gentlemen-at-Arms, the Scottish Archers and the Indian attendants carrying maces stood round as Their Majesties' bodyguard. The Indians wore scarlet robes embroidered with gold and had white turbans striped with gold upon their heads.[39]

Lady Haig had arrived at the Durbar before her husband and found their tents waterlogged, the boxes holding her Durbar dresses floating in water. She took prompt and practical action to remedy the problem, but contracted dysentery, as a result, she thought, of sleeping in a damp tent, and she nearly died of the disease on the way home from India, which they left on 23 December. Just before their departure Haig was made a Knight Commander of the Indian Empire.

'THE BEST COMMAND IN THE ARMY' AND 'THE UGLIEST MAN IN THE ARMY': ALDERSHOT AND HENRY WILSON

There was a poignant aspect to the Haigs' return from India: when, on a railway platform, they met their children for the first time after three years of separation neither the adults nor the youngsters recognised each other. The situation must have been a sadly common one in those days of service in the subcontinent. Once the children realised what was what, they proved to be unmanageable. Haig, recalling his own childhood, was inclined to leave them alone to settle down: Lady Haig was made of stronger stuff:

> I hated being stern with them. But it was no good, so I went in steeling myself to be firm. As the child remained obstinate, I finished by picking her up and laying her across my knee to spank her. 'Don't pull my nightie up, 'cos it hurts more' came from the child, and when I administered the smack she simply laughed and remarked to the nursery-maid, 'poor mummy'. She knew that I minded most, but I got her to bed eventually. There was one sad thing which worried me every night: that child refused to kiss me until quite a month after I had been at Radway. I realised to the full what it must mean to mothers whose husbands are in the Indian Army, and to have to leave their children so long and so often.[1]

Initially, the Haigs stayed at the Queen's Hotel in Farnborough. There were many German waiters in English hotels at that time, and it is indicative of the spy fever in the years before the war that Haig became convinced that one of the waiters had been tracing a drawing in his desk.

Haig took over his new command, 'the best command in the Army', on 1 March 1912. Throughout his time as a senior officer, Haig enthusiastically supported the *theory* that a general should expect to take over a new staff on his appointment, staff appointed on merit and not on the basis of the general's personal whim. But he never submitted himself to the practice, and perhaps no sensible general on taking on a new appointment would wish to be without people of ability and experience with whom he is used to working. Haig's problem was that he tended to hang on to people whose merit was very doubtful, simply because he was comfortable with them. Before he had even left India he was intriguing with Kiggell to have officers from the subcontinent appointed to positions at Aldershot, and when he arrived there he brought with him several members of his Indian staff, including his ADC, Captain H.D. Baird, and his assistant military secretary, Captain John Charteris. The team was known without great political propriety as 'the Hindu invasion'.

His loyalty to Charteris, in particular, was to prove unfortunate in the later stages of the war. Charteris was a Scot, the son of the senior Professor of Materia Medica at Glasgow University. He was brash and untidy, and liked to start the day with a brandy and soda. G.S. Duncan, a sensitive observer, said: 'I knew him well. A man of abounding vitality, he tended to be bustling and boisterous; and his loudmouthed exuberance made him none the too popular [*sic*] with his immediate colleagues, and with others up the line and at the War Office.' He was known amongst Haig's staff as 'the principal boy' and appears to have been a licensed jester in a circle that was otherwise sober and discreet. (Haig's confidants seem to have had a special interest in pantomime: after he became Commander-in-Chief, they called the army commanders 'the Wicked Barons'.) Often Charteris was the object of jokes as well as their instigator, as in his soaking by Haig in the fire-damaged Government House at Aldershot, where he for once seems to have failed to see the full comedic content of the situation. He was totally loyal to his Chief and sought to please him in every way: indeed his ultimate failure, as Haig's intelligence chief, flowed from his desire to tell the field-marshal what he wanted to hear. His loyalty earned Haig's confidence. He was highly intelligent. Although he did not go to Camberley, he was at the Quetta Staff College, where he was the most outstanding graduate of his year, 1909. His problem was essentially that he was not a trained or natural intelligence officer. It was a position for which he was not qualified, and Haig kept him in that position when his inadequacies had been very well exposed.

He was unpopular with his colleagues and with the army commanders. Burgess, who was appointed as his secretary in 1916, described him as 'really a horror of a man'. Towards the end of his time as Haig's intelligence officer, he became so unpopular with the army commanders that he was known as the 'U-Boat'.

Whatever his colleagues thought of him, Charteris comes across in his writings as likeable, able (he was fluent in both French and German), humorous and self-deprecating. In relation to Haig they consist of two volumes of biography, *Field-Marshal Earl Haig*, (1929), *Haig* (1933) and his recollections of his time with Haig during the war in diary form, *At GHQ*. *Field-Marshal Earl Haig* is not free from idiosyncracies, and is certainly biased towards his subject, of whom he was genuinely fond, but what is surprising is how reliable it is and how sound his judgements are. *At GHQ* was published in 1931. Charteris had not kept a diary during the war, and the artificial diary that he now published was based on papers, notes and letters written at the time, particularly the letters that he wrote to his wife daily, sometimes several times a day. In his preface he concedes that where records were incomplete he has amplified them from his recollections, but he asserts that 'In the main the book is in the words written at the time.' He lays himself open to the charge that the book is an exercise in hindsight. It does indeed have a remarkably *ex post facto* feel to it. The entry for 30 June 1916, for instance, on the eve of the opening of the Somme, reads as follows:

Once more the eve of battle. We do not now expect any great advance, or any great place of arms to fall to us now. We are fighting primarily to wear down the German armies and the German nation, to interfere with their plans, gain some valuable position and generally to prepare for the great decisive offensive which must come sooner or later, if not this year or even next year. The casualty list will be big. Wars cannot be won without casualities. I hope people at home realise this.[3]

This sombre prediction sounds as if it had been tailored after the event to fit in to a downgraded idea of what the Somme was about. But the manuscript letter to his wife of the same date is in identical words, and his letter to her the following day is equally realistic and in similar tone to the 'diary' entry:

The attack this morning has, so far as present reports go, done fairly well. But it has only really begun. There will be weeks of hard fighting, I think. Remember that this is <u>not</u> an attempt to win the war at a blow and do not be disappointed if things do not move as rapidly as some people will want.[4]

A study of the manuscript letters suggests that the published account is, by and large, an authentic record of the events, and of the mood at GHQ. The letters are worth reading for their own sake. Charteris was not in great danger of being killed by a bullet although he was seriously ill on several occasions; but these loving letters to his wife are a poignant expression of the pain of separation. The only 'Douglas' in them is their infant son, and generally the letters are less about the war than concerns about her cold, Douglas' health and other domestic news, her blue nighties, her swimsuit. They generally begin simply, 'My Darling' and go on to tease her about the girls in his billet who are flirting shamelessly with him, very forward and in fashionably short skirts. They have 'no shame in running after an elderly married man like myself'.' They turn out to have a combined age of sixteen years.[5]

The letter in which he remembers his wedding to Noel is worth quoting at a little length:

> Can you imagine how impatiently I waited for my bride to come from her room and away with me to London? . . . Do you remember the dinner at the Savoy? . . . Do you remember at last, my beloved, how you came to me and all of you, all of you, darling, belonged to me and all of me belonged to you, and we fell asleep, my Noel, for the first time husband and wife – Noel and John – my Noel and your John. Surely the world turned more slowly on its axis that night, my Noel, for you and I had fulfilled the first part of our destiny. We had pledged ourselves to one another . . .
>
> And that darling was the first time I had ever seen you perfectly happy. I can close my eyes and picture you in my mind and I see you then with my eyes. It is the most vivid of all my memories of you. And after that memory, child, comes another very clear to me but so sad, of you standing on Victoria Station platform weeping as the train carried me off to France again in February . . .
>
> Goodnight, my girl . . . I love you, love you, love you.[6]

One of the great attractions of the Aldershot command for Haig was that it was a big one: it was composed of the 1st and 2nd Divisions and 1st Cavalry Brigade, and therefore offered the opportunity of handling by far the biggest concentrations of troops that were available in Britain, where manoeuvres on a French or German scale were unknown.

Haig's first manoeuvres, held in East Anglia, were disastrous. Haldane had just been succeeded as Secretary of State for War by Colonel J.E.B. Seely. Things went badly for Seely from the start, when his horse went lame and he kept the King waiting. When at last a replacement was found, Seely was horrified to find that his horse had seized the King's foot in its mouth.

In the mock battle, Haig commanded 'Red Force' which had

landed on the Norfolk coast and was advancing on London. 'Blue Force', blocking the road to London, was commanded by Lieutenant-General Sir James Grierson, who proved infinitely the better general, hiding his troops from Haig's aerial observation. Haig's troops, by contrast, had all been seen from the air by Grierson – all the more surprising in view of Haig's particular interest in aerial warfare. The Chief Umpire was Johnnie French, but neither he nor the other umpires and judges were able to disguise what had happened. It was a bad start to Haig's command, the more embarrassing because he was observed not only by the King and Seely, but also by General Foch, and a Russian delegation led by the Grand Duke Nicholas, plus the ministers of defence of South Africa and Canada. At a post-manoeuvre conference, chaired by the King, Haig could not, in the light of events, read the speech he had prepared, and he attempted to extemporise, a fatal attempt for someone as inarticulate as he. He became not only unintelligible, but so dull that the Cambridge University delegates fell asleep. Haig's carapace of self-confidence was not, however, penetrated: he recorded in his diary: 'I think my remarks well received.'

It is noticeable that in 1913, when another major exercise took place, Haig used many more aircraft. This exercise too, however, was not without its problems. On this occasion, Haig was playing the role of corps commander under French. Henry Wilson made a minor criticism of Haig's role which, he said, 'left a gap of three miles in the centre of the line.'[7] Haig himself criticised French in stronger terms: 'Sir John French's instructions for moving along the front of his enemy (then halted on a fortified position) and subsequently attacking the latter's distant flank, were of such an unpractical nature that his Chief of the General Staff [Grierson, for the purpose of the manoeuvres] demurred.' Some slight modifications in the orders were permitted, but Grierson ceased to be French's CGS on mobilisation, and was very soon transferred to another appointment in the BEF. The diary entry, written very much after the event, reflects Haig's increasing criticism of his old Chief.

Despite these relatively minor setbacks, these were happy days for

Haig. He had time to develop the tradition of 'Search-light Tattoos' which had been inaugurated by his predecessor, and viewing 'with some misgivings the growing tendency of the younger officers to seek their relaxation in drawing rather than in more virile exercise, [h]e even went so far as to throw the weight of his influence against the *Thés Dansants* which were introduced at the Officers' Club.'[8] Charteris describes the routine that he established:

For the first time in his married life he was settled in a real home. Government House, if not palatial, was spacious, and in those pre-war days it stood in country surroundings. Happy in the reunion with his family, Haig set himself to the just admixture of the life of a serving officer and a country gentleman. His private means, though not great, were sufficient to enable him to meet the demands on his income. He entertained frequently, but not extravagantly . . .

Golf replaced polo as his chief means of physical exercise. His attack on the citadel of golf was characteristic. He spared no pains to conquer its difficulties. He was determined to succeed. He took lessons from a professional. He practised assiduously. Each stroke was treated as a separate and all-important problem. He was not content until he felt that he had acquired the utmost proficiency within his scope. His ball never left the fairway. His play was as consistent as that of Colonel Bogey himself. If his official handicap was never very low, he was a most difficult opponent to beat . . .

The days passed evenly. The early hours of the morning he spent on horseback, supervising the training of the units of his command: when the inspection was over, he would indulge in a sharp gallop across country and took a mischievous pleasure in evading the staff officer and escort who accompanied him. Riding either alone or with one companion, ahead of the others, and with perfect knowledge of every inch of the ground, he would suddenly increase his pace, and make an abrupt turn, taking advantage of either a fold of the ground or a path through one of the spinneys, and if those behind failed to follow, he would be delighted. But when, often after a long search, they succeeded in rejoining him, there was always the same question with quite unmoved face: 'Did you not see which way I went?' Only those who were long with him knew of the pleasure this little amusement afforded him, and in France they would seek to lighten his burden of anxiety by purposely allowing him to succeed in evading them. At 11 o'clock he reached his office at Army Headquarters and worked there until lunchtime. From lunch to tea was play-time – either golf, or tennis, as the days grew warmer – or sometimes he preferred the role of onlooker and watched the games of some section of the Command. After tea two hours were devoted to reading, and this brought his day's work to a close. The hours after dinner were spent with his household, which comprised, in addition to his family, his immediate personal staff, his military secretary and his ADCs. There were the usual number of official dinners to officers in his Command – generally two each week.[9]

This résumé of Haig's daily routine discloses a régime that is still fairly relaxed, and a pace of life that seems remarkably gentle in the context of the events which were taking place. Within the army, and particularly within the War Office circles in which Haig moved, the certainty of an early and difficult war with Germany was pretty well accepted, and the events that were to bring that war succeeded each other at some speed. The Agadir crisis in 1911 concentrated the minds of politicians and soldiers on the prospect of war. Indeed, they did not need much concentrating: ever since the Boer War, publication of the Esher Report in 1904, the launching of the *Dreadnought* in 1906, the Enquiry into the Likelihood of Invasion in 1908, and Haldane's Reforms, the pace of preparation had been accelerated. These concerns were shared with the French, Britain's colleagues, if not her allies, in the Entente Cordiale. The Liberal government, with its tradition of avoiding foreign entanglements and with its many pacifist supporters, could not deal very directly with France, but did so through the offices of Colonel Repington, the very influential military correspondent of *The Times*. The French were indirectly asked for their views on Anglo-French cooperation. Recognising the respective strengths of the two countries, France indicated that she would leave naval strategy to Britain, but that Britain's military contribution should be coordinated with that of France and under the same direction as the French armies.

Repington's name will occur frequently in the course of this narrative, and a brief biographical note is justified. Charles À Court Repington came from a rich, aristocratic background, which gave him, perhaps, the confidence that enabled him to view politicians and senior army officers with a degree of contempt. At the Staff College he was regarded as a brilliant student and he had a distinguished and courageous military career until he was invalided out of the army in the course of the South African campaign. After his marriage he had many affairs, including a lasting but unfaithful relationship with Lady Garstin, which became widely known while he was still in the army. He was required to give a written promise 'upon his honour as a soldier and gentleman' to have no more dealings with her, and his parole was handed to his colleague Henry Wilson. He chose, for reasons which he thought justified his behaviour, to break his parole, and was tried for that breach and required to resign. It was Wilson's conduct, and not his, which he thought culpable.

Thereafter his role was as an influential journalist, principally for *The Times*. His critics often regarded him as Northcliffe's mouthpiece, but he retained his professional independence. His views were fairly orthodox: he was in favour of a General Staff, he feared a German 'bolt from the blue', he was an unequivocal 'westerner', he was uncritically hostile to almost all politicians and disliked by many. The left of the Liberal Party, in particular, referred to him as 'the gorgeous Wreckington'.

Staff talks began between Britain and France in 1906, but gathered impetus in 1910, when Henry Wilson became Director of Military Operations. Wilson is an interesting figure and an attractive one – except in a physical sense. 'Ugly' Wilson, 'the ugliest man in the British Army' as a result of a wound he received from Burmese bandits, was tall and quizzical and was characteristically to be found bent over his interlocutors, engaging them with irresistible geniality. He failed twice for Woolwich and three times for Sandhurst and only obtained a commission by the back door route of two years in the Militia. But he was far from being without brains, and passed for entrance to Staff College with no difficulty. He was a protégé of Roberts and worked with him during and after the South African war: his rapid ascent was resented by some. By 1895 he was the youngest staff officer in the army. He was profoundly sociable, and enjoyed the company of politicians, a trait that caused him problems during his military career. Haig and many others were suspicious of him, regarding him as foxy and unreliable. Charteris recorded: 'DH thinks Wilson is a politician, and not a soldier, and "a politician" with Douglas Haig is synonymous with crooked dealing and wrong sense of values.'[10] 'The ready wit, the hearty laugh, the almost unfailing charm of the exuberant Irishman produced no impression but distrust in the mind of the cautious Scotsman.'[11] Wilson, for his part, was generally supportive of Haig, contrary to what the latter thought, and never plotted against him. He was, broadly, a loyal and trustworthy supporter. Esher, who knew him well, said that he was always loyal to the man he was serving.[12] He was however always a little baffled by Haig. Haig never succumbed to his charm, or understood the need for the personal skills that Wilson had in such great measure. Wilson could never, for instance, comprehend why Haig did not really engage with those outside the narrow confines of his staff and the trusted confidants on whom he relied for information and assessments of morale. That was a fair observation, but Wilson quite wrongly went on to claim that while Haig regularly met senior commanders, his visits to subordinate units were few, formal and brief. He despaired: 'I never can get inside his head.'[13] Wilson had many friends in the army, and also many enemies. Some blamed him for appearing to foment the Curragh incident and then failing to support the mutineers. But his interest in politics and politicians, his command of big and broad ideas (as in his masterly lectures as Commandant at Camberley), separated him from his more pedestrian colleagues, and earned their distrust. Sir Sam Fay complained that he could argue with total conviction that a horse chestnut was the same thing as a chestnut horse, and that he got an erection whenever he came within a mile of a politician.[14] He was loathed by Major-General Sir Edward Spears, who compared him to Quint: 'the semi-spooky, entirely evil valet, in Henry James' *The Turn of the Screw.*'[15]

Churchill, in his history of the Great War – *The World Crisis* magnificently written, its arguments supported by an impressive mass of data, and everything radiating from the engaging egotism which prompted Balfour's excellent quip: 'I hear that Winston has written a book about himself and called it *The World Crisis'* – recalled the skills that made Wilson popular with politicians and his ability at making complicated military issues clear to laymen:

He wantonly pronounced grotesquely the names of French towns and Generals. In discussing the gravest matters he used the modes of levity. 'Prime Minister,' he began one day to the War Cabinet, at a meeting which I attended, 'Today I am Boche.' Then followed a penetrating description of the situation from the standpoint of the German Headquarters. On another day he would be France or Bulgaria, and always out of this adaptation there emerged, to my mind, the root of the matter in hand. But some Ministers were irritated. He did not go so far as Marshal Foch, who sometimes gave a military description in pantomime; but their methods of displaying a war proposition had much in common.

I can see him so clearly as I write, standing before the map in the Cabinet Room giving one of his terse telegraphese appreciations. 'This morning, Sir, a new battle.' (The reader will recognise it when it comes.) 'This time it is we who have attacked. We have attacked with two armies – one British, one French. Sir Haig [his flippant name for the Commander-in-

Chief] is in his train, Prime Minister, very uncomfortable, near the good city of Amiens. And Rawly is in his left hand and Debeney is in his right. Rawly is using 500 tanks. It is a big battle, and we thought you would not like us to tell you about it beforehand.'

Churchill then permits himself to stray from his narrative:

We should be thankful that the future is veiled. I was to be present at another scene in this room. There was no Henry Wilson. The Prime Minister and I faced each other, and on the table between us lay the pistols which an hour before had drunk this loyal man's blood.[16]

There is a touching little note in manuscript in the Kiggell papers which tells us something about Wilson's charm, how – unlike Haig – he was loved by the French even when he was laughing at them, and something too about Kiggell's own lack of confidence:

A spell-binding lecturer – always joking and amusing and informal – the only General who could meet politicians ('the Frocks') on level terms – he fascinated the French and could say outrageous things to them (e.g. 'We can't trust you French an inch' caused much laughter coming from him. What would have been the effect from Haig?!) I think the only VIP I ever felt completely at ease with.[17]

After the war he did what he should perhaps have done earlier, and went into politics, saying that he wanted to make mischief. He became Irish Secretary. He left that office hated by the Fenians, and on 21 July 1922, having performed the official unveiling of a war memorial at Liverpool Street Station, returned to his flat, wearing his full military uniform and sword. As he reached his doorstep a Fenian fired a pistol at him at short range, but missed. Wilson did not take advantage of the missed shot and take refuge in his flat. He turned and advanced on his assailant with drawn sword and died under the impact of a second bullet. A Roman death.

One of the things about Henry Wilson which most of his brother-officers neither understood nor approved of was that, unlike most of them, including certainly Haig, he actually liked the French. Thus Charteris:

> [Haig] had a high opinion of General Wilson's intellectual ability, but he did not trust his judgement. Wilson had fallen under the influence of the French General Staff Officers – and, indeed, of the French nation. His temperament was almost Latin in its principal qualities.[18]

The view was honestly held by some of colleagues that his attitude amounted to treachery, and that his loyalties truly lay with France and not with Britain. This was of course nonsense, but he did find, as did many others, much to admire in the French military machine, particularly in the early part of the war. He also got on well with the French people.

Although Wilson liked talking to politicians, both those in power and those in opposition, he used politics to advance his policies, rather than his career.

Not only did the Cabinet know nothing of the talks between the British and French staffs in which Wilson was intimately involved: the War Office and the Admiralty were even ignorant of each other's plans. The Committee of Imperial Defence itself was split between those of 'the Blue-Water School', who saw Britain's maritime defence as effective and conclusive, and the 'Bolt from the Blue Party' who were concerned about military action, particularly the risk of invasion. In this vacuum, Wilson and his colleagues enjoyed considerable freedom. Wilson's philosophy was to see the two armies operating in the same theatre, and in very close proximity, the British Expeditionary Force on the left flank of the French army. He spent much of his leaves in the years running up to the war visiting France and cycling over the Franco-German frontier. He came to know France, the French countryside and the French people as a result of these visits, studying in great detail the topography of the ground where fighting might be expected. If it had not been for his work, it is difficult to think how mobilisation would have proceeded: no one else gave the matter of the geographical deployment of the expeditionary force any great thought. So personal was Wilson's contribution to the planning that to the French he was 'Général Dooble-vay', and the British Expeditionary Force was 'l'Armée Wilson'.

The confusion with which Britain approached 1914, and the debt she owed to men like Henry Wilson, is encapsulated in Haldane's record of what happened when the government had to react to Agadir:

> At a meeting of the Defence Committee . . . the Prime Minister . . . was enquiring into our joint war plans. Sir Arthur Wilson [First Sea Lord] unexpectedly said that the plan of the Admiralty for the event of a war with Germany was quite different from ours [the Army's]. They wanted to take detachments of the Expeditionary Force and to land them *seriatim* at points on the Baltic coast, on the northern shores of Prussia. We of the War Office at once said that such a plan was from a military point of view hopeless, because the railway system which the Great General Staff of Germany had evolved was such that any division we landed, even if the Admiralty could have got it to a point suitable for debarkation, would be promptly surrounded by five to ten times the number of enemy troops. Sir John Fisher appeared to have derived the idea from the analogy of the Seven Years' War, more than 150 years previously, and Sir Arthur Wilson, his successor had apparently adopted it. The First Lord (McKenna) backed him up. I said at once that the mode of employing troops and their numbers and places of operation were questions for the War Office General Staff and that we had worked them out with the French. The results had been periodically approved in the Committee of Defence itself. Sir William Nicholson [CIGS] asked Sir Arthur whether they

had maps at the Admiralty of the German strategic railways. Sir Arthur replied that it was not their business to have such maps. 'I beg your pardon' said Sir William, 'If you meddle with military problems you are bound not only to have them, but to have studied them.' The discussion became sharp; I of course, agreeing *ex animo* with the utterances of the CIGS. He had a rather too sharp tongue, and I remember that on a previous occasion Sir John Fisher had said to me that he wished I would enjoin "Old Nick" not always to stamp his hoof on his (Sir John's) toes.

The Prime Minister was clear that the arrangements made must be carried out in accordance with the plan of the General Staff. But the Admiralty were evidently not convinced when the meeting came to an end. The difficulty had its origins in the fact that the Navy then possessed nothing like a General Staff. Sir John Fisher had always objected to having one . . . He did not realise that in the 20th century it is impossible to conduct military operations successfully either at sea or on land, without close preliminary study on an intensive scale.[19]

Colonel Hankey, Secretary of the Committee of Imperial Defence, recorded the role of Henry Wilson at the meeting that Haldane was describing. Wilson set out the General Staff plan for the deployment of the Expeditionary Force: it appears that this was the first time that the Committee had heard its details. 'When the Committee adjourned for lunch, there was no doubt that Henry Wilson had made a profound impression, which I am the more ready to admit, because he had entirely failed to carry conviction in my own mind.'[20]

In Terraine's words:

The result was the acceptance of the (Henry) Wilson plan, and *without any full discussion or realisation of its implications*. That this is what occurred is shown by the facts that, when war broke out, and those implications came closer into view, it transpired that neither the recent CIGS (French), not the C in C of I Corps

(Haig) were fully aware of what had been decided; two cabinet
ministers (Morley and Burns) resigned as soon as they understood; and a number of other ministers (chief among them
Churchill and Lloyd George) were never able to bring themselves to accept those implications, with which they should have
been familiar for years.[21]

Thereafter, plans continued for war. Churchill took over the navy and
began to create a Naval Staff. Hankey drew up the War Book, a
compendium of every detail of the procedure that would require to be
followed once it was decided that war should be declared; but the
crucial question of where Britain's contribution would be in the
event of war was not discussed again until the Council of War on 5
August, the day after the declaration of war.

In this narrative it is appropriate that only a brief mention should
be made of the Curragh incident, which occurred in March–April
1914. At this time, almost 100,000 volunteers had come together in
Ulster, having declared themselves bound, with signatures written in
some cases in their own blood, to resist the establishment of home
rule for the whole of Ireland. Ireland seemed on the brink of civil war,
and the position of the army was critical. On 16 December 1913, the
Minister for War, Seely, told senior officers of the army, in strangely
chosen phrases, that they were not bound to obey orders which were
not 'reasonable under the circumstances' and, simultaneously, that
they must not 'pick and choose'. He attempted to synthesise these
instructions by telling them that they would only be asked to support
the civil power 'if the police are unable to hold their own'.

A surprisingly high proportion of officers in the army were Anglo-
Irish or from Ulster, and there was little support amongst such people
for the use of force to impose the Home Rule Bill on the north of
Ireland. Henry Wilson was one of these Ulstermen, and felt strongly
enough about the issue to disclose confidential information to the
Conservative opposition and to the Ulster Volunteers. In March
1914, General Sir Arthur Paget, the commander of the troops in
Ireland, reacted to War Office orders by assembling his officers at the

Curragh, the great military base near Dublin. He told them that those among them who were domiciled in Ulster could 'disappear' if their units were ordered north; they would subsequently be reinstated. Any other officers who were not prepared to enforce the new legislation in Ulster were required to say so and face dismissal. Brigadier-General Hubert Gough (the brother of Haig's Chief of Staff, John Gough) said he would prefer to be dismissed than to serve in the north, and his example was followed by fifty-seven of the seventy officers in 3rd Cavalry Brigade.

John Gough immediately told Haig that he would follow his brother's example. Haig went to London and to his old chief, Haldane, now Lord Chancellor. The Cabinet had to try to resolve a crisis which only arose as a result of the inflammatory instructions to Paget. The response was that soldiers were not to be faced with hypothetical questions but, equally, they could not dictate their terms to the government as to which orders they would carry out and which they would not. Hubert Gough, now in London, asked the government to confirm its position in writing, and this was done. The formula as it stood gave, of course, no comfort to the Ulster-minded officers on the point that concerned them: were they to be asked to enforce the Home Rule Bill if it became an act? Henry Wilson recognised this lacuna and sought the further assurance that no question of coercing Ulster would arise. Seely, in a further example of War Office incompetence, gave the required assurance by precipitately adding two paragraphs to the document to which Asquith, Haldane and the Cabinet had devoted so much careful thought. This addition, known as 'the peccant paragraphs', effectively contradicted the rest of the document. They were repudiated and Seely resigned, to be followed by French and Sir Spencer Ewart, the Adjutant General, who had initialled the paragraphs. Wilson sought opinion from the Army at the Staff College point-to-point (somehow the locus seems appropriate for such an urbane intriguer) and he told French that there was no alternative to his resignation, just as Haig told Ewart. French's resignation was given with a string round its leg, and it was understood that he would be brought back when war broke out, as many, but not all, expected it to do. That was the end of the crisis, although it might well have been repeated on a much bigger scale if Ireland and the Home Rule Bill had not been displaced a few months later by the outbreak of war: the issue that had caused the 'mutiny' had still not been addressed. Haig, for instance, although not at the centre of the crisis, and disapproving of the army's intervention into a political role, articulated an ambivalent position when he held a meeting of GOCs of divisions and brigades on the day of Seely's resignation: 'I pointed out the danger of disruptions in army and empire and begged them to induce regimental officers to give up dabbling in politics. We were all united to do anything short of coercing our fellow citizens who have done no wrong.' But coercing their fellow citizens is exactly what the army would have been required to do if it became necessary to enforce the provisions of the Home Rule Bill in the north.

The Curragh bomb was not the explosion it might have been, but particles of shrapnel did do serious damage. The incident led to great personal bitterness between brother officers (Lord Roberts cut Sir John French, for example). Secondly, the intervention of the army into politics to the extent that it had done and to the extent that it threatened to do created an atmosphere of mistrust, particularly between the Liberal Party and its principal representatives on the one hand, and the army leaders and the Establishment on the other, and this was to cause enormous personal difficulties for Haig during the war, and to imperil the efficient prosecution of the British war effort.

Even if they did not know where they were going to play, the identity of the players was known. In November 1912 Seely and French had become convinced that war was likely to break out. On 8 November Wilson and French drew up a list of appointments, which were confirmed by the Army Council on 12 November. The two corps composing the BEF were to be commanded by Haig and Smith-Dorrien. Allenby was to command the Cavalry Division. Grierson was to be CGS. A few days later Smith-Dorrien was replaced by Sir Arthur Paget, and on 17 November a meeting was held to discuss strategy, with French, Haig, Grierson, Wilson and Paget present. Wilson was not impressed and wrote of 'some amazing contributions to strategy and a general want of knowledge and clear thinking which make me hope we don't go to war just at present.'[22] Haig was developing doubts about French's abilities, but he was not the only one to do so: Wilson was clear that Sir John did not have the necessary intellectual skills.

WAR. THE ARMY SEARCHES FOR ITS ROLE. THE GREAT RETREAT. FIRST YPRES. HAIG ON THE MENIN ROAD

When the Archduke Franz Ferdinand was assassinated at Sarajevo on 28 June 1914, Haig took the event more seriously than the Foreign Secretary, who did not refer to it in the House of Commons until 10 July. Even at Aldershot Haig was alone in taking a keen interest in the repercussions of the murder.[1] He had his staff prepare an appreciation of the consequences, as soon as he heard of the assassination. Their conclusion ruled out a major conflict. Events proved them wrong, but as these events unrolled, the machinery that Haig and Haldane had established for the run up to war operated smoothly. The 'precautionary period' orders were received at Aldershot on 29 July and by the time that full mobilisation took place, such was the efficiency of the system that Haig had nothing whatsoever to do.

On 30 July, French had been sent for by the CIGS and told privately that if an expeditionary force were sent out, he would command it. Since the Curragh incident his position had been uncomfortable, and he was not confident that the assurances of the CIGS could be relied upon. Ramsay McDonald said years later that on the night of 2 August 1914 he was at the house of Sir George Riddell, the newspaper proprietor. 'After supper they went upstairs to Riddell's smoking room. The telephone bell rang, and Riddell picked up the receiver. All they heard was: "That you Johnnie? How are you? . . . Oh yes it is going to be war . . . Oh yes. Fancy you not having heard. You are to command it all right." It was Sir John

French at the other end, who was learning of his command from the proprietor of the *News of the World.*[2]

War was declared on 4 August. The Germans had made no secret of what their plans were. Edward Spears, for instance, had been told by a German staff officer in Berlin of the detailed implications of the Schlieffen Plan, and was even shown a drawing of the advance through Belgium. Spears told the British military attaché – who did not listen to him – and also the French attaché.[3] There was much less certainty about what the British were going to do. On 5 August a quite remarkable Council of War took place at 10 Downing Street. It was not any established committee that met, but a comprehensive assembly of both key Cabinet ministers and a large number of eminent men, some of whom were certain to be involved in the conduct of the war, such as Sir Charles Douglas, CIGS. French, the Commander-in-Chief of the Expeditionary Force, Sir Archibald Murray and Henry Wilson, French's sub-Chief of Staff, Haig, in command of I Corps, and Grierson in command of II Corps were there. Slightly more peripheral, but also present, were Sir John Cowans, Quartermaster General, Sir H. Sclater, Adjutant General, Sir Stanley Von Donop, Master General of Ordnance, and Sir Ian Hamilton, Inspector-General of Overseas Forces. Even more exotic were Kitchener, not yet Secretary of State, that post being occupied briefly once more by Haldane, and the 82-year-old Lord Roberts. The purpose of this extraordinary meeting was, at this very late stage, to decide what the Expeditionary Force was to do. Haig's record of the meeting is one of the parts of his diary which he appears to have rewritten, or at least written retrospectively, probably to cast the role of Sir John French in an unfavourable light. Sir John, unaware of the detailed though unofficial understanding between the British and the French regarding the deployment of 'l'armée Wilson', suggested that the Expeditionary Force would best be sent off to somewhere that had never been discussed, Antwerp, to liaise with the Belgian, and possibly the Dutch, army. The suggestion was the more bizarre in that the neutrality of the Netherlands had not been violated.

Understandably, Wilson was aghast at this 'ridiculous proposal'.

Haig's contribution to the discussion cannot be ascertained with certainty. His diary for August 1914 is not available until the thirteenth day of that month. His account of the meeting is contained in a memorandum headed 'Mobilisation', which was written after the war:

> Sir John French gave in outline a prearranged plan which had been worked out between the British and French General Staffs. Briefly stated it was hoped that the Expeditionary Force would mobilise simultaneously with the French, and would be concentrated behind the French left at Maubeuge by the 15th day of mobilisation. Then the intention was that we move eastwards towards the Meuse, and act on the left of the French against the German right flank. We were now however late in mobilising, and so this plan was no longer possible. He spoke about his hopes of now going to Antwerp and operating with the Belgian and possibly Dutch armies.

Haig recorded: 'Personally, I trembled at the reckless way Sir J. French spoke about "the advantages" of the BEF operating from Antwerp against the powerful and still intact German Army!' Wilson's diary record sums up the conference as 'an historic meeting of men mostly ignorant of their subject'. As well as referring to 'the desultory talk on strategy', he records the ignorance of some of the speakers who believed 'that Liège was in Holland'.[4]

The Antwerp expedition was effectively sabotaged when Churchill, as First Lord, said that the navy was not in a position to guarantee safe passage.

Then, according to Haig, the CIGS, Douglas, pointed out that plans had already been made for embarkation at Newhaven, Southampton and Bristol, with landings at Le Havre, Boulogne and other French channel ports. The French had arranged rolling stock and railway timetables to co-ordinate these plans, which could not now be changed.

Haig persisted, though it was not now necessary to do so, with a number of points that emphasised the fact that Britain should be fighting alongside the French rather than the Belgians. Then to broader issues:

> I also made these points: 1st. That Great Britain and Germany would be fighting for their existence. Therefore the war was bound to be a long war, and neither would acknowledge defeat after a short struggle. I knew that German writers had stated in their books that a modern war in Europe would not last more than a few months. In my opinion that was what they had hoped for and what they were planning to make it. I held that we must organise our resources *for a war of several years.*
>
> 2nd. Great Britain must at once take in hand the creating of an army. I mentioned one million as the number to aim at immediately, remarking that that was the strength originally proposed for the Territorial Force by Lord Haldane. Above all we ought to aim at having a strong and effective force when we came to discuss peace at a Conference of Great Powers.
>
> 3rd. We only had a small number of trained officers and N.C.O.s. These must be economised. The need for efficient instructors would become at once apparent. I urged that a considerable proportion of officers and N.C.O.s should be withdrawn forthwith from the Expeditionary Force . . . *Lastly*, my advice was to send as strong an Expeditionary Force as possible, and as soon as possible, to join the French forces and to arrange to increase that force as rapidly as possible.

The contribution was not particularly contentious, although it is interesting that Haig, with a few others, was already looking at a long war. He did not address the critical problem of where the Expeditionary Force should be placed in relation to the French army. After the war French, in his controversial and bitter *1914*, said that Haig 'Suggested postponing any landing until the campaign had actively opened.' Haig resented and denied this suggestion, which was probably false, though Haig's papers are at their most suspect in relation to the Council of War and his part in it. His manuscript diary for the period 29 July to 13 August does not survive, either in its original or its typed form, and what does survive in typescript is the post-war 'Mobilisation' memorandum, a composite entry covering several days, not the usual daily record. Did he destroy a manuscript version? If so, was that because it did not support the story he wanted told? The likeliest explanation seems to be that he had not kept a manuscript record for the days in question rather than that he destroyed it: if he had wanted to do a cover-up he would presumably have recreated a bogus daily record, rather than change the form to a single account of the days covering the mobilisation period. In a 'Memorandum of Opinions expressed by me at the War Council Meetings held at 10, Downing Street, on the 5th and 6th August 1914', which was signed 'Field-Marshal' – after the war – Haig wished to put on record that

> I certainly never 'suggested', as Field-Marshal Lord French states on page 6 of his book, 'postponing any landing until the Campaign had actively opened, etc . . .' On the contrary, I definitely stated that 'our best policy' at the time 'was to be ready to do as the French wished us [*sic*]'.[5]

He acknowledges that his contemporaneous notes were given at the time to Hankey. Hankey did not preserve them but on 25 July 1919 sent *his* notes to Haig, saying that he could not see anything to support French:

> [Y]ou will see that my own summary was as follows:-
> > The trend of his [Haig's] remarks was that our best policy at the present time was to be ready to do as the French wished us [*sic*].

In the immediately pre-war period, Haig had come to think that the BEF should be used as the nucleus of a greatly expanded army, rather than being dispatched to France on its own and in its entirety. In a letter he wrote as late as 4 August 1914, for example, he said:

> I agree that we ought not to dispatch our Expeditionary Force in a hurry to France. Possibly had there been a chance of support-ing her at the very beginning, our help might have been decisive. That moment seems to have been allowed to pass. Now we must *make* an Army large enough to intervene decisively – say 300,000.[6]

At the Council he realised that such a delay was impossible, and, in any event, the delay he had formerly talked of was not of the type that French alleged he advocated at the Council. It was however what Wilson recorded him as urging: Wilson's diary says that Haig wanted to wait for up to three months, to allow a build-up of forces from the Empire.[7] But reliability is not the hallmark of Wilson's diaries, and Haig's account is supported not only by Hankey, but also by Charteris, who indicates that his chief did want to weigh the arguments for delay as against immediate embarkation before making his decision. It is revealing that Haig was confident enough to appeal to third party witnesses for support. As well as Hankey, he wrote to Ian Hamilton. The latter chose not to become involved, but did not contradict him.

The whole nature of the meeting, and Haig's own vague and fluid position, points up the sloppiness of the preparations for war, and the failure to join up the plans that were being made at the War Office with the Admiralty, the government and even with senior army commanders. It is remarkable that disaster did not ensue. At any rate and inevitably, the end of the meeting was a vindication of the Wilson plan: that the Expeditionary Force should go to Maubeuge, stopping at Amiens, as Wilson characteristically put it, for '*dix minutes pour une tasse de café*'. Haig and Kitchener considered Mau-beuge too exposed and would have stopped for good, and not just for a cup of coffee, at Amiens.

Indeed, Haig's reaction to the news that he was to go to Maubeuge was one of some consternation:

We are to detrain . . . some 60 or 70 miles to the east of Amiens! In view of ignorance still existing regarding the enemy's movements, the rate of his advance into Belgium, and his intentions, it seems to some of us somewhat risky to bring our concentration so close to the enemy . . . I have an uneasy feeling lest we may be thoughtlessly committed to some great general action before we have had time to absorb our reservists. Any precipitate engagement of our little force may lose us the small value which our highly trained divisions do possess not only as a unit in battle, but also as a leaven for raising the moral of the great National Army which the Govt. is now proceeding to organise.

It was indeed a 'little force' that was going to France: initially the Expeditionary Force consisted of four infantry divisions and one cavalry division, the two remaining infantry divisions following fairly swiftly. France, by contrast, started with sixty-two infantry and twenty cavalry divisions and Germany with eighty-seven and eleven. It is not easy to see how Britain thought that they were going to make a significant influence on the outcome of the war on land. Great as the prescience of men like Haig and Haldane had been, given that they had so long foreseen a long and difficult war with Germany, perhaps they should have argued more forcibly for a much larger expeditionary force. It would, however, have done no good.

On 11 August the King and Queen visited Aldershot. Haig recorded that the King 'seemed delighted' that French had been given command of the BEF. Haig dampened the King's delight by telling him

at once, as I felt it my duty to do so, that from my experience with Sir John in the South African War he was certain to do his utmost to carry out orders which the government might give him. I had grave doubts, however, whether his temper was sufficiently even or his military knowledge sufficiently thorough to enable him to discharge properly the very difficult duties which will devolve upon him during the coming operations with the Allies on the Continent. In my own heart, I know that French is quite unfit for this great command at a time of crisis in our Nation's history. But I thought it sufficient to tell the King that I had 'doubts' about the selection.

He went further in his diary of 13 August:

[The] uneasy feeling which disturbs me springs, I think, from my knowledge of the personalities of which our high command is composed. I have already stated somewhat briefly my opinion of Sir John French's ability as Commander in the Field. His military ideas often shocked me when I was his Chief of Staff during the South African War . . . With all this knowledge of the Chief . . . behind me, I have grave reasons for being anxious about what happens to us in the great adventure upon which we are now going to start this very night. However, I am determined to behave as I did in the South African War, to be thoroughly loyal and to do my duty as a subordinate should, trying all the time to see Sir John's good qualities and not his weak ones.

It has to be remembered that many of the diary entries that relate to French were revised after the war as a result of the contents of *1914* and of Haig's falling out with French in 1915. Although he confided in his diary that 'His military ideas often shocked me when I was his Chief of Staff during the South African War', his reservations about his chief were not voiced or recorded during that war.

On the following day, 14 August, Haig and his staff were joined at the Dolphin Hotel in Folkestone by Henrietta and Willie Jameson, who had driven down from London with a case of champagne. Haig boarded the *Comrie Castle* and set off for France. His arrival was inglorious: he stuck in the lift on the way up to his hotel bedroom. As Commander of I Corps, Haig commanded two divisions, First Division under Major-General Lomax and Second Division under

Major-General Monro. II Corps was to have been commanded by
Grierson, Haig's adversary in the pre-war manoeuvres and a serious
rival in any contest for promotion, but the latter died on his way to
war and was replaced by Horace Smith-Dorrien.

The instructions that French received from Kitchener, on his
appointment as Secretary of State, were full of tensions and at times
almost contradictory. If French had been inclined to agonise over his
responsibilities, which he was not, he would not have been reassured
to be reminded that

> It must be recognised from the outset that the numerical
> strength of the British Force and its contingent reinforcement
> is strictly limited, and with this consideration kept steadily in
> mind it will be obvious that the greatest care must be exercised
> towards a minimum of losses and wastage.
>
> Therefore while every effort must be made to coincide most
> sympathetically with the plans and wishes of our Ally, the
> gravest consideration will devolve upon you as to participation
> in forward movements where large bodies of French troops are
> not engaged and where your Force may be unduly exposed to
> attack.
>
> Should a contingency of this sort be contemplated, I look to
> you to inform me fully and give me time to communicate to you
> any decision which His Majesty's Government may come to in
> this matter. In this connection I wish you distinctly to under-
> stand that your command is an entirely independent one, and
> that you will in no case come under the orders of any Allied
> General.

He was not to risk substantial losses. He was to obtain government
approval before taking significant independent action. He was to
react sympathetically to the plans and wishes of the French. He was
entirely independent of them. To make matters worse, the French did
not know what his instructions were. Indeed, they actually believed,
Joffre in particular, that French had been specifically instructed to act

on their orders, and when he periodically refused to do so, they concluded that his government was simply too weak to order him to do so.[8]

Towards the end of August French became increasingly concerned about the continued French retirement. He was out of sympathy with both Joffre and Lanrezac, and he wished to come out of the line and withdraw behind the Seine to refit. Joffre remonstrated, even President Poincaré implored him to remain in the line, and Kitchener decided to come out to France to put backbone into the Commander-in-Chief. In the military hierarchy, little things can matter a lot, and Kitchener appeared in his field-marshal's uniform. There was nothing particularly surprising about this: a field-marshal technically never retires from the army, and Hankey recorded that Kitchener 'lived in uniform at the time' – as indeed he did himself throughout the war. But he came not as a field-marshal, with the power to give orders, but as Secretary of State, and while a Secretary of State, with the support of his Cabinet colleagues, can appoint and dismiss Commanders-in-Chief, until they *are* dismissed they are sovereign in their command. French told Kitchener that while

I valued highly his advice and assistance, which I would gladly accept as such . . . I would not tolerate any interference with my executive command and authority so long as His Majesty's Government chose to retain me in my present position.[9]

At the end of the day Kitchener gave more than advice and assistance: he ordered French to remain on the line, and French accepted the order. He did so without good grace. He asked Churchill to '*stop this interference* with field operations. Kitchener *knows nothing* about European Warfare. Of course he is a fine organiser but he never was and never will be a commander in the field . . .'[10]

First Corps' initial contact with the enemy was at the beginning of the Great Retreat from Mons. Haig was wakened at 2 a.m. on the morning of 24 August to learn that the Germans were moving forward and threatening the British Army, which was no longer supported by the French to their right. Although he had been ordered to cover the retirement of II Corps to his left, Haig decided that this was impractical. First Corps had suffered only forty casualties, whereas Smith-Dorrien was engaged in a major action. Haig may have feared that the Germans were seeking to outflank the whole BEF. At any rate he ignored GHQ's order to support II Corps' retirement. He treated the order with derision: 'I Corps to cover retirement of II Corps! . . . This seemed impossible, as I was much further to east, and not being allowed to pass through Maubeuge had to make a flank march in face of the enemy!' Instead, he moved south, meaning to maintain contact with the French and achieve a regrouping of the BEF as a whole. That was all very well, but by abandoning Smith-Dorrien and II Corps he risked the destruction of the BEF as a fighting force. On the previous day Smith-Dorrien, heavily engaged with the Germans, had requested assistance: 'The battle is won, if you only send a battalion or two.' Haig was not as optimistic as Smith-Dorrien and only belatedly sent him three battalions. Now a staff officer was sent to Smith-Dorrien 'to co-ordinate the retreat'[11] and by dawn the retreat of the whole of I Corps was underway. In the course of the next eighteen hours Haig was continuously on the move, attempting to establish a secure line of retreat. By the evening of 24 August, Haig was with French at GHQ. In his account, he found French with 'no very clear plan on holding this wretched Bavai position . . . I pointed out to Sir John that if halted for a day at Bavai the whole force would be surrounded by superior numbers. He agreed and ordered the force to continue its retreat.'

Smith-Dorrien was left to his own initiative. At Mons on the previous day, French had announced: 'the BEF will give battle on the line of the Condé Canal'. Smith-Dorrien had asked, reasonably enough: 'Do you mean to take the offensive or stand on the defensive?' French consulted with his Chief of Staff, Sir Archibald Murray, and then replied: 'You do as you are ordered, and don't ask questions.' Now Haig, thinking that the enemy had inserted himself between him and II Corps, further distanced himself from the rest of the Expeditionary Force. When he heard that Haig had said that he was unable to reach Le Cateau, where Smith-Dorrien was, Wilson, disgusted, commented: 'He ought to be *made* to go on to Le Cateau.'[12] On the following day, the anniversary of Crécy, Wilson learned that Smith-Dorrien had come to the conclusion that he had no choice but to turn and fight the Germans at Le Cateau. Wilson could only communicate with Smith-Dorrien by making use of a telephone at the nearest railway station. Without waiting to put on his leggings, Wilson rushed off to the station, six inches of bare leg showing. He told Smith-Dorrien that if he stood and fought, there would be another Sédan. Smith-Dorrien replied that he had no choice. 'In any case, it's too late to break off now. The battle has begun. I can hear the guns firing as I am speaking.' Wilson's reply was typical: 'Then good luck to you. Yours is the first cheerful voice I've heard these three days.'

Smith-Dorrien's decision was probably the right one: at any rate, he won the battle of Le Cateau and for the second time held up the German Army. He did so by disobeying French's order, and the Commander-in-Chief was not pleased.[13] Haig never acknowledged that Smith-Dorrien had been right to fight at Le Cateau. Nor did he acknowledge that Smith-Dorrien could only have extricated himself by sacrificing one of his three divisions.[14] John Terraine attributes this to Haig's awareness that 'he was conscious of having fallen below his own standards.'[15] Others have gone further and have accused Haig of acting (or rather not acting) out of jealousy. That is far-fetched, but the episode was not the high point of Haig's war.

Haig established his headquarters at Landrecies, and here a German advance guard surrounded them. For once he lost his marmoreal imperturbability and displayed some symptoms of anxiety. He asked Smith-Dorrien for reinforcements, which the latter was unable to give him. He ordered the whole town to be organised for defence. Secret papers were to be destroyed. The evidence of his alleged 'panic' is scanty. Charteris says: 'For once he was quite jolted out of his usual placidity.' Edmonds claimed that Haig had 'lost his head'. Haig misread the gravity of the situation in which he found himself. He said that they would sell their lives dearly. If this is panic, it sounds fairly heroic panic. Terraine comments: 'It was not customary for Haig to use such dramatic language. This was one of the rare moments during the war, when he was caught "off balance", and the reason for it may quickly be discerned in his shaky physical condition'.[16] One of those present said that Haig's only sign of worry was that he stroked his moustache more than usual.

The fighting at this stage was fluid, as it was not later, and the fluidity engendered confusion. In fact, the situation was not as serious as it appeared. Perhaps Haig should have known that; one of his favourite observations was that in war things were never as good or as bad as first reports made them out to be. The Coldstream Guards, with whom Haig had billeted himself, rose to the occasion, and the German attack was repelled. As Haig and Charteris drove off their driver took a wrong turn and headed for enemy lines, where the car was challenged by German soldiers. Haig's war came close to being a very short one.

Haig left Landrecies with the fighting continuing, and his immediate and perhaps unduly pessimistic reports to GHQ were to the effect that the position of I Corps was 'very critical'. Soon he even asked for help from the beleaguered II Corps. French, already far from sanguine, responded by ordering I Corps to retreat. Smith-Dorrien was still expecting support from Haig, who was now to move not towards him, but away from him. Later in the day Haig did make an offer to support Smith-Dorrien, but no response was received. By that time II Corps were very much occupied in their heroic and successful fight.

If Haig was less in control at Landrecies than usual, the explanation may be simple. Two days earlier he had picked up a gastric infection and refused treatment. Eventually Charteris prevailed on him to see the Corps Medical Officer, Colonel Ryan. 'DH was at his worst, very rude, but eventually did see Ryan, who dosed him with what must have been something designed for elephants, as the result was immediate and volcanic! But it was effective, for DH ultimately got some sleep, and in the morning was better though very chewed up, and ghastly to look at. He wanted to ride as usual, but Ryan insisted on his going in a car that day.' In fact he was so weak that he had to be carried out of the house in the arms of his faithful batman, Secrett.[17] It was just a few hours later, at 4 p.m. on 25 August, that he reached Landrecies. By 26 August, Charteris describes Haig in much more typical form at a brigade headquarters:

> A good deal of shelling, but not many casualties. Shell-fire was rather nerve-wracking at first, but it is extraordinary how many miss. The Brigade Commander was very rattled and nervous, and DH was walking him up and down, holding his elbow and soothing him, just like a nurse with a nervous child. It was an interesting study in psychology. DH was showing no signs of his customary curtness at anybody who fell short of requirements . . . all this after a night without sleep, and heavy with great anxiety.

The Great Retreat lasted from 24 August to 5 September. The bearing of the troops in the course of a march of 200 miles was remarkable. They were never demoralised, nor was there any of the atmosphere of defeat. Lieutenant (later Major-General Sir Edward) Spears, who had seen the Belgians in retreat, was amazed by the confident and orderly bearing of I Corps. Haig was well aware of the strain on the troops: 'The men were daily becoming weaker from want of rest, and from not having sufficient time properly to prepare their food.' He took a practical step to lighten their load: 'the extreme measure' of reducing by half the ammunition carried by the column. More importantly, probably, he also took pains to be seen on the march, not in a car, but in the saddle. Charteris records: 'His headquarters moved at the rear of the main columns in close touch with the rear guards but each day he himself rode along the whole length of the line. His uniform was neat as in peace time; his face immobile; his horse fully groomed; and his presence gave confidence and strength to all who saw him.' Haig knew exactly what he was doing: at this time, confidence 'was more than I felt often, but I dared not show all that I knew and felt. It was the most anxious time. The

Regular Officers and indeed the Brigade and Divisional staffs knew very little, or did not understand how nearly surrounded we were.' Even John Gough complained in the course of the march, as Haig recalled a few months later, when Gough was killed:

> After dinner at Mareuil he in his impetuous way grumbled at my going on retreating and retreating. As a number of the Staff were present I turned on him rather sharply and said 'That retreat was the only thing to save the Army, and that it was his duty to support me instead of criticising' . . . He was very sorry, poor fellow.

The bearing of the men of I Corps was observed by a French officer, and contrasted with II Corps: 'The men of the I Corps were tired and suffering from the extreme heat, but they marched in perfect order. The regiments went by ceaselessly singing *Tipperary*'. Second Corps 'presented a striking contrast to the I Corps, the men looked harassed, there was some disorder and some units were intermingled. Nobody was singing'.[18]

The satisfactory way in which I Corps managed its retreat was not achieved by accident or even by Haig's behaviour during the retreat. Before the war he had noted with approval how the French trained for manoeuvre in retreat, and he had encouraged active preparation for such manoeuvres during his time at Aldershot.

In the course of the Retreat he had little support from GHQ, where morale was at a very low level. The Chief of Staff, Sir Archibald Murray, who had never fully recovered from a serious stomach wound he sustained in South Africa, fainted at his desk on hearing the news of Smith-Dorrien's predicament at Le Cateau. Wilson issued orders to I and II Corps to abandon their baggage and 'hustle along', orders which were either countermanded on receipt or destroyed before dispatch. Against this background, Haig asked for permission to assist the French General Lanrezac in his operations at St Quentin which were to form the Battle of Guise. Sir John French replied: 'Commander in Chief does not approve of any active operations on the part of our I Corps tomorrow and has already ordered a halt for one day's rest.' Haig asked if he could then support the French with artillery. French's reply was terse: 'The Commander in Chief repeats the order that no active operations of any arms except of a defensive nature will be undertaken tomorrow.' Early on the morning of 29 August, Haig received a follow-up from French: 'Please be good enough to inform C-in-C how it was that any confidential promise of support by I Corps was made to General Lanrezac or why any official exchange of ideas was initiated without authority from Headquarters.' Haig: 'I do not understand what you mean. I had initiated no "official exchange of ideas" . . . The extrication of this Corps from the false position in which it was placed still demands greatest exertion from us all, and my sole objective is to secure its retreat with honour to our arms. I therefore beg you will not give credit to such allegations as the one under reference without first ascertaining whether it is true or not'. Sharp words between the brother officers who had huddled together on the floor of the train from Ladysmith.

On the conclusion of the Great Retreat, Haig was anxious to see the army transfer its momentum into advance. He sought to curb the spirit of caution which had been engendered by the Retreat. His ability to sense the new climate, and to move on the offensive, was crucially demonstrated again in 1918. Peremptory written orders were issued for energetic action. 'And by repeated personal visits to the headquarters of subordinate formations, Haig inspired his corps anew with both spirit and method of offensive warfare.'[19]

Eventually I Corps took part in its first proper engagement: the Battle of the Aisne. The move to the Aisne had to be carried out in conditions of the utmost secrecy. Unfortunately, some despatches from journalists eluded the censor and appeared in England in advance of the move. The War Book prepared under the directions of Hankey provided for every conceivable eventuality during the war, including even this, and there was immediate simultaneous action on the part of all the censorship authorities, together with exercise of the *droit de prince*, under which all ships were prevented from leaving

British shores. This was the only time in the course of the war that this machinery was used.[20]

Haig had begun to move forward tentatively on 7 September, so tentatively that he can be criticised for the slowness of the advance. Haig was concerned by reports of a heavy German force to his front and wrongly thought that the French had suffered a significant reverse. He ordered a halt on 9 September, just a day after being ordered to continue his advance to the north. Again there was delay in advancing to the elevated Chemin des Dames a few days later. Haig's actions can be explained, but the failure to secure this ridge meant an end to the possibility of an Allied victory in open warfare. On the following day contact was made with the Germans. Haig himself was so far forward that he was within range of enemy machine-gunners and he and his party had to shelter behind tombstones in a churchyard. The advance continued until 13 September, when I Corps crossed the River Aisne and met the Germans in force on the edge of the Chemin des Dames Ridge. Surprisingly for a cavalryman, Haig did not ensure that there was adequate or perhaps any reconnaissance in the front of I Corps on the night of 13–14 September. 'As a result of this the advance guards of both divisions were forced to deploy on the morning of 14th in the confusion of surprise, from cramped valleys.'[21] Neither side was able to turn the flank of the other, and the consequence was the sort of stalemate that was to characterise the Western Front for the rest of the war. The battle of the Aisne was marked by Haig's use of aeroplanes to direct fire. He also made use of a partially destroyed aqueduct to move his guns to the north, so that I Corps alone was able to push through. This was Haig's first command of a substantial body of troops in action.

In the course of the fluid fighting that had prevailed until now, the BEF had been dislodged from the sector of the line it was intended to occupy. On 30 September French asked Joffre for his agreement that the Expeditionary Force should move to the French left, based on the Channel ports. Haig liked the idea but had difficulty in seeing that it would be easy to withdraw, when he was in such close touch with the enemy. Joffre agreed, and when the manoeuvre went ahead it did not do so without difficulties: it was associated with an attempt, which proved unsuccessful, to relieve Antwerp, under siege by the Germans. A British Naval Division which was disembarked at Dunkirk for this purpose had to withdraw to the Ypres sector.

Almost as soon as he arrived in France, Haig began the practice that was to continue through the war, and sent copies of his diary to Lady Haig. The diary was in the form of a duplicating notebook, and a carbon copy went off, generally each day, by King's Messenger. Lady Haig was utterly discreet, in the sense that the content of the diaries was never communicated unintentionally. Frequently, however, Haig authorised her to pass on the content to a specific recipient. Writing to Lady Haig on 19 September 1914, Haig told her that although his diaries were otherwise strictly private, they might be shown to Lord Stamfordham for the King. A few weeks later Lady Haig was approached by Clive Wigram, Stamfordham's assistant, suggesting that the diaries should in future go direct to Buckingham Palace and would then be passed on to her. She wrote to Haig, 'and a very forceable reply came back at once, saying that he had arranged to send dictated reports to His Majesty but, as regards the diaries, they were written for me alone and he intended to continue to write them for me.'[22] It is interesting that Wigram knew that copies of the diaries were reaching London.

Lady Haig had other concerns at this time. 'We were warned officially that the water might be poisoned and that in our households we should only use aerated or bottled water. Curiously enough, I noticed at the Queen's Hotel the same waiter who had copied Douglas's map when we first went to Aldershot. As this waiter was constantly talking to soldiers, I thought it my duty to report the matter to General Hamilton Gordon, who had succeeded my husband at Aldershot, and he immediately had the man interned.'[23]

The responsibility for the planning of the First Battle of Ypres was French's, not Haig's, and this is not the place for a detailed account of those aspects of the conflict with which Haig was not concerned. On his way from the Aisne to Ypres, Haig visited Sir John French's headquarters at St Omer. He was struck by the plight of the refugees and 'gave them two doz. "Oxo" soup squares for which they seemed most grateful.' He also met Sir Henry Rawlinson, now in command of IV Corps. Rawlinson, who was a close friend of Wilson, was, like his friend, regarded by Haig as being a little foxy. Charteris reported that Rawlinson 'was flying an enormous Union Jack on his car, and DH's first remark was rather caustic – "I thought only the King and the C in C are permitted to fly the Union Jack." Rawlinson's reply was that it helped to encourage the inhabitants. I shall be interested to see whether he is still flying it when we see him again!' Haig's interfering officiousness must have grated. Military life sometimes encourages a perpetuation of the schoolboy's love of hierarchy.

French was now in an optimistic phase. He underrated the strength of German defences and on 19 October ordered Haig to advance from the Ypres sector to capture Bruges and Ghent. Haig had a better appreciation of the situation on the ground. On 22 October he ordered his Corps 'to prepare for the attacks which there could be little doubt would be made upon us . . . From yesterday's operations I have come to the conclusion that the enemy was in considerably greater strength than had been anticipated by Sir John French when he gave me my instructions at St. Omer.' In addition to being on the spot, Haig had his own Intelligence Section. He had become unhappy with the quality of intelligence that he had received from GHQ during the Battle of the Aisne, and put Charteris in charge of a new section of his own. Charteris's intellectual ability was often transmuted into intellectual arrogance. He was opinionated, and also in sufficient awe of Haig to withhold bad news and possibly from time to time to manufacture good news. These fatal qualities were not immediately evident, and for the moment, in his advanced headquarters at Hooge Château to the east of Ypres, Charteris preened himself: 'we actually know more about what is happening on our own front than GHQ does . . . There is . . . an accommodating German Corps Commander who sends out constant messages and orders to his units by wireless, without coding them. I suppose he thinks we do not know any German! . . . I'll give him a drink if I ever see him when the war is over.'

Throughout the Retreat, Johnnie French had displayed a dismaying lack of consistent leadership. He was as brave as any soldier could be, but as was said by Fortescue, he and his staff simply lost their heads. Precipitate and excessive reaction to events was what caused him to threaten to pull out of the line, and it meant that he did not effectively control and coordinate events at Mons and Le Cateau. It was Haig who provided leadership in the Retreat, and Robertson who was responsible for the practical planning, laying out supplies of foodstuff and fodder on the route of the march. The same lack of steadiness was evident at Ypres, and led the French to believe then, as they have continued to do, that the British Commander-in-Chief had framed an order for a retreat to the west of the town. Almost certainly he did not, but he vacillated. Joffre dealt with him bluntly, Foch more subtly: 'You have only to tell him that he has just saved England; that will put him in all his good humour again.'

First Ypres did not therefore assist French's long-term prospects, but it was a good battle for Haig. In what is known as the third phase of the battle, a huge German attack by a new army under General von Fabeck fell mainly on Haig's Corps and Allenby's Cavalry. The German Order of the Day of 29 October expresses the spirit of the attack: 'The breakthrough will be of decisive importance. We must and will conquer; settle forever with the centuries-long struggle, end the war, and strike the decisive blow against our detested enemy. We will finish with the British, Indians, Canadians, Moroccans and other trash, feeble adversaries, who surrender in great numbers if they are attacked with vigour.'

The importance the Germans attached to their attack is reflected in the fact that the Kaiser himself arrived on 31 October. By this stage, in the words of the Official Historian:

The line that stood between the British Empire and ruin was composed of tired, haggard and unshaven men, unwashed, plastered with mud, many in little more than rags. But they had their guns, rifles and bayonets, and, at any rate, plenty of rifle ammunition, whilst the artillerymen always managed to have rounds available at the right place at critical moments.

In reality, a shortage of artillery ammunition had already been reported by French to London. He was told to economise. The first German attack captured Messines (though it was later retaken by the London Scottish, the first Territorial Battalion to take part in the battle). Haig's line across the Menin Road was vulnerable and Gheluvelt, at the centre of the road, was threatened by the second attack. In the chaos of war and the absence of effective communications, rumours came back to Haig first that the line was holding and then that it had broken. British artillery was pulling back and German shells were moving forward. There was a stream of wounded soldiers returning from Gheluvelt.

Haig recognised the responsibilities that weighed on his divisional commanders. He had found Lomax squashed into a two-roomed cottage, and he moved him and Monro into his own headquarters at Hooge Château while he himself moved his headquarters to Hellfire Corner. There, at 12.45 p.m. on 31 October, in the face of the German onslaught, Lomax, commanding 1st Division, had to tell Monro, commanding 2nd Division, 'My line is broken.' Thirty minutes later the news got even worse.

At his advanced headquarters at Hellfire Corner, White Château, Haig received the news that not only had the 1st Division's line been broken, but also that Hooge Château had been hit by four large shells: General Lomax was mortally wounded, General Monro stunned, and seven of the staff officers of the two divisions had been killed. Though Haig's motives for establishing both commanders in one HQ had been for the best, his judgement in bringing two divisional commanders together had clearly been questionable.

Haig's reaction to the stress of these events showed him at his best. Almost all the commanders, however resolute, and from Joffre down, were rattled when they first experienced the realities of this new, industrial war. Even many of Haig's most uncritical supporters for some reason feel constrained to say that at Landrecies he had underperformed but now at any rate he was invincibly resolute. Rather than take the easy route of telling the broken forces to hold firm and hoping that all would be well, he ordered a controlled retirement to the shallow trenches of the first of a series of prepared fall-back lines.

This dangerous manoeuvre was mistaken by some of the French for the implementation of Johnnie French's general withdrawal. More importantly for Haig's reputation, it was the subject, after the war, of one of Edmonds' malicious, irresponsible and fallacious communications that are unsupported by evidence or anything that he wrote in the Official History. In 1931 he told Liddell Hart that the official account concealed

> the way the French learnt definitely of Haig's order to retire . . . Haig was actually suffering a 'scare' similar to that of Landrecies. He had drawn up orders for a general retirement to the line of the ramparts and canal at Ypres. (This was recalled under persuasion of one of his staff before it reached its recipients and the copies of it were afterwards destroyed.)[24]

Edmonds' story has been demonstrated convincingly by John Hussey[25] not only to be unsupported by evidence, but to be at odds with what evidence is available.

Now French appeared. He had driven from Ypres in the face of traffic hastening in the other direction. 'It was a regular débacle. The heavy field guns were trotting. When a heavy field gun trots you may be sure things are pretty bad.' He had to abandon his car and make his way to Haig's headquarters on foot. 'They have broken us right in and are pouring through the gap,' Haig told him. A fall-back position had been selected, but the chances of reaching it in order were low. French had no reinforcements to offer Haig. Haig was 'very white but quite calm.'[26] 'Sir John was full of sympathy and expressed his gratitude for what the Corps, as well as I myself, had done since we landed in France. No one could have been nicer at such time of crisis but he had no reinforcements to send me, and viewed the situation with the utmost gravity.' Muttering about the lack of 'French help', Sir John went off to visit Foch. Haig remounted and was about to go back to the Front when the news came that

Gheluvelt had been retaken and the line re-established. 'Can you imagine what that felt like?' said Charteris, 'It was just as if we had all been under sentence of death and most suddenly received a free pardon . . . Everyone else was as excited as I was, except DH who pulled at his moustache and said "he hoped that it was not another false report".' It was not. A counter-attack by the Worcesters had succeeded. An ADC caught up with the Commander-in-Chief's car and gave him the news. 'The Worcesters have saved the Empire,' said French.[27] Haig was more cautious. It was in these circumstances that he mounted his charger and in the words of the Official History was to be seen, 'moving up the road at a slow trot with part of his staff behind him as at an inspection, doing much to restore confidence.' Charteris was on the spot: '[W]ith his personal staff and escort, he rode slowly up the Menin Road, through the stragglers, back into the shelled area, his face immobile and inscrutable – saying no word, yet by his presence and his calm restoring hope to the disheartened and strength to the exhausted troops.'[26] The heroic image of this ride became one of the few celebrated cameos of Haig to emerge from the war. It is doubtful whether he saw more than confusion around him, but he certainly put heart into his troops.

There followed a slightly quieter period – 'quieter' only relatively. Activity continued on both sides and in particular the German artillery bombardment of Ypres was stepped up. Haig himself had a narrow escape when he was looking at a map under a glass candelabrum. A shell hit the house and the candelabrum fell, narrowly missing his head. Charteris reported that 'a couple of signallers were killed at HQ at the same time. He was quite unperturbed – and we prevailed on him to change his HQ, as once the German artillery had got range of the château it was certain to be struck again.'

Foch was in optimistic mood and French was always easily infected by Foch's confidence. Haig was irritated that French (and Foch) did not appreciate how worn down by battle his troops were. On 9 October a meeting took place between Foch, French and Haig. Charteris says that there was a good deal of straight talk. DH was very emphatic that the French custom of very high-placed officers issuing energetic orders and leaving it at that, without themselves taking active steps to see that they were carried out, was useless . . . He urged that they must go forward and take a personal grip of things. Our own GHQ is not very much better. Sir J. French himself goes round Divisional Headquarters, but very few of the Staff Officers ever seem to come as far forward even as Corps HQ. DH himself errs, I think in the other extreme. He is constantly in extreme danger of being hit; he goes everywhere on horseback. I do not know what would happen if he were knocked out.

Typically, Haig was taking more risks than he should have done, particularly if he recalled the fate of Generals Lomax and Monro.

By the end of November, the battle had come to an end. It had been indecisive in the sense that neither side had broken through, but it was full of lessons. The Official History says that

The old British Army was gone past recall, leaving but a remnant to carry on the training of the New Armies. The allies had held their line against the German attacks by the superior shooting by the French 75s, and by the British both with gun and rifle; the skill in the use of ground, the employment of cavalry as a mobile reserve; and the bold and skilful use in counter attack of small reserves drawn, as a rule, from parts of the line that General Haig and other leaders judged might be thinned for the benefit of more vital sectors.

It was at Gheluvelt that the British musketry, sixteen rounds per minute, sometimes up to thirty a minute, was mistaken by the Germans for machine-gun fire.

The price that the army paid for its achievement was enormous. Charteris wrote on 16 November:

It is the saddest thing in the world to see the remnants of the units as they come back – just a skeleton, the men unshaven, haggard, worn out and plastered with the accumulated mud of the trenches. But there is pride mixed with sadness. I do not believe any other troops in the world could have done what our men have done.[29]

First Ypres had been a critical battle in the history of the war. It was the first time that elements that were to characterise the subsequent period of the conflict came together. Perforce there had been a commingling of British, Belgian and French units, and an essential and difficult cooperation between the British and French commands, in which Haig had taken a key role. Losses, and losses of high-quality troops, had been suffered on a terrible scale. Haig had learned much. If Ypres had been lost, the forward Channel ports would have gone or been at risk. Supply routes would have been extended and the Channel approaches exposed. Falkenhayn had not however persisted after the 31 October setback, when Haig had proved equal to resisting his onslaught. With an enhanced reputation for his active command at Ypres, Haig took away the lesson that in future there was a need for massed machine-gun batteries and much more high explosive.[30] He had also seen that Johnnie French was almost an irrelevance and that at times his inconsistency could make him a positive nuisance.

On 20 November Haig was promoted to full General and took five days' leave in England, where he met the King, who was 'most complimentary'. He and Lady Haig had lunch with the elderly Empress Eugénie and after the meal he inspected an officers' hospital which Lady Haig was running. They spent his last afternoon with the children at the zoo. 'The houses were locked up before they came away, so that they did not see the monkey house, a great disappointment to both Xandra and Doria, but they saw every other kind of animal very well and fed them.'

Disputed Appointments. Neuve Chapelle

If a bullet had pierced that immaculately pressed tunic as he moved up the Menin Road at a slow trot, Haig would have died a quintessential British hero, in the line of Nelson and Gordon. At that stage his career recorded no fault. His slow start would have been forgotten, his performance in the Sudan and South Africa would have been remembered for its gallantry, he would have been seen as a great reforming officer and a future commander, his loss to his country incalculable.

His war, as 1914 drew to a close, had been a good one. First Corps had been spared the mauling that Smith-Dorrien's II Corps had suffered at Le Cateau, and, at a personal level, Haig had escaped the controversy which surrounded Smith-Dorrien. His leadership in the Great Retreat from Mons had been inspiring. He may or may not have been rattled after his experience at Landrecies, but, if so, the consequences had been insignificant. He had been warmly congratulated by French for his contribution at Ypres.

Tensions had emerged in his relationship with his old chief, but the latter's stock was not so high as it had been at the beginning of the war. His authority had been undermined by excesses of both optimism and pessimism, and the quality of the intelligence on which he based his decisions was questionable. Grierson, Haig's victor in Red Force against Blue Force, and a serious contender for the succession if French were to be removed, had died in the first days of the war, and Smith-Dorrien's survival as a rival was in doubt.

On Boxing Day 1914 there was an extensive reorganisation of the military machine and Haig was placed in command of First Army, which now consisted of I Corps, IV Corps and Indian Corps. Smith-Dorrien commanded Second Army consisting of II, III and V Corps.

Before he went to London Haig found French in apparently poor physical health. He 'had had a severe attack of heart, and doctors had ordered him to take things more easily.' On his return, when he found French looking better, Haig took the opportunity of expressing his lack of confidence about the GHQ staff. French said that he had asked Kitchener to replace Murray, the CGS, with Wilson. Murray had been in a difficult position every since his collapse during the retreat from Mons. His confidence suffered and he found it difficult to deal with subordinates who had witnessed the incident. In the past he had been a calm, equable staff officer (although Haig described him as 'an old woman'), but now he was difficult to work with and the atmosphere around him was uncomfortable. He discussed resignation with his colleagues, and it was clear that if he did resign, Wilson was the likely successor. Haig had earlier been a critic of Murray, but his suspicion of Wilson was a stronger emotion, and his reaction now was that Wilson 'has been intriguing to get poor Murray withdrawn', and he proposed William Robertson, QMG, rather than Wilson, who 'had no military knowledge'. Charteris, 19 December 1914:

> DH told me yesterday that the C-in-C had informed him that he had sent a Staff Officer to London to arrange for Wilson to become CGS in succession to Murray, whose health had broken down. French asked DH's view and got it straight – that Wilson was always to the neck in intrigue, and so far, seemed always to have subordinated the interests of the British Army to those of the French Army. DH said he had suggested *Robertson* (now Q.M.G.) to succeed Murray; he said that the whole Army had complete confidence in Robertson. By the 'whole Army' he meant, of course, the commanders, for few of the regimental

officers neither know or care who is CGS. I am still quite sure
that K. will never agree to Wilson.[1]

For his part, French would have liked Haig as his Chief of Staff, but
the latter would not give up his command to take that post. In the
meantime Murray went on leave and Wilson briefly took his place as
Acting Chief of Staff. The atmosphere at Headquarters was markedly
better during Murray's absence. Wilson's role as a successor was
confirmed by French. Far from intriguing, Wilson repeatedly encouraged French to look at the whole field before making an
appointment, to 'take his Army List, and pick the best man he
could find and put him in as Chief of Staff.'

But the succession was not quite as simple as it seemed. French
returned to England to find Asquith against Wilson because of the
Curragh incident and Kitchener against him because the appointment would alienate Wilson's opponents in the army. French gave
way in the face of the combined opposition of the Prime Minister and
the Secretary of State, though later, after the war, he apologised to
Wilson for not resigning over the incident, 'and the two old friends,
who had never let the incident cloud their relationship for more than
a few hours, clasped hands without another word.'[2]

Wilson's case was taken up at this stage by the French, for whom
'Général Dooble-Vay' was a very special person. The French government threatened to take the matter up through diplomatic channels.
Wilson said that he did not want to be the subject of an international
incident but Colonel Repington reported to Haig that Wilson had
been intriguing with the French government to get himself made
Chief of Staff. Haig believed the story and reported it to Charteris,
although in fact the French approach to the British Ambassador had
been made before the meeting at Chantilly at which Wilson was
supposed to have made his pitch.

French encouraged Wilson to make one last try: 'You are such a
brute, you will never be polite to people you don't like. Now, I am
going to get Asquith out here. Why don't you make love to him?'[3]
But Asquith took his time coming out and before then Robertson

had been appointed as Haig had wished. The incident confirmed
Haig in his prejudice that Wilson was an ambitious intriguer. When
Asquith did eventually arrive, by which time Wilson had declined a
proffered knighthood, the Prime Minister remarked to French at
dinner, with surprisingly little social grace, that 'it is a curious thing,
Field Marshal, that this war has produced no great generals.' Wilson
quickly replied, 'No, Prime Minister, nor has it produced a statesman.'

At Christmas Leopold Rothschild had sent out fur-lined gloves
and 1820 brandy for Haig and his staff. Lady Haig sent presents for
all the staff and servants. Haig and his entourage

> spent a cheery evening in spite of the uncertainty of the future.
> Doris's Xmas presents had reminded us that my Corps Staff was
> 'a family party' and had greatly touched us all at this high
> season. I felt truly thankful to the Higher Power for having been
> permitted to command the I Corps during the whole period of
> the past four critical months of the war, and to have done so
> with conspicuous success.

Following these changes, Haig reorganised his own staff, appointing
John Gough as his Chief of Staff and Charteris as Army Intelligence
Officer. Haig's systems were described by General Butler:

> D.H. always visited some corps, divisions or brigade HQ every
> day whether a battle was in progress or not . . . As regards to the
> First Army Staff it was our rule that
> (a) every staff officer had to go out once every day (or night) and
>   visit some unit, and
> (b) every portion of the front held by the army had to be visited
>   at least once every day.[4]

Critics of the command in the First World War frequently assert that
Haig, and his staff, knew little of what was going on in the front line
and were comfortably sheltered from danger in luxurious châteaux,

far behind the front. It is irresponsible for a Commander-in-Chief to put himself in a position where he may unnecessarily be killed, but it has already been noted that Haig, if anything, took far too many risks with his personal safety. Equally, the systems in place ensured that staff officers were closely in touch with battlefield conditions. Staff officers have work to do which can only be done in offices behind the front, but the procedures that General Butler describes ensured that they were very closely in touch with what was going on.

Haig told Charteris on 11 February that Gough, Haig's Chief of Staff, was to be promoted and get a division at home. Gough had often said to Haig 'that we were wasted together as I did not need the help of a Staff Officer such as he, while he could well be doing more necessary work by keeping some feeble general straight', but Haig very much valued his advice and his friendship. 'In many ways DH is his own Chief of Staff. He knows so much more about fighting than any of the Staff, and he goes round the divisions and brigades so constantly that his Chief of Staff has little to do, except to see that things go smoothly.'[5] Charteris' remark is interesting in two ways: it again emphasises just how close Haig, as an army commander, was to forward units. Secondly, he points out how much of Haig's time was taken up with matters that were arguably staff responsibilities. He sees Haig's practice as meritorious but there could be another view. Later, when Haig became Commander-in-Chief, in charge of a huge army on a scale unimagined in peacetime, of which the fighting troops were only one component, there was no staff machine to organise the vast array of administrative and commissariat and logistical requirements. Haig necessarily took control of this process, and did so very well, but it was a function which should not have been left to the commander of the fighting forces.

Very soon after these appointments Gough was hit by a sniper. After a lunch with his old regiment he inspected a company in line, and he attracted an opportunistic shot as he walked away. He died shortly afterwards. Haig was more affected by this casualty than any other single death in the course of the war. Lady Haig wrote, 'Douglas was dreadfully upset over the death of General Gough.

He told me of his anxiety when Gough was being operated upon in an attempt to save his life, and how his poor wife arrived just in time to get the news of his death.' Gough had been with Haig since the beginning of the war and in addition to being a calm and efficient staff officer he formed a close friendship with Haig. He had been ready to decline the command of his New Army division in order to remain with Haig. Much as Haig disliked losing his personal staff he did not stand in the way of Gough's promotion. Now, according to Charteris, 'for almost the only time in the war he allowed a personal incident to interfere with the normal routine of his work.' A staff officer was sent to bring Gough back from the front line trenches to the operating theatre, and the Chief Surgeon of the Army, Sir Berkeley Moynihan, was ordered to await him there and try to save Gough's life by an operation. 'In spite of all that human care and skill could do Gough died early the following morning.'[6] Haig's heart was not worn on his sleeve, and the words in his diary are measured and controlled, but it is not difficult to look below the surface and discern the emotion below. His promotion of John Gough's brother, Hubert (Eton and Sandhurst, the youngest of the army commanders, arrogant and disliked), and his later defence of him in the face of great criticism is thought by some to have been due to his affection for John.

Already, in 1915, frustrations were being generated by a war which no one could control. From the Western Front, French was complaining to the press that he did not have the resources to enable him to deliver a victory. At home, the very possibility of victory on the Western Front was being called into question. Churchill was urging the Dardanelles Expedition, Lloyd George was arguing for the removal of most of the Expeditionary Force to another theatre of war, Lord Fisher was speaking of transferring part of the army to the Baltic, there was talk of coordinated action with the Greek and Bulgarian armies in Turkey. Even Kitchener was starting to refer to the German lines as a sort of fortress which would never be carried. The French were considering operations in the Balkans. But Haig stood firm: 'We ought not to divide our Military Force, but concentrate on the decisive point which is on this front against the main German Army.' He had concluded that victory depended almost entirely on possession of adequate supplies of high explosive.

The 'battles' of the First World War are the names given to the different phases of the fighting that continued from 1914 to 1918. The start of these offensives is usually clear enough. When each finished is more difficult to say: usually the intensity of an offensive reduced before the commander 'closed down' the battle, and, conversely, activity would continue even after that date. There was always fighting going on somewhere on the Front, and the division of this constant activity into 'battles' is, in terms of both time and geography, arbitrary and sometimes misleading. But in the case of the great offensives the names are appropriate, and even in other cases nomenclature does facilitate an analysis of events. In 1915 the battles in which Haig was involved were Neuve Chapelle, Aubers Ridge, Festubert and Loos.

The initial plan for early 1915 was to move the British element to the coast and there operate in conjunction with the navy. At this stage, Haig's plans incorporated 'an unlimited amount' of high explosive. On the face of it, Haig, contrary to what some of his critics say, appears to have embraced the significance of modern artillery. In reality, at this stage in the war but not later, it was the effect of the weapon on morale that appealed to him.[7]

Joffre was not anxious to see the British withdrawing from a central role in defending the line. The report that the Germans were withdrawing troops to the Eastern Front reassured French that the war would be over before June, when the New Armies would take the field and he satisfied Joffre by agreeing on a joint action which would knock the Germans out. It was to consist of a main Franco-British attack in Champagne and Artois, with a subsidiary British attack at La Bassée. Haig was told to prepare for an attack near Neuve Chapelle, initially on 15 February, but subsequently postponed, and the coastal attack was abandoned.

As so often, the battle that was fought was not the battle that had originally been planned. On French's orders, Haig prepared for an attack designed to capture Aubers Ridge, which lay about sixty feet higher than the British trenches, The attack involved capturing the heavily defended village of Neuve Chapelle and its associated woodland, and was to be simultaneous with but independent of the French operations. While he was formulating his plans, Haig learned that there was to be a French attack under General Maud'huy on his right. Next he learned that this attack was dependent on his taking over trenches from the French. Haig thought that he lacked sufficient troops both to relieve the French and to proceed with his own attack, and for a time it looked as if the plan would be abandoned. In the event, Haig and French reverted to the original plan of an independent British assault, essentially designed to improve the line. The battle was the first pre-planned formal operation (of a sort that was to occur from now on), and was not an encounter battle like those that had marked the early days of the war.

The Battle of Neuve Chapelle, with its attack on Aubers Ridge, began on 10 March. On tactics Haig clashed with Rawlinson, IV Corps Commander, who had dragged his feet at the planning stage, attempting to delegate responsibility to his divisional commanders. The latter wanted to attack incrementally, nibbling away over a series of days. Similarly, Haig's Artillery Commander wanted a compartmentalised bombardment over four days. In both cases they were overruled by Haig who wished to 'compress the fire into a sudden outburst for three hours – and follow it with a sudden rush of our infantry.' He was still thinking in terms of *arme blanche* fighting. Rawlinson's preference was for just thirty minutes. In the event, and after a conference on 5 March, the decision was for a wire-cutting bombardment of ten minutes, then thirty-five minutes directed on the German trenches, followed by a 'barrage' in its real sense of a barrier, to hold German reinforcements away from Neuve Chapelle. Finally, twenty-five minutes on Neuve Chapelle itself. His élan broke through. He thought it 'desirable', as he explained to Rawlinson, 'to make our plan in the chance of surprising the enemy and with the definite objective of advancing rapidly (and without any check) in the hope of starting a *general advance.*'

The exchanges between Haig and Rawlinson are interesting: Rawlinson had a blinkered, limited view of what the whole battle was about, restricting himself to planning, when he got round to it, for the capture of the village. Haig urged on him the necessity of thinking in wider terms:

> The advance to be made is not a minor operation. It must be understood that we are embarking on a serious offensive movement with the object of breaking the German line and consequently our advance is to be pushed vigorously . . .
>
> The idea is not to capture a trench here, or a trench there, but to carry the operation right through; in a sense surprise the Germans, carry them right off their legs, push forward to the Aubers . . . Ridge with as little delay as possible, and exploit the success thus gained by pushing forward mounted troops forthwith.

The tactics he was urging were still those of the early stages of the war.

It was just four days before the start of the battle that Rawlinson responded by asking his divisional commanders to look at the possibility of an advance beyond Neuve Chapelle.

The battle was not a success. The brief barrage did ensure that there was a very real element of surprise; and the British forces were double those of the defenders. The Indian Corps, if not the British, cut the wire in their front. So at the end of the first day, the situation looked hopeful. But by the following day the Germans had reinforced Aubers Ridge and were even able to counter-attack. After a few more days the battle was called off. The ammunition used at Neuve Chapelle exceeded that expended in the two and a half years in South Africa; but had given out after two days.

The hurricane bombardment had not been effective against distant objects. The lesson that was taken out of this was that a much heavier bombardment was required. But, as so often in the early part of the war, the process of reacting to events led into a blind alley, in this case the aim of wholesale destruction as opposed to the neutralisation of targets. In the course of the battle Rawlinson had made repeated and hopeless attacks against the strong German defence, which failed because of the lack of associated bombardment. He drew out of the experience at Neuve Chapelle a confidence in the capacity of conventional artillery which was to prove dangerously false on the Somme:

> The lessons we have learned at Neuve Chapelle are . . . that it is always possible by careful preparation and adequate Arty support by heavy Howitzers to pierce the enemy's line provided always that his wire entanglements can be cut by the fire of our field guns, and it can always be so cut if it is visible and not protected by earth works.[8]

The repercussions involved some bitter recriminations between Rawlinson, Haig and French. Rawlinson commented on the battle as follows:

> I think DH would have been better advised to content himself with the capture of the village instead of going on with the attack on the 11th, 12th and 13th for the purpose of trying to get the cavalry through. I advised him to do this in the first instance but he and Sir John were so obsessed with the cavalry idea that he would not listen. Had he been content with the village we should have gained just as much ground and reduced our casualties by three quarters.[9]

Rawlinson recognised that while the enemy's line could be broken, there was no prospect of an effective breakthrough by infantry or cavalry. He fell back therefore on the doctrine of 'bite and hold' which he set out in a letter to Wigram on 25 March:

> What we want to do now is what I call, 'bite and hold'. Bite off a piece of the enemy's line, like Neuve Chapelle, and hold it

against counter attack. The bite can be made without much loss, and, if we choose the right place and make every preparation to put it quickly into a state of defence there ought to be no difficulty in holding it against the enemy's counter attacks and inflicting on him at least twice the loss that we suffered in making the bite.[10]

He qualified his doctrine in two important respects: the army did not yet have enough artillery ammunition to apply the doctrine, and it did not 'result in any decisive victory which could affect the final issue of the war & it only very slowly forces the enemy's line back towards their own frontiers.'[11] It was predicated on a long, 'wearing-down' process. The doctrine was unimaginative, as was the implication that it was for the most part the only sensible way of making war on the Western Front. It was, however, an important insight, but one which Haig, with his hopes of more dramatic action, never wholly shared. It would be some time before Haig accepted 'bite and hold' if he ever truly did. This may or may not be to his credit, but it does not sit comfortably with the view of him as an attritional commander. A year later, as preparations were made for the Battle of the Somme, Rawlinson's plans for an attritional, bite-and-hold campaign were replaced by distant objectives and an engagement of manoeuvre.

The lesson that French took from the battle he conveyed to the War Office:

I have the honour to state that our experience at Neuve Chapelle and again this week and that of the French near Arras show clearly that it is possible to break through the enemy's defences, provided sufficient artillery ammunition of the proper nature is available and sufficient troops are resolutely employed.[12]

An investigation into the battle suggested that the British Forces had not pushed forward quickly enough, and when Haig asked Rawlinson why, he was told that Joey Davies, Commander, 8th Division, had been dilatory in advancing. When Haig then asked French to recall Davies, the latter said that he had been acting on Rawlinson's orders. Rawlinson admitted that this was the case. For his bad judgement compounded by a lack of candour French would have dismissed him, had not Haig pleaded that he had 'many other valuable qualities for a commander in active service', and that his punishment should be limited to a reprimand. Rawlinson was confident that Haig would be fair to him ('I know I shall get justice from DH'), and he was, but the incident was critical. Ever afterwards Rawlinson was acutely conscious that his continued employment (something that mattered greatly to him) depended entirely on Haig's goodwill. The consequence was that he was dangerously loath to express disagreement with Haig's views. On the Somme, for instance, he managed to persuade Haig to abandon the planned hurricane bombardment, but did not risk telling him that he had insufficient guns. He went on to agree with Haig that what shells were available should cover several lines of German defence rather than being limited to the primary target.

Rawlinson was an enthusiastic correspondent, and following the battle had been in touch with, amongst others, Wigram, for the King's ear, and Kitchener. In the course of the discussion about his 'unfair' treatment of Davies, he protested to Kitchener:

> If we had not tried to do too much our losses would have been one quarter what they were & we should have gained just as much ground but the idea of pushing through the Cav[alr]y which has just been seized hold of by our leaders, all Cavy Officers, was the origin of our heavy losses.[13]

In the battle, the British had advanced 1,000 metres at a cost of 12,000 men. 'So many good fellows no more; but it can't be done without incurring loss,' said Haig. Rawlinson thought that Haig 'looked for too much – he expects to get the cavalry through with the next push but I very much doubt he will succeed in doing more than lose a large number of gallant men without effecting any very great purpose. I should be content with capturing another piece out of the

enemy's line of trenches and waiting for the counter attack'.[14]
Slightly strangely, French regarded the battle as a success. He
congratulated Haig, but then he went on to order Haig to rewrite
his report of the battle so that, said Haig, it 'reads as if the action
taken was on the orders of the GHQ!' The words at the beginning of
the report, 'General Officer commanding the I Army' were to be
replaced by the words 'Commander-in-Chief.'

> The whole thing is so childish, that I could scarcely have
> credited the truth of the story had I not seen the paper. The
> main thing, however, is to beat the Germans *soon*, and leave to
> the British public the task of awarding credit for work done
> after peace had been made.

The following day, French thought that he would put matters right
by telling Haig that he had been recommended for a GCB. Haig was
not to be tempted off the high ground: 'I told Sir John that my one
thought was to finish the war as soon as possible, that the decorations
did not enter into my mind, all I wanted was responsible work;
decorations always come to people along with old age.' For Haig, one
of the lessons of Neuve Chapelle was what could be done with
adequate artillery. 'I think the main lesson of Neuve Chapelle is that
given sufficient ammunition and suitable guns we can break through
the enemy's line whenever we like!'[15] But the inference that the
heavier the bombardment the better, pointed again towards obstruction rather than neutralisation.[16] The lesson he learnt was also
flawed, in that the wire at Neuve Chapelle on the British front
had *not* been cut, although Rawlinson allowed him to think it had
been, rather than inviting opprobrium by reporting that it had not.

Haig was not the only person who was to be frustrated by the lack
of artillery ammunition, but he expressed his annoyance with
characteristic vehemence:

> In my opinion, given sufficient High Explosive gun ammuni-
> tion we could drive the Germans out of France in six weeks.

> Instead of having 30 rounds per day per gun and Howitzer, we
> only have 7. It is a disgraceful state of affairs to be in this
> situation after over 7 months of War. How can we order Officers
> Commanding Corps to 'press on with vigour' and at the same
> time say 'mind you must not expend more than 7 rounds a gun
> in a whole day!'

Later Haig became convinced that the problem was simply that
industrial workers were taking too many holidays, or drinking too
much.

> I don't suppose it would be possible to make such people sober
> by any regulations. The best thing, in my opinion, is to punish
> them with the chief offenders . . . Take and shoot two or three
> of them, and the 'Drink habit' would cease I feel sure. These
> sub-people don't care what the King or anyone else does – they
> mean to have their drink.

While Haig's proposed remedy was extreme, the problem was real
enough. Britain was producing 22,000 shells a day compared with
100,000 for France and 250,000 from Germany and Austria.[17]

Haig appears disillusioned at this stage. The lack of ammunition
was bad enough: 'More than serious it is completely preventing us
from profiting from our success by driving back the enemy before he
can reorganise and strengthen his position.' Now he discovered from
a visit to GHQ that resources were actually being diverted from the
French Front to the Dardanelles. He had been clear for some time
that exotic adventures were not justifiable. Kitchener had told him in
January 1915 of the objectionable proposal

> that the New Army might be better used elsewhere than on the
> French Frontier. A suggestion had been made of co-operating
> with Italy and Greece. I said that we ought not to divide our
> military force, but *concentrate on the decisive point* which is on this
> Frontier against the German main army. With more guns and

ammunition and more troops, the allies were bound in the end
to beat the Germans and break through.

When Haig now took a few days leave, he spent it golfing at
Folkestone. He declined meetings with the politicians and, strangely
for him, asked to be excused from attending on the King. By sulking
in his tent, or, more prosaically, in his hotel in Folkestone, where he
and Lady Haig were registered as 'Colonel and Mrs Brown' and spent
their time golfing, he indicated a subtle degree of detachment from
the conduct of the war, and a disillusionment with its political
direction. In response to a letter from Sir Clive Wigram, asking if
Haig was going to be in London, Lady Haig said that she insisted
that he remained in Folkestone.[18] 'I think you are very wise to keep
the General at Folkestone,' replied Wigram. 'Should his presence in
England reach the ears of HM, I will explain everything – my
"bouch" is "close" [*sic*].'[19]

He was not however too downhearted to enjoy April Fool's tricks,
mainly at the expense of Charteris, on his return to his headquarters.

13

THE APPROACH TO LOOS

Haig was now perceived increasingly as the man of destiny, and his Folkestone leave may have represented an attempt to manage this mood. In January Repington, 'much doubted whether we would ever get a general sufficiently fearless of public opinion to incur the losses which must be suffered in any attempt to pierce the enemy's fortified front.' Haig chose to reply, saying that 'as soon as we are supplied with ample artillery ammunition of High Explosive, I thought we could walk through the German lines at several places.'[1] His initiative in replying to the Colonel is interesting: first, he reveals his view of the simple, quantitative value of the possession of high explosive, as opposed to its skilful use; secondly, he is implicitly criticising the politicians for not supplying adequate shells; and thirdly, he is putting himself forward as the fearless general for whom Repington was looking. His approach to Repington is a dramatic tergiversation for someone who had hitherto (and subsequently) abominated journalists, including, specifically, Repington. He despised those who used journalists to promote their careers and when Wilson described him as 'a Famous General' in the course of the dramatic successes of the last three months of the war, the Hundred Days, Haig turned aside the compliment: 'For that must we not have pandered to Repington and the Gutter Press!'

Back in France he received an increasing stream of visitors

including Asquith, Haldane, Curzon and Kitchener. He received them politely and discreetly.

At this stage in the war the French were regarded by many British politicians, including Lloyd George, as having better generals and more professional soldiers than the British, with their lack of militaristic tradition, and their small regular army. Haig was of a different view. In April 1915 he wrote of 'Foch & Co.':

> These French leaders are a queer mixture of fair ability (not more than fair) and ignorance of the practical side of war. They are not built for it by nature. They are too excitable and they never seem to think of what the enemy may do. And they will not see a nasty situation as it really is, and take steps to meet it.

He was gratified, therefore, by the visit of Foch ('regarded in the French Army as their most capable general!') in order to 'study the method of attack adopted by the British at Neuve Chapelle.' No less gratifying was the information that the Kaiser considered the '1st Army Corps under Douglas Haig . . . the best in the world'. It is intriguing to reflect that in the civilised and small world of pre-war professional soldiering, the Kaiser and Haig had met and talked and drunk each other's health and Haig's wife had been a maid of honour to the Kaiser's aunt, Queen Victoria, who had died in her nephew's arms.

The veneer of civilisation had proved thin, and courtly decencies had quickly given way to the evils of total war. In April 1915, very soon after the close of the Battle of Neuve Chapelle, the Germans opened the Second Battle of Ypres. The battle was marked by their use of gas, chlorine: the first time that this new weapon had been deployed in the war. It did not bring them the breakthrough they had hoped for, and thereafter the battle was conventional and grim. Haig was not directly involved: the British line was held by Second Army under Smith-Dorrien. French underestimated Smith-Dorrien and was now repeatedly criticising him behind his back. Smith-Dorrien had annoyed French by not withdrawing at Le Cateau, in the retreat from Mons, and now he annoyed him even more by doing the opposite. The point of the salient was vulnerable. He withdrew from it and then asked for permission to do so. He and French were equally short-tempered. S-D's nickname amongst the troops (apart from the inevitable 'Doreen') was 'Smithereens', reflecting his volatility. Concerns about his self-control, and even his sanity, had ruled him out as Commander-in-Chief in India after O'Moore Creagh. But French's will prevailed and Robertson had to intimate to Smith-Dorrien, "Orace, yer for 'ome.' There was no substantial reason for his dismissal, and his treatment was pretty shabby. As Commander-in-Chief at Aldershot from 1907 to 1912 he had done more than Haig to form the BEF, and by his stand at Le Cateau he saved half of it from destruction. He was sent to command the British Forces in East Africa, and was replaced in France by Plumer – who was shortly authorised by French to withdraw to a new defensive line, just as Smith-Dorrien had wanted to do.[2] French had never liked Smith-Dorrien: he was jealous of him, with a resentment that had its roots in 1907, when Smith-Dorrien replaced French in the Aldershot command and insisted that the cavalry learn to fight on foot and to shoot straight. This, from an infantry officer, caused French great irritation. There were other areas of conflict. Smith-Dorrien was most uxorious, and disapproved of French's lifestyle: 'There are too many whores around your headquarters, FM!' When Sir James Grierson, initially the Second Army Commander, died of a heart attack immediately after arriving in France, French had at once wired to Kitchener: 'I recommend that Lieutenant-General Plumer may be appointed to fill vacancy caused by unfortunate death of General Grierson', a telegram which crossed with one from Kitchener, appointing Smith-Dorrien. French, always ready for a fight with Kitchener, protested:

> I had already wired you asking to appoint *Plumer* in his place, when your wire reached here . . .
> I very much hope that you will send me Plumer . . . *Plumer*. Do as I ask you in this matter. I needn't assure you there is no 'pressure' of any kind.

French's protests were too late, and in any event, Smith-Dorrien was a perfectly reasonable appointment. In December 1914, Plumer was given command of V Corps, under Smith-Dorrien, where he remained until French finally contrived Smith-Dorrien's dismissal.

Asquith, on a visit to First and Second Armies, had reported to French that he found Haig's command much the better of the two. French attributed this to the fact that Smith-Dorrien was inclined to interfere with his brigadiers and subordinate commanders, so that no one knew what he wanted. Haig made the point that he had had the advantage of having had two divisions under his command for two years at Aldershot. He and his officers had evolved a common 'doctrine'.

Plumer was aware of the irony in a situation which saw his first action as army commander as the very one that had led to his predecessor's dismissal. He wrote to his wife:

> Things have not been made better by Sir John French slighting Sir Horace [Smith-Dorrien], and taking practically all my force away from him and leaving me independent of him. It is the last thing I wanted. It is not fair because Smith-Dorrien and I were in absolute agreement as to what should be done, and I am only doing now what I should have been doing if I had remained under Smith-Dorrien. He, Smith-Dorrien, feels it very much of course, he came to see me yesterday and had a long talk.[3]

In May the main allied attack planned by Joffre in Champagne and Artois, of which Neuve Chapelle had been a subsidiary component, opened up. Haig's role within it was another attack on Aubers Ridge. Neither French nor Haig had any great enthusiasm for such an assault at this stage, and would have preferred to wait for further supplies of artillery ammunition. They were pressed, however, to draw German reserves from the French Front.

Despite the fact that Haig, now reinforced with three more Territorial divisions, had a huge numerical superiority, ten divisions against three German divisions, the attack went very badly.

The assault took place on 9 May. It was preceded by an artillery bombardment of only forty minutes. At Neuve Chapelle the German trenches had received a huge bombardment from heavy guns. In the planning for Aubers Ridge, the front was extended from an initial 600 yards to 1,500 yards, without a consequent increase in heavy guns. Only the original 600 yards were attacked by 6-inch howitzers. Secondly, compared to Neuve Chapelle, a much larger proportion of guns was directed not on the German front line, but on positions behind it. The infantry advance was halted by uncut barbed wire and savage machine-gun and rifle fire: the artillery barrage had been far too short to cut the wire, and the Germans had prepared exceptionally effective defensive positions, with well-concealed machine-gun placements. The Official History also criticised an inadequate provision of large calibre shells, poor quality ammunition and difficulties in ranging: 'so that the British Gunners were unable to hit their targets and the counter-batteries and machine-guns were not silenced . . . According to British aeroplane reports the registration before the battle was useless.' The Official History, of course, was written long afterwards and with the benefit of hindsight; Haig identified the problems precisely at the time:

1. The defences in our front are so carefully and so strongly made, and the mutual support with machine-guns is so complete, that in order to demolish them a *long methodical bombardment* will be necessary by heavy artillery . . . before Infantry are sent forward to attack.
2. To destroy the enemy's material, 60-pdr *guns* will be tried, as well as the 15-in., 9.2 and 6-in. hows. Accurate observations of *each shot* will be arranged so as to make sure of flattening out the enemy's 'strong points' of support, before the Infantry is launched.[4]

The 9 May attack cost Haig 145 officers and 9,400 men. The French did better, with a barrage that lasted four hours, and Sir John French was optimistic that German reserves had been so depleted by the

French attack that victory was assured when Haig's assault was renewed.

That assault, near Festubert, took place on 15 May. This time there was an artillery bombardment which lasted no less than two days and launched 100,000 shells, the '*long methodical bombardment*' of which Haig had written on 11 May, intended to destroy the German machine-gun nests. Further, the assault, the first night attack of the war, began at 11.30 p.m. The Battle of Festubert represented an attempt, after only six days, to apply at least some of the lessons learnt on the first day of Aubers Ridge. There was still no breakthrough, despite the element of surprise achieved by the night attack; most of the German line held firm. A resumed attack on 17 May was launched in heavy rain and mud. The supply of shells was soon exhausted and the troops by now were worn out. The Germans had had the opportunity to construct defences in depth. In the course of the ten days of the Battle of Festubert, however, some gains were made and at the cost of 'only' 60 per cent greater losses than at Aubers Ridge on one day.

In retrospect, the loss of 710 officers and 15,938 men (against German losses of some 5,000) scarcely seems a matter for congratulation, but at the time it appeared that Haig was devising a tactical formula that might deliver success. Charteris recorded that as early as April, Lord Esher was at his headquarters: 'his chief characteristic is that he is always close friends with those that matter. So his visit probably means that DH's star is in the ascendant.' By this stage Esher was operating, unofficially as ever, as an observer of the British armies (Esher's son was Kitchener's ADC), and he interpreted this role in the widest of senses. In June Asquith arrived. 'Mr. Asquith was most enthusiastic about all he had seen,' said Haig, 'and on bidding good-bye, he asked me to write to him whenever I could spare the time.'

After a visit to French's headquarters, Esher recorded that 'The FM [French] said today "It is a solemn thought that at my signal all these fine young fellows go to their deaths." This tenderness does Sir John infinite credit, for warriors are commonly made of sterner stuff; yet he is a warrior.'[5]

French was unusual, and a little like Churchill, in simultaneously exulting in command and feeling the pain of its consequences. Haig put the pain aside, to be dealt with after his task was completed; French did not, and could not. On one occasion he wrote:

> I spoke to one battalion 2 Shropshire LI, which lost 20 officers – 8 of them killed! It seems horrible butchery. I talked with a young subaltern whose voice got quite husky when he spoke of it. It is rather an awful thing to *miss* so many comrades so suddenly. Poor boy, he *felt* it.

It was at this time that French formed his liaison with Winifred Bennett, his final, intense relationship, he elderly, portly and short, she, over six feet tall, but his 'little darling'. On the eve of the Battle of Neuve Chapelle, he wrote to her: 'Tomorrow I shall go forward with my War Cry of "Winifred".'[6]

He could confide to her the cost of command:

> I sometimes people my room with these glorious friends (all boys compared to me!), who have gone over. That 'Silent Army'. Alas, alas! The room is getting too small to hold even my intimate friends. Dear old 'Bobs' was with us in that same room the night before he died – perfectly well and enraptured by being amongst us.[7]

For French the responsibility for the losses which hurt him so much lay in the lack of high explosive. With that issue he associated the War Office and Kitchener, whom he now routinely referred to as 'the Arch-Fiend'. Wilson, close to French since the Curragh Incident, said Kitchener was as great an enemy of the BEF as Moltke or Falkenhayn. French:

> I have more trouble with the War Office than I do with the Germans. While they are fiddling Rome is burning. What we want is more and more High Explosive ammunition and they

do nothing but squabble amongst themselves. I devoutly wish we could get rid of Kitchener at the War Office – I'm sure nothing will go right whilst he is there. It is so hard to have enemies in *front* and *behind*.[8]

When Kitchener visited First Army Headquarters on 8 July, Haig recorded that: 'He explained how he found it difficult to get Sir John French to comply with any of his suggestions. Whereas in bygone days F. obeyed his smallest suggestion. However, he (K) was ready "to black French's boots" if need be, in order to obtain agreement and win the war!' But French's dislike for Kitchener went far beyond practical issues: he had an unreasoning and bitter hatred of the Secretary of State. Kitchener's sentiment towards the Commander-in-Chief was simply of contempt. He told Haig of the difficulties that had arisen between him and French and asked him, in Haig's words:

to assert myself more, and to insist on French proceeding on sound principles. I replied that that was easier said than done – and in any case it was more his affair to control Sir John French than mine. I had really to do as I was ordered by Sir John, and French had much more self-confidence now than when I was with him in South Africa.

Without actual disloyalty Haig could hardly have said more to keep the anti-French pot boiling. That the pot was boiling is shown by Charteris' report on a further visit by Esher to First Army Headquarters: 'Esher says that in "political circles" there is considerable speculation as regards the length of Sir J. French's period of command, and as to his probable successor.' To be fair to Haig, his sniping at French was not entirely unprovoked. As far back as 24 April Charteris recorded that Haig was 'rather afraid that he may be sent to India as C-in-C. Indeed Sir J. French made the suggestion to him. I imagine it originated either with Wilson or Rawlinson, both of whom would, I think, like to see DH out of France, with a view to the possible reversion of the Command-in-Chief should French go for

any reason'.[9] It is just as likely that the suggestion would originate
from French himself, as he must have been aware that the main risk of
his deposition lay in replacement by Haig.

On 15 May Repington wrote in *The Times* that 'the want of an
unlimited supply of High Explosive shells was a fatal bar to our
success.' Repington said 'these words were my own, and were not
suggested by Sir John French.' But French recorded that after Aubers
Ridge: 'I immediately gave instructions that evidence should be
furnished to Colonel Repington . . . who happened to be then at
headquarters, that the [lack of] vital new High Explosive shells had
been a fatal bar to our army success on that day.'[10]

The shells crisis, stimulated by French, resulted in the fall of the
Liberal government, the formation of the first coalition government
and the establishment of the Ministry of Munitions under Lloyd
George. But political support for French in London was weakening.

Richard Holmes has captured the anti-French mood of the time
very well:

> News from France flooded into Buckingham Palace in an
> unceasing flow as an astonishingly large number of officers
> wrote to the King's private secretaries on one pretext or another.
> Haig, Robertson and Smith-Dorrien were in regular contact
> with the palace, and some Corps Commanders – and even the
> occasional Division Commander – did not hesitate to add their
> loyal pennyworth when the mood took them. The King had
> never been one of Sir John's warmest admirers, and on 1st July,
> after a long talk with Robertson, he noted that 'it would be
> better for all concerned if the C in C were changed'.[11]

These difficulties were alluded to on 15 July, when the King
conferred the GCB on Haig:

> [The King] referred to the friction between Sir John and Lord K
> and hoped I would do all I could to make matters run smoothly.
> He said he visited the Grand Fleet last week where all the

admirals were on the most friendly terms with one another. In the King's opinion, the Army would be in the same satisfactory state and there would be no back-biting and unfriendly criticism of superiors if the officer at the head of the Army in the Field – a most splendid body of troops – was fit for his position! He (the King) criticises French's dealings with the Press, *The Times*, Repington and Lord Northcliffe, etc. All most unsoldierlike and he (the King) had lost confidence in Field Marshal French. And he had told Kitchener that he (K) could depend on his (the King's) support in whatever action he took in dealing with French. The King's one object was efficiency. He was approving of any action to ensure the Army being in as fit a state as possible to end the War. I pointed out that the time to get rid of French was immediately after the retreat. Now the army was stationary and could practically be controlled from London. The King hoped that I would write to Wigram, and said that no one but he and Wigram would know what I had written.

In the course of this same visit to London, Haig met Kitchener:

He was most affable, and . . . wished me to write to him on any subject affecting the Army and in which I thought he could be of assistance. He would treat my letters as secret, and would not reply, but I would see my proposals given effect to and must profess ignorance when that happened! . . . At both my interviews today, I was urged to write regarding the situation and doings with the Army in Flanders to Lord K. The King quite realised the nature of such conduct on my part, because he told me he had said to Lord K with reference to it 'if anyone acted like that, and told tales out of school, he would at school be called a sneak.' K's reply was that we are beyond schoolboy's age!

Following the publication of the edited version of Haig's diary in 1952, he was much criticised for his apparent disloyalty to French and for intriguing against him. Terraine powerfully defends Haig against these charges. He argues that initiative for secret communication did not lie with Haig; he did not press for French's removal, but said that the time for it had passed; he did not approve of the secret letter procedure; he could not have resisted instructions from Kitchener, or from the King, the Head of the Army; 'Public School morals did not offer a complete solution to the problems of national survival in a global war.'[12] The defence is skilful but is not, I think, finally persuasive. Haig's behaviour at this time has to be looked at in the context of his enthusiasm for confidential letters to his superiors throughout his military career, and if he did not press for French's removal in July 1915, he would quite soon afterwards avail himself of the opportunities for secret correspondence that had been offered to him. But ultimately the real defence for Haig's behaviour depends on whether he is thought to have been furthering his own career or, as he always insisted, doing what was in the interests of the army and his country.

The final stage in the Battle of Aubers Ridge had taken place on 15 June: Joffre asked for British assistance to draw the Germans from the Vimy Ridge sector, where the French were under pressure. French authorised a minimal attack which Haig allotted to IV Corps under Rawlinson. Casualties amounted to 3,811 men and there were no gains. Thereafter, First Army was not involved in any major operations, although a directive from French in February 1915 stressed the importance of local attacks

with a view to gaining ground and of taking advantage of any tactical and numerical inferiority on the part of the enemy. Such enterprises are highly valuable and should receive every encouragement, since they relieve the monotony and improve the moral of our own troops, while they have a corresponding detrimental effect on the moral of the enemy's troops and lead in a variety of ways to their exhaustion and general disquiet.[13]

During this quieter period, visitors continued to arrive at Haig's headquarters. One was Kitchener on a mission to repair good relations with the Commander-in-Chief. Haig took Kitchener right to the front line and sought to impress on him the nature of the new type of warfare that was taking place: siege warfare. Another was Ben Tillett, the leader of the dock strikes of 1889 and 1911 and founder of the Dockers' Union, later the Transport & General Workers' Union, together with Monsieur Bruhl, the French socialist. Haig handled this well. Both men had made clear their hostility to militarism in every form, but he disarmed them by giving the clearest of orders that they were to be shown everything they wanted to see and were to have the chance of meeting men of all ranks whenever they came across them: officers were to make themselves scarce so that there could be a free exchange of views. He himself met them at the beginning of their tour and told them what he had done. This was a rare public relations and political victory for Haig: Tillett returned to London hugely impressed, and thereafter supported and sustained the army in the field in every way that he could.

A visit in the following month by Lloyd George's new munitions committee was not so satisfactory when Haig discovered that at least one member was under the impression that the army still used the solid cannon balls of Waterloo days.

Unimpressed by the quality of some of his interpreters, Haig took steps at this time to improve his French. Charteris reported that: 'he therefore enlisted the services of his French liaison officer and for two hours a day sat down studying French – working out exercises and compositions, much in the same way as any public schoolboy works at the language at home. He made rapid progress and at the end of the summer was able to converse fluently.' The Hon. Neville Lytton and Edward Spears, both fluent French speakers, also gave Haig high marks for his command of the language.[14] Charteris went so far as to claim that Haig was actually able to 'express himself far more coherently and accurately [in French] than in English'; this is very much a Charteris comment, and should be regarded with suspicion.

All his life his mind had worked faster than his tongue, and he had contracted a habit of breaking off a sentence and leaving the rest to the imagination of his listeners. Even if the sentence did chance to have an end, as often as not he would have omitted the verb. Only Staff Officers who thoroughly understood their Commander's mind could grasp his meaning from his spoken word.

While this was the case when he spoke, no man had a greater command of forcible expression in writing than had Haig. He wrote without effort and with hardly a correction, and it appeared to be the same brain cell that functioned when he spoke a foreign tongue. His speech in French came slow, definite, in perfect grammar, and with every sentence simply and clearly enunciated.[15]

Smith-Dorrien had the reverse of this problem and a staff officer is said to have remarked: 'If Haig could only speak as clearly as Horace and if Horace could only write as clearly as Haig, I would be better able to understand what was in their minds.'[16] Smith-Dorrien's peculiarity was strong language, allied to his violent temper (due, his son said, to persistent trouble from his teeth). Haig's *learned* communication skills were better than those which were instinctive.

There is something of the feeling of a man preparing for future responsibilities in these French lessons. It is at this time also that Haig established private links between the First Army headquarters and French intelligence and concentrated on intelligence on the state of the German Army.

As the summer of 1915 came to a close, the time approached for the major battle which Joffre wanted. The initiative for what was to be the Battle of Loos lay very much with the French. The war, in all its different theatres, was going badly for the Allies, and a major victory was required. In any event, Joffre had great confidence that he could deliver a victory. His requests of Britain were so readily accepted by Kitchener at this time that it has been suggested that the latter wished to make himself an acceptable candidate as a Supreme Commander for the Allied Forces. The evidence for this is sparse, although the Official History says: 'It is believed that Lord

Kitchener himself had anticipated a call to this post.' There are other suggestions, but much the most likely seems the simple one: that Britain must be seen to be supporting her Ally. In any event, after the Dardanelles, the Secretary of State was anxious to see something positive done. Churchill described Kitchener's demeanour when he brought him the news of the offensive:

> He looked at me sideways with a very odd expression on his face. I saw he had some disclosure of importance to make, and waited. After appreciable hesitation he told me that he had agreed with the French to have a great offensive in France. I said at once that there was no chance of success. He said that the scale would restore everything, including of course the Dardanelles. He had an air of suppressed excitement like a man who has take a great decision of terrible uncertainty, and is about to put it into execution.[17]

The main attack was to be in Champagne, with a powerful secondary attack in Artois, where the British would co-operate with Foch's Army Group. The British were not at all enthusiastic about the choice of area, and French wished to attack near Ypres. There were however over sixty French divisions committed to the battle, as against only six British, and Joffre, after the war, noted that: 'At my request, [French] relinquished this plan and acquiesced in mine. In a spirit of real as opposed to conventional discipline, he subordinated his will to the wishes expressed by me "in my capacity as Commander-in-Chief".'[18] Joffre was not Commander-in-Chief of the British armies or the Allied armies and could not give direct orders to his British allies, and French was acknowledging the discipline of reality rather than military discipline. British generals – French, Haig, Robertson – had a rooted, emotional rather than entirely rational, objection to taking orders from French generals. The absence of a Supreme Commander was to create problems until the very last months of the war. Although the French army was very much greater than the British, the British fleet was by far the more significant. France and Britain were therefore more or less equal allies; and they had for hundreds of years been bitter military rivals. Such an equal partnership made for a prickly relationship: things were different in the Second World War, when there could be no doubt about the relative strengths of the British and American contributions to the war effort. Later, and under the stresses of the war, Haig, subject to some caveats, would be ready to subordinate himself to an Allied Commander-in-Chief who was a Frenchman. The rationale was that while Foch happened to be a French general, his authority derived not from that fact, but from the fact that he was the Allied Supreme Commander, directing both French generals and British generals.

For the moment it was with Joffre, rather than Foch, that French and Haig had to deal. Many British generals were suspicious of their French allies. For example, Robertson: '[The French] are unstable people. Easily elated, and still more easily depressed.'[19] While, according to Johnnie French: '*Au fond* they are a low lot, and one always has to remember the class these French generals mostly come from.'[20] Haig shared these suspicions in regard to the French in general, and was far from immune from the institutionalised anti-French prejudice which permeated the British army, but that did not stop him from being on good terms with a number of individuals (including Lyautey and Clemenceau), and for the most part he enjoyed tolerably good relations with both Joffre and Foch and indeed had some respect for each of them. Despite his marked differences from Joffre – Haig was fit, trim, always immaculately presented, whereas Joffre was almost obese, genial and ponderous – there was a certain affinity between the Scots countryman and a general who was Catalan, rather than French, in the same way as Haig was Scots rather than English. Haig quoted General de Vallières as describing Joffre as 'an underbred individual', but he himself never used language of this sort of his colleague, even when he turned up at Haig's headquarters 'with a beard of four days' growth!' Joffre was kindly, slow-spoken except in moments of excitement; and, just as Haig retained a strong Scottish accent,

Joffre's accent was in the rich, meridional tone of the Mediterranean. When an interview went well, Joffre heaved himself out of his chair and took from a cupboard in the wall of his room a present for his visitor: a pipe inscribed, '*Souvenir du Général en Chef* J. Joffre'. When things didn't go so well, he tapped himself on the back of his head and murmured, 'Pauvre Joffre!' He could scarcely read a map.

Though agreement in principle had been reached, detailed arguments about the ground continued. In mid-June French agreed with Foch on a British offensive on First Army's extreme right. Haig was ordered to investigate and on 23 June reported that the ground was very unsuitable: German defences were strong and the terrain unpropitious: 'an attack on Loos is not practical unless the enemy is dislodged from Lens, which is a massive ruin organised as defended localities and coal heaps.' French, despite some doubts, and only after examining the ground himself from Notre Dame de Lorette, decided that Haig was right. As late as 23 July, when Rawlinson passed his Loos plans to him, Haig was arguing for a fresh attack on Aubers Ridge, rather than any adventures in the Loos area. French conceded that '[T]he actual terrain of the attack is no doubt difficult, as it is covered with all the features of a closely inhabited flourishing mining district – factories – slag heaps – shafts – long rows of houses – etc., etc.'.[21]

On 9 July Haig was back in England for Lady Haig's birthday. This time there was no question of not speaking to the King. Colonel Wigram wrote to Lady Haig, saying: '[T]hat for Imperial reasons it would be a good thing if Douglas were to see His Majesty whilst he was at home.'[22]

On 20 July French told Clive, the British liaison officer at French headquarters, to inform his French colleagues that he had given up the idea of attacking the Loos area. But ultimately, despite his well-argued representations, French had to give way and on 28 July wrote in his diary that he had decided to leave the direction of affairs 'in the hands of the Generalissimo . . . I have asked the C-in-C to give due weight and consideration to the points I have just put forward and then to tell me what he wishes me to do and I *will do it*.'[23] Haig's reaction was that: 'Sir John seems now to have . . . put himself and the British Forces unreservedly in Joffre's hands!' He did not yet understand the constraints involved in working in partnership.

French still tried to limit his commitment, by telling Haig that the attack was to be made chiefly with artillery and no large force of infantry was to be used. Joffre was not however going to be bought off in this way: 'You will certainly agree with me that [British] support can only be effective if it takes the form of a large and powerful attack, composed of the maximum force you have available, executed with the hope of success and carried through to the end.'[24] But the final British decision was made by Kitchener, who came out to visit Joffre, French and finally Haig, whom he told that: '*He had decided that we must act with all our energy, and do our utmost to help the French, even though by doing so we suffer very heavy losses indeed*'. [Haig's emphasis.] Kitchener appears to have been motivated largely by his fears of imminent Russian collapse and the need to take pressure off the Eastern Front.

Haig became more bullish about prospects as the battle approached, and his earlier reservations about the terrain were forgotten. His relationship with Rawlinson was still not comfortable. Rawlinson had received a fairly sharp rebuke from Haig when the plans for Neuve Chapelle were being drawn up: he had accepted unquestioningly fairly second-rate plans produced by a subordinate officer, and without Haig's stimulus would not have formulated a workable plan for himself. This time Rawlinson found his plans, which were limited and cautious, overturned and replaced with much more ambitious ones, which he viewed with concern. The responsibility was not all Haig's. Joffre's insistence on large-scale support had obliged French to require from Haig that the attack be on as wide a front as possible and that heavy losses must be tolerated. Rawlinson's plan had originally been to capture the German front line. To that had been added attacks on Loos and Hill 70. Now the objective was two miles to the east of Hill 70, involving the capture of the German second line, something Rawlinson had argued could not be done without fresh troops. So far the expansion of the objectives had not been Haig's responsibility. But now he urged his Corps Commanders to go further, on to the plain of Douai, which implied a major breakthrough. Privately Rawlinson thought that breaking the German second line would be unlikely ('It looks to me as if we may be here for the winter'[25]), but he did not feel able to voice his concerns to Haig, and that fact is a criticism of Haig's method of command.

It was in these circumstances that Haig came to fight a battle which he did not want on ground which he would not have chosen. It was, however, a battle which would bring him the prize of commanding the British armies in France.

14

Loos: Destruction of the BEF and Creation of a Commander-in-Chief

John Terraine described the Battle of Loos as 'the true beginning of the martyrdom of the British Army.' By the time the battle had finished, the destruction of the old, highly trained and professional Expeditionary Force was complete. Throughout the war the British army was handicapped by a desperate shortage of properly trained staff officers, and after Loos almost a third of the Staff College graduates had been killed. Sir John French must have been conscious that if it went badly (and his instinct had told him that it would go badly, even if latterly his natural optimism took over), it could well mark the end of his military career. Churchill had told him as much. He had argued strongly against Loos in Cabinet 'till I was suppressed', and urged Sir John to alter his plans. 'In my small way, I tried my best to stop it. I warned Sir John French that the new battle would be fatal to him.'[1]

The battle was however a political necessity, not only to comply with Joffre's wishes, but, more generally to provide a collective reassurance to the French, who had become sceptical about their Ally's commitment, and doubted that Britain really had the heart for a fight. The ambivalent spirit in which French and Haig contemplated the battle is reflected in their agreement that they should tell as little as possible to Kitchener about the plans for Loos. Lady Haig, who was now knitting all of her husband's ties (in silk, plain and purl stitch), recorded that they thought that they might as well tell the Germans about their plans as tell the Cabinet.[2]

As the start date for the battle, 25 September 1915, approached, Haig gradually became more optimistic about prospects. Rawlinson, who immediately before the planning for Loos began had settled in his mind that the only way forward was attack on a wide front, following massive bombardment, with the objective of limited bite-and-hold nibbles, also became infected by the ambitions of his army commander and the Commander-in-Chief. He told his wife that a winter campaign might not be a certainty, and that he understood that the Germans were having difficulties: 'an early peace is advised as the only way to save the country.' To his corps commanders he acknowledged that the army was required to attack before it was fully ready, but still thought that they could 'get on the enemy's rear and cut his communications.'

The German use of gas at Second Ypres had been greeted with horror and revulsion by the British press as a barbarous and inhumane breach of all the rules of war, but Britain lost no time in exploiting this breach. Haig has repeatedly been criticised for his alleged resistance to technological advances. This is one of the many myths that surround him. In fact, he had a boyish enthusiasm for any invention that would help to shorten the war. He was conscious that the fighting conditions were different from anything that the army had experienced before, and that new methods were necessary. In the development of some new departures he was personally involved. For the most part new techniques were evolved at army level or below, but he was always receptive to radical proposals. It is true that he had originally been sceptical about the feasibility of using gas. He recorded, shortly before Second Ypres that:

Lord Dundonald arrived from England. He is studying the conditions of War in the hope of being able to apply to modern conditions an invention of his great grandfather for driving a garrison out of the fort by using sulphur fumes. I asked him how he arranged to have a favourable wind![3]

But he reacted swiftly and pragmatically and wrote to Robertson shortly before the battle: 'In my opinion, under no circumstances should our forthcoming attach be launched without the aid of gas.'[4] His diaries at this stage, as at others, disclose how excited he was by gadgets and gizmos. He draws fascinating little Heath Robinson sketches to illustrate the devices that have intrigued him. He took a great interest in the detailed characteristics of the different types of gas, and advocated placing cylinders under the front parapet of trenches to protect them from enemy fire. At a meeting on 25 June 1915 with the assistant to the Minister for Munitions, (now Lloyd George) and two generals, he stressed the new types of armament the war was showing to be necessary: a small-calibre gun for counter-battery work like a naval five-pounder, new bomb mortars to supplement heavy artillery, a trench mortar to throw 100-pound shells of high explosive up to 500 yards, captive balloons to supplement aircraft observation, daggers or short bayonets for use in trenches. 'A *lighter* machine gun, with tripod and gun in one part, is a necessity. Mobility is most important.' He noted that there were fourteen types of hand grenades in use: they should be rationalised down to two. A couple of months later he noted that the French had produced excellent smoke bombs, and he ordered the production of similar devices in Britain.

Criticism for fighting where he did at Loos is misdirected. He considered the ground, 'flat as the palm of my hand,' to be quite unsuitable for infantry advance, and back in June, in the early planning stages of the battle, told Hubert Gough and General Birch: '*I had no intention of ordering any infantry under my command to attack until the hostile position was thoroughly prepared*, so they were not to under-estimate [ammunition requirements] merely to please GHQ! If we had not enough ammunition now, we must wait until it accumulated.'[5] The required ammunition had not materialised by 25 September, and gas was one way of improving British prospects in the face of massive German defences. Ahead of the battle, French complained that 'the Arch-Fiend' was depriving him of shells. Another Haig innovation (vetoed by French), designed to accommodate the French plans, was to have been a surprise attack without a bombardment on the day of the battle. Wilson had a key part in the veto, pointing out that the Germans frequently mended their fences during the night and that without a brief bombardment, Haig might be faced by uncut wire.

Cylinders containing 150 tons of chlorine gas were available. The problem of course was the wind, which could as easily blow the gas back on to the British lines as on to the Germans. The weight of the responsibility for giving the order to open the taps was enormous. The night before the battle was 'an anxious night, wondering all the time what the wind would be in the morning! The greatest battle in the world's history begins today. Some 800,000 French and British troops will actually attack today.'

Ernest Gold, FRS, a Fellow of Trinity College, Cambridge, and Britain's most distinguished meteorologist, had been brought across and attached to Haig's headquarters with the rank of captain. The significance of his discipline to modern warfare was recognised by the fact that his initial staff of three had risen to 120 by the end of the war. Just before midnight the wind was blowing on to the British trenches. At midnight itself, there was no wind at all. Haig calmly went to sleep while Captain Gold and the intelligence service monitored reports from instruments placed at intervals over the whole area of the front. At 2 a.m. he was awakened to be told that the weather reports from the front itself were unfavourable, but that from more distant readings Captain Gold was able to predict that a favourable breeze would spring up just before dawn. He went back to sleep, until 4 a.m., when he went to the meteorological station with Alan Fletcher, his ADC. Charteris had noted Haig's ability to make a decision and then clear his mind: 'He is amazing. You can awaken him at night to hear unpleasant news and authorise some important order; he is alert at once, clear-headed and decisive, and asleep again almost before one has left his room.'[6] Gold remained confident, but from the immediate area there were still no readings to support him. On the previous evening, Haig had sought to postpone the start of the battle and had been very upset to be told that this was now impossible;[7] now he delayed his decision for as long as possible. Surrounded by his staff, with Gold occupied in his calculations, Haig remained silent and only moved from time to time to look at his watch. The tension in this silent tableau which lasted for a full hour must have been unbearable. Then one favourable reading was received, and it was reinforced by more homely evidence than anything that Captain Gold and his weather stations could provide:

> I went out at 5 am. Almost a calm. Alan Fletcher lit a cigarette and the smoke drifted in puffs towards the north east. Staff Officers of Corps were ordered to stand by in case it were necessary to counter order to attack. At one time, owing to the calm, I feared the gas might simply hang about *our* trenches. However, at 5.15 I said "Carry on". I went to the top of our wooden lookout tower. The wind came gently from south west, by 5.40 it had increased slightly. The leaves of the poplar trees gently rustled. This seemed satisfactory. But what a risk I must run of gas blowing back upon our own dense masses of troops!

A clear, leader-like decision had been made. Haig believed that even a bad decision was better than indecision.[8] The reliance on gas was misguided. Haig had told his Corps commanders that it would cause panic in the German ranks, although it was known that the Germans he faced were experienced troops, equipped with gas respirators. Why should they panic when the British and Canadians had not done so at Ypres? And on the strength of the supposed effect of gas, a huge reduction in artillery, compared to Neuve Chapelle, was accepted. There, in thirty-five minutes, five shells with a total weight of 288 pounds fell on each yard of enemy trench. At Loos, over a period of forty-eight hours, only 7/10th of a shell weighing sixty-two pounds fell per yard on the trenches under attack. Wire-cutting guns were also reduced, as against Neuve Chapelle. Further, the hurricane bombardment was not repeated, and the Germans had an opportunity to repair damage before the attack.[9]

What then followed was frightful. In the course of the next three weeks (and another three weeks remained thereafter before the end of the battle), 2,013 officers and 48,367 other ranks were casualties, and a further 800 officers and 15,000 men were killed or missing. German losses were less than half those of the British. 'Such,' wrote the Official Historian, 'was the tremendous sacrifice made by all ranks to support our French ally.' The reference to 'our French ally' was telling: the French, on whose insistence the battle took place, did not meet with success in Champagne, and consequently did not draw the Germans away from the British sector.

On the first day of Loos, Haig's First Army was committed in full to the attack. Despite Fletcher's cigarette smoke, one flank was affected by British gas blowing back, and the other flank became bogged down. A lot had been asked of Captain Gold: the nature of the front meant that the wind had to blow in different directions at different places for the gas to be effective. By the following day, 26 September, the advance in the centre had been checked. The battle continued, at the request of the French, for some weeks; at the end 8,000 yards of German front had been taken and in places British troops had advanced over two miles, the largest advance made by the Allies since the war had settled into its trenches. The gains were of little real value.

Within the larger picture, there was huge heroism by elements of the old Expeditionary Force – and by New Army Divisions, which were playing their part in the war for the first time. The 9th and 15th (Scottish) Divisions of the New Army fought with incredible courage. The future Major-General Robert Hilton, a forward observation officer in the battle:

A great deal of nonsense has been talked about Loos. The real tragedy of that battle was its nearness to complete success. Most of us who reached the crest of Hill 70 and survived were firmly convinced that we had broken through on that Sunday, 25th September 1915. There seemed to be nothing ahead of us but an unoccupied and incomplete trench system.

All we needed was more artillery ammunition to blast those

clearly located machine-guns, and some fresh infantry to take over from the weary and depleted 'Jocks'. But, alas, neither ammunition nor reinforcements were immediately available, and the great opportunity passed.[10]

Charteris says, 'Haig was entirely unaware of all the mental reservations which were to influence the Commander-in-Chief's actions and . . . disposed the whole of I and IV Corps in the front line for the first assault, relying on the vital and essential support of the General Reserve to carry the attack forward when the first impetus of his own two Corps was exhausted.'[11] But Haig was certainly *not* entirely unaware of these mental reservations, and indeed Charteris' account in the biography is at odds with his diary entries. Haig was however absent from a meeting between Foch and French on 24 September. Joffre's overall instructions required commanders to move reserve troops immediately in rear of points of attack at the same time as those in front. French told Foch that he would not be putting his reserve troops under Haig's command before the battle.

The tragedy of Loos for French and Haig and, more importantly, for the soldiers who fought and died in the battle, was that in the centre of the First Army attack there *may* have been a missed opportunity for a major advance. At that point, on the first day of the attack, the German defensive strength was limited and came very close to breaking, as cooks and clerks and orderlies and staff were thrown into defence. Transport was brought forward for the retreat that appeared imminent. What would have happened in there *had* been a breakthrough will never be known. It might have been crucial, but the subsequent history of the war shows that breakthroughs were very difficult to exploit.

The reason that apparent success could not be exploited was that reserves were not available, and this issue is critical to an appreciation of the battle, and to the subsequent relationship between Haig and French. Haig had stressed the importance of having a reserve readily available as early as 17 August: 'I discussed the forthcoming attack with Sir John, and said that the Front on which we attacked and the distance to which we go will depend on the orders and Reserves which he gives me.' When he learned shortly afterwards that the reserve was represented by General Haking's XI Corps, which consisted of two New Army Divisions that had not even arrived in France, Haig immediately objected. On 18 September he asked French to have the 'General Reserve (which the C in C retains under GHQ) with the head of its two divisions at Noeux les Mines and Verquin respectively by the *morning* of the 25th. Sir John seemed to think that was too close up.'[12] Haig was told that the Reserves would advance more slowly than he wanted and would remain further back from the line than he wished. He enlisted the aid of Kitchener on the following day, but found the latter insensitive to the difficulties of moving troops through congested areas. Foch was next to be approached: he agreed with Haig and, with Joffre's support, made representations to French. Haig took comfort from vague assurance by French that 'he would release XI Corps to support me on the earliest possible moment'.[13]

In view of the importance which Haig was subsequently to attach to the issue of the reserves, he should in the time that was left to him have raised the matter much more firmly with French, and perhaps with Kitchener, and at least have put his protest on record. Instead, he complained to Robertson and Haking, but took refuge in the vague belief that 'the three divisions will, *I hope*, be close up in the places where I have arranged to put them, and will go forward as soon as any opportunity offers.'[14] Charteris, more realistically, recorded on 24 September that 'everything possible has been done – except the three Reserve Divisions. They are too far back. If our first attack gets through we shall want them at once. It is the first real break between [Haig] and Sir John French. Last week DH might have asked Kitchener to overrule French, and I am sure K would have done so. I wish he had. It is so vital. But, after all, it may go right.'[15]

French ultimately ordered XI Corps forward, but not until after dark on 24 September, although he had assured Haig that the reserve would be in position by daybreak on 25 September. The move was not accorded priority and was held up in badly controlled traffic. The situation was not assisted by the fact that French, in a desire to be close to the action, was twenty miles ahead of his Chief of Staff and Headquarters. When Haig was Commander-in-Chief he tempered every commander's wish to be as close as possible to the action with the realisation that effective communications were a prerequisite in modern warfare. The reserve could not be put into the attack until 26 September, by which time they were not facing the shaken and disorganised defence which had been envisaged.

Haig set out what, in his view, followed, in a letter to Kitchener dated 29 September:

My Dear Lord Kitchener

You will doubtless recall how earnestly I pressed you to ensure an adequate Reserve being close in rear of my attacking division, and under my orders. It may interest you to know what happened. No Reserve was placed under me. My attack, as has been reported, was a complete success. The enemy had no troops in his second line, which some of my plucky fellows reached and entered without opposition. Prisoners state the enemy was so hard put to it for troops to stem our advance that the officers' servants, fatigue men, etc. in Lens were pushed forward to hold their second line to the east of Loos and Hill 70.

The two Reserve Divisions under C-in-C's orders, were directed to join me as soon as the success of First Army was known at GHQ. They came in as quick as they could, poor fellows, but only crossed our old trench line with their heads at 6 pm. We had captured Loos 12 hours previously, and Reserves should have been at hand *then*. This, you will remember, I had requested should be arranged by GHQ, and Robertson quite concurred in my view and wished to put the Reserve Divisions under me, but was not allowed.

The final result is that the enemy has been allowed time in which to bring up troops and strengthen his second line, and *probably* to construct a third line the direction in which we are heading, viz, Pont-à-Vendin.

I have now been given some fresh divisions, and am busy planning an attack to break the enemy's second line. But the element of surprise has gone and our task will be a difficult one.

I think it right that you should know how the lessons which have been learnt in this war at such cost have been neglected. We *were* in a position to make this the turning point of the war, and I still hope may do so but naturally I feel annoyed at the lost opportunity.

We were all pleased to receive your kind telegram, and I am, Yours very truly, D. Haig.

After the battle Haig became increasingly convinced that the presence of fresh and immediately available reserves could have made all the difference. With them: 'we could have walked right through. GHQ refuses to recognise the teachings of the war as regard the control of Reserves.' Given French's very obvious reluctance to release troops, perhaps Haig should have husbanded his own reserves for a follow-through but he chose to be optimistic that the general reserve would arrive speedily, and used his own reserves for the initial attack; this optimism flew in the face of all the evidence. Had he wished he could have drawn seasoned troops from other parts of his command.

The carnage at Loos was frightful:

The Germans were as impressed as other observers. They saw an 'entire front coloured with the enemy's infantry.' They stood up, and some stood even on the parapet of the trench, and fired into the approaching wave of infantrymen as they advanced over open ground. The machine-guns were able to open fire at 1500 yards' range. 'Never had machine-guns had such straightforward work to do . . . with barrels becoming hot and swimming in oil, they traversed to and fro along the enemy's ranks. One machine-gun alone fired 12,500 rounds that afternoon. The effect was devastating. The enemy could be seen falling literally in hundreds, but they continued their march in good order and without interruption.' Eventually they reached the unbroken wire of the Germans' second position. 'Confronted by this impenetrable obstacle the survivors turned and began to retire.'

The Germans were taken aback by the efficacy of their machine-guns. They called the battle the Field of Corpses of Loos, *der Leichenfeld von Loos*. One German regimental diary commented, following the failure of the fifth British attack, as the wounded men worked their way back to the British lines, 'No shot was fired at them from the German trenches for the rest of the day, so great was the feeling of compassion and mercy for the enemy after such a victory.'[16]

French's reluctance to transfer XI Corps to Haig and to bring the reserve further up was not gratuitous obstructiveness. As early as 24 September he had written: 'In view of the great length of line along which the Army is operating I feel it to be necessary that I should keep a strong reserve under my own hand.' Additionally, he was aware that the divisions were inexperienced New Army troops which might require gentle handling. Haig was regarded as a 'thruster who had to be kept under restraint'.[17] At the same time it is necessary to recognise that French was increasingly out of his depth, as the scale of the war intensified, and was isolated at his headquarters at Lillers, twenty-five miles from his Chief of Staff, and with no direct telephone link.

Sir John French possessed qualities that made him a more attractive personality than Haig, and perhaps a better leader of men, though a poorer Commander-in-Chief. After the battle he could be seen riding unaccompanied amongst the troops and on the second day of the battle he visited a dressing station at Nouex les Mines, and talked to his wounded men. ('Dead, dying and badly wounded all mixed up together. Poor dear fellows they bear their pain gloriously and many of them gave me a smile of recognition.') He enjoyed the love and loyalty of his troops in a way that Haig never did, but by temperament he was a regimental commander.

While Britain attempted to comply with Joffre's requests and renew the advance, until finally bad weather put an end to plans for a further offensive, the battle between Haig and French continued. The talk of wounded officers who returned to London revealed that all had not gone well at Loos. Some of the reports were critical of Haig. Repington met an officer at lunch at Prince's Grill just back from France who 'was very interesting. Admitted that the whole attack had been a failure and laid the blame on Douglas Haig, who had been dreadfully aged.'[18] But the bulk of the attacks were directed against French. The Official History records that Haig's reputation was enhanced as a result of Loos and that French had made serious mistakes.

Haldane was sent out by the Cabinet on 9 October to interview witnesses on the spot to see what had gone wrong. Haig, as would be expected, spoke with unrestrained candour:

I gave him all the facts. The main criticism to my mind is the fact that the Reserves were not at hand when wanted. The causes for this seem to me to be:
1. Neither the C-in-C nor his staff fully realised at the beginning (in spite of my letters and remarks) the necessity for reserves being close up before the action began.
2. The two divisions were billeted in depth a long distance from where they would be wanted, and no attempt was made to concentrate them before the battle began.
3. When the course of the fight showed that reserves were wanted at once to exploit VICTORY the two divns. were hurried forward without full consideration for their food etc. with the result that the troops arrived worn out at the point of attack and unfit for battle.
4. But the 21st and 24th Divns. having only recently arrived in France, with staffs and commanders inexperienced in war, should not have been detailed for this work. It was courting disaster to employ them at once in fighting of this nature. There were other divisions available as shown by the fact that they arrived three days later upon the

> battlefield, namely the 28th Divn., the 12th Divn. and
> the Guards Divn.

I also felt it my duty to tell Lord Haldane that the arrangements
for the Supreme Command during the battle were not satisfactory. Sir John French was at Philomel (near Lillers) 25 miles
nearly from his CGS who was at St. Omer with GHQ. Many of
us felt that if these conditions continued it would be difficult
ever to win! Lord Haldane said that he was very glad to have had
this talk with me, and seemed much impressed with the serious
opinions which I'd expressed to him.

Whatever he said to Haig, Haldane reported back to London that no
blame for failure could be attached to Sir John French and that the
relationship between him and Haig had simply become overheated.
As against that, intelligence from captured prisoners and others
tended increasingly to suggest a seriously missed opportunity,
probably overstated by Charteris: 'We had in fact broken the German
line as clean as a whistle. For four hours there was a glaring gap; then
it was gone.'[19]

Churchill, by contrast with Haldane, intended to write to Asquith
in a different sense on 4 October 1915, although in the event the
critical part of the letter was excised by him:

> Sir Douglas Haig in spite of his feeble powers of speech is
> incontestably the most highly educated & intellectually gifted
> soldier we possess; & he has solid achievements in the field
> behind him. His science with Lloyd George's drive and pene-
> trating insight wd thus secure what we now lack altogether –
> *viz.* an efficient composite brain for war direction with military
> affairs.[20]

Robertson, in London for talks with the Cabinet, was contacted by
Stamfordham, on the orders of the King, and asked if he did not
think that it was time for French to go. Robertson had already
criticised French to Hankey and Kitchener. On this occasion he

remained studiously loyal to his chief despite his own views, but when he returned to France on 17 October he asked Haig what he should say. Haig

> told him at once that up to date I had been more [than] loyal to French and did my best to stop all criticisms of him or his methods. Now at last, in view of what had happened in the recent battle over the Reserves, and in view of the seriousness of the general military situation, I had come to the conclusion that it was not fair to the Empire to retain French in command on this main battle front. Moreover none of my officers command-ing Corps had a high opinion of Sir J's military ability or military views; in fact, they had no confidence in him. Ro-bertson quite agreed, and left me saying 'He knew now how to act and would report to Stamfordham.'

A week later the King, in France visiting the army, asked Haig to dine with him.

> After dinner, the King asked me to come to his room, and asked me about Sir J. French's leadership. I told him that I thought the time to have removed French was after the Retreat, because he had so mismanaged matters, and shown in the handling of the small Expeditionary Force in the Field a great ignorance of the essential principles of war. Since then, during the trench warfare, the Army had grown larger and I thought at first there was no great scope for French to go wrong. I have therefore done my utmost to stop criticisms and make matters run smoothly. But French's handling of the reserves in the last battle, his obstinacy and conceit, showed his incapacity, and it seemed to be impossible for anyone to prevent him doing the same things again. I therefore thought strongly, that, for the sake of the Empire, French ought to be removed. I, personally, was ready to do my duty in any capacity, and of course would serve under anyone who was chosen for his military skill to be C-in-C. The

King said that he had seen Generals Gough and Haking that afternoon, and that they had told him startling truths of French's unfitness for the command. General Robertson also told him that it was 'impossible to deal with French, his mind was never the same for two consecutive minutes.'

Gough and Haking told the King that 'everyone had lost confidence in the C-in-C'. Haig 'entirely corroborated what the other two had said, but went much further and said that the C-in-C was a source of great weakness to the army, and that no one had any confidence in him and the war.' The pointless flourish about being personally ready to do his duty in any capacity was one that leaped to Haig's lips in such situations.

It was in the course of this visit that the King was thrown from Haig's horse when it was disturbed by cheering soldiers and suffered quite serious internal bruising. Although the King reassured him, Haig was greatly embarrassed by the behaviour of his horse, which had always proved docile in the past. Alan Clark in *The Donkeys* has drawn attention to (and exaggerated) the amount of space Haig's devotes in his diary

> to an account of, and apologia for this incident . . . On and on rambles the text, as we read that it was a chestnut mare, that Haig had ridden her regularly for over a year, that she had been tried the day before with cheering men and people waving flags, but hats – not flags – were waved, that the grass was wet, that the ground was slippery, that the King seemed to clutch the reins *very firmly* (a tricky passage, this), and to pull the mare backwards, that the cheering would upset any horse at such a distance, and so on.[21]

During his visit, the King wrote to Stamfordham: 'The troops here are all right, but I find that several of the most important Generals have entirely lost confidence in the CIC and they assured me that it was universal and that he must go, otherwise we should never win this war. This has been my opinion for some time.'[22]

What happened next was that French unwisely published a very partial account of the battle in his Despatch in *The Times* on 2 November. Haig was furious about its content, particularly regarding errors in the times at which the reserve divisions were transferred from GHQ to his control. An exchange of correspondence resulted in the receipt by Haig of two letters on 8 November, one ordering that the correspondence should cease and the second saying that the Despatch was 'substantially correct' and did not call for amendment. Haig ignored the order and eventually, at a meeting on 10 November, French effectively climbed down and promised to forward Haig's letters to the War Office, giving him sight of the covering letter. Haig had gone so far as to send a criticism of GHQ, together with copies of the relevant orders, to Lady Haig, who passed them, via Stamfordham, to the King.

Rawlinson was no less enthusiastic in seeking a replacement for French, with whom his relations had always been difficult. While the Battle of Loos was still underway he was claiming that a wonderful opportunity had been lost because of the lack of reserves. He directed his campaign through Derby, who was told that:

If the Cabinet did not take steps to strengthen the General Staff at home and to change the command of the army in France we shall go very near losing this war . . . Now in my opinion the only hope we have of avoiding further strategical mistakes is to appoint Robertson . . . to a supreme position at the War Office . . . and to appoint Sir John to the command of the troops in the British Isles replacing him here by Douglas Haig. If you do not do this you will continue to have vacillation and indecision at home and no hope of accomplishing any decisive success on the Western front. Cannot you use your influence at home to bring these changes about?[23]

The momentum of events and opinion was now strongly biased against French. In *The Times* on 2 November Repington (well disposed to him) had praised his qualities as a commander, and even implied that he rather than Haig should have had direct control at Loos, but French was dead in the water, and the continuing machinations had to do less with him than with relatively minor players.

Kitchener was presently on a visit to the Middle East and in his absence Asquith was acting as Secretary of State for War. Under Kitchener the *Imperial* part of the General Staff had almost ceased to exist, and the General Staff itself, on which Haig had lavished so much care earlier in his career, was marginalised, as Kitchener arrogated most of its functions to himself. Kitchener was aware of the view that he monopolised power and would not allow the General Staff to take part in a strategical direction of operations, but he maintained it simply was not true. His assertion need not be taken as definitive, as the syllogistic premises on which his views of military propriety rested were unusual. In his role as Secretary of State, he was simply one of twenty-four fellow-members of the Cabinet, but he felt separated from them, a professional soldier standing apart from a collection of civilians: 'It is repugnant to me to have to reveal military secrets to 23 gentlemen with whom I am barely acquainted.' Moreover, if he were to impart secrets to the Cabinet: 'they would all tell their wives – except Lloyd George, who would tell other people's wives.' When Esher lunched with him on 14 November Haig urged that Kitchener should be disposed of and sent perhaps to India as Viceroy. '[S]ome blood letting [was] . . . necessary for the health of the body politic!' Part of Haig's concern was that Kitchener, currently interested in the Mediterranean and Egypt, 'by his masterful action . . . will give that sphere of the operations an undue prominence in the strategical picture.' Haig wanted no diversion of resources from the Western Front.

Haig and Esher agreed that 'Robertson should be appointed CIGS and to advise the War Committee of the Cabinet direct (not through S of S for War).' The effect of this and various other proposals which Esher and Haig discussed: 'it is hoped, will be to strengthen the Imperial General Staff, and keep it free from the administrative details carried out in the War Office. The CIGS can then devote his whole time to thinking over the war and its problems – will advise the cabinet, and will be in a position to keep in closer touch with the French.'

Haig had earlier suggested that either he or Robertson – it did not matter which – could become the new CIGS. This was almost certainly a disingenuous suggestion, though some commentators have suggested that Haig as CIGS and Robertson as Commander-in-Chief might have been a better arrangement than the other way round. That suggestion does seem bizarre. Churchill, stung by the later revelation that Robertson had described the Cabinet as 'poltroons', *toED*: 'Spiritless cowards, mean-spirited, worthless creatures, (ravens) referred disparagingly to 'General Robertson (who had never himself at any time led even a troop in action, and whose war duties involved him in no more risk than many clerks).'[24]

Immediately after his meeting with Esher, Haig went to London and on 23 November relayed their proposals to Asquith. ('The matters we discussed were of such vital interest to the Empire that I never alluded to my own affairs, and the differences which I had with Sir. J. French'.) He briefed Bonar Law and his Chief Whip, Lord Edmund Talbot, on the following day. On the day following that, Haig and Lady Haig were invited to lunch at 10 Downing Street. There he had the intimidating experience of finding himself next to Margot Asquith. Lady Haig noticed that 'her tirade of questions, certainly very astute and clever, just bewildered his calm Scots mind. He must have felt very embarrassed and he did the only thing possible under the trying circumstances. He simply left the questions unanswered, casting many a worried look across the table to me.'[25]

Kitchener, now returned from the Mediterranean, told Haig that he had written to the Prime Minister recommending that Haig succeed French. Esher was dispatched to tell French that his command was at an end. (Asquith's note ran: 'I entrusted to Lord Esher as an old and most attached friend of Sir John French the duty of conveying to him my views and decision that owing to the strain of the previous months he was no longer able to conduct the campaign.') He was allowed the opportunity of resigning voluntarily with the reward of a Viscountcy and appointment as Field-Marshal, Commander-in-Chief, Home Forces. Sir John took the news badly. He said he could think of nothing he had done to deserve the blow, and that no successor would have a better control of the army. Esher wrote to Asquith, 'I know you will make things as easy for him as possible. He is a poor man, and he has served his country well.'[26]

As for Haig, on 10 December 1915:

> about 7 pm I received an envelope from the Prime Minister marked 'Secret' and enclosed in *three* envelopes! It was dated 10 Downing Street December 8th 1915 and ran as follows: 'Sir J. French has placed in my hands his resignation of the Office of Commander-in-Chief of the forces in France. Subject to the King's approval, I have the pleasure of proposing to you that you should be his successor. I am satisfied that this is the best choice that could be made in the interests of the Army and the country.'

The King did of course approve of Haig's appointment. He wrote to his new Commander-in-Chief and – redundantly – told him to write. Haig of course did as he was told; John French had only written infrequently and in stilted fashion to his titular commander. Haig had been close to King Edward, but was closer to King George. French, like many others, had more respect and affection for the old King, with whom he corresponded on the niceties of etiquette that obsessed Edward, such as the correct dress for inspecting the Corps of Commissionaires. After Edward's death, he wrote to Esher: 'I do think of our old days in King Edward's time and what a difference he made in all our lives. I hope he *knows* how we think of him.'[27] Esher never wavered in his veneration of the institution of the monarchy, but his unqualified admiration for Edward VII was never transferred to George V, whom he increasingly found commonplace, stupid and *bourgeois*.

There was no real alternative to Haig as French's successor. Bridges said that 'Popular opinion pointed to Haig as the *prétendant,* though Plumer would probably have had the army's vote. But happily the choice of Commander-in-Chief was not part of our duty.'[28] Haig had already leapfrogged Plumer when he was appointed to Aldershot, and was promoted above him in November 1914. His experience of current warfare was unchallenged. Two years later, when Haig was himself in danger of being sacked and replaced, it was still Plumer who was his main rival. Repington then wrote that 'One plot is for Haig to be called and put in French's place [in command of the home forces] and Plumer to have command in France', and some weeks later he quoted a senior military colleague: 'Plumer is considered a lucky general by the troops. Haig has the army's confidence, but they seldom see him. They would prefer Plumer if there were to be a change.'[29] The views of Bridges and of Repington's friends are of no evidential value in themselves, but they do fit in with the general mood of contemporary and military opinion. Plumer's reputation steadily increased as the war went on and he would have been Haig's obvious successor; but there was never any significant move to have him take the succession. Plumer was arguably a better army commander than Haig would ever have been, but Haig was a better Commander-in-Chief than Plumer would ever have been.

French's resignation was effective from 17 December and Haig met him on the following day at St Omer (there was a joke by French that his title would be 'Lord St Omer'):

He did not look very well and seemed short of breath at times. He expressed a wish to help me and the Army in France to the best of his power at home. Then he said that 'There was a delicate personal matter' which he wished to speak about. This was that he wanted to give Winston Churchill an Infantry Brigade. This had been vetoed but he was anxious that Winston should have a battalion. I replied that I had no objection because Winston had done some good work in the trenches and we were short of Battalion COs. I then said goodbye. Winston Churchill then appeared and I told him what I had said to French.

Churchill wrote to Clementine that night:

Haig came to see French who told him the whole position. I was called in and had an interview with Haig. He treated me with the utmost kindness of manner & consideration, assured me that nothing wd give him greater pleasure than to give me a Brigade, that his only wish was that able men shd come to the front, & that I might count on his sympathy in every way. He had heard from Cavan of the 'excellent work' that I had done in the trenches . . . I was greatly reassured by his manner wh. was affectionate almost. He took me by the arm and made the greatest fuss. I used to know him pretty well in the old days when he was a major & I was a young MP, but I am bound to say the warmth of his greeting surprised me . . . So I am back on my perch, again with my feathers stroked down.[30]

Churchill accompanied French as he relinquished his command, and wrote later, 'His pain giving up his great command was acute. He would much rather have given up his life.'

Haldane wrote to his mother in December 1915 to tell him that Haig had replaced French:

You will I expect be sorry to see that your old friend Sir John French, who is to become Viscount French, has been removed from the command in France and is to be succeeded by Haig. I know them both intimately. We owe a great debt to French for his courage and leadership during the critical first months of the war. He is a leader in a way in which Haig can never be, for Haig is too reserved and too inarticulate to be able to make a personal appeal to men. But on the whole I think the change is justified. Haig's character is yet more solid than French's and he is technically far better equipped. I owe a great deal to his sound judgement and wide knowledge both of principles and detail, which were invaluable to me in getting my reforms through. He is, I think, best equipped to deal with the new type of warfare which has come upon us.[31]

French was not an 'educated' soldier: his approach was instinctive, full of panache and flair. He was a soldier's soldier, at his best in the cavalry dashes of the South African War. He conveyed enthusiasm and a reassuring *impression* of professional knowledge that carried him forward in the army. While he was ambitious, he had a genuine love for his country and the army. He had been bitterly depressed, immediately before the war, to think that he would never be in command again, and he was equally upset, and far more bitter, when he was obliged to resign his command. He did not have a big enough view, nor did he have the administrative gifts, to command the British armies in France, but he was not negligible. He was loved by the troops, who cheered him all the way to Boulogne and on to the ship that took him back to England, and he was highly respected by military experts too. Haldane and Esher thought well of him, even though they recognised that it was correct that he should be superseded by Haig.

The most interesting commentator on French's military abilities was Haig. Generally people were either strongly for or against French, but Haig was both. He was greatly impressed by French in the early stages of his own career, and severely critical after 1914. He may simply have seen French first as a benefactor and then as a rival, or his views may have changed because he saw him first in command of limited cavalry forces and later responsible for the combined strength of several armies. Haig was in no personal doubt that his motive for turning against his chief was altruistic: he considered him woefully inadequate for the position he occupied. He was quite clear that French deserved to be dismissed and after the end of the war he referred to French's having been '*recalled* from the command . . . for *incompetence*'. In his memoirs, *1914*, French came close to acknowledging his own shortcomings: 'No previous experience, no conclusion I had been able to draw from campaigns in which I had taken part, or from a close study of the new conditions in which the war of today is waged had led me to anticipate a war of positions. All my thoughts, all my prospective plans, all my possible alternatives of action, were concentrated upon a war of movement and manpower.' He arguably apprehended this contrast between the war that was being fought and the war for which the army had prepared faster than Haig, but he did not draw practical conclusions from that apprehension.

The bitterness that persisted between the two comrades was sad, though it did not last for ever. 'I would not receive Viscount French in my house. I despise him too much personally for that.' Even eighteen months later, when French pressed the claim of a senior officer to a Division, Haig's reply was cold: 'I will give Bingham's claims such consideration as I can, but as you know, Divisional vacancies do not occur frequently, and I have a large number of brigadiers highly recommended for advancement, and who have commanded their Brigades in all the hottest fighting during the last 18 months . . .'[32] Haig's reply did not reciprocate the warm personal remarks that had been contained in French's letter.

Field-Marshal Lord Chetwode was surprised by Haig's bitterness:

He owed everything to French, who brought him out of nothing to prominence in South Africa, and was behind him in all his subsequent big appointments. I grant you that the two men were poles apart in their temperaments. French was a man who loved life, laughter and women, whereas Haig was a dour Scotsman and the dullest dog I ever had the happiness to meet . . . French was full of imagination, and to my mind a man who might have done big things in open warfare. He was a lucky general, and inspired the greatest confidence in his troops. Haig never got anywhere near his troops or officers during the war, with the exception of his immediate and personal entourage . . .[33]

Robertson's appointment was announced on the same day as Haig's. Haig's response fell below the level expected of him:

I am sure that it is good for the government and the country to have such a man in authority at the War Office at this time. He means very well and will succeed I am sure. How much easier, though, it is to work with a gentleman.

This about the man whose appointment he had recommended, and whose son, Brian, was Haig's ADC. Even allowing for the attitudes of the time, pretty appalling.

From now on until 1918, the relationship between Haig and Robertson was important. William Robertson is the only man in British military history to have proved the truth of Napoleon's *dictum* about the marshal's baton in every soldier's knapsack. Indeed, he not only rose from the rank of private soldier to field-marshal, but did so despite the handicap of starting from a lowly social background: his parents were said to have been illegitimate. His father was a village tailor and postmaster in Lincolnshire, and Robertson himself, after leaving school at the age of thirteen, went into domestic service as a footman. When, as a result of his efforts and ability, he obtained a commission, he increased his handicap by choosing to be gazetted in the cavalry, where his background and poverty distinguished him all the more from his brother officers, who were from the upper middle classes if not from still more rarefied strata of society, and all possessed of private incomes. In India he lived a very different life from his colleagues: self-disciplined, focused on his profession, working while others slept. He learned not just Hindi, which was usual, but also, which was very unusual, four other oriental languages, Urdu, Persian, Punjabi and Pashtu.

By retiring early to bed and leading an abstemious life I avoided the rather common and injurious habit of sleeping during the day, and utilised the time in learning Hindustani. My munshi, or teacher, a man of a stout and lethargic type, was quite content with whatever progress his pupils made, or did not make, provided he regularly received his monthly pay of 10 rupees. To keep awake when teaching after his mid-day meal was entirely beyond his powers, and he could not understand why I should wish to work while other Sahibs either took their lessons in the evening or not at all. By degrees I caused him to see that this was not my method of doing business.[34]

Later he learned French and German (he undertook translation of
German heavy artillery regulations at one stage in his career). He won
many prizes, in tent-pegging, swordsmanship, fencing and other
contests including the prize for the best officer-at-arms.

> These achievements, such as they were, were mainly due to
> keeping myself physically fit - not an easy thing to do in the
> plains of India unless one is blessed with a strong constitution,
> and is careful to safeguard it by temperate habits and suitable
> exercise.
>
> I claim no credit for pursuing these habits, because I had not
> the wherewithal to do otherwise. Water was the only drink I
> could afford, while for smoking I had to be content with a fixed
> amount of tobacco and cheroots at two shillings a hundred. It
> was not altogether agreeable to be seen drinking water at the
> mess when others were drinking champagne, or to defer
> smoking to leaving the mess because pipes were not allowed,
> but it had to be done.[35]

From India he went to Staff College. He was not an exact contemporary of Haig, but he valued the training that they had in
common, as he recalled when he wrote of his time as CIGS:

> In the case of Haig the exchange of views and the transmission
> of the War Cabinet's instructions were comparatively easy, since
> we could meet at frequent intervals and discuss matters verbally
> [*sic*]; but here also [as in the case of more distant commanders]
> the work of both of us was facilitated by our Staff College
> training, and, as with . . . the other Commanders . . . , there
> was never, so far as I know, any material difference of opinion
> between us in regard to the main principles to observe in order
> to win the war.[36]

After Staff College he was appointed to the Intelligence Staff of the
War Office, and later worked in Intelligence during the opening of

the South African War. His career thereafter proceeded unchecked to the highest of ranks.

Despite his proficiency in such a wide range of foreign languages, he never lost his regional English accent. As has already been seen, when he told Horace Smith-Dorrien that he was being removed from command of the Second Army, he is famously said to have announced, "'orace, yer for 'ome.'[37] (Considerable scholarship has been devoted to the suggestion of an alternative reading, comprehensible to Smith-Dorrien as a cavalryman: "'orace, you're thrown". Another version, *ben trovata* rather than scholarly, is: 'Well, 'Orace, I'm afraid you 'ave to 'op it'.) He was universally known as 'Wully'; except when Northcliffe turned against him and named him 'Wooly'.

Robertson had a sense of humour and could be self-deprecating in a way that Haig never was. (There is an agreeable lightness of touch in Robertson's writings.) When Robertson was CGS at GHQ in France, the GSO 1 (Operations) was Colonel G.M. Harper, the military abbreviation for whose post was O(a). When he was asked what this stood for, Robertson replied 'old 'Arper'. He modestly claimed that he had only made one good joke in his life: 'I was crossing the Channel during the war, together with Lord Rhondda, the Food Controller. It was very rough and, seeing my companion violently sick over the ship's side, I went over to him and said, "I say, Rhondda, I don't think you are much of a Food Controller!".'

Although able, ambitious and intelligent, he displayed in discussion or argument a lack of social confidence that led him to be laconic and abrupt. In Cabinet, when Lloyd George would say to him, 'I've heard it said that . . .', and put to him a proposition with which he disagreed, he simply slammed his ruler on the table and said, 'I've 'eard different.' Despite that, he was reasonably adept, as CIGS, at handling the politicians, and despaired of Haig's insensitivity and lack of political finesse. In other respects Robertson's qualities were not unlike Haig's. He was a capable organiser and made the General Staff a highly efficient machine, through which he came to dominate strategical control on all fronts. He had *gravitas* and authority founded on ability and military knowledge, but that knowledge, according to his critics, was entirely book-learned, and he would not deviate from the principles that he expounded slowly and deliberately. Spears told Wilson to give French words an English pronunciation, otherwise Robertson would not understand them. French politicians were frustrated by his stolid intransigence, and called him 'General Non Non', and to the mercurial and imaginative Lloyd George his principles were platitudinous. But Hankey, who as Secretary of the War Cabinet knew him and understood him as well as anyone, found that 'Taking him all in all he was within his limitations a rugged, dogged, able and likeable man'.[38]

Throughout his time as CIGS, and indeed to an extent before that, he and Haig worked in the closest of associations. Not only were they inevitably in close contact in their respective military offices, but they were by far the two most powerful advocates of a Western policy, and required continually to confer and coordinate their arguments to resist the attacks of the Easterners and waverers in the Cabinet. Although they sometimes seem to be an inseparable double-act, the Tweedledum and Tweedledee of the Western Front, there was no real affection between them nor any lasting social contact. As long as Robertson was CIGS he did everything he could to support and protect Haig, but when he was in danger of deposition, Haig did nothing to defend Robertson. After the war Lord Milner gave a dinner for the army commanders. Haig made a speech in which he praised Wilson, Robertson's successor, whom he disliked, distrusted and wrongly suspected of consistent intrigue against him. He made no mention of what Robertson had done as CIGS. As Robertson left the Senior Service Club, his response was, 'I'll never go farting with 'Aig again.' Whatever the precise meaning of this utterance, it seems clear that he was not pleased with Haig.[39]

Robertson came to his new post as a convinced Westerner, reinforced in that position by the views of the Prime Minister: Asquith had told him, in connection with developments in Persia and Afghanistan, that he did not care what happened there, so long as Germany was defeated in Europe. He had strong views on the proper constitutional role of the Chief of the Imperial General Staff. He insisted that all operational orders issued to Commanders-in-Chief to give effect to the government's military policy be sent by the CIGS and not in the name of the Army Council, over the signature of the Secretary of the Council – 'a civilian'. He was bringing to his new office, whose function was ill-defined, an expanded concept of his role as CGS at GHQ. There the CGS was officially defined as the Commander-in-Chief's 'responsible adviser on all matters affecting military operations, through whom he exercises his functions of command, and by whom all orders issued by him will be signed.'

Robertson's requirement, that operational orders were to be signed by him and not the Secretary of the Army Council, was not acceptable to Kitchener, who said that it would be impossible for him to remain as Secretary of State for War without full executive power and with his functions curtailed to the feeding and clothing of the army. He said that he would be prepared to resign as Secretary of State, but might continue as a member of the War Council. Kitchener was passing through Calais on the night that Robertson received this response. Robertson drove to Calais, to meet Kitchener's train. It was about to leave, so he jumped in and continued the discussion with the Secretary of State until two in the morning. He had wanted to alter the existing system of issuing orders for two reasons. First, because of delays on the part of the Army Council, which consisted at that time of eight members, four military and four civil, later with three further military members. 'My second objection to this sham system was that it prevented the General Staff at the War Office from being recognised as the Great General Staff of our Armies at the Front, and in my opinion this recognition was essential.'[40]

Ultimately, after discussion and a little redrafting, Kitchener accepted the force of Robertson's proposals, which were incorporated in a long letter to the Secretary of State dated 5 December 1915. They were approved in an Order in Council of 27 January 1916. This change was followed by various other structural changes in the direction of the war. The Committee of Imperial Defence was replaced by the War Council (which became the Dardanelles Committee) and then by the War Cabinet. Hankey was successively Secretary of the Committee of Imperial Defence, The War Council, the Dardenelles Committee and the War Cabinet, and in due course became the secretary of the Cabinet itself, which until then, even in war time, had not had a secretariat. Hankey created the War Cabinet and its procedures. Its authority overrode that of all government departments, which were required to report to it. The War Cabinet's decisions were to be implemented as soon as the minutes were initialled by the Prime Minister. When Lloyd George, as he frequently did, failed to give them his imprimatur, Hankey simply issued them anyway. Each of these changes marked an improvement on what had gone before, but even the War Cabinet was imperfect, and Britain's machinery for waging total war remained unsatisfactory to the end. The Secretary of State for War, the First Lord and the Foreign Secretary were not members of the War Cabinet and had to be brought in specially, as also had others. Despite these peculiar omissions, there were too many members. Robertson recorded that 'My experience leads me to add that the War Cabinet did not by any means provide a complete remedy for the evils from which its predecessor had suffered.'[41] Churchill, observing these defects, drew crucial lessons from them when he created his own command structure in 1940.

When Churchill, given a battalion by Haig after he had been offered a brigade by French, achieved supreme power in May 1940, he was 'conscious of a profound sense of relief. At last I had the authority to give directions over the whole scene.' In his memoirs he shared with the public the fact that, 'I felt as if I were walking with destiny, and that all my past life had been but a preparation for this hour and for this trial.'[42] Haig would have felt that it was beneath him to share his intimate thoughts in this way and he revealed little in his letters and diaries about his emotions, except to say to his wife: 'I can honestly say that no one in this army has been so highly tested as I have been in this war.' His niece, Ruth du Pree, wrote to congratulate him and said that all he required now was Bemersyde and a son. 'You have made the name of Haig illustrious – hitherto it has been celebrated merely by reproducing its species and keeping Thomas the Rhymer's prophecy true!' Haig's reply was downbeat: 'There has been no celebrated man in the family, and the quicker it dies out the better'.[43] But he must have seen his appointment as Commander-in-Chief as the vindication of a life spent in the advancement of his military career. The late start, the difficulties in reaching Sandhurst and the Staff College, were forgotten. The ascetic self-discipline of his years in India, the study of the teachings of the great soldiers, the long days at the War Office where he had moulded the army that was now his to deploy: all had been worthwhile. What he had achieved was the result of ambition, application and a belief that it was his duty to play his part at as high a level as he could in safeguarding and defending a country and empire whose values he uncritically accepted. He had complete confidence in his ability to deal with the task he had been given, and no doubts about the way in which the task should be tackled: he assumed the Supreme Command with a sense neither of triumph nor of diffidence.

15

HAIG'S COMMAND

The year 1916 marked an entirely new phase in Haig's career. It is not too difficult to assess his performance as an army commander. He had done pretty well, recognising that he was involved in a new type of warfare, and making intelligent attempts to react to the circumstances in which he found himself. The remainder of his military career is much harder to assess. As Commander-in-Chief, French (now Viscount French of Ypres: he had gone quietly, taking the peerage and command of the Home Forces), had not performed adequately. He was thrown off his stride by the nature of the war he found himself fighting, he did not understand his role in the Anglo-French alliance, he lacked steadiness, and was too readily affected both by successes and failures. Crucially, he lacked the authority that was required to impose his will on his command. But, large as that command was, the forces at his disposal were of a scale comprehensible to commanders of the past. The difficulty about making a judgement on Haig is that his command was now increasing hugely, as the New Armies became available.

The scale of the resources at his disposal gave Haig an obvious advantage over French, who had been asked to direct a twentieth-century total war with nineteenth-century *matériel* and manpower. On the other hand Haig was required to command sixty divisions on the Somme. Montgomery had eleven at Second Alamein, and

Montgomery had the advantage of being able to concentrate on his role as an Army Group Commander, leaving administrative concerns to Alexander, as Theatre Commander. Haig effectively combined both roles.[1] He commanded numbers of men that no British general had ever had at his disposal before, and none has had since. There is nothing against which to measure Haig. From the outset of his command he had to fight to defend his strategy, but there was no realistic alternative. The losses on the Western Front were terrible, and the conditions under which men fought the unremitting, dehumanised war of attrition remain an affront to humanity. Haig could not see how the Germans could be defeated except on the Western Front, 'where they are'. Though his emotions repeatedly hankered after movement and dash, in principle he accepted without reservation a strategy of wearing down the enemy at a cost in his own men's lives that would not be greatly different from the price paid by the enemy. His critics, and even his friends, did not see below the surface, and referred to his lack of imagination. An increasingly disenchanted Lloyd George ('I never met anyone in a high position who seemed to me so utterly devoid of imagination [as Haig]') felt that there *must* be an alternative to the Western Front. As early as 1 January 1915 he had written a paper for the Committee for Imperial Defence, entitled 'The War – Suggestions as to the Military Position'. It was a thoughtful reaction to the stalemate that was being encountered:

> There is a real danger that the people of Great Britain and of France will sooner or later get tired of long casualty lists explained by monotonous and rather banal telegrams from headquarters about 'heavy cannonades', 'making a little progress' at certain points, 'recovering trenches', the loss of which has never been reported, etc., with the net result that we have not advanced a yard after weeks of heavy fighting.

He advocated an attack on Austria, in conjunction with an attack on Turkey.

Unless we are prepared for some project of this character I
frankly despair of our achieving any successes in this war. I can
see nothing but an eternal stalemate on any other lines. The
process of economic exhaustion alone will not bring us a
triumphant peace as long as Germany is in possession of these
rich allied territories. No country has ever given in under such
pressure, apart from defeat in the field. Burke was always
indulging in prophecies of victory as a result of France's
exhaustion. The war with France went on for twenty years
after he indulged in his futile predictions . . .[2]

Churchill, who was much less personally frustrated by Haig and never
entirely lost his respect for him, had seen the Dardanelles as an
alternative, and continued to look for a route to victory that did not lie
through the trenches of France and Flanders. But the weight of the
German military machine was on the Western Front, and no one has
yet been able to suggest a realistic means for the Allies to maintain a
defensive presence there while simultaneously bringing sufficient force
to bear on the Central Powers elsewhere. The Dardanelles, Salonika
and even Italy offered no serious prospect of ultimate victory. The
carnage in France and Flanders, and a type of static warfare in which
little room was left for individual skill or initiative, and where men in
their thousands did not even die soldiers' deaths but drowned in the
mud or were vaporised by high explosive, inevitably produces the
reaction that such a state of affairs is intolerable and unacceptable and
that no one who presided over it can be militarily competent. The
reaction is understandable but without a basis in logic.

Criticism, indignation, anger is still often directed against Haig
not for anything for which he was personally responsible, but because
he is the symbol of an appalling war and of warfare formed by the
industrial age in which dehumanised masses were carried to their
deaths by conveyor belt. The nature of that war was already well
established before Haig became Commander-in-Chief. In the first
five months of the war almost four and half million casualties were
sustained by the European powers. By the time Haig became

Commander-in-Chief, Britain's casualties totalled half a million. France, with a population 15 per cent less than that of Britain, had sustained almost two million casualties. The disparity between these figures is the reason for the major role which Britain was to play in the battle for which Haig was now preparing: the Battle of the Somme. That has long been known and understood. What is less easy to understand is why, against the background of these appalling statistics, it should be Haig who is singled out as a butcher.[3]

The most that can be argued is that Haig, as one of the principal planners for the war, should have foreseen the possibility of stalemate and sought to devise a strategy which would avoid it. With hindsight, Haig's successors tried to do that when they planned for the invasion of Europe in the Second World War. Churchill's planning for D-day and indeed the deferral of the opening of the Second Front was informed by his determination to avoid the type of warfare he had seen a generation earlier. Haig never doubted that war with Germany, when it came, would be on a scale quite different from anything that the world had seen. He was one of the minority that recognised that the war would continue for many years. But he expected this titanic struggle to be of the same nature as earlier conflicts, characterised by mobility and dominated by cavalry. Neither he – nor anyone else – challenged the view that given the existence of the Schlieffen Plan and the French Plan 17, the conflict would take place in the west. Many commentators thought that the scale of the contest would be such that the struggle could not be long lasting. Haig drew the opposite conclusion. But no one could see an alternative to a massive clash on the frontiers of France and Germany. In assessing how well Haig discharged his role as Commander-in-Chief of the British armies in France, one has to keep in mind not only what he did, but also what else he could have done and whether there was any plausible case for an alternative.

Both the Allies and the Central Powers entered 1916 determined to see an issue in the course of the year. The previous year had been one of recognition of the realities of trench warfare, and of experiment, reaction and adaptation. Falkenhayn, the Kaiser's Chief of

Staff, concluded, even before the end of 1915, that France had reached breaking point. The break itself would be achieved by a concentrated offensive and a single target which would: 'compel the French to throw in every man they have. If they do so the forces of France will bleed to death.' The consequence would be that 'England's best sword is knocked out of her hand.' The target was to be a fortress with a special, almost mystic, significance for France: Verdun.

Generally, the activity of the Germans in these months, so far as not directed towards their plans for Verdun, consisted of improving their defences. The Allies' essential concern, expulsion of the Germans from the parts of France and Belgium that they occupied, meant that their barbed wire and dug-outs were far less substantial than the German equivalents. In certain areas in the early months of 1916, the Germans did mount local attacks. On 14 February they seized an important British artillery observation post known as The Bluff, an artificial mound two miles south of Ypres in the sector commanded by Plumer. Four days later, Haig visited Second Army Headquarters and

[s]poke to General Plumer alone; he admitted that the defences were bad but said that he had been short of men, and the weather had been bad, etc. that he had withdrawn troops to train by my orders. I pointed out that before the Loos battle we had made 16 miles of trenches in open ground and under close view of the enemy. He then said he was quite ready to go if I thought it desirable. He was only too anxious to do what was best. He behaved altogether in such a straightforward way and is such a thorough gentleman that I said I would think over the matter and let him know tomorrow. I added that it is a matter of no small importance to get rid of an army commander. At the same time this is no time to have any doubts about anyone's capacity to discharge his duty. I got back to St. Omer in time for lunch. After thinking over the matter I wrote to Sir H. Plumer that I wished him to continue in his Command and to do his

utmost to strengthen his defences with as little delay as possible. If, however, after a reasonable time I found little improvement in the general arrangements and conditions of the 2nd Army, I should feel it my duty in view of the great task which lies before this Army, to ask him to resign of his command . . .

Haig had firmly intended to dispose of Plumer: he had warned Robertson, whom he had asked to 'try and give Plumer some other job so as to let him down lightly'. A letter from Haig to the King suggests that he had already voiced his misgivings to the Palace. Haig's relations with Plumer were never easy. Plumer was always his main potential rival, and that is an obvious possible explanation for the *froideur*, but it is one for which there is no supporting evidence. Plumer had been the Staff College examiner who reported unfavour-ably on him. Again, Haig may simply have thought of Plumer as one of yesterday's officers, discredited by some time on half-pay in the course of his career. The first period of half-pay started in November 1905, when it was thought that he had resigned in protest against Haldane's policies, though it seems likely that he was dismissed because he was too closely identified with the unpopular reforms of Arnold-Forster. From then onwards he was at pains to emphasise his loyalty to his superior officers and identity with the military estab-lishment.[4] Despite his efforts, he spent another two years on half-pay between 1909 and 1911. Haig was always impatient of older officers standing in the way of the promotion of able, younger men. Plumer was in fact a mere four years older than Haig, although in appearance more elderly than that. But four years were enough for Haig with his strange hang-up about age: Plumer was almost always referred to in the diary as 'old' Plumer.

Plumer, for his part, at least after the 1905 half-pay period, was the most loyal of army commanders. It was a point of honour to him, even after the war, never to criticise his brother officers, never to seek to justify his own conduct, and never to enter into any controversy. One of the reasons, although Haig did not know it, that Plumer was later to decline the opportunity to succeed Robertson as CIGS was that he did not wish to have to take a part in what then seemed likely, the dismissal of Haig. Had he wished to, he could almost certainly have intrigued to succeed Haig early in 1918. As it was, his relationship with the Commander-in-Chief was correct, but never close: there was none of the friendship that existed between Haig and Gough or Rawlinson. But Plumer was far from alone in having a distant and correct relationship with his Commander-in-Chief. At Messines, and in some stages of Third Ypres, he was to achieve, on the basis of meticulous planning, some of the most complete victories of the war, but Haig always remained grudging and condescending.

In the follow-up to the loss of The Bluff, Haig kept Plumer on a very short rein. Perhaps mindful of Haig's complaint that he was too kind to his generals, Plumer wanted to remove General Turner, commanding the 2nd Canadian Division, and Brigadier-General Ketchen, commanding the 2nd Canadian Brigade. Haig refused his request, though probably for good political reasons.

The Allies braced themselves for heroic efforts in 1916. France vastly increased her industrial output and in particular her production of shells. Although almost 80 per cent of those of military age had already been conscripted (as opposed to less than 50 per cent in Germany), France managed to create twenty-five new infantry divisions in the year to the spring of 1916. Britain's production of armaments increased too, particularly after Lloyd George became Minister for Munitions. Kitchener's New Armies were coming on stream and by spring 1916 there had been a tenfold expansion in the size of the army, with seventy divisions under arms.[5]

In a sense, 1916 began at the allied conference at Chantilly at the end of 1915. At the time of the conference Sir John French was still Commander-in-Chief, but shortly after his resignation Haig paid a formal visit to Joffre and expressed his agreement with the general scheme that had been agreed. Joffre had argued for limited attacks by the French armies followed by a major Allied attack. Haig accepted the plan and selected for Britain's part of the offensive the area between the Somme and Vimy Ridge, or alternatively an area in

Belgium and Northern France between the Lys and the sea. As always he was attracted by the possibility of joint military and naval operations. But Joffre's insistence on an attack south of the Somme meant that was where Britain would fight.

It is suggested that Haig thought that his Somme offensive could end the war. In his more considered moments he never did believe that, but separately from Chantilly, he had already, in an appreciation of his own, envisaged a final offensive in 1916, although in 'the early autumn, when the British Armies would have reached the high-water mark of their strength, equipment and training'.[6] The advancing of the British element of 1916 to meet the requirements of the French meant that the early autumn plans were forgotten.

On Sunday 2 January 1916 Haig attended the Church of Scotland service in St Omer, held in what had been a dingy little concert hall at 116 Rue de Dunkerque. The chaplain was a young Scot, George Duncan. Duncan had studied classics at Edinburgh and Cambridge Universities. He then decided to go into the ministry of the Church of Scotland. To that end he spent three more years at Edinburgh, a winter at St Andrews University and three summers at German universities. In the summer of 1914, as the war was breaking out, he was carrying out postgraduate studies of the New Testament at Heidelberg, and was able to find his way back to Britain only a week before the outbreak of war. He was to become, in effect, Haig's chaplain for the rest of the Great War. In the memorial issue of the British Legion *Journal*, Duncan recalled that he was closely associated with Haig as a chaplain for all but the first two weeks of Haig's time as Commander-in-Chief, 'and every relation I had with him led me to admire him as I admired no other man on earth.'[7] He was a highly intelligent man, who ended his career as Regius Professor of Biblical Criticism and Principal of St Mary's College, St Andrews. He was perceptive and sensitive and his book, *Douglas Haig as I Knew Him*, published in 1966, in an attempt to correct what he regarded as a false impression given by work such as Alan Clark's *The Donkeys*, is an important and revealing analysis of Haig's psychology.

Despite the influence of his mother, until now religion had not played a particularly large part in Haig's life. Although he had been brought up in the Church of Scotland, he had largely attended Anglican services (in India, for instance, he did not attend the Church of Scotland services) but he was not an assiduous attender in any church, and Sundays were often devoted to golf.

Haig recorded his first visit to the St Omer Church of Scotland in his diary:

> Service was held in a school up a stair. A most earnest young Scotsman, George Duncan, conducted the service. He told us that in our prayers we should be as natural as possible and tell the Almighty exactly what we feel we want. The nation is now learning to pray, and nothing can withstand the prayers of a great united people. The congregation was greatly impressed, and one could have heard a pin drop during the service. So different to the coughing and restlessness which goes on in church during peacetime.

To George Duncan's surprise, the Commander-in-Chief appeared the following Sunday:

> I attended the Scottish church at 9.30 am. The clergyman (George Duncan), is most earnest and impressive. Quite after the old covenanting style. 'Whatever your work is,' he said, 'Do it well, and have God always with you'. He was well aware of the difficulties of praying in the Barrack Room, etc; that was not essential, but constant communing with God for a regular period was necessary every day – when walking or when doing work. Such a habit gives one added strength. Pray without ceasing.

Thereafter Haig attended every Sunday unless he was absent from GHQ, and when at the end of March 1916 he transferred his headquarters to Montreuil, Duncan was moved with him.

A family group *circa* 1865. Douglas is in front, to his mother's left. His father's magnificent beard prompted cat-calls at political meetings. (© *Trustees of the National Library of Scotland*)

Douglas Haig about three years old. He had to be bribed with the present of the pistol to pose, and he wears skirts. His interest in weapons persisted. (© *Trustees of the National Library of Scotland*)

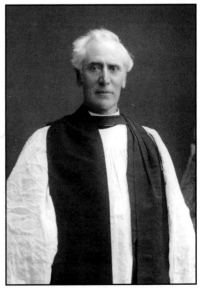

The Rt Revd John Percival. A great Victorian educator and first headmaster of Clifton. He had 'the grace of a marble statue' and on sight the artist G.F. Watts wished to paint his portrait. His moral impact was no less powerful. (© *National Portrait Gallery*)

Haig's statue at Clifton. (*Author's collection*)

His mother, Rachel, was devoted to her children. Her deepest concerns were for her youngest son. (© *Trustees of the National Library of Scotland*)

His sister Henrietta took great pains to promote Haig's career. Her social connections and the wealth that her marriage to William Jameson brought allowed her to assist in many practical ways. (© *Trustees of the National Library of Scotland*)

'Daisy', Countess of Warwick. Very rich, very beautiful, very aristocratic and finally very socialist. Haig's lover and the Prince of Wales' mistress. (© *National Portrait Gallery*)

Doris Haig. Haig and Dorothy Vivian were engaged within 36 hours of meeting and married a month later. For the rest of her life this beautiful and intelligent woman devoted herself to her husband and his memory. (© *Trustees of the National Library of Scotland*)

Haig (left) with Haldane during their time at the War Office. Haldane's work in these years entitles him to be regarded as by far Britain's most important Secretary of State for War. (© *Getty Images*)

Sir John French and Mrs Winifred Bennett, his 'little darling'. (© *Imperial War Museum*)

An unforgettable image from Richard Attenborough's film adaptation of *Oh! What a Lovely War*. Haig (John Mills) leapfrogs over his old comrade Sir John French to command the British Armies in France. (© *BFI*)

The official image. Sir William Orpen's portrait of Haig for Brasenose College, Oxford. Long after Haig's death it was defaced by undergraduates with the graffito, 'Murderer of 1,000,000 men'. (© *Bodleian Library, University of Oxford*)

Reginald Brett, second Viscount Esher, the aesthete who was so closely involved in the preparation for war. (© *National Portrait Gallery*)

Above. Churchill and 'Wully' Robertson. Wully had many good qualities, but he was everything that Churchill was not: stolid, unimaginative and conservative. The body language is expressive. (© Getty Images)

Left. David Lloyd George. For most people, by the end of the war Lloyd George was a twinkling Welsh Wizard, 'the man who won the war.' Haig always saw him as a fire-brand rabble-rouser, unscrupulous and intent on bringing down the existing social order. (© National Portrait Gallery)

For most of the war Haig's headquarters were near Montreuil-sur-Mer. This statue in Le Square Douglas Haig replaces an earlier one, destroyed in the Second World War. After publication of his diaries, which revealed anti-French sentiments, the statue was decorated with pigs' heads, whisky bottles and chamber pots. (*Author's collection*)

Haig's headquarters in the Chateau de Beaurepaire were modest by the standards of the times. (*Author's collection*)

Henry Wilson, 'Ugly Wilson', in a typically endearing pose. (© *National Portrait Gallery*)

Colonel Maurice Hankey. Austere, dazzled by Lloyd George, the designer of much of the war's administrative machinery, as well as of modern Cabinet government. (© *National Portrait Gallery*)

John Charteris. As his principal intelligence officer he sustained Haig with an unreliable appraisal of German strength and morale. This photograph was taken in 1926, by which time he was Conservative MP for Dumfriesshire, interesting himself in agriculture, animal welfare and war veterans. (© *National Portrait Gallery*)

In the Second World War generals frequently drove their own jeeps. The almost mediaeval aspects of this picture of Haig congratulating Canadian troops tend to blind us to the incredible feat of modernisation over which he presided. (© *Imperial War Museum*)

Haig at work on his headquarters train with his secretary, Sir Philip Sassoon. (© *Imperial War Museum*)

Haig with Joffre (left) and Foch, walking in the garden at Beauquesne, August 1916.
(© *Imperial War Museum*)

Foch bogged down on the Western Front. His British allies (Haig and Sassoon) fail to come to his aid.
(© *Imperial War Museum*)

The Doullens Conference. Haig respected Clemenceau but cannot have approved of his head-gear. (© *Imperial War Museum*)

The Doullens Conference chamber, untouched since 1918. Haig sat on the chair nearest the camera. An unconvincing representation of him can be seen in the modern stained glass. (*Author's collection*)

The Great Victory March of 1919. Haig was moved by the reception he was accorded by the crowds.
(© *Trustees of the National Library of Scotland*)

Haig's body lies in state in St Columba's Church, Pont Street, London before the funeral service in Westminster Abbey. (© *Getty Images*)

Haig and his wife lie side by side in the grounds of the ruined Dryburgh Abbey, with the same simple headstones as mark the graves of his men who are buried in France. (*Author's collection*)

On my first two Sundays at Montreuil the congregation was so
small that we read the hymns instead of singing them. Before
long, however, I could count on a congregation of about 20,
including a number of men from the Commander-in-Chief's
escort of Lancers under the command of a much loved Scottish
officer, Captain George Black, on whose suggestion the men of
the escort expressed a readiness to attend worship with their
Chief. The Commander-in-Chief himself was invariably present, accompanied perhaps by his assistant military secretary,
Lieutenant-Colonel Alan Fletcher, his Private Secretary, Sir
Philip Sassoon, and one or two other members of his personal
staff; and a few Senior Staff Officers attended from time to time.
Apart from these the congregation consisted almost entirely of
private soldiers. There was no formality or parade as the
Commander-in-Chief arrived and took his seat in that little
wooden hut on the ramparts that now served as our church. As
for myself, I was in no sense a staff chaplain. I was simply the
Presbyterian chaplain attached to GHQ troops, and as such I
remained to the end of the war, a chaplain of the lowest grade,
unattached to any other unit and with my initial rank as
Captain.[8]

De Groot and others, including Sir John Keegan, have made much of
the influence of George Duncan and of their interpretations of Haig's
religious beliefs. Thus Sir John Keegan:

Haig, in whose public manner and private diaries no concern for
human suffering was or is discernible, compensated for his
aloofness with nothing whatsoever of the common touch. He
seemed to move through the horrors of the First World War as
if guided by some inner voice, speaking of a higher purpose and
a personal destiny. That, we now know, was not just appearance. Haig was a devotee both of spiritual practices and of
fundamentalist religion. As a young officer he had taken to
attending séances, where a medium put him in touch with

Napoleon; as Commander-in-Chief he fell under the influence
of a Presbyterian chaplain whose sermons confirmed him in his
belief that he was in direct communication with God and had a
major part to play in a divine plan for the world. His own
simple religion, he was convinced, was shared by his soldiers,
who were inspired thereby to bear the dangers and sufferings
which were their part of the war he was directing.[9]

The last sentence is accurate, but neither Haig's diaries nor Duncan's
evidence supports the idea of a personal destiny. Certainly, Duncan's
ministry, and a stronger religious belief than he formerly had,
supported Haig hugely in carrying the increasingly heavy burdens
that he was required to assume. In a post-war letter to Duncan he
said, 'I had a hard trial before I came across you at St. Omer',[10] and he
made certain that Duncan stayed with him throughout the war.
When the latter suggested that he ought to move on, feeling that a
change would be good for Haig and for himself, Haig vetoed the
proposal. '[H]e put his hand on my shoulder and said quite simply:
"If you are of help to me, I hope you will be satisfied." '[11]

Duncan and Haig would have been equally astounded by the
suggestion that the latter had 'fallen under the influence' of the
former. The relationship was a formal one. Duncan was sometimes
invited back for lunch at GHQ and occasionally had long talks with
the Commander-in-Chief, but his role, while important, was a
strictly limited one and was complementary to, rather than the
cause of, Haig's evolving thoughts on religion. Haig was irritated by
sectarian dissension and by any occasion when, in his view, the
churches failed to emphasise the purpose and nature of the war. Later
he came to urge both on the archbishops and the King the idea of an
imperial church, to bind the Empire together and support its values.
He returned to this idea of an imperial church from time to time. On
22 July 1917, the Archbishop of York, Cosmo Lang, spoke to Haig:

about the necessity of opening the doors of the Church of
England wider. I agreed and said we ought to aim at organising

a great Imperial Church to which all honest citizens of the Empire could belong. In my opinion, Church and State must advance together and hold together against those forces of revolution which threaten to destroy the State.

After his command had ended, he pressed the scheme on George V.

I urged the King to press for the formation of a great-minded Imperial Church, to embrace all our Churches, except the Roman Catholics [because their allegiance went beyond the Empire]. This would be the means of binding the Empire together. In my opinion the Archbishop of Canterbury had missed his opportunity during the war, and not a moment's time should be lost now in getting to work and organising an imperial body of control, consisting of bishops, moderators etc . . . Empires of the past had disappeared because there was no church or religion to bind them together. The British Empire will assuredly share that fate at no distant date unless an Imperial Church is speedily created to unite us all in the service of God.

In May 1916 Haig asked the Archbishop of Canterbury:

Firstly: that the chaplains should preach to the troops about the objects of Great Britain in carrying on this war. We have no selfish motive, but are fighting for the good of humanity. *Secondly*: the chaplains of the Church of England must cease quarrelling amongst themselves. In the Field we cannot tolerate any narrow sectarian ideas. We must all be united whether we are clerics or ordinary troops. We have no selfish motive but are fighting for the good of humanity.

This view was absolutely unquestioned in Haig's mind. Charteris was aware of the paradox that in Germany, as in Britain, sincere clergymen supported the war; but for Haig the moral issue was very clearcut. In April 1917 Charteris recorded:

We had a regular Scottish Sunday. DH took me to church in a little wooden hut in the village. The sermon was to the effect that we all had to believe that God is working in us for a definite purpose; all very cheering if you are quite certain that the purpose is our victory. But it is difficult to see why a German preacher could not preach just such a sermon to Hindenburg and Ludendorff. All the same, DH seems to derive an extra-ordinary amount of moral strength from these sermons. We discussed it after lunch, for all the world as one used to do as a boy in Scotland. Then suddenly DH switched off to a paper which he is preparing for the War Cabinet at home, and was back in 1917 and at war.

While it is true that Germany was an authoritarian state, aggressive and without a developed parliamentary democracy, the causes of the war were complex and the objectives for which it was being fought were far from black and white. Yet Haig had no difficulty in identifying the war as a crusade in which Britain was fighting on behalf of the rest of the world. That is why he would not be troubled by Charteris' reflections. Britain was fighting a good war; Germany was not.

Haig's religion, as it reappeared in 1916, was close to his mother's confident Christian fatalism. It was this which enabled him to carry his burdens so lightly. Setbacks did not matter, because in the end all would be well. But this view rested on his confidence that the objectives for which he was fighting were the right ones, and would thus be supported by God, rather than on a belief in his own personal destiny or his relationship with God. Duncan deals with this question very forthrightly:

I have often been asked the question: 'How far is it true that Haig regarded himself as God's appointed agent for the win-ning of the war?' Never during the whole time I was with him did I hear language of that kind from his lips. I am also certain that, if ever he allowed himself to entertain such a thought, he did so in all humility, not out of egotism or wishful thinking, but with a sober grasp of the situation as he saw it. For what was his position, viewed in a strictly matter of fact way, apart from any religious interpretation that might be put upon it? Our country was facing the greatest crisis it had known for 100 years, a crisis which he had long foreseen, and for which he had rigorously prepared himself. Now that the hour had come he found himself, at his country's call, in a position of supreme responsibility, in which his plans and decisions would go far to determine whether the final issue would be victory or defeat, with all that the issue seemed to imply for the future of our country, for the cause of justice and freedom, and for the progress of humanity. He knew, too, that he had the confidence of his colleagues in the field, and also (despite the distrust of the Prime Minister) the confidence of the country as a whole. Would it be surprising if, in such circumstances, he humbly traced in his position the working of the divine Providence?

In his Presidential candidature Lincoln declared on one occasion, when replying to an ignorant attack made on his religious position: 'I see the storm coming, and I know that His hand is in it. If He has a place and work for me, and I think He has, I believe I am ready. I am nothing, but truth is everything.' Lincoln's thoughts might well have been Haig's, though Haig would probably have kept his thoughts to himself. To suggest (as has sometimes been done by men who never shared his responsibilities or fathomed the depths of his character) that a sense of divine mission was allowed by Haig to close his mind or to cloud his judgement is a matter of travesty, false in fact and scurrilously unjust to a character rare in ability. With some, no doubt, belief in a divine 'call' leads easily to fanaticism. But Haig was no fanatic. There was about him a mental balance which was associated not a little with his stern sense of duty; and like other devout men down the ages he heard in the call of duty the voice of God. He takes his place with those heroic figures (like Moses and Joshua in the Scripture records, or like

Cromwell and Lincoln in the story of the nations) who in some critical hour of history begin by recognising the need for action in the situation which confronts them, and then, in a spirit of obedience and faith in God, find themselves braced to meet it with courage and resolution, and in so doing draw strength from unseen sources.[12]

Before leaving George Duncan, it is worth looking briefly at his final analysis of the Commander-in-Chief:

In personal character – his austerity and reserve, his nobility of outlook and behaviour, his rigid adherence to principle, his quiet self-confidence firmly rooted in his trust in God – Haig takes his place alongside that great soldier of the south, Robert E. Lee. But in the military policy which he pursued with unwavering determination his prototype was Ulysses S. Grant. While other Federal Generals were hesitant and bewildered, Grant saw clearly that if the formidable Confederate Army was to be defeated, he must hold it in an inexorable grip. He must follow it wherever it went, attack it even in strongly entrenched positions, and he must never allow it time to rest or recuperate. His losses were inevitably heavy; and for that reason he was accused, as Haig was, of incapacity and callousness. So far from being callous Grant had, like Haig, a singular delicacy of feeling and he was deeply sensitive to the suffering and loss which his policy entailed. But as a Commander the one thought that possessed his soul was the necessity to bring the war to a victorious end. He was convinced that this could be done, and could only be done, by steadily undermining the enemy's will to fight, and inflicting on them losses which could not be replaced. And the event proved him to be right.[13]

It was in January 1916 that Haig started to get to know not only George Duncan, but also Lloyd George. The pair of them had frequently met before. Lloyd George had formed a favourable view of Haig; but Haig disliked all politicians and thought Lloyd George one of the poorer examples of the profession. After a January meeting, when Lloyd George and Bonar Law both came to his headquarters, he recorded, 'Mr. Bonar Law strikes me as being a straightforward, honourable man . . . Lloyd George seems to be astute and cunning with much energy and push; but I should think shifty and unreliable. He was most anxious to be agreeable and pleasant and was quite delighted at my having arranged for his two sons to stay and see him. They seem quite nice boys.' Charteris was given a grilling on intelligence work that lasted two hours:

> Lloyd George led the cross-examination, and it was very severe. He was astonishingly quick at grasping points, but, curiously enough, could not read a map . . . But whatever else may be said of the 'little man', there is no doubt that he has genius. He dominates. One strange physical feature draws one's eye when he is not talking – his curious little knock-kneed legs. When he is talking one would not notice if he had no legs or no arms, his face is so full of vitality and energy, and, after all, it is from the chin upwards that matters.[14]

Lloyd George, for his part, reported: 'Things are much more businesslike than in French's time. There is a new spirit. Haig seems very keen on his job and has a fine Staff.'[15] His letter of thanks to Haig was enthusiastic: 'My visit, if you will permit me to say so, left on my mind a great impression of things being *gripped* in that sphere of operation; and whether we win through or whether we fail, I have a feeling that everything which the assiduity, the care, and the trained thought of a great soldier can accomplish, is being done.'[16]

The staff to which Lloyd George referred was led by Kiggell, the recipient of Haig's Indian correspondence, as CGS. Kiggell worked in this capacity until the extensive and not voluntary reorganisation of General Headquarters two years later:

but it is hard to resist the conclusion that Kiggell never was, nor aspired to be, more than a mouthpiece for Haig. He was an efficient Staff Officer, and Haig respected his opinion when offered; but in two years Kiggell made little mark on the Army, remaining always a shadowy figure in the background, assigning orders, circulating papers, minding the machine . . . In truth a distinct weakness of Haig's period of command is the lack of a forceful and energetic personality at his side until the last month of the war, when Sir Herbert Lawrence joined him.[17]

Major-General J.F.C. Fuller was even more critical of Haig's staff. Kiggell, he said, was: 'A highly educated soldier but a doctrinaire. He possessed knowledge, but little vision, and at the Staff College he appeared to me to be a dyspeptic, gloomy and doleful man. I cannot imagine that his influence on his Chief was in any way decisive or beneficial'.[18] Kiggell sometimes had to be involved in little matters, as well as big ones. A letter from him to Major-General Hickie shows that even as Commander-in-Chief Haig remained a stickler for military etiquette. Kiggell wrote to Hickie to tell him 'demi-officially' that the Commander-in-Chief had motored through his troops and although a large union jack flew from the car, the men were 'far from alert in coming to attention and saluting.'[19]

General Butler, as Deputy Chief of Staff, Brigadier-General Davidson as Head of Operations, and Charteris, as Head of Intelligence, all came with Haig from First Army. There was criticism at the time of the youth of the appointees, and it remains a criticism that they were too much in awe of their Chief because of their inexperience. In general, throughout the war, Haig was – commendably – ready to promote able young officers. As early as November 1914, he had been pressing for the promotion of able men from the ranks as company commanders. He urged the War Office to send out young students, who understood the crisis in which the country was placed. Six months later he was discussing with the Prime Minister the removal of some of the older Major-Generals in order to make room for young people of ability. In the same month, July 1915, he secured French's agreement to accelerating the promotion of able subalterns as local captains and majors. A study of age profiles within the army shows that his policy met with much success; and it would have met with much more but for prejudice at the War Office. All the same, it is difficult not to feel that his own staff appointments were not made so much on the basis of ability as on the fact that Haig was familiar with the men and did not want change.

The Montreuil headquarters were in a château, just outside the town. Le Touquet was not far away, but Haig had no time for the frivolous diversions that it offered, and did not visit it until the war was in its last phase, and his confidence in victory was secure. What he did do was to instruct the military police to expel from the town the female friends of some of his officers, who had been installed there because Montreuil itself was out of bounds to them.

Charteris describes the routine at Haig's HQ in some detail:

Only his Chief of Staff and his personal ADCs shared his mess with him. Except at rare intervals he seldom visited the Headquarters Offices. The Heads of Department had definite days and hours for their interviews with him . . . All the threads led direct to the one large room in the Chief's own Headquarters, where at a desk (on which there was hardly ever a single paper) he controlled the whole of the vast and intricate ramifications of the growing British Army . . .

He rarely used the telephone himself. He cherished an ineradicable belief that conversations were inaccurate and liable to be distorted over the telephone, and that the agency of a third person using the telephone on his behalf ensured greater care and accuracy.

Each day he saw the heads of the chief branches of the Staff, and each day his own doctor found an opportunity of visiting him. His personal servant – Sergeant Secrett – kept almost as close a watch on the Chief as the Chief did on the Army. If he was late in going to bed, if he omitted his physical exercises, if his rest was disturbed and his appetite failed, Secrett reported it to Colonel Ryan, and Ryan exercised all the authority of a house physician in a great hospital on a recalcitrant patient. Senior Officers whose whole day was coloured by a word of praise or blame from the Chief, would listen with amazement to Ryan 'telling off' the Chief. 'If you don't sleep you won't last,' Ryan would say sternly. 'I told you to go to bed at 11.' And the Chief would reply mildly – though with a suspicion of a twinkle in his eye: 'All right, I'll be good.'

Punctually at 8.25 each morning Haig's bedroom door opened and he walked downstairs. In the hall was a barometer, and he invariably stopped in front of the instrument to tap it, though he rarely took any particular note of the reading. He then went for a short four minutes' walk in the garden. At 8.30 precisely he came into the mess for breakfast . . . At 9 o'clock he went into his study and worked until 11 or half past. At half past eleven he saw Army Commanders, the Heads of Departments at General Headquarters, and others who he might desire to see.

The main administrative elements of his Headquarters were housed in the Cadet School, where officers built a tennis court which is still used by the Montreuil Tennis Club. The communications centre was in a room above the Theatre, on the town's Grand' Place, more formally the Place Général de Gaulle. In 1995 the area immediately in front of the Theatre was named Le Square Douglas Haig. On it stands an equestrian statue of Haig. The original statue was inaugurated in 1931 in the presence of Lady Haig, but was overturned and then broken up by German soldiers in 1940. Their action was unauthorised and attracted official disapproval. Just four years after the Liberation, it was decided that the statue should be replaced: the original sculptor, Landowski, had kept the mould, and the effigy was recreated with three tonnes of bronze taken from the British Zone in Germany. The inauguration of the new statue involved two days of ceremonies at Montreuil, at the great British War Cemetery at Étaples, and at le Touquet, where they included a gala evening at the Casino, of which Haig would hardly have approved.

Soon afterwards, Blake's edition of the private papers, with their comments on the French, appeared. French veterans were infuriated by what they read – particularly in relation to morale in the Army – and there were demonstrations and demands for removal of the statue, or at least the removal of Haig's name from the plinth, so that the monument might simply serve as mark of respect to the British army and Anglo-French collaboration. Before the hullabaloo died down, the statue had been surrounded by rum and whisky bottles (empty), and festooned with pigs' heads and chamber pots.[20]

Haig's family maintain that the representation of his charger is so accurate that a wound on its flank can be seen, supporting the argument that it was the King's poor handling of the horse that led to his being thrown. The charger's flanks do indeed ripple with muscle and sinew, but it requires some imagination to identify the royal cicatrice.

The Montreuil headquarters are once again a private house, the Château de Beaurepaire. Far from conforming to the image of palatial surroundings for the generals, the Château Beaurepaire is a modest building, the adjunct to a nearby farm, and it must have struggled to accommodate Haig's staff. It is very different from the sort of base that Eisenhower would occupy in the Second World War.

After he took over as Commander-in-Chief, Haig instituted weekly meetings with all his army commanders. The meetings took place at a different HQ each time, and he and the commanders moved off as soon as the meetings were over: they were not to be allowed to degenerate into 'luncheon parties'.

Haig's private secretary, Sir Philip Sassoon, was an integral part of the retinue at GHQ until the end of the war (and even after it, when he continued to act on Haig's behalf in delicate negotiations). On the face of it, Sassoon was everything that Haig should not have liked: intellectual, brilliant, an exotic and artistic millionaire. But even if Haig himself did not contribute to the gaiety of his headquarters, he enjoyed wit in others and the sophistication that Sassoon lent to his circle.

Sassoon was totally loyal to Haig, despite their differences in background and attitudes. He was a darling of London society, humorous, with a love of harmless gossip. He was amused, in a kindly way, by Haig's earnestness and by his habits and tastes. His own inclination was for the treasures and *objets de vertu* with which he filled his houses in Park Lane, Port Lympne and Trent. Kenneth Clark described Sassoon's 'idiosyncratic and infectious *style*. He moved quickly and always seemed to be in profile, like an Egyptian relief.'

His mind moved equally quickly, and as his most unexpected comments were made without any change of inflection, they often took people by surprise. He saw the ridiculous side of Port Lympne. Going round the house we came upon a particularly hideous bathroom, panelled in brown and black zig-zags of marble. Philip said without altering his tone of voice, 'It takes you by the throat and shakes you.'[21]

Sassoon wrote of himself:

Of course the sort of house I like & pine for has no comforts, nothing but stone floors and stone walls, moth-eaten 14th century fragments – draughts – and a few stiff chairs against the wall with a string attached across to prevent anyone from sitting down on them. You would think it easy to realise this ideal. But it isn't, and I find myself the reluctant possessor of Park Lane with its *leitmotiv* of sham Louis XVI, Lympne which is Martini *tout craché*, and Trent which isn't even Lincrusta when my period is Merovingian or Boiling Oil. *Le Monde est toujours mal arrangé.*[22]

This marvellous third Baronet, of Indian and Sephardic Jewish descent, comes straight from the pages of Saki, and there must have been a huge part of his life which he could not share with Haig. Later he was to be Lloyd George's PPS.

The whole day was mapped out in a regular routine. Haig had lunch at one and then either motored or rode to another headquarters. On his return his horse would meet his car, so that he could spend the last few miles on horseback. When not motoring he spent the afternoon riding, always accompanied by an ADC and an escort of 17th Lancers. On his return he stopped about three miles from home and walked the rest. Then a bath, physical exercise and a change from riding gear into trousers. He then worked until dinner at 8 o'clock, returning to his desk after dinner, and working until 10.45. Charteris has a wonderful phrase to describe Haig at the head of the table: 'DH never shines at dinner, but . . . kept silence merrily.'[24]

Charlie Carrington described Haig's retinue on one of the afternoon rides:

[A] fine sight he was, as I saw him once near his advanced headquarters at Beauquesne, with a trooper riding in front bearing his Union Flag, a group of red-tabbed officers at a decent interval, and an escort of Lancers with fluttering pennants.

The twenty-first-century reaction is of astonishment at this panoply of quasi-medieval splendour, but what he was doing was nothing more than would be expected at the time. Carrington goes on to say that he does

not think he enjoyed pomp – a simple, thoughtful man. It is when I compare Haig's GHQ with Eisenhower's SHAEF that front-line jealousy begins to rise in me. While Eisenhower was in Algiers the current joke was that he had more officers on his staff than Washington had soldiers at Valley Forge, and the Byzantine luxury of the successive resting places of SHAEF as it traversed Western Europe was disquieting.[25]

It was against this background that Haig prepared for the great offensive of 1916. What had been agreed at Chantilly was a massive

coordinated attack on all fronts: Russian, Italian, French and British
– all were to be engaged in assaults. Haig made it clear that although
he was not under Joffre's orders, that was not important, 'as my
intention was to do my utmost to carry out General Joffre's wishes on
strategical matters, as if they were orders.' He met Joffre on 17
January when 'he was most open, told me of the shortage of men in
France and of the highly unsatisfactory state of munitions. I got the
impression that Joffre felt that the French Army could not do much
more hard fighting.' An investiture followed when Haig received the
Grand Cordon of the *Légion d'Honneur*, and Sir Henry Rawlinson and
Henry Wilson were invested as *Grands Officiers*. '[Joffre] . . . placed
the ribbon of the Order round my neck . . . and . . . before I quite
realised what was going to happen, kissed me on both cheeks! I could
hardly refrain from laughing. Then Rawlinson's turn came . . . He
was duly kissed, and the long Henry Wilson had to bend down for
the little fat "Generalissimo" to perform this part of the ceremony!'

The government's instructions on relations with the French were
spelled out a *little* more clearly to Haig than they had been to French.
His orders made cooperation with the French more prominent.
Kitchener's instructions of 28 December 1915 provided that 'the
defeat of the enemy by the combined Allied Armies must always be
regarded as the primary object for which British troops were
originally sent to France, and to achieve that end, the closest cooperation of French and British as a united army must be the
government policy.'

All the same, the inherent contradiction that lay in the instructions to French were carried forward in Haig's. '[But] I wish you
distinctly to understand that your command is an independent one,
and that you will in no case come under the orders of any Allied
General further than the necessary co-operation with our allies above
referred to.' Thus the armies were a united army, but were also not a
united army. What it meant was that Haig was responsible for the
safety of the British Army but did not have the right to decide where
and how it would operate.[26]

In the course of the months of preparation for the offensive, Haig had a few days' leave at Deal with his family. Haig and Lady Haig were resting beside the sea, leaning against some rocks, while the children played nearby. They noticed that the passers-by were examining Haig with interest, and were surprised, as he was not usually noticed. Then they found that the children had chalked on the rocks above their heads the words 'THIS IS SIR DOUGLAS HAIG'. In the course of this visit Haig had an audience of the King, whom he met again in the course of the Somme, when George V came to Cassel. In deference to the King's wartime teetotal policy, no drink was provided and Haig was amused by Joffre's horror when he was offered the choice of lemonade or ginger beer. The King felt that Haig could do more to improve his relationship with Nivelle and the French generally; and he spoke to Wilson of the unfortunate hostility to the French at Haig's headquarters.

Haig never drank heavily, but he was not in favour of total abstinence (he was of the view that total abstainers always had some sort of mental problem) and he disapproved of the King's repudiation of alcohol for the duration of the war. The King's stance may have assisted the production of munitions, but it made life difficult for his ministers. Haig got off quite lightly: when he had informal lunches *à deux* with the King, at which the King helped him to food as his son would help Churchill a generation later, the field-marshal was allowed a cider cup. Rosebery on one occasion suffered such an attack of hiccups as a result of drinking ginger beer that he could not speak a word to the Queen. Asquith found meals at the palace a most painful experience. At Haig's headquarters fine wines and spirits (thanks to Leo Rothschild) were served, but even there Asquith could suffer. Sir Philip Sassoon wrote to Lady Haig:

> The old man is in great form. At dinner last night he kept on shoving his empty brandy glass to try to attract Sir Douglas' attention but in vain! and he was at last reduced to asking for some more! We told the Chief that he had been very unkind and had obviously turned a blind eye on purpose. Old Joffre came to lunch on Sunday and I have never seen him so well and cheery.

'His Majesty isn't here today' he said gleefully as he drained a large bumper of wine![27]

On another occasion Asquith fared better; Haig reported to his wife:

You would have been amused by the Prime Minister last night. He did himself fairly well – not more than gentlemen used to drink when I was a boy, but in this abstemious age it is noticeable if an extra glass or two is taken by anyone! The PM seemed to like our old brandy. He had a couple of glasses (big sherry glass size!) before I left the table at 9.30, and apparently he had several more before I saw him again. By that time his legs were unsteady, but his head was quite clear, and he was able to read a map and discuss the situation with me. Indeed he was most charming and quite alert in mind.

The great offensive was not to function as planned. Verdun, and its huge drain on the strength of the French army, was a critical factor thrown in to Joffre's planning. (But it is important to remember that the Somme was planned before Verdun, and not as Haig later argued, to take pressure off France at Verdun.) The Italian offensive did not succeed. France suffered from an increasing lack of manpower, and the British contribution accordingly became more important. Limited British objectives came to be replaced by virtually unlimited ones, but without an increase in resources. Initially Haig resisted a request from Joffre that he should take over a part of the line held by the French tenth Army, but as Verdun began to have an increasing impact on France, he relented. He knew that France had resources for only one major offensive in 1916 and could probably not stand another winter's war. Joffre saw Britain as bearing the burden of the 'wearing out' fights ('*batailles d'usure*'), reserving to France the climactic effort. A diversionary – or possibly alternative – attack at Arras was contemplated, but in the event the British choice was to strike on the Somme. 'Thus,' said Charteris, 'we became for the first time the chief partner in a big attack'.[28]

The view that Haig only subsequently thought of and represented the Battle of the Somme as a wearing-down offensive, rather than one which might end the war, is false, although he did later emphasise the former role. As the plans for the battle went ahead there were grounds, although diminishing ones, for hoping for outright victory, but this optimism grew less as the demands of Verdun forced Joffre to scale down the attack and cancel plans for turning south and rolling up part of the German line. To the end of his life, Haig believed that if all available troops and materials had been concentrated in the Somme, and not in other theatres, there could have been victory in 1916. Equally, to the end of his life he thought that the Somme justified itself in terms of its effect on enemy morale. His supporters can point for confirmation of this view to Ludendorff's *War Memoirs*. Where there is so much room for allegations about *a posteriori* Haigian justification of the Somme and its purpose, it is as well to recollect the very clear *a priori* statement of his aims in a letter to Lord Bertie, the Ambassador in Paris, of 5 June 1916. They were:

1. Train my divisions . . .
2. To make arrangements to support the French . . . attacking in order to draw off pressure from Verdun, when the French consider the military situation demands it.
3. But while attacking to help our Allies, not to think that we can for a certainty destroy the power of Germany this year. So in our attacks we must aim at improving our positions with a view to making sure of the result of campaign next year.

Haig moved forward to advanced headquarters for the first great battle in which he would command the British Army. They were in the Château du Valvion, on the outskirts of a village called Beau-quesne. Duncan had dinner with the Commander-in-Chief two nights before the battle opened:

We were a small party; and as we sat at dinner there came from the adjoining room sounds of a piano – a little girl was playing her five-finger exercises. I thought by contrast of the 'sound of revelry' that preceded Waterloo. Here was a Commander-in-Chief who, rather than cause undue inconvenience to the legitimate owner of the house, was willing that she and her little daughter should continue in possession of a few rooms.[29]

His own personal staff officers had moved with him, but the bulk of the General Staff remained behind. Amongst those who moved with him was Charteris:

The battle had been planned to begin on June 28th but heavy rain on the 26th, 27th and 28th compelled it to be postponed until July 1st. As early as the 24th the artillery bombardment had opened, and continued without intermission and in increasing severity until the infantry attack was launched. On the 29th the weather cleared, the sky was still overcast, but there were long intervals of sunshine.

To an onlooker the scene was one of strange and awful grandeur. Overhead more than a score of observation balloons hung in the sky, aeroplanes circled like birds of prey; on the ground there was nothing but bare desolation, stark ruins that once had been villages, and gaunt skeletons of trees; the roar of the guns and the crash of the shells shook the ground as the gigantic artillery duel continued; as far as the eye could see into the enemy lines no sign of movement or life could be discerned save the flash of the guns.[30]

16

THE SOMME

For those who know little of Haig, he remains for ever and inescapably associated with the Somme, and in particular, its first day. His name prompts a Pavlovian recollection from those who remember nothing about him that beyond the fact that there were 60,000 victims on that first day. There were indeed something like 58,000 casualties on that first day, 1 July 1916, a third of them killed, and that figure is frequently cited as being entirely sufficient proof, on its own, of Haig's incapacity and callousness. (It may be an irrational reaction, but it seems particularly poignant that some 30 per cent of the casualties suffered by the British were incurred behind their own front line.) For the revisonists, Peter Simkins has referred to the 'tyrannical hold' that the first day on the Somme has on history and the popular imagination, a phrase that has been applauded by his colleagues.[1]

The scale of the losses on that first day was so great, so appalling, that they cannot be brushed aside with a phrase, however neat. And yet in truth the losses were an indictment not of Haig, but of the collective military orthodoxy of the time, and if his handling of the Somme is open to criticism, that criticism has more to do with other aspects of the battle. In Haig's lifetime, such criticism as there was of him was directed to the later stages of Third Ypres, rather than to the Somme. The Somme was the first and only time that Britain engaged the main body of her principal enemy in a continental war. Its uniqueness means that there is nothing against which to measure it. At the time, the reaction to the battle was generally favourable, subject to the caveat that it had perhaps gone on too long. A year later, for instance, *The Times* reported the start of the Battle of Arras by saying, '[T]he enemy will suffer more than we, and we shall break him here as we broke him on the Somme'.

The pace of events after the attacks on Verdun earlier in the year was fast. Two weeks before they began, when asked whether, in principle, Britain would relieve the French tenth Army, Haig replied in the affirmative to Joffre. Joffre then asked him when he would do so. Haig replied, 'Next winter.' Then Verdun. As Duff Cooper put it:

> [o]n February 21st the blow fell. Nothing like it had ever before been seen in military history. The whole concentrated endeavour of German military thought, German technical ingenuity, German courage, devotion, discipline and efficiency were directed in one vast, desperate effort against that section of the French Front which will be forever memorable under the name of Verdun. It was the second great effort of Germany to win the war. It was a supreme test of French heroism and French endurance, a test from which France emerged scarred and battered, but triumphant.[2]

Six days later Haig recorded: 'I telephoned to General Joffre that I had arranged to relieve all his 10th Army and that I would come to Chantilly tomorrow to shake him by the hand, and to place myself and troops at his disposition.' On 1 March Fourth Army came into official existence under Rawlinson. Haig had been suspicious of Rawlinson, who had all the articulateness that Haig lacked. He was ambitious and Haig thought he was an intriguer. Despite that he gradually came to acquire Haig's confidence. Fourth Army completed the relief of the French Tenth Army in the early part of March, and British troops now stretched continuously from the banks of the Yser to the Somme.

Haig was still not happy about launching an immediate attack. When he mentioned 15th August, Joffre at once got very excited and shouted that 'the French Army would cease to exist if we did nothing till then!' The rest of us looked on at this burst of excitement, and I then pointed out that in spite of 15th August being the most favourable date for the British Army to take action, yet, in view of what he had said regarding the unfortunate condition of the French Army, I was prepared to commence operations on the 1st July or thereabouts. This calmed the old man . . .

It was agreed that three weeks' notice of the exact date of the attack would be given.

During the preparation for the battle Haig pressed for the use of tanks. When he read a paper, on Christmas Day 1915, in which Churchill argued for the use of 'caterpillars' Haig was immediately captivated by the idea. Churchill had started experiments with tanks while he was at the Admiralty and they were now being developed under the control of Colonel Swinton. Haig met Swinton at the War Office on 14 April 1916, and was told that he could have 150 tanks by 31 July. He said he needed fifty for 1 June, and Swinton was pressed to provide them and to arrange for the necessary training. He was 'to practise and train tanks and crews over obstacles and wire similar to the ground over which the forthcoming attack was to be made'.[3] In the event the fifty tanks were not available for the opening offensive, and it was only in the later stages of the battle that tanks went into action, and then only in very small numbers. Additionally, not nearly enough development had taken place. They were vulnerable to artillery fire, and many broke down. Charteris recorded in his diary that: 'The tanks were led in one place by an officer on foot carrying a red flag, just as in the pre-motor days, and by a marvel he escaped unwounded'.[4] The result of their premature deployment at the Somme was the loss of secrecy and surprise before sufficient numbers were available to make a significant contribution to the battle. With hindsight, it would have been better to wait until 1917, when 350 tanks would have been available. At the time, in the desperate later stages of the battle, even a little seemed better than nothing,[5] but if Haig can be criticised in relation to tanks, the criticism should be not that he was a technophobe, but that he was too recklessly enthusiastic in grasping at what new technology could offer.

Robertson telegraphed Kiggell on 16 September asking how the tanks had performed. Kiggell replied on 17 September:

Consider that the utility of the tanks has been proved. It has been established that the magnitude of the success on the 15th in certain localities was directly attributable to the employment of tanks. Further there is no doubt that their employment minimises loss among the attacking troops. On the 15th approximately 48 tanks deployed. Of these 30 started. Of these 21 did good work. Four were hit by artillery fire in movement. Of the remainder breakdowns were chiefly attributable to either mechanical trouble and to inexperience of drivers and the very difficult conditions.[6]

Equally false is the idea that Haig did not understand or appreciate the values of the machine-gun. As Director of Staff Duties, he had argued for more of them in the Expeditionary Force, and now he not only pressed for the destruction of enemy machine-guns by artillery fire but also tried to stimulate the use of machine-guns in the offensive. 'I think units have hardly begun to realise yet the great addition which they have recently received to their fire power by the provision of Lewis machine-guns and machine-gun batteries.' At one of the army commanders' meetings in the middle of March he returned to the subject:

After considering the situation in the front of each army in turn, we discussed the use of Lewis machine-guns in an advance. A few of these guns can develop as great a volume of fire as a considerable number of infantry. They are far less vulnerable and can find cover more easily. I emphasised the necessity for

Company and Platoon Commanders being trained in the use of these guns in tactical situations. At present only a comparatively few officers of infantry realise the great addition of fire power which has been given them by the formation of machine-gun companies and Lewis gun detachments.

As far as artillery was concerned, Haig encouraged new methods, and experts worked on a variety of techniques: preparatory bombardment, creeping barrage, counter-battery fire, counter preparation, sound ranging and flash spotting. Progress in these specialist fields was steady, rather than spectacular, and it was not till the last year of the war that all of this research came together; but piece by piece the lessons of modern warfare were being learned. Sound ranging, for instance, had already been in place for a year when the Somme offensive began and every part of the line was now covered by sound range sections, which were able to ascertain the distance to enemy batteries by calculations based on the noise from their shells. (The War Office was initially unable to issue suitable chronometers and Leo Rothschild, in one of his many generous gifts, presented the army with a number of gold chronometers.)

Although Haig bore ultimate responsibility for the conduct of the battle, its nature was dictated by the proliferation of agencies involved in making plans and executing them. Joffre had envisaged a slow battle of attrition, but not an attempted breakthrough. Rawlinson agreed, requesting a long bombardment. Haig had not yet fully accepted the evidence of the importance of artillery, and only reluctantly agreed. The use of a long period of bombardment obviously removed any element of surprise but by now the flow of munitions was much greater than in 1915, and bombardment on a scale which Haig could only have dreamed of a year earlier seemed full of promise. Rawlinson wanted the attack to start before dawn, but the French objected and he gave way. Thus 'the place, the date, the hour – all these had been decided by the French.'[7]

It was at 7.30 on the morning of 1 July that the huge barrage came to an end and on sixteen miles of front the British moved forward into bright sunshine. Haig had wanted small parties to go out after the bombardment to check on the state of the German wire, but his corps commanders, on the basis of observation and Royal Flying Corps reports, said this was unnecessary. According to Duff Cooper, Haig also wanted the infantry to advance in small units, lying down between rushes. As early as December 1914, he had told one of his brigadiers that 'no advance is ever to be made in mass or in rigid lines when under fire'.[8]

The picture of the soldiers of the first day of the Somme advancing across No Man's Land in parade-ground lines, dressing from left to right, is therefore partly a myth. In the smoke and heat of the day, no one, not even Philip Gibbs, who claimed to observe the phenomenon, could really see the detail of what was happening. It seems to have been John Buchan who promoted the notion of the measured advance of the extended lines.[9] He did so to emphasise the heroism of the day; others seized on the image to depict the callousness and stupidity of the commanders. But research has revealed that at divisional and brigade level, advances were certainly not always made in waves. Tactics had evolved in ways that were appropriate to the circum-stances, and as well as the wave, 'blobs' and 'worms' were used in infiltrationary tactics.[10]

Some commanders did require long waves moving forward at regular intervals. 'Rushes' were awkward, but not impossible, for men carrying sixty-six pounds of kit. The real problem however was that the technique was difficult for the New Armies to master. What was involved was 'Fire and Movement', two lines of men, just five yards apart, moving alternately, and lying down between moves, those moving supported by the fire of the others. Strict control was needed otherwise cohesion was lost and friendly fire resulted. There was evidence from the previous year that the lightly trained troops of the New Armies could not cope with this method of movement, which of course became the norm in infantry training.

And so some men did move at a slow walk, and could probably not have done more, shoulder to shoulder in straight lines. *Fourth Army Tactical Notes* have often been cited as being responsible for this slow march to death. But the *Notes* were not prescriptive and units were free to adopt their own tactics. They acknowledged that 'there can be no definite rules as regards the best formation for attack' and recommended that 'small columns, which can make use of the folds of the ground to cover their advance, are preferable during the preliminary stages of the advance.' At most there could have been more direction to subordinate commanders to adopt 'infiltration' as opposed to 'wave' tactics, of which army commanders were perfectly aware.[11] But as a matter of fact the divisions that sustained the lowest numbers of casualties appear to have been those which did advance at a slow walk. The lower casualties were probably due to a more effective artillery barrage in certain areas: a good creeping barrage was the key to success. Conversely, some divisions, such as those of VIII Corps, which did not attack in waves had very high casualties.

The failures of the artillery bombardment are well known: the German defences on the Somme were far more extensive than had been realised and their dugouts were deep and well constructed; shrapnel, rather than high explosive, had been used, and barbed wire entanglements, far deeper than had been expected, were frequently uncut. The advancing British troops were cut down by undamaged machine-guns. They fell like hay cut by a scythe.

They were Kitchener's New Armies. They came from civilian life, some in the army only for months before they advanced into that hail of machine-gun bullets. They came to the army inspired by duty and patriotism. The army received them as a 'mere collection of divisions' but welded them into a unified fighting force. They learned the discipline of the military machine and accepted it to the full, as they marched in parade ground precision to their deaths. That was what they had been trained and formed to do: they had not been trained to operate as flexible troops, capable of individual thought and initiative. That was to come before the end of the war, but these men died as automata.

Some aspects of the artillery failure can be excused by lack of experience, some but not all. Rawlinson had originally planned an attack to a depth of 1,250 yards. Haig required this to be doubled, without any increase in artillery support. Probably too much was expected of the artillery: at this point in the war it remained fairly unsophisticated: the pattern of 100 shells fired by a 60-pounder gun was a narrow rectangle, 4 yards wide by a remarkable 39 yards long, and until more accurate shelling was possible, anything like total destruction of defensive positions was impossible. Rawlinson agreed to this unfortunate extension of the line of his attack despite his experience at Neuve Chapelle, Aubers Ridge and Loos. The result was that the preliminary bombardment on the Somme was only half as intense as that which much thinner German defences had faced at Neuve Chapelle. Throughout the battle, Rawlinson was too ready to suppress his doubts in the face of his habit of deference to Haig. He frequently revealed a lack of confidence in Haig's plans and often unjustified ambitions when he addressed his own officers, but he only rarely confided these views to the Commander-in-Chief. The exchanges between Haig and Rawlinson in the planning before these battles show a lack of constructive engagement: Rawlinson should have pressed his arguments more strongly, and Haig should have encouraged him to do so. This last criticism can also be directed at Rawlinson himself in his relations with his corps commanders: he did not see it as his responsibility to ensure coordination.

As things advanced in the course of that first day, both Haig and Joffre had some reasons for optimism. By the early afternoon, 18th and 30th Divisions had pretty well completed their tasks. To the south of the Somme the French had also made significant advances. But in the event, there was no breakthrough, and the first day was just one of the 141 days of the battle. Haig was always inclined to be carried away by optimism when battles were immediately imminent and often also in their early stages. He wrote to his wife on 8 July: 'In another fortnight, with Divine Help, I hope that some decisive results may be obtained.' Again, on 14 July, when he was so encouraged by success in the south that he was telling his wife that cavalry might be pushed through the German lines:

This morning very early our troops surprised the enemy, and have captured some 4 miles of his *Second Line*.

This is indeed a very great success. The best day we have had this war and I feel what a reward it is to have been spared to see our troops so successful! There is no doubt that the results of today will be very far reaching.

It is interesting to contrast these accesses of enthusiasm with his wearing-down philosophy. But the latter was not an *ex post facto* argument, advanced to excuse a failure to break through. He was committed to wearing down the enemy (to an extent that almost blinded him to breakthrough when it did occur), but he always tended to hope for the bonus of a major advance.

It was some days after 1 July before Haig became aware of the scale of losses. Separated by a barrage of German artillery shells which runners from the front and staff officers from the rear could penetrate only with difficulty, Headquarters remained in ignorance of detailed conditions on the front. It is worth making a conscious effort to remember, in a time when sophisticated wireless and electronic communications are taken for granted, just how primitive the means of communication were throughout the First World War:

The maintenance of communication on the West [*sic*] Front particularly in the forward area, was very difficult owing to the heavy shell-fire, mud and exposure which were experienced, and as no one means could be relied on any alternative methods had to be provided. Telegraph and telephone by wire and cables, wireless telegraphy, telegraphy through the ground (power buzzer) visual signalling with electric lamps, helios and flags, carrier pigeons, messenger dogs, message-carrying rockets, firework signals, motor-cyclists, despatch riders, mounted or-derlies, cyclists, and finally runners were all employed in turn according to circumstances. The telephone cables, being too vulnerable overground, had sometimes to be buried to a depth of six or eight feet to protect them from shell-fire, a task which entailed the digging of hundreds of miles of trenches. In 1917 some 80,000 miles of telephone wire were buried in this way.[12]

There are some engaging photographs of dogs with drums attached to their backs, running forward, laying out telephone cables to advanced posts. Sensibilities at home, however, were respected. Although cinema film showed men hit and falling in battle, no mention of the role of the dogs and the dangers they faced was permitted in Britain.

Haig noted in his diary at the end of the day: 'Hard fighting continued all day on front of 4th Army. On a 16-mile front of attack varying fortunes must be expected.' Even at the end of the second day, Haig still understood that he had lost a total of 40,000 in both days, instead of nearly 60,000 on the first day alone. In reality, the first day had been a disaster. There was some progress on the right. Elsewhere gains were small and the words used in the Official History to describe the 31st Division's advance could apply to many parts of the line: 'The extended lines started in excellent order, but gradually melted away. There was no wavering or attempting to come back, the men fell in their ranks, mostly before the first hundred yards of No Man's Land had been crossed.' Haig thought that the (limited) losses of which he was aware had resulted in a shaking of German resolve. His orders now to Rawlinson were to concentrate upon his right and exploit success there. Rawlinson did not agree and Haig resorted to making it an order. When he met Joffre on 3 July, the latter shared Rawlinson's scepticism:

> General Joffre exploded in a fit of rage. *He* could not approve of it. He *ordered* me to attack Thiepval and Pozieres. If I attacked Longueval [on the British right], I would be beaten, etc. etc. I waited calmly until he had finished. His breast heaved and his face flushed! The truth is the poor man cannot argue, nor can he easily read a map. But today I had a raised model of the ground before us . . . When Joffre got out of breath, I quietly explained what my position is relative to him as the 'Generalissimo'. I am

solely responsible to the British Government for the action of the British Army; and I have approved a plan and must modify it to suit the changing situation as the fight progresses. I was most polite. Joffre saw he had a mistake, and next tried to cajole me.

At the end of the day, Haig parted company with Joffre on good terms: he genuinely liked this Frenchman.

Edward Spears became the most famous liaison officer with the French during the war. He was brought up in France, improbably the son of a commission agent, and his flawless French made him an obvious candidate for liaison work when war broke out. He admired the French army, and the courage of the French soldier. He was himself a brave man, frustrated by the fact that he was not directly involved in the fighting: all the same he was wounded four times and won the Military Cross before he became head of the British Military Mission to the French War Office in Paris in 1917. He had an interesting career after the war, publishing two excellent books about his experiences, becoming a Member of Parliament and playing a crucial part in the Second World War as Head of the British Mission to the Free French. In 1918 he married a no less remarkable woman: Mary Borden, a Chicago heiress (though the Borden fortune disappeared in the crash of 1929). She had come to France to work in Dunkirk in a typhoid hospital. She then set up her own mobile hospital at the Front, where she met Spears. She received the *Croix de Guerre* and was made a member of the *Légion d'Honneur*; in the Second World War she again ran field hospitals in the French Middle East. She also found time to write at least twenty-three books.

Spears now visited Rawlinson's Fourth Army and 'when I saw how badly our left had got on I felt bitterly disappointed.' Spears contrasted the French gains south of the Somme with the British losses. He noted the French tactics of self-contained platoons moving forward, 'elusive as quicksilver', while the British walked into the oncoming fire. His reaction was extreme, perhaps unbalanced, although understandable: 'Some English General wants an English victory, never mind 200,000 more men killed.' He had to listen to the criticisms his French colleagues made of the British. 'Perhaps they could not stand shellfire.' 'They had lost the courage of their race.' He sent an account of French tactics to GHQ, where a totally opposite view was held: the French, said Charteris, 'were not up to our level.' Spears caused great offence when at dinner at GHQ he said that British cavalry officers should volunteer for the infantry: the best French infantry officers came from the cavalry. One cavalry officer stormed out of the room accused, as he felt, of a lack of courage. Spears was desperate to be involved in actual fighting and had to be threatened with court martial if he did not throw himself fully into his liaison work. He was close to breaking. On 9 August he wrote, 'I think I will shoot myself.' His appropriation of national guilt was unnecessary: General Fayolle sent his congratulations to Haig on his progress.[16]

Only two of Haig's corps commanders in the Battle of the Somme had commanded even a division in peacetime, but they did learn, and the terrible losses of 60,000 men on the first day reduced to a daily average of 2,500.

On 11 July Falkenhayn gave the order to suspend offensive operations at Verdun. This was not the achievement of the Somme offensive, as Haig was to argue: the scale of the attacks on Verdun had already reduced very significantly before the battle began. The purpose of the Somme as a means of relieving pressure on Verdun had been nullified.

Between 2 and 13 July the Battle was characterised by narrow-front attacks without adequate artillery preparation. The next significant offensive was on 14 July. This took the form of a night attack by Rawlinson, and demonstrates that Haig was no inflexible theorist. His experience of night attacks in the South African War had shown him that they were risky, particularly with large numbers of troops. When Rawlinson first put the proposed to him Haig squashed it very swiftly and then 'I declined to discuss the matter further.' For once Rawlinson bravely did not accept this and approached Haig again via Kiggell, but received the response that: 'I considered that the experience of war, as well as the teachings of peace, are against the use of *large masses* in night operations, especially with inexperienced Staff Officers and young troops.' Rawlinson and his staff still stood firm, and it is a tribute to their determination, as well as to Haig's flexibility, that another phone call followed, as a result of which Haig said that he would go into their proposals and reply in the morning. In the morning, he reviewed the plan and then put four questions to his staff:

1. Can we take the position in the manner proposed?
2. Can we hold it off to capture?
3. What will be the results in the case of a failure?
4. What are the advantages, or otherwise, of proceeding methodically . . .?

This was typical of Haig's approach at a meeting. He used similar tactics when dealing with politicians and the Cabinet. He had the capacity to analyse a proposition and identify the crucial premises on which it rested. Usually the process was applied negatively, and he would hammer at the dialectical flaw which he had identified. His technique is essentially a forensic one: it works well in a court of law, but it tends to be sterile and not provocative of lateral thinking or imaginative concepts. On this occasion he accepted the answers he was given and the early morning attack went ahead – and with some success. Cavalry was able to move forward and some squadrons actually charged across the open ground that had been reached. The gains of 14 July were much more extensive than those of 1 July, and the losses were much more modest. But after the initial delight with which the British reviewed the situation on 15 July, they had to face a rallying German army that imposed heavy losses in the course of interdicting exploitation of what had been won.

All the same, Charteris made an interesting entry in his diary on 18 July:

Another stage of the battle was over; we hold four miles of the crest of the ridge. One cannot help comparing this battle with the Aisne, when for nearly a month we strove to gain the Chemin des Dames ridge and made no progress. In this battle, in three weeks we are on the ridge.

The next part of his entry reflects an awareness of the vast technical changes since the beginning of the war:

How different it all is from 1914. Then we had no heavy artillery, little ammunition for our light guns, no hopes of reinforcements. This time, ample artillery, and reinforcements coming out regularly. Even more remarkable is the progress of the scientific side of war. Observation balloons, aeroplanes, air photographs, sound ranging, listening-in apparatus, Secret Service. On the Aisne each corps only had one officer for 'I' work. Now there is one with each brigade and division, and all together 17 at Army Headquarters, and every corps is asking for a larger staff. It is the same in every other branch. War is a science. GHQ are now controlling a far bigger and more intricate business than any industrial concern in peace-time. As time goes on it will get bigger still.[14]

After the 14 July attack, Rawlinson came to recognise that artillery bombardment was the critical element in success. The battle now consisted generally not of great offensives, but of a continuous series of struggles that moved back and forth along the whole line. This phase gives the lie to the 'tyranny of the first day' argument. Between 15 July and 14 September, Fourth Army suffered 82,000 casualties in the course of capturing 2 square miles: casualties were 40 per cent higher in the capture of a smaller area than on 1 July.[15]

The capriciousness of Haig's judgement and his vulnerability to accesses of optimism are encapsulated in his memorandum to Rawlinson and Gough of 2 August:

To enable us to bring the present operations (the existing phase of which may be regarded as a 'wearing out' battle) to a successful termination, we must practise such economy of men and material as will ensure us having the 'last reserves' at our disposal when the crisis of the fight is reached, which may – and probably will – not be sooner than the last half of September.[16]

This sort of inconsistency abounds in Haig's thinking and pronouncements until 1918, when his judgement becomes much more sound. Here, in August 1916, he is characterising only *the current phase* of the Somme as a wearing-down battle. Earlier and later he said and was to say that the whole battle was of that nature. This mental confusion was mirrored by an unusual confusion in his orders at this time, which made it difficult for Rawlinson to know what was expected of him. Preparations were to be 'careful and methodical'; at the same time they were to be 'pushed forward without delay'. Rawlinson was told to harbour his resources, but at the same time 'a sufficient force must be employed to make success as certain as possible.'[17] The 2 August memorandum suggests that Haig thought that something really significant, possibly even the end of the War, was imminent. By 7 September he was telling Rawlinson that Third and Fifth Armies had been asked to carry out operations on their fronts. Even Second Army and Dover Patrol were to be involved. His objectives were almost unlimited.

What in fact followed was important, but was not on the grandiose scale that Haig had dreamt of. It was in the next major attack, on 15 September, that tanks were used for the first time. The background to their deployment was hardly propitious: Rawlinson had never seen a tank, and Haig had difficulty in inducing him to share his enthusiasm for their use: once he thought he had done so, he sent Rawlinson off to the seaside for two days' rest before the battle. He seems to have thought that the French too possessed this new weapon, only to discover that Foch had never even heard of it. He was always in favour of leaving much to 'the man on the spot'.

There are sound reasons for such an approach, and in any event, from a practical point of view, the scale of Haig's command made it difficult for him to impose complete uniformity across all his armies. But he should have done more to ensure that tanks were used in the way that Colonel Swinton had recommended. The biggest success in the 15 September engagement was at the village of Flers, where, instead of being scattered and vulnerable, thirteen tanks were engaged in mutually supporting actions. A possible breakthrough here failed because there was no follow-up. Haig was personally impressed by the tanks, even though only forty-eight had been available. On 18 September, again in the grip of technical enthusiasm, he suggested to Admiral Bacon, in command of the Dover Flotillas, that 'in view of the successes obtained by the tanks, . . . he should carry out experiments with special flat-bottomed boats for running ashore and landing a line of tanks on the beach with the object of breaking through wire and capturing the enemy's defences . . . The Admiral was delighted with the idea, and is to go to the Admiralty with a view to having special boats made. I asked him also to urge the loan of sufficient personnel from Navy for manning 100 tanks.' Hardly an unimaginative response to the challenge of technology. Indeed, on the following day, Haig asked the War Office for 1,000 tanks. At its highest the largest number of tanks he was ever able to deploy at one time was 534.

Haig was an enthusiast, but he was in a minority of what we now see as advanced thinkers. Even the German high command, usually innovative, was not impressed by the tank, and only a dozen German tanks were ever in action. To be fair to the sceptics, it should be remembered that at this stage in the war (and even by the end) tanks were very vulnerable creatures compared to the Second World War machines. On 18 September only eighteen out of the forty-nine in France were able to take part in the battle: mechanical problems were common. The crews had a miserable time inside the tank, suffering from sea-sickness and choking on carbon monoxide and petrol fumes. They had to endure an average temperature of 51.7 degrees Celsius.[18] The armour of their swaying prison was easily pierced. The Mark 1 tank then available had a maximum speed on the battlefield of about half a mile per hour.

The period from 15 to 30 September marked the most successful phase of the battle. It was characterised by the dispatch of many messages designed to put heart into Rawlinson, who was sceptical about the achievability of Haig's aims. Haig certainly did not share the view that the battle was to consist in limited operations conducted within range of his artillery and designed to wear down the enemy by killing the largest number at the lowest cost. His orders of 29 September were ambitious, as was his diary entry of 30 September – part of it so ambitious indeed that it was marked for Lady Haig, 'Please do not copy this part'. Rawlinson would have had to advance twenty-four miles, six times what they had achieved in three months, Gough much the same, and Allenby some twenty miles. In formulating these plans, as in his readiness to envisage imminent German collapse, Haig, in his impetuous mode, was displaying a serious lack of judgement and a continuing failure to grasp the new nature of war.

German reinforcement and bad weather put paid to grandiose dreams. Attacks on 1 October did result in quite substantial advances, but as rain began to fall in the course of the day – and it continued to fall for the next four days – mud made further advance impossible, and within the week the divisions had been thrown back to their starting point. Further attacks took place throughout October, without any gain at all. The army was bogged down, and the approach through the quagmire behind the front line led to moral and physical exhaustion in the troops that came forward. Haig insisted on continuing to attack. The objectives for even the first day had not been achieved. As he always tended to do, and as he always logically could do, he maintained that he required to attack to assist the French, who were also still fighting, and whose wing he did not wish to leave undefended. He told Rawlinson that he intended to continue attacking throughout the winter.

But in these weather conditions, and with no successes to show for the monstrous losses, even Haig could not persist forever. The final substantial action in the battle was the capture of Beaumont Hamel on 13 November and on 18 November the battle was officially closed down.

What is history to make of the Battle of the Somme, this sombre four months of battle which, with Third Ypres, through the writings of Owen and Sassoon and the others has formed forever our picture of the First World War? And what is history to make of Haig's part in it? The final British casualties were approximately 432,000, of whom 150,000 died and 100,000 were too badly wounded to fight again. Prior and Wilson compute that the fighting capacity of 250,000 men, or twenty-five infantry divisions, was thus lost to the British army.[19] The German losses have been the subject of scholarship, debate and dispute. A reasonable estimate is 230,000. The battle wore down the British army more than the German army by a ratio of almost two to one. Hardly any ground had been gained.

What we make of it depends on what it was meant to do. The initial concept of it as part of a huge war-winning onslaught in every theatre had been abandoned. Haig was for the most part guarded in what he expected of the battle. His despatch said that its objectives had been, first, to take pressure off Verdun, secondly, to keep the Germans away from the Russian Front and thirdly to wear down the German Army, and he claimed that in each of these objectives the battle had succeeded. As far as the first objective is concerned, the Somme was planned, as has been seen, before Verdun began. Additionally, Germany began taking troops away from Verdun before the battle had really developed. The battle was not effective in pinning down Germans on the Western Front: 15 German divisions were in fact moved to the Russian front.

What about wearing down? The 2 August memorandum that saw just the first part of the operations as the wearing-down phase was obviously false. Haig's earlier view was that the whole of the battle was to be a wearing-down exercise, and in his *Final Despatch* he characterised everything up to the last 100 days of the War – and perhaps even much or all of that last period too – as one continuous process of wearing down. If that view of the wearing-down process is valid, then the Somme was effective – though at a colossal price. 'On an overall view of the Somme battle,' said George Duncan, 'Haig did not doubt that it was a notable victory. Apart from relieving the pressure on Verdun it had forced the German Army and its commanders to face the possibility of defeat.'[20] And after the war, Ludendorff ascribed to the wearing-down effect of the Somme the radical cause of British victory. But even if the Somme can be justified on the 'overall view' to which Duncan referred, the piecemeal attacks of July and August, and the assaults on High Wood, for example, resulted in numbers of casualties out of all proportion to ground gained, and some phases of the battle cannot be justified even on an attritional basis.

Much of the value of the Somme was in its educational function. At every level commanders learned lessons, and learned them very quickly; though in recognising this one must always remember just how expensive their education was. In the dawn attack of 14 July, the shelling was much more concentrated than it had been on the first day when 22,000 yards of front and 300,000 yards of supporting trench were shelled. Thirteen days later the figures were just 6,000 and 12,000. In the cavalry advance which followed, the cavalry dismounted and entrenched and had machine-gun support which silenced a German machine-gun. They might have done more with more cavalry reserves and artillery support. Haig is often criticised for seeing the role of cavalry still in *arme blanche* terms, but here cavalry was used as mounted infantry.

Such was the determination to learn lessons that *Preliminary Notes of the Tactical Lessons* were issued in July, while the battle was still under way. At divisional level and by GHQ itself many series of notes were produced. After the battle had ended such documents were followed, early in the following year, by SS143, *Instructions for the Training of Platoons for Offensive Action,* and SS144, *The Normal Formation for the Attack.* These publications emphasised the importance of a platoon as a tactical unit, organised into different specialities. Germany is usually credited with being first to make the move to more specialised units, but SS143 and SS144 predate the

German *Der Angriff in Stellungskreig* of January 1918.[21] In these papers, and the thinking they reflect, lies the genesis of the transformation of the British army which would deliver victory two years later.

Ludendorff was not alone in attributing significance to the Somme. Captain von Hentig, a German staff officer, wrote:

> The Somme was the muddy grave of the German Field Army and of its faith in the ability of the German leaders. The German Field Command, which entered the war with enormous superiority, was defeated by the superior technique of its opponents.[22]

Similarly the German Official History recorded that the heavy loss of life affected Germany much more heavily than the Allies. Falkenhayn was now replaced by Hindenburg, with Ludendorff as his very active deputy.

Of course the tactical direction of the British forces was not free from flaw. The coordination of units and of artillery supporting different units was poor. As far as Haig himself was concerned, his tactical view lacked a coherency because of his readiness, despite all his emphasis on wearing down, to convince himself that break-through was just round the corner. He was not consistent in his view of attrition. He was still at the beginning of his learning curve. Rawlinson had already applied his 'bite-and-hold' tactics in the previous year and would have preferred this to be the basis of the Somme offensive. By mid-September, perforce, that was what was happening on the Somme, but often in the form of inadequate penny-packet actions where the losses were high. Haig was wrong, too, in allowing attacks on narrow fronts, which left dangerously exposed flanks. In the final Somme battles he returned to over-ambitious objectives, because, as so often, he allowed himself to think that the Germans were about to break. He insisted on the use of tanks when the vehicles were too few and too unreliable and thus destroyed their surprise value, although Gary Sheffield argues that 'critics such as

Lloyd George, who subsequently attacked Haig for revealing the secret of the tank before large numbers became available, displayed a tenuous grip on the realities of a Western Front in September 1916. For the BEF, fighting as the junior coalition partner in a *Materielschlacht*, the battle had to be a case of 'maximum effort'.[23] It is certainly true that even if the build-up of a huge tank fleet could have been achieved in secret, the new weapon could scarcely have been deployed in force without small-scale trials.

These faults are not overwhelming. The dreadfulness of the Somme was the fault not of Haig but of modern warfare. After the terrible losses of the first day, losses continued at a level that is a reproach to mankind, but not hugely different from the average losses in the later battles of the war. Gary Sheffield is correct when he concludes that:

> For the allies, the Somme was not a 'victory' in the traditional sense, but it was certainly a success. Moreover it is difficult to avoid the conclusion that the Battle of the Somme was an essential precondition to the allied victory of 1918 . . . The Battle of the Somme was not a victory in itself but without it the *Entente* would not have emerged victorious in 1918.[24]

At a very early stage the scale of the Somme losses caused concern at home. Robertson, seeking government approval for the offensive, had known little of Haig's actual plans, and blandly assured Colonel Repington that Haig was 'a shrewd Scot who would not do anything rash.'[25] Robertson was taken aback by the losses on the first day, writing privately to Rawlinson and Kiggell, urging caution and commonsense. He expected Haig to transfer the action to Second Army and the Ypres sector when the offensive appeared to miscarry, and he became frustrated by the lack of information he received from GHQ, which certainly made his contact with ministers difficult: 'I have seen several Cabinet Ministers and the first question has always been how you are getting on and what you propose to do next. As regards the first I have said that you are getting on very well, but that it would be a slow business. As regards the second I have been able to say that I do not know what you propose to do next, that being the truth.'[26] Haig was irritated by the suggestion that he should keep Robertson updated on a weekly basis.

Robertson writes again to Haig, pressing him to repair relations with Joffre, and particularly Foch, 'with whom you do not deal to the extent that French was accustomed to do', and to work with the French in exploiting successes on the south front. 'We have these Germans this time for a certainty if we take the chances now offered. Good luck.'[27] In a postscript he tentatively requests an indication of Haig's plans even in general terms. He wanted these plans for mutual and foreign opinion, but especially for the War Committee: 'If you could send me a short letter which I read to the War Committee I am sure it would be to the General [*sic*] interest and to your interest in particular'.[28]

By 29 July, he was writing:

> The powers that be are beginning to get a little uneasy in regard to the situation. The casualties are mounting up and they are wondering whether we are likely to get a proper return for them. I do my best to keep the general situation to the front, and to explain what may be the effect of our efforts . . . but they will persist in asking whether I think a loss of say 300,000 will lead to really great results because if not we ought to be content with something less than we are now doing, and they constantly enquire why we are fighting and the French are not.

Haig's reply made use of a favourable report from Charteris on the state of the German Army, and pointed out that the July losses were only '120,000 more than they would have been had we not attacked.' He concluded that he expected to be able to maintain the offensive well into the autumn.

Kitchener had gone down on HMS *Hampshire* on 6 June (Haig: 'How shall we get on without him?') and was now replaced as War Secretary by Lloyd George ('a mere civilian'), who instructed Robertson to 'send a message to General Sir D. Haig that he might count on full support from home.'

But that full support was being eroded. Churchill circulated a Cabinet paper critical of Haig's methods and Robertson reported to Haig on 6 August that there was disquiet amongst 'Winston, French, Fitzgerald and various "degommed" people [who] are trying to make mischief.' 'Degommed' or sometimes 'degummed' was the adjective used at the time to describe commanders who had been sent home in disgrace. The most eminent of these people was French, whose office at Horse Guards, according to Richard Holmes, 'became a clearing-house for gossip from France as generals, most of them with their own axes to grind, passed through London'.[29] The King intervened, first to tell Haig that 'a regular cabal' of dismissed generals was criticising him, and then on 25 November to summon French to Buckingham Palace to warn him to stop his criticisms of Haig. In October, French had gone out to France, on Lloyd George's instructions, for a series of meetings with the French generals, returning to report to Lloyd George and not to the CIGS. Foch reported to Henry Wilson that French was trying to find the reason for the Somme losses and lack of progress, but assured Wilson that he had declined to discuss British generals behind their back. French was to 'receive every attention due to a British Field Marshal', but at a personal level, Haig had nothing but contempt for his old friend, whom he refused to see. He sent instead his ADC, Lieutenant-Colonel Alan Fletcher. 'I despise him too much.' So much for a friendship described by French with some prolixity in the inscription he placed on a gold flask given to Haig in 1902: 'A very small memento, my dear Douglas, of our long and tried friendship proved "in sunshine and in shadow." JF'.

In September General Maxse, the Commander of 18th Division, came to lunch:

He had heard from his brother Leo (Editor of the *National Review*) that certain politicians had banded themselves together with the object of having me removed from the Command of the Armies in France. General Maxse wished to know whether I thought he ought to urge his brother to take action in the matter. I saw him along with General Kiggell, and I said that I had no dealings with the press personally. But my policy had always been to give the press as free a hand as possible. To show them everything, to allow them to talk to anyone they chose, and to write what they liked, provided no secrets were given away to the enemy. In the present case I saw no reason to depart from this policy. If his brother chose to come to France and to go around the Army and see whether —————————'s statements were true or false, he was free to do so in the ordinary way. I at any rate could take no part in a press campaign against anyone. All my time was taken up in thinking out how to beat the enemy of Great Britain – I mean Germans.

The last sentence is very Haigian, but he was always conscious of intrigue and attempts to get rid of him. No one was entirely frank about what they did and said. On 17 September Foch came to visit Haig and then went out with him into the garden. He told Haig about Lloyd George's recent visit to his headquarters and explained that Lloyd George had begun

by saying that he was a British minister and as such he considered that he had a right to be told the truth. He wished to know why the British, who had gained no more ground than the French, if as much, had suffered such heavy casualties . . . LG also asked his opinion as to the ability of the British generals. Foch said 'LG was sufficiently patriotic not to criticise the British Commander-in-Chief', but he did not speak with confidence of the other British Generals as a whole . . .

Unless I had been told of this conversation personally by Gen. Foch, I would not have believed that a British Minister could have been so ungentlemanly as to go to a foreigner and put such questions regarding his own subordinates.

In Henry Wilson's diary it appears that Lloyd George was even more ungentlemanly than Haig thought, and criticised the Commander-in-Chief by saying that 'he gave Haig all the guns and ammunition and men he could use and nothing happened. Foch said that Lloyd George was *très monté* against Haig, and he did not think Haig's seat was very secure.'

It appears from Charteris' diary that GHQ was well aware of the plots and criticism. To his credit, Haig's reaction was fairly detached and Olympian. He had come, despite his scruples, to use public relations in the shape of the press to secure his position. He certainly used his royal connections. But beyond that he confined himself to making ringing patriotic assertions of which the subtext was that he was too high-minded and preoccupied by the cares of his great office to concern himself with the (very much lesser) people who sought to displace him. He did not resort to petty counter-attacks: his bile was largely confined to his diary.

The politicians were already beginning to call Haig 'The Butcher', but Esher sought to defend him. On 3 August, just back from the Front, he wrote to Hankey, asking him to tell the Prime Minister that the battle was going well. He urged Haig to explain that the casualties were justified by the enhanced morale amongst the surviving troops. He visited Haig at fortnightly intervals, and reported back to London about achievements that could not be measured on the map. His judgement on military matters, though generally sound, was not always above criticism. At about this time he was picking out Major-General Montgomery (who would be Field-Marshal Sir Archibald Montgomery-Massingberd, and Chief of the Imperial General Staff) as a future Commander-in-Chief. He was the handsomest soldier he had seen in France.

Just a year ago I picked out Douglas as the future C-in-C because of his blue eyes and knowledge and Scottish coolness. So now I feel sure that Mongomery is *the* soldier who will command the British armies of the future, after Douglas and Rawly have given up their charge. He is very tall, and has the frankest face you would wish to see; dark blue eyes, and a delightful smile. His capacity is obvious after two minutes' talk in spite of his disconcerting charm. They say he is tenacious, and even masterful.[30]

Haig naturally took care to present his case in the most favourable light, and this is reflected in his final report on the great battle of 1916:

> The . . . picture is full of encouragement and promise. The enemy's losses have undoubtedly been very heavy – far heavier than those of the Allies – and there is convincing evidence of a sensible depreciation in his moral. From this evidence it is safe to conclude that an appreciable proportion of the German soldiers are now practically beaten men ready to surrender if they could find the opportunity, thoroughly tired of the war, and hopeless of eventual success . . . [E]ven German discipline, obedience to authority and love of country will not suffice to enable the German Commanders to enforce their will if the majority of their men lose courage and confidence, and as we know beyond doubt that many of them have done.

Robertson too drew optimistic conclusions from the Somme months, despite the fact that it had caused him so much criticism from the politicians, and in spite of the fact that he was aware of the attacks on the 'Western' Generals who had advocated the battle. ('[We lacked] imagination in our plans, we were too wooden in our ideas and too heavy-footed in our movements.') He looked back on the Somme as being a definite stage on the road to victory. He considered that the outcome of the war was thereafter no longer in doubt, and he deprecated as *naïf* the politicians' propensity to measure success in terms of 'kilometres of ground gained, with little or no regard to the moral ascendancy our troops had established'.[31]

Laffin has argued in *British Butchers and Bunglers of Word War 1* that very soon after the fall of the Somme, but only afterwards, the argument was developed that Britain was not looking for break-through, only wearing-down. This view can be seductive in the light of the suspiciously retrospective feel about a number of passages in Charteris' diaries, but a detailed comparison of the book with his contemporary writings dispels the suspicions. Haig does inject some *ex post facto* thinking in his Despatch after the battle, and ahead of it he allowed himself his usual moments of over-optimism. But before the battle he said plenty to support the view that he did see it as a wearing-down exercise – though it would have been a delightful bonus if something more dramatic came of it. True, Rawlinson had said that all that was necessary on 1 July was for the troops to stroll over and take the German trenches after the British guns had finished with them, but as early as 5 July Robertson wrote to Kiggell in terms remarkably consistent with what Haig was to say later:

The more I think of it the more I am convinced that at any rate until we get through the enemy's defences the road to success lies through deliberation. All last year I preached this doctrine. I maintained then and still maintain, that nothing is to be gained but very much is to be lost by trying to push on too rapidly. Before the war our theory was that anybody who could make ground should make it. This is a dangerous theory until we get through the enemy's trenches. People who can and do push on in front of the general line seldom or ever [*sic*] stay there. They are usually cut off or at any rate driven back. The fact is that the whole line must go forward together . . .

If the above view is sound it follows that the objectives must be exceedingly limited. In fact limited to such a distance as there is reasonable prospect of the whole line being able to reach. This theory tends to what is absolutely necessary includ-ing the concentration of artillery fire.[32]

An objective proof of the effectiveness of the battle was that by 12 December 1916 the Central Powers submitted a note to the neutral states and to the Vatican, to say that they were willing to negotiate a peace. The terms proposed were crazily unacceptable, but the fact remained that Germany now thought that outright victory could not be taken for granted.

There are many flaws in Haig's handling of the battle. But most of the British failures flowed from the fact that Haig was commanding an army group of sixty divisions, whereas before the war at Staff College no training or thought had been given to anything bigger than the six-division Expeditionary Force. In advance of the battle he erred in demanding the capture of an excessive depth of trench and accordingly the huge artillery barrage was dissipated over too much ground. The targets he gave to his divisions were too ambitious, even for the huge weight of artillery. The necessity for the use of high explosive shells, rather than shrapnel, in cutting wire was not generally known. While the problem of uncut wire on 1 July has been exaggerated in traditional accounts of the battle, there were areas, such as Beaumont Hamel, where the problem did exist. It was difficult to establish in advance how effectively wire had been cut, and aerial surveillance was unsatisfactory, but Haig may have been too ready to accept the assurance of his army commanders that the bombardment had cut the wire. On the other hand he is often unfairly criticised for overruling his army commanders, and if he could not rely on their advice, it is difficult to see what he could have done: he could hardly have inspected the wire himself. The main criticism of his handling of the Somme is that he allowed the battle to drag on in terrible weather conditions. He was pressed to do so by Joffre and when the battle was closed down Joffre attacked him for not continuing to a decisive victory: France for her part in fact moved on to the attack at Verdun as late as 15 December, with significant success. In reality, Haig often ignored French entreaties, and could easily have closed the battle down much earlier without criticism from London, where the politicians were increasingly dismayed by the scale of the losses. The prolongation of the battle was largely due to Haig's desire to make improvements in the line and to launch local attacks, and to his fatal weakness for sensing that the Germans were on the point of collapse. Joffre in his memoirs described this period as 'a series of disconnected actions both costly and unprofitable'.[33] The reason for the line straightening was not just a desire for tidiness: it increased the effectiveness of artillery support. But it cannot be justified by the losses suffered. The prolongation of the battle was a mistake.

Deceit and Misinformation: The Calais Conference Backfires on Lloyd George. Arras

In the span from the close of the Somme in November 1916 to the close of the Battle of Arras, in the late spring of 1917, Haig was increasingly preoccupied by political issues, both at home in Britain and in France.

At home, the vast power of the Northcliffe machine was responding to and fomenting anti-government feeling. 'The discontent which began to manifest itself throughout the country was fanned to fever heat by the powerful agency of the Northcliffe press. There were thirty-three members of the cabinet. One morning the streets were placarded with posters of the Northcliffe *Evening Journal* bearing the legend, "Wanted! Twenty Three Ropes".'[1] While the German peace proposals were not officially discussed, there were members of the Cabinet who would have liked to explore them. Amongst them was Lord Lansdowne, who submitted a paper to his colleagues, urging that the Allies should make peace now unless the relative departmental heads were certain of victory by the autumn of 1917. Later he was to follow this document with the famous letter to the press. Northcliffe refused to publish it in *The Times,* but it appeared in the *Daily Telegraph.* Lansdowne's doubts were echoed by other Cabinet ministers, who thought it necessary to ask Robertson for his view on the *possibility* of a 'knock-out blow'. His reply was confidently disdainful: 'Quite frankly, and at the same time respectfully, I can only say I am surprised that the question should be asked. The idea had not before entered my head that any member of His Majesty's Government had a doubt in the matter.'[2] Lloyd George, Carson, the *Morning Post* and others worked to bring down Asquith, and at the beginning of December Northcliffe's campaign achieved its objective and Asquith fell, to be replaced by Lloyd George. Haig wrote to his wife: 'You seem to have great excitement at home, making a new government. I am personally very sorry for poor old Asquith. He has had a hard time and seems to have more capacity and brain power than any of the others.' Asquith of course never interfered with Haig's plans. It has been said that he would have regarded it as at least as constitutionally improper to question the judgement of professional soldiers as to put pressure on the law officers. (Lincoln must be the generals' favourite: when Grant was appointed to command the Union Armies in 1864, Lincoln told him, 'I neither ask nor desire to know anything of your plans. Take the responsibility and act, and call on me for assistance.' And that despite the fact that Lincoln had prepared himself for the military conflict by sitting up late, night after night, studying Jomini and Clausewitz.)

Haig was unhappy to see Lloyd George as Prime Minister, but the new Secretary of State for War was Lord Derby, already an acquaintance, and one with whom he found it easy to work. Derby was a loyal supporter of the army, although uninspired. Hankey described him as 'a flabby jelly' and 'a poor wobbly thing'. Haig did better. He wrote to Lady Haig on 14 January 1918: 'A very weak-minded fellow, I'm afraid and, like the feather pillow, bears the marks of the last person who sat on him.' Dictionaries of quotations attribute this neat turn of phrase to Haig, and only Haig, but it sounds far too good to be a Haig original. While he had little personal liking for Lloyd George, at this stage their professional relationship worked perfectly well. On 31 December 1916, when Haig was dining with Esher in Paris, Esher said that he thought the new Prime Minister 'a dangerous experiment'. He asked 'Would you trust him to bring up your daughters or to do any business for you?' Haig replied that he would not have chosen Asquith, nor many of his predecessors – Disraeli for instance – to bring up his daughters, but that they had been fairly satisfactory Prime Ministers.[3] Again, pretty good for Haig.

The King, who took a close interest in his army and its generals, had wanted for some months to make Haig a field-marshal in order to enhance his position against his enemies. This unusual honour in the case of a serving general was conferred late in December. Early in the New Year Haldane sent his congratulations:

> You are almost the only military leader we possess with the power to think, which the enemy possess in a highly developed form. The necessity of a trained mind, and of the intellectual equipment which it carries is at last recognised among our people. In things other than military they have, alas, most things still to learn, but in the science and art of war a trying experience has dictated the necessity of a gift such as yours won by the hard toil of the spirit.

His next paragraph is particularly interesting:

> If I had my way, you would have taken the place at the head of a real Great Headquarters Staff in London on 4th August 1914. But with Kitchener, who knew nothing of these things, this was impossible. What we needed then was by taking thought to penetrate the obscurity of the future and survey the conceivable theatres of war as one whole.

Haldane's observation here points at once to Haig's strengths and his suitability for control of the sort of Great Headquarters Staff that Haldane had in mind. He had been intimately implicated in the creation of the Imperial General Staff in the years before the war and understood exactly what such an organisation was meant to do. He had the administrative abilities which would have enabled him to run a Great Headquarters Staff on the German model; although it must remain a question whether he had sufficient breadth of vision to fulfil the strategic aspects of such a position. In the circumstances in which he now found himself, he was in France, and Robertson, a limited man who saw himself as the agent of the army in Whitehall, rather than as its director, was in the London position of which Haldane spoke. Haig, as the more influential of the two and the most powerful military voice in the army, was to an extent fulfilling (as he was expected to do, even by an increasingly antagonistic Cabinet) some of the functions that properly belonged to an officer at a distance from any one of the theatres of war. It was too much to expect Haig, as Commander-in-Chief of the British armies in France, to argue anything other than the primacy of the Western Front. The fact that he was probably right in doing so should not obscure the conflict of interest that existed. To the end of the war, Haig's position was ambivalent: he was required to make policy as well as to execute it. He was frequently requested to advise the government on the overall direction of the war. Not entirely of his own choosing, although he was not averse to the role, he thus occupied an important function in urging and advocating the strategy for the conduct of the war as a whole, rather than simply implementing policy in his own theatre. That was not his fault, but it had much to do with the frustrations between him and the politicians.

Haig was not the only general to receive a Marshal's baton in 1917: Joffre received one also. In his case it was a consolation rather than a reward. A conference of the Allied military leaders took place at Chantilly on 15 November 1916, and it was already apparent by then that the ascendant star was that of Nivelle. The French government under Briand was in difficulties and sought to improve its position by moving Joffre on 13 December to a sinecure as 'Technical Adviser', replacing him with Nivelle. Foch, too, became an 'Adviser', protesting as he went, 'I want to kill Boches. I want to kill Boches.'

Joffre and Foch were sacrifices to France's growing war-weariness. She had been carrying by far the major part of the war effort on her shoulders. Her casualties were vast: 800,000 men in 1914, 380,000 in 1915 and 495,000 men in 1916. The will of both the civil community and the army to continue the war was beginning to crack. Haig was aware of this and it was a major factor in the decisions which he made throughout his period of command, but possibly a factor he exaggerated after the event.

The conclusion of the November 1916 Chantilly conference, the last major piece of planning in which Joffre was involved for the time being, was to try to do in 1917 what had not worked in 1916, and to attack the Germans simultaneously on all fronts. The German possession of interior lines of communication meant that she could throw her forces rapidly from one front to another. She was able to make use of this capacity to defeat Romania. It was critical to keep Germany tied down on the Western Front, if she were to be deterred from Balkan expansion. There was to be an allied attack on Bulgaria, and Germany had to be engaged on the Western Front. Haig indicated that he was prepared to launch an attack as early as February, but would prefer to operate on a larger scale in May.

The western-minded Haig and Robertson were aware that Lloyd George was inclined to look east. He had never been enthusiastic about the Dardanelles, favouring a campaign in the Balkans, but on 12 December Robertson wrote to Haig:

> Our new PM is well on the move. He is at last convinced than Salonika is wrong and is going to tell Briand so next week . . . Though he is off Salonika he is *on* Egypt, and wants to get to Jerusalem. For this he is hankering after two divisions from France for the winter. He is also after lending some of your big guns to Italy for the winter. I have done my best with him and in company with you I have no doubt we can keep him all right. I want him to get the division from Salonika but that will be difficult and opposed by all the allies.[4]

France, and in particular General Sarrail, was not to agree easily to abandoning the Salonika campaign, even though Nivelle was in favour.

The seeds of friction between Lloyd George and Haig were being sown, and their first green shoots began to appear when Lloyd

George, passing through France, had a meeting, in Haig's absence, with Kiggell, who reported:

> Lloyd George began talking about the merits of the relative fronts – taking the line that we only thought of our own side; that we had not really effected much there and he did not believe we could; that we must strike against the soft front and could not find it in the west; that much of the Somme loss was useless and the country would not stand more of that sort of thing; and so on. In fact he poured out a lot of heretical amateur strategy of the most dangerous and misleading kind and was far from complimentary to what had been done by our armies here. He ruffled me so thoroughly that I argued vehemently with him and I fear without displaying the respect due to his high office. I told him he had better make peace at once if England was going to take up the line that heavy losses could not be allowed, and that everything he sent to other theatres before we had all we wanted would reduce our chance of winning the war . . . Robertson threw in a contribution now and then backing me up, but said little. Afterwards he told me privately that he had to meet that sort of stuff all day and every day, and was doing his best against it though he feared he thought he could do more than he could.[5]

Visitors continued to flow to Haig's headquarters during the preparation for the spring offensive. 'Mr. John Masefield came to lunch. He is a poet, but I am told he has written the best account of the landing at Gallipoli.' Another visitor: 'Mr. Bernard Shaw (the author and playwright) came to lunch. An interesting man of original views. A great talker! On sitting down to lunch I at once discovered he was a vegetarian. As if by magic, on my ordering it, two poached eggs appeared, also some spinach and macaroni, so he did not fare badly'. Hilaire Belloc arrived: 'An English MP, but very French in appearance.'

A more eventful visit took place when a group of French journalists interviewed Haig on 1 February 1917. They regarded the visit as an interview, although Haig denied that that was what it amounted to, saying that he 'merely talked platitudes and stated my confidence in a victorious termination of the war.' Haig was now, at Esher's urging, seeing journalists, French and British, and Charteris was supposed to censor the articles from a military standpoint. He assumed that Haig would then see the copy before it was published and be satisfied that it reflected his views. This had not happened and the article, as it appeared, was in much more outspoken terms than Haig would have wished or used. It scorned 'sham' German peace proposals or, for that matter 'an incomplete victory, a premature or halting victory [which] would enable German militarism to make ready its revenge'. There was also a reference to his view that the war would be won in the west. The determination of politicians to win the war was questioned and there were references to munitions shortages. This Lloyd George regarded as an attack on him, in his capacity as former Minister of Munitions. The article was published in *The Times*, with a translation, and there was uproar in London. Derby sent a telegram, wanting to know what was to be said. In the House of Commons, Philip Snowden referred to Haig's 'blazing indiscretion [which] had shaken the confidence of many people in his judgement and common sense.' Major Lytton, who was in charge of foreign press correspondence, was summoned to London and faced a grilling by Lloyd George and Lord Curzon.

Characteristically, Haig simplified and personalised what was a serious crisis that would not have occurred if his Headquarters had been better run:

> Lloyd George seem[s] to resent my bulking large in the public eyes at all. He wishes to shine alone. As for Curzon, it seems that he still has a grudge against the soldier and would like to reintroduce a new system with a Military Member as at Simla . . . The attacks seem to have been made by discredited socialists and 'peace at any price' people.

Again, to Lady Haig, Lloyd George was

> slipping down the hill in popular favour, and is looking about to find something to increase his reputation as the man of the hour and the saviour of England! . . . I am doing my best and have a clear conscience. If they have someone else who can command this great army better than I am doing, I shall be glad to hand over to him and would be *so happy* to come back to my darling wife and play golf and bring up the children.

Derby identified Charteris as having been responsible for the débacle. He advised Haig to give the responsibility for censorship to someone else and suggested that Haig should decline further interviews. He ended his letter, 'I am not in any way exaggerating the effect the interview has had not only on the Cabinet, but on the people of this country.' Haig scribbled in the margin of the letter: 'Possibly correct as to the Cabinet, but absolute rubbish as regards the people'. It was difficult to dent his self-esteem.

The extent to which Haig relied on Charteris is at first difficult to understand. He had described him as 'dirty and fat' (obesity was always a serious criticism as far as Haig was concerned) and he cannot have approved of his pre-breakfast brandies or his bawdy jokes. Charteris was, however, intelligent and in some areas able and he had good administrative capacities, and Haig made use of him for a wide range of tasks. Part of the problem was that the combination of intelligence work (which Charteris did not enjoy) and propaganda work was an undesirable one. Esher noted that: 'The one is mainly a system of falsehood while the other aims at the exact truth. It is corrupting for the furnishers of truth that they should be engaged in manufacturing lies.' The suggestion that he deliberately set out to mislead Haig has been discredited, but by accident or by design, because he tended to let Haig hear what he wanted to hear, Charteris consistently gave an inaccurate picture of German morale and of the German economy. He relied greatly on the testimony of prisoners of war, an intelligence which is usually regarded with great suspicion.

The poor quality of Charteris' intelligence appreciations was compounded by the fact that Haig did not deal in the subtle shades of grey that are the stuff of morale assessments, but seized on what seemed to him indicative of collapse or revolution. Desmond Morton, one of his ADCs, testified that 'Haig hated being told any information, however irrefutable, which militated against his pre-conceived ideas or beliefs.' Later in 1917 Haig wrote to Robertson, agreeing with various points that the latter had made but adding:

> the only point on which I am not in accord with you is the desirability of issuing such pessimistic estimates from your Intelligence Branch. They do, I feel sure, much harm, and cause many in authority to take a pessimistic outlook, when a contrary view, based on equally good information, would go far to help the nation on to victory. Personally I feel we have every reason to be optimistic, and if the war were to end tomorrow, Great Britain would find herself not merely the greatest power in Europe, but in the world.

While his optimism is commendable, his approach to intelligence was dangerously plastic.

Charteris was responsible in July 1916 for nursing a new and important contact, surprising in view of what the King had said about French's dealings with the press and Haig's own prejudices. Haig now chose to solicit the influence of Lord Northcliffe. Charteris writes: 'Confident in their belief of the favourable opinion that a personal interview with Haig made on all who came in contact with him, and with the co-operation of personal friends of Lord Northcliffe, Haig's Staff arranged the visit and the interview between these two men, each great in his own sphere.' (There is conflict between Charteris' different accounts about the date of this *démarche*, which in one case he gives as 1915. The evidence is much stronger for 1916.) Charteris says that the meeting was arranged without Haig's knowledge, but that cannot have been the case. He says that the officers who had arranged the meeting 'awaited the result with some trepidation, but its success exceeded their highest expectations'.[6]

They might well have had trepidations. Haig's contempt for journalists and the press was even greater than his contempt for politicians. The interview must have been painful to him, because his classical concept of a great military leader precluded him, like Coriolanus, from submission to the approval of the public. An appeal to the press was something unworthy of a great general. Northcliffe, for his part, had enormous power as the proprietor of a vast press and he used that power overtly, in a direct way that is unimaginable today. Moreover, he was unpredictable, mercurial and by the end of his life clinically insane. He was interested in phrenology. Kitchener was no use: 'A tall man with a narrow forehead.' Lloyd George, himself an amateur phrenologist, was not acceptable: 'It's his big head on a little body that I don't like.' The conformation of Haig's cranium was, however, ideally that of a general. 'Lithe and alert, Sir Douglas is known for his distinguished bearing and good looks. He has blue eyes and an unusual facial angle, delicate features, and a chin to be reckoned with.'

Northcliffe was unimpressed by Asquith: 'We are not at law with Germany, we are at war with her.' He savagely attacked Kitchener for failing to provide enough shells. He brought down Asquith's ministry, but soon tired of Lloyd George. On one occasion he burst into the War Office and roared at Lloyd George's secretary: 'I don't want to see him – you can tell him from me that I hear he has been interfering with strategy and that if it goes on I will break him.' Politicians, including Lloyd George, for whom Northcliffe was: 'the mere kettledrum of Sir Douglas Haig and the mouth-organ of Sir William Robertson', did fear that they could be broken by him. He was thought to be planning a bid for dictatorship, a risk which Lloyd George took seriously. It was partly to keep him harmlessly busy that Lloyd George first sent him to the United States as a leader of the British War Mission, and then appointed him Director of Propaganda in Enemy Countries.[7]

Churchill assessed him thus:

There can be no doubt that Lord Northcliffe was at all times animated by an ardent patriotism and an intense desire to win the war. But he wielded power without official responsibility, enjoyed secret knowledge without the general view, and disturbed the fortunes of national leaders without being able to bear their burdens. Thus a swaying force, uncertain, capricious, essentially personal, potent alike for good or evil, claiming to make or mar public men, to sustain or displace Commanders, to shake policies, and to fashion or overthrow Governments, introduced itself in the absence of all Parliamentary corrections into the conduct of the war.[8]

With his impeccable phrenological credentials, Haig made a favourable impression. For the moment he was the one indispensable man, and (until equally precipitately – Northcliffe took against Haig) the enormous power of the Northcliffe empire swung into action to support Haig and promote his cause. Kitchener did not receive the same consideration: Northcliffe told Beaverbrook, another press baron, although not in the Northcliffe league, 'to go on attacking Lord Kitchener, day in, day out, till he had driven him from office.'[9]

For the moment Haig saw the press, personified in Northcliffe, as his ally, and further visits were encouraged. Lady Haig had voiced some concern about Northcliffe's presence at GHQ. Haig reassured her: 'I myself was much exercising my mind whether to receive him or not. As a matter of fact, a man more unlike the *Daily Mail* than Lord Northcliffe is, it is difficult to imagine.' Some days later he wrote again to her: 'Lord Northcliffe lunched today, I quite like the man; he has the courage of his opinions and thinks of doing his utmost to win the war.' Before Northcliffe left headquarters he told Haig just to let him know if anything appeared in *The Times* 'which was not altogether to my liking.' He reassured Haig that his *bête noir,* Repington, 'had now no influence with *The Times*; they employed him to write certain articles but he (Lord N.) knew he was not reliable.' In September 1916, Northcliffe was back again and Haig suggested that he see something called a 'tank', which Northcliffe thought was a storage device of some sort. He was persuaded to climb into the tank, but the turret was of a smaller circumference than his girth. The tank crew pulled his feet, and Northcliffe's assistant, Steed, sat on his shoulders. Like a lobster squeezing itself into a pot, he does not seem to have appreciated that getting himself out might be more difficult than getting himself in, and the exercise was only achieved at the cost of several buttons.

In just two months since he had become Prime Minister, Lloyd George had become by now overtly critical of the Commander-in-Chief. On 24 February the War Cabinet concluded that 'Haig is the best man we have, but that is not saying much . . . As between Haig and Nivelle, LG [intends] to support the latter.'

Nivelle had a mesmeric effect on politicians, particularly British ones. His mother was English and he spoke her language – and with a reassuringly upper-class accent. He came, supplanting Joffre, from two successes at Verdun, achieved by concentrated fire power. He was an artillery officer and he was convinced that he could produce what he called '*rupture*': a vast artillery onslaught would destroy all resistance, the French would advance under a continuous barrage, bypass any remaining resistance and move into open country. Communicating enormous confidence, he undertook to be in Laon in forty-eight hours.[10]

Kiggell recorded that:

[A] recollection of [The Chantilly conference] is that I gather (my recollection is indeed that General Joffre said so to Sir D. Haig) that the French – shaken by Verdun and much disturbed by their dwindling manpower, the feeling of growing weakness & the fear that their voice, in consequence, would not carry full weight in the later stages of the war, & in the eventual peace, – were averse to undertaking any offensive themselves on a decisive scale and wished the British to carry out the main offensive with which the French would co-operate to the best of their power, though they could not afford to risk great losses . . .

When General Nivelle's plans were approved this situation

was entirely altered. The French attack became the main one &
the British were ordered to conform, both in time & other
respects . . .

It is also relevant to note that there was evidence beyond what
one heard at the Chantilly Conference of depression in France
owing to dwindling manpower, of anxiety lest a weakened
France should lose any share of eventual glory, of a desire to
conserve the strength of the army in consequence & of nervous-
ness regarding renewed German attacks on the French Front.
These symptoms could not be disregarded in estimating what
might be expected of France & the French Army and what part
we should probably have to play in breaking down the German
resistance.[11]

The site for Nivelle's attack was to be on the Aisne, with the
British to the north at Arras and Vimy. The British contribution was
to be split, partly to the north of the Somme and partly to the south
in the sector previously occupied by the French Sixth Army. Haig
was unhappy with the idea of the southerly attack, but felt he had no
alternative but to agree so as to draw off German reserves when
Nivelle broke through on the Aisne. He was given a sweetener: if the
main French attack failed he was promised support for an attack
through Belgium, liberating the Channel ports, including Zeebrugge and Ostend which were thought to be the main bases for the
U-boats which were increasingly harrying British shipping. Again,
Haig was attracted to his long-held notion of an attack along the
coast, preferably with support from the Royal Navy.

He was not uncritical of Nivelle's plan. His idea of a breakthrough
still involved an attack on a broad front, broad enough to allow a full
army to advance. There was also friction about manning the line:
France wanted an arithmetical division of the whole of the Western
Front in proportion to a numerical strength of the two armies. Haig
wanted to recognise the 'strategic nature' of different sectors of the
front.

The Allies' planning throughout the war was repeatedly thwarted by events, and now as the Allies planned the great offensive, the Germans were close to withdrawing from their positions along the very front between Arras and the Aisne on which the attack was to take place. As far back as September 1916 the Germans had started work on a new line, behind the Somme battlefield, which would shorten their existing line and release ten divisions for service elsewhere. Initially France was less confident than Britain that this withdrawal would take place. As it became ever clearer to Haig that it would, he decided to extend his attack to take in Vimy Ridge, which was not affected by the German withdrawal. Nivelle was against this but Haig said that not to include Vimy would be a blow in the air. By 18 March the new German line, generally known in Britain as the Hindenburg Line, and consisting of stretches named after the heroes of the Sagas, Wotan, Siegfried, Hunding and Michel, was fully occupied. The British and French walked over the deserted and devastated ground in front of them and then dug in their new front line opposite the Hindenburg defences. The withdrawal to the Hindenburg line did not substantially alter Nivelle's plans: in his sector the line stopped short of the Chemin des Dames, where he would attack, and in the British sector the line did not reach Arras or Vimy.

Joffre's intention at Chantilly had been for the great Allied offensive to be, again, on the Somme. Between them, Nivelle and the Germans had changed that.

Lloyd George welcomed Nivelle's plan which he outlined in detail at a Cabinet meeting in London on 15 January. Nivelle was fluent where Haig was inarticulate, and the Cabinet was captivated by his promises. After the meeting Haig was told by Lloyd George, perhaps unnecessarily, that he must be cooperative with Nivelle.

But what Lloyd George wanted went beyond cooperation. His confidence in Haig may have been dented by the French journalist crisis, and he now wished formally to subordinate him to Nivelle. Under the pretext of wanting to discuss the problem of railway communications in France, he convened a meeting at Calais with, amongst others, the French Prime Minister, Briand, and War

Minister, Lyautey. This conference, the Calais conference, was one of the pivotal episodes in the command structure in the First World War.

The atmosphere of the conference was saturated with deception and a lack of candour. Haig arrived expecting a routine but important meeting in relation to railways. Robertson had been aware that the agenda would include 'the operations of 1917', but he had no knowledge of what that entailed. On 19 February Lloyd George had met the assistant French military attaché, Berthier de Sauvigny, and told him that he regarded Nivelle as the only person capable of winning the war in 1917. 'It is necessary in the last resort that he should be able to make use of all the forces on the French Front, ours as well as the French armies.'

> The prestige which Field Marshal Haig enjoys with the public and the British Army will make it impossible to subordinate him purely and simply to the French Command, but if the War Cabinet realises that this measure is indispensable, they will not hesitate to give Field Marshal Haig secret instructions to this effect, and, if need be, to replace him.[12]

To make 'this measure . . . indispensable', France had to make the necessary demand at Calais. Ahead of Calais the War Cabinet met with Robertson significantly absent. His absence was clearly contrived. Hankey telephoned him to say that unless he had any special question to bring forward he need not attend the Cabinet meeting, an unusual occurrence. Derby was told that the purpose of the conference at Calais was simply to get signatures to confirm the conclusion of the recent London conference regarding the offensive, and also to discuss transport. According to some accounts Derby was also absent from the Cabinet meeting. This was not the case, but he was assured that at Calais nothing of moment was to be discussed. Far from that being the case, Curzon subsequently reported that at the Cabinet meeting the subordination of Haig to Nivelle had been agreed on the following basis:

1. The French had practically twice the number of troops in the field that we had.
2. We were fighting on French soil to drive the enemy off French soil.
3. Independent opinion shows that without question the French Generals and Staffs are immeasurably superior to British Generals and Staffs, not from the point of view of fighting but from that of Generalship, and of the knowledge of the science and art of war.
4. The War Cabinet did not consider Haig a clever man. Nivelle made a much greater impression on the members of the War Cabinet.[13]

The deceit and misinformation that preceded the Calais conference even involved delaying the submission of the Cabinet minutes to the King until after the conference had taken place.

Haig now proceeded innocently towards a conference that, Duff Cooper said, would 'always be the high-water mark of ineptitude of civilian interference with the conduct of military operations. It has no parallel in history.' Terraine talks of the episode in terms of 'plot' and 'conspiracy'. How crystallised the plotting was remains doubtful. Major-General Sir George Arthur, captivated by the charming Nivelle, says that he 'was a gentleman to his fingers' tips and a loyal comrade, but he was under the baneful influence of his military secretary, one Colonel Alençon. This officer was one of the very few Anglophobes in the French Army.'[14] Nivelle was not as loyal as all that. He had scribbled a note ('*Évidemment on ne peut pas compter sur lui {Haig}*') on a document which had been unfortunately forwarded to Haig's headquarters. It certainly was understood between Alençon and Berthier de Sauvigny that Lloyd George would be glad to see Haig subordinated to Nivelle. Later, when all was in the open, the French sought to convince Esher, whom Haig had summoned in this moment of crisis, that they assumed that Robertson and Haig had been told what Lloyd George's plans were. In their account it was they, the French, who had modified the scheme, recognising that it was inconceivable that the British armies could be commanded by French officers. Briand claimed that Lloyd George, rather than the French, had been responsible for the plan. What Nivelle envisaged was an arrangement which would relieve Haig of strategic command, with orders being passed to the armies from Nivelle through a British Chief of Staff.

In the months preceding the conference, Haig had become increasingly disenchanted by Nivelle's plans, and had sought to attack them on the basis that the French railway system was inadequate for the attack. So, ironically, it was he who was responsible for the calling of a conference at Calais. When the conference opened, the question of railways and transport, the pretext for the conference, lasted less than an hour. Lloyd George then sent the technical experts away. Tea was brought in and then the conference moved into secret session. Haig recorded that Nivelle had outlined the plans for the offensive and

concluded by saying that he would answer any questions which LG cared to put to him. But LG said, 'that is not all – I want to hear everything', and to Briand he said, 'tell him to keep nothing back' and so forth 'as to his disagreements with Marshal Haig.'

Nivelle looked surprised but said nothing of moment at this stage. Haig spoke and indicated disagreements with Nivelle, particularly in regard to the latter's reservations about the attack on Vimy Ridge. Lloyd George again attempted to get Nivelle to speak out. He said that he did not understand about strategy and tactics but did want to know 'what the respective responsibilities were'. Nivelle, who had made such an impression of sophistication and *finesse* when he addressed the War Cabinet, seems to have had cold feet. Lloyd George was reduced to the cruder tactics of asking the French, as the conference adjourned for dinner, for a statement of what they wanted. The French withdrew, and prepared a typewritten statement. Hankey recorded his reaction, when Lloyd George showed it to him:

Lloyd George handed me the document and said 'What do you think of it?' It fairly took my breath away, as it practically demanded the placing of the British Army under Nivelle; the appointment of a British 'Chief of Staff' to Nivelle, who had powers practically eliminating Haig and his Chief of the General Staff, the scheme reducing Haig to a cipher.[15]

The degree of Nivelle's involvement in the detail of the plan is not clear, and even Haig, in calmer moments, did not attribute the idea to him so much as to Lloyd George and Briand. According to Hankey, the plan was put down in writing by the French after Lloyd George had pressed Nivelle in the way that Haig described, and while Lloyd George and Hankey went for a walk through Calais. But Haig was too generous in his assessment of Nivelle: President Poincaré's diary suggests that *Projet d'Organisation* had been drafted at his headquarters a week before the conference – perhaps indeed by Nivelle himself.

Robertson's reaction to the plan was well-nigh apoplectic. Haig remained outwardly calm. Both immediately confronted Lloyd George who took the wind from their sails by saying that he had War Cabinet approval. Haig said that 'it would be madness to place the British forces under the French' and that 'he did not believe that our troops would fight under French leadership'. Lloyd George's response was distinctly below the belt: 'Well, Field-Marshal, I know the private soldier very well, and there are people he criticises a good deal more strongly than General Nivelle!' Haig and Robertson were now requested to put forward their own alternative scheme. They withdrew and conferred in Robertson's room. Hankey raised the temperature further by telling them that Lloyd George had not received full authority from the War Cabinet. Haig and Robertson 'agreed we would rather be tried by Court Martial than betray the army by agreeing to its being placed under the French . . . And so we went to bed, thoroughly disgusted with our government and the politicians.'

That night was the only one in the war in which Robertson's sleep was disturbed. 'He was in a terrible state and ramped up and down the room, talking about the horrible idea of putting the "wonderful army" under a Frenchman, swearing that he would never serve under one, nor his son either, and that no-one could order him to.'[16] He was not the only one to have a disturbed night. Lloyd George slept badly, and Hankey had to sit up all night to draft a formula to try to retrieve the situation.

When they rose the following morning ('Glass rose slightly,' Haig noted. 'Fine but dull'), Lyautey asked Haig to speak to him and Nivelle. They reassured him that they were conscious of the 'insult offered to me and the British Army by the paper which Briand had had produced' and told them that they had not seen the document until recently – in Lyautey's case not until he boarded his train for Calais. According to Spears, however, Nivelle had been well aware of the proposals, which had been gestating in Paris since the previous year.[17] Haig was given to understand that the paper had been drawn up in Paris with the approval of Lloyd George and Briand. He now prepared a paper for Robertson in which he took the view that there were only two alternatives: to leave matters as they were, or to place the British army in France entirely under the French Commander-in-Chief, involving the disappearance of the British Commander-in-Chief and GHQ. 'So drastic a change . . . [seemed] to me to be fraught with the gravest danger . . .' He signed his paper, as usual, 'D. Haig, FM, Commanding British Armies in France'. Such statements, over his signature, could not be ignored by any politician. An hour later Robertson handed in yet another paper, this one prepared by Lloyd George. It proposed that in an initial period Haig was to follow Nivelle's instructions in preparing for the coming battle, but was to be free to depart from them if he thought the safety of the army endangered. During the battle itself the army was to act entirely under Nivelle's orders. Haig objected to this second part and obtained 'a free hand to choose the means and methods of utilising the British troops in that sector of operations allotted by the French Commander-in-Chief.' Nivelle agreed to this and also to the important provision that the British and French War Cabinets should each judge when operations were deemed to have concluded.

> Finally I signed the Agreement, but wrote above my signature: 'I agree with the above on the understanding that while I am fully determined to carry out the Calais Agreement in spirit and letter, the British Army and its C-in-C will be regarded by General Nivelle as Allies and not as subordinates except during the particular operations which he explained at the Calais Conference.

After returning to his headquarters, Haig strengthened his position by writing to the King, a reflex action for him in any such circumstances, setting out the position and concluding with an unconvincing assertion that if the War Cabinet wanted to dismiss him they should do so now. As he expected, a telegram from the King arrived containing resounding reassurances.

> His Majesty appreciates the reasons which led you, at the request of the Prime Minister, to sign the Calais Agreement, but feels that your having done so it would prudent not now to discuss these terms, but to take advantage of the period before the 'move' begins to clear up with General Nivelle all points upon which you are doubtful or not satisfied. Apparently this would not be difficult as the King understands that General Nivelle more than once during the Conference disclaimed any dissatisfaction on his part or any desire for the holding of the Conference.
>
> The King begs you to dismiss from your mind any idea of resignation. Such a course would be in His Majesty's opinion disastrous to his army and to the hopes of success in the coming supreme struggle. You have the absolute confidence of the Army from the highest to the lowest rank: a confidence which is shared to the full by the King.[18]

Robertson, with his emphasis on constitutional propriety, found the whole episode very disturbing. On 3 March he wrote to Haig in a letter marked 'personal':

> Since yesterday I have thought further over the matter and am rather anxious. I am bringing the question before Cabinet . . . I want to get along with the war without trouble, but I fear trouble in the future and therefore am wondering whether we ought not to thrash out the matter more now. We ought not to have <u>signed</u> the document. Still we did, and the only thing is to put it quite clear. We shall probably discuss {it in the Cabinet] on Tuesday . . . I think you may have great difficulties in carrying out the hybrid arrangement. I trusted to Nivelle to play the game. It all depends upon him and I hardly dare trust him.[19]

In the event discussion in Cabinet was delayed for some time. Robertson to Haig 6 March 1917:

> The whole difficulty has arisen because the Cabinet took the decision without first obtaining military opinion, and then the proposal was sprung upon you and me at 10 o'clock at night. We have not heard the last of this yet by any means.[20]

The whole episode was strangely ill thought-out, a rare example of political machinations by Lloyd George which went wrong. In the long run a united command proved to be essential, but at Calais Lloyd George went about achieving it in the wrong way – and with the wrong men. Nivelle's political performance at Calais was disastrous, and his military performance a few months later was to be no better. When he got back to London Lloyd George told Frances Stevenson that Nivelle had 'floundered about most hopelessly'; but he himself had performed just as badly. Almost 100 years later we may find it strange that what was still very much the junior military partner in the military alliance should find it objectionable that the senior partner should act as Commander-in-Chief. The historical enmity between England and France was still strong in 1917, and Haig's and Robertson's frank dislike of the French was not untypical of attitudes throughout the army. What is less explicable is the turn-around in Haig's fortunes. Barely a year after his appointment as Commander-in-Chief, he had lost the confidence of the Prime Minister and indeed of many members of the War Cabinet. Lloyd George had reacted strongly and swiftly against Haig since becoming Prime Minister. From now until November 1918 the war was conducted on Britain's part by a Prime Minister and a Comman-der-in-Chief who despised each other. The way in which Haig was treated by the Prime Minister and many of the members of the Cabinet from the end of 1916 onwards is astounding. In the Memorial Issue of the British Legion *Journal*, a publication under-standably filled, for the most part, with anodyne encomia, Robertson made a remarkable excursion into controversy:

> The point I wish to emphasise is the great handicap under which he [Haig] laboured in the discharge of his duties. I refer to the lack of confidence displayed by certain Ministers in regard to his qualifications for the post he occupied, and the consequent omission to give him at all times that genuine and whole-hearted support which every Commander has the right to receive from those who employ him. In the most favourable circumstances a Commander-in-Chief in war carries a very heavy burden, and there is no one to whom he can look to for help and sympathy in time of stress except to his Ministers. If they fail to sustain him and in the fullest possible measure, the burden may become almost insupportable.
>
> Lord Haig's experiences in this respect were probably more discouraging than those of any British Commander before him . . .[21]

The Cabinet could have dismissed Haig if they wished. As they never thought it in the national interest to do so, they should have given him their support. Instead Lloyd George and some others made their hostility, lack of confidence and even contempt quite evident. That Haig was able to carry on in such circumstances, and with no more bitterness than he evinced, reflects not only his impenetrable self-confidence but also a certain nobility of spirit.

On 28 February Robertson wrote to Haig:

> A story at the War Cabinet this morning gave quite a wrong impression. He [LL.G.] accused the French of putting forward a monstrous proposal, and yet you and I know that he is at the bottom of it. I believe he equally misled the Cabinet last Saturday. Derby is telling Balfour the whole truth. The former talked of resigning last night. He was furious and *disgusted*. He spoke up like a man for you this morning and insisted on a letter of confidence and explanation being sent to you . . . These things always happen in war. But they are worse now than ever. Still I can't believe that a man such as [Lloyd George] can remain for long head of any government. Surely *some* honesty and truth are required.[22]

Haig duly received a missive, saying that the only object of the Calais conference had been to secure 'a clearly defined unity of control' and 'it was in no sense an aspersion on the ability and qualifications of Sir Douglas Haig in whom the War Cabinet continued to entertain full confidence.' A covering letter from Derby was in warmer language.

The repercussions of the Calais conference continued for a long time, and indeed almost immediately Haig received a request from Nivelle requesting the appointment of Wilson as head of the British Mission at Beauvais. Wilson was always suspect in Haig's eyes, but what he particularly objected to were 'the very *commanding* tones' of Nivelle's letter, 'a type of letter which no gentleman could have drafted, and it is also one which certainly no C-in-C of this great British Army should receive without protest.' He asked the War Cabinet to tell him 'whether it is their wishes that the C-in-C in command of this British Army should be subjected to such treatment by a junior *foreign* Commander.'

One of the objections Haig put forward to Wilson as liaison officer with Nivelle was on the basis of his rank. Robertson knocked this spurious objection on the head: 'It was agreed at the Conference that a more senior officer should be appointed and you did not demur. I think that if you say, as you are quite justified in saying if you so desire, that Wilson would not be suitable, your wishes would not be opposed, and at any rate you would have a clear cut case which we here could support.'[23]

Wilson was in Russia at the time of the Calais conference but returned to hear that Haig and Robertson suspected him as having been one of those behind the plot. As usual they did him less than justice. Although Haig told him to his face that the French were asking for him 'in order to make a cat's paw' of him, he pressed Haig to establish a clearer definition of the latter's relationship with Nivelle. For himself, Wilson said, 'Rather than accept an equivocal position, I would prefer to go on half-pay and I *will* go on half-pay'. Haig ended up by addressing Wilson by his Christian name and begging him to accept the position he had been offered. Wilson recorded in his diary, 'and all the time, while I am helping Haig all I can, I realise more and more that he is quite unfit for the post of C-in-C.'.

Haig noted, not without some satisfaction, the continuing German withdrawal to the Hindenburg line which meant that 'the advisability of launching Nivelle's battle at all grows daily less' and his conclusion was that there might be a German attack, making use of the troops that had been released by the shortening of the line. He thought the likeliest attack would be at Ypres. Thus 'the folly of definitely placing the British C-in-C under the orders of the French . . . becomes more marked'. He stressed in a letter to Nivelle that the released German reserves might attack on the Flanders front, which was of particular importance to Britain's security. He referred to his responsibility for the safety of his armies. Nivelle noted in the margin of Haig's letter: 'that responsibility is mine, since the British government has so decided'.[24]

Nivelle insisted on his offensive, and on a full British contribution.

For Haig, Nivelle was going 'beyond the letter and also the spirit of the Calais conference'. Frustrated by Haig, Nivelle went behind his back and told Lloyd George that the situation would not improve until Haig was replaced – perhaps by Gough. Haig was genuinely misreading German intentions, which were, for 1917, to avoid large-scale operations on land, leaving it to the U-boats to win the war, but Lloyd George believed that he was knowingly misrepresenting events to win support for his plans for a Flanders campaign.

As Haig's resignation was canvassed in political circles, Hankey, increasingly Lloyd George's adviser on a wide range of political issues, warned his chief that Haig's departure would bring together the Tories, the Asquithian Liberals, the Irish and others, including 'court and society influence'. At the same time, the court party, represented by Wigram, who visited GHQ on 9 March, feared that Haig's resignation might allow Lloyd George to make an appeal to the country and 'come back as a dictator'. There was much talk at this time of dictatorship. The coalition government, responding to the desperate needs of the times, was exercising powers, with the consent of an acquiescent parliament, which Hankey, for instance, regarded as exceptional, though executive freedom was far less then than in the Second World War or indeed than it is now, in peacetime. The idea of a dictatorship had not yet been discredited as it would be in the 1930s, nor had the very word 'dictator' acquired a pejorative sense, and there were many who thought that it would be a worthwhile expedient in the context of the conditions of the national struggle for survival. Thus Hankey:

> *March 2nd* [1917] Then I had to see Bonar Law, to whom I spoke of Robertson's misgivings *re* the Calais arrangements. Bonar Law replied that he didn't like them much himself, but he regarded Lloyd George as dictator and meant to give him his chance, so acquiesced.[25]

At the same time, there were fears on the right, which Haig certainly shared, of an imminent Bolshevik revolution. For Haig, as for many Tories, even the more gentle elements of the left were potential

Bolsheviks. For Wigram and those whom he represented, the army was an instrument of social stability and 'breaking it up and distributing it amongst the French armies' was a threat to the monarchy. The King himself warned Haig on 11 March 'not to resign, because Lloyd George would then appeal to the country for support and would probably come back with a great majority, as LG was at present very popular it seems. The King's position would then be very difficult.'

Haig returned to London, finding Robertson so upset by 'the Calais Conference and its results' that he was confined to his bed. After a visit to Buckingham Palace, where he received assurances of the King's support, he prepared a lengthy memorandum for submission to the War Cabinet. It contains an interesting comment on his view of the French psychology: 'It is natural that France should hope to emerge from the war with national triumph and as great a position as possible in the eyes of the world.' His submissions in relation to the detail of the Calais agreement, mostly of a face-saving nature, were accepted by Lloyd George and, with some minor alterations, by Nivelle. It was recorded:

that while the British Commander-in-Chief has been directed to conform to General Nivelle's instructions under certain defined conditions, it is desirable that General Nivelle should address his instructions in the form of requests to an equal and not as orders to a subordinate,

that the conditions laid down in the Calais agreement referred specifically to certain defined offensive operations and did not give the French Commander-in-Chief any right to dictate to the British Commander-in-Chief on other offensive operations or on such questions as the defence of the remainder of his front, or the measures taken and dispositions made therefor,

that in case of difference of opinion the British War Cabinet reserves to itself the right to decide as to whether any given conditions fall under the terms of the Calais Conference or not.

This visit to London was for the purpose of attending a second Anglo-French conference on 12 and 13 March. Nivelle's tone *had* been high-handed, and his language unacceptable. A telegram from Briand to the British government complaining that Haig was trying to derail Nivelle's plan brought most of the Cabinet behind Haig and Robertson. The frustration of Lloyd George's Calais plans was now complete.

The time wasted in addressing these personal and national vanities, with all the attendant semantic face saving, is in itself a powerful argument for a supreme allied commander.

But despite the distractions, planning for the now imminent offensive continued. Haig's relationship with Allenby, his Staff College rival for the Mastership of the Drag Hounds, and now commanding Third Army in the offensive, was never easy. Haig may have seen Allenby as a rival. At the end of the year, after Arras, Charteris recorded that there was a rumour that Allenby and Plumer had both been offered 'the reversion of DH's job'. The rumour seems most improbable, certainly in the case of Allenby, who had been 'degummed' after Arras. Allenby, for his part, thought that Haig was jealous of him and of his wide range of knowledge and interests. He was a shy man who attempted to disguise his shyness behind a fierce exterior. He was concerned for the well-being of his men, but intolerant of minor breaches of discipline: it was often remarked in the course of the war that the units where discipline was strongest had fewest casualties. The weight of his responsibilities appears to have resulted in an inability to distinguish between those rules and regulations that really mattered, and those that did not. He could bring the whole weight of his disapproval to bear on a cavalryman who had not properly adjusted his chinstrap. Gough said that while Allenby was in France, he had no ideas and 'would apply orders rigidly without reasoning'.[26] At the same time, it was said that a dressing down from Allenby felt like being blown from the muzzle of a gun, but that when one regained the ground, Allenby bore no malice.[27]. His fierce demeanour brought him the nickname, 'the Bull'; inevitably the one senior officer who faced up to him,

Lieutenant-General Sir John Keir, was known as 'the Toreador'. He was dismissed.

The meetings between Haig and Third Army Commander were difficult. Charteris described them, maybe more for effect than for the sake of accuracy:

> Allenby shares one peculiarity with Douglas Haig. He cannot explain verbally, with any lucidity at all, what his plans are. In a conference between the two of them it is rather amusing. DH hardly ever finishes a sentence, and Allenby's sentences, although finished, do not really convey exactly what he means. Yet they understand one another perfectly; but as each of their particular Staffs only understands their immediate superior a good deal of explanation of details has to be gone into afterwards and cleared up.
>
> I remember hearing Lord Kelvin lecture. He had just the same peculiarity, and had a sort of Greek chorus in the form of an assistant who explained in very broad Scotch exactly what Lord Kelvin meant. The only difference then was that the comments and chorus went on at the same time as the main motif. At these Army conferences no one dares to interfere, and all clearing up has to be done afterwards.

Although Charteris rather enjoyed playing up Haig's poor communication skills, it must be realised that his picture was only slightly exaggerated. Haig was almost as poor in oral as he was good in written communication. His weakness was noted by many, as also his need to fall back on gestures in an attempt to make his points. His failure to make himself understood by his political masters can be seen from time to time.

The last conference of the Allies before the offensive took place on 6 April at Compiègne, with Henry Wilson joking and putting his cap on the wrong way round, saying he would walk into the conference as a German and terrify everyone.

Before the battle began, Haig interfered in what he regarded as grand tactics. Allenby's intention had been to give the Germans as little warning of the offensive as possible, limiting shelling to a hurricane bombardment of forty-eight hours, with breaks only to allow the barrels to cool down and the men to eat. Haig wanted a more conventional bombardment, lasting five days. Allenby's plan was very possibly not technically feasible and Haig was supported by his artillery expert, Major-General 'Curly' Birch, as well as by several of Allenby's subordinate commanders. Allenby's artillery expert, Major-General Holland, who had been responsible for recommending the two-day bombardment in the first place was manoeuvred out of the way by being given a corps to command.

The British attack began on Easter Monday, 9 April 1917: the French offensive was to begin a week later. The bombardment, which did run for the five days that Haig wanted, was delivered by 2,800 guns. Although the period of the bombardment was shorter than on the Somme, the number of shells delivered on the German defences was twice as many. The Canadians, north of Arras, took the important dominating feature of Vimy Ridge after three hours of heavy fighting. To the east of Arras, and with the advantage of a network of cellars and caverns in the old town which allowed the troops to move forward unseen to the front line, Third Army advanced three and a half miles, the biggest gain since the trenches had been dug in 1914. To the south of the River Scarpe, the advances were less extensive.

By the end of the first day the success of the British and the Canadians appeared remarkable. Captain Cyril Falls described the Easter Monday attack as 'One of the great days of the war . . . among the heaviest blows struck by British arms in the western theatre of war.' In the course of the day, Third Army took 5,600 prisoners and the Canadians a further 3,400. Ground had been taken with relatively few casualties and the way seemed open for further advance. But the weather was appalling. The advance had begun in sleet, and rain and snow succeeded. The terrain was chalk which had been rendered into mud. A planned pause of two hours checked the advance. Some further advances were made in the north on 12 April.

Thereafter little happened until 16 April, when the French Aisne offensive began.

The British component of the attack was of course the minor one; Nivelle's part, the major component, proved disastrous. On the first day alone, the French suffered 40,000 casualties, a French Somme. Nivelle continued to attack until 20 April, before finally abandoning the offensive on 9 May. France had suffered 187,000 casualties compared to a German total of 168,000.

Haig urged Allenby, held up to the east of Arras at Monchy, to push forward on the north of the Scarpe, and then move south-east behind Monchy, so as to turn the German flank. He found it very difficult to get divisional commanders to go forward and take control of operations. By 12 April he concluded that the opportunity had been lost: 'I pointed out that the enemy had now been given time to put the Drocourt-Quéant line into a state of defence.' It is not obvious that Allenby needed urging from Haig. Immediately after the 9 April advance, Allenby had ordered his army to continue the advance. On 10 April Haig met Allenby at St Pol and told him to continue forward where he could. On the following day, although things were by now not going well, Allenby was still optimistic – unrealistically so – and his order for the day was full of adrenalin: 'The Army Commander wishes all troops to understand that 3rd Army is pursuing a defeated enemy and that risks must be taken.' As late as 14 April Allenby still wanted to push on, but there was a remarkable 'mutiny' by three of his divisional commanders, who criticised him and formally represented to General Headquarters that his attempt at narrow advances left vulnerably exposed flanks. Haig upheld their appeal and ordered a suspension of operations.

The frustrating aspect of the matter was that the subordinate British contribution to the offensive, intended simply to take pressure off the French, was the one which in the event demonstrated more potential for success, if not a success which could be translated into victory.

Limited action was renewed on the British Front on 3 May, as Haig tried to encourage the French to continue their fight, but the

offensive was over by the end of May. The Germans had suffered
badly at Vimy, but by the time the battle was closed down the
British had lost 150,000 men, against just over 100,000 lost by the
Germans. The prolongation of the battle, to support the French,
delayed operational planning for Third Ypres, and ensured that it
would be fought in autumnal weather, rather than in the excellent
summer weather of May, June and early July 1917.

Arras is the forgotten battle of the First World War; but it
delivered significant local success as well as incurring losses as great
as any of the better known conflicts. The daily loss rate was 4,076 at
Arras, compared with 2,963 at the Somme, 2,323 at Third Ypres and
3,645 in the Hundred Days battles of 1918. On 10 April Charteris
recorded in his diary that 'the attack has been a complete success'. On
the following day:

> DH is enormously pleased with our success. Yesterday we made
> a lot of ground, and have got as far as we had originally intended
> to go. I have never seen DH so stirred by success before. It
> means a great deal to him personally, though I do not think that
> weighs much with him. After all this trouble at Calais,
> however, there is no doubt in any of our minds that the Prime
> Minister would have got rid of him out of hand unless this show
> had been a success. It is a success, indeed it is more than a
> success, it is a victory.

Critically he goes on: 'The one unfortunate thing about it is that
strategically it loses much of its value owing to the delay in the
French big battle.'

Lloyd George did not want to have enemies. He liked to be liked,
and did not fight when there was not an object to be fought for. On 7
May he came out to France with Lord Robert Cecil and Hankey.
Charteris reported that:

> the Chief was summoned away during dinner by an urgent
> message and called me to his chair at the head of the table. I sat

between and presided over, the PM of Great Britain on my right, and the Acting Foreign Minister on my left. Lloyd George made merry at the situation, but was most charming all the same. He can fascinate in a way I have never known any other man fascinate, and he enjoys doing it! You have to take hold of yourself, shake yourself and make yourself remember all his misdeeds, or you would become a 'chela'. He is amazingly sharp witted, and full of energy, fire and go. At present his line is outspoken praise of everything in the British Army in France, and especially of DH. He compares us now with the French, very much to the disadvantage of the latter, and says he trembles to think what would have happened if we had been held up with them. I longed to point out that if the Calais conference agreement in its first form had held, we probably *should* have been held up just the same . . . Lloyd George finished up by giving an extraordinarily amusing imitation of Robertson at a Cabinet meeting. It was a wonderful bit of mimicry, and kept us all in fits of laughter.

Allenby did not long survive the battle: by June he had been degummed and relieved of the command of Third Army. The records are opaque, referring to his dismissal as being because of his conduct in command of Third Army 'and many other reasons'. It is not clear what these 'other reasons' were. He was far from happy to be dismissed, and on making a courtesy call on his successor, General Byng, 'broke down very badly'. He was sent to Palestine, at that time regarded as distinctly a side show: as things turned out he went on to achieve a distinction in Palestine which eluded him in France, his victory at Megiddo, in particular, being regarded as exemplary.

The other commander who was a casualty of the battle was Nivelle. He had been very specific in his promises and he was not allowed a second chance. Indeed even before his campaign opened, Briand had resigned as Prime Minister to be replaced by Poincaré, and Lyautey was replaced as War Minister by Painlevé. Neither man supported Nivelle, and Painlevé in particular was hostile to his strategy and would have cancelled the offensive if he could have done so. His protégé was Pétain. In 1914 Pétain was fifty-eight, about to face retirement, a colonel from the Chasseurs Alpins who was as obscure militarily as he was socially. But in 1918 he was a Marshal of France, with the prestige that prompted his nomination as early as 1936 as a leader of his country with dictatorial powers.[28] In 1940, of course, he became that leader.

His rise through the army in the early years of the Great War was attributable to qualities that he shared with Haig. He entered Saint-Cyr, the military academy, with difficulty, placed 403rd out of 412 entrants. He was recognised early as being hard-working and thoughtful, with his own ideas on tactics and strategy. Unlike Haig, he enjoyed great success with women. But like him, he was regarded by most men as dull and unattractive. In the war he came to despise politicians, and to embrace attritional warfare: 'Success will in the end belong to the side which has the last man.' Now he succeeded Nivelle. Even before his dismissal, Nivelle had been left in no doubt about his government's lack of confidence in him. On 6 April, when the British were about to attack at Arras, there was a bizarre meeting at Compiègne in the drawing-room coach of President Poincaré's train. Nivelle faced hostile speeches from Painlevé and Pétain, and amongst his own generals the best that Franchet d'Esperey could say was that the French part of the offensive could not be abandoned now that the British part had begun. Nivelle challenged his critics by saying that if he did not have the support of the government or his subordinates he had no alternative but to resign. He was immediately reassured that he should think of no such thing; but the lack of enthusiasm for him and his offensive amongst his fellow countrymen at the Compiègne meeting is a dramatic contrast with the enthusiastic reception he had enjoyed in London a few months earlier. Just before Nivelle's removal, Frances Stevenson wrote in her diary:

> Nivelle has fallen into disgrace, and let D[avid Lloyd George] down badly after the way D had backed him up at the beginning of the year. Sir Douglas Haig has come out on

top in this fight between the two chiefs, and I fear D will have
to be very careful in the future as to his backings of the French
against the English.[29]

Pétain's first task, as Nivelle's successor, was to address the problem
of the mutinies in the French Army. As early as February, he had
reported on what he regarded as a dangerous climate, essentially of a
political character. He considered that revolutionaries, anarchists and
syndicalists were attempting to promote strikes and sabotage. Early
in May, two regiments that had suffered badly on the first day of the
offensive refused to return to the Front. Their attitude was an
ambivalent amalgam of syndicalism and repudiation of war, with
slogans such as 'Down with the War! Death to those who are
responsible!', compounded by comparison of their pay with that
of munitions workers. The mutinies spread through the Fourth,
Fifth, Sixth and Tenth French Armies, the units that had taken most
punishment in the offensive. Civilians struck in sympathy. The
soldiers, who had displayed immense courage under fire, were not
in reality mutineering; it was more a withdrawal of labour, an
attempt to make a considered statement to the effect that current
strategy was a failure. The French did not refer to the phenomena as
mutinies but as *'mouvements collectifs d'indiscipline'*. Pétain quelled the
discontent skilfully, combining sympathetic treatment of the ordinary soldier – leaves, with transport provided, rest camps, recognition
of individual effort – with a shift in tactics and a substitution of
limited objectives for grandiose schemes. But punishment was meted
out too: special military tribunals were set up and found 3,427 men
guilty of mutinous offences. Between 500 and 600 were sentenced to
death, some 30 to 32 shot and about 100 exiled to the colonies. The
extent of the mutinies was not publicised. Haig was aware of the
phenomenon in general terms, but not of its full extent. He was
reinforced in his long-held conviction that the capacity of France to
remain in the war was questionable.

From a very early point in the war, he had been pessimistic about
the ability of the French Army to continue the fight. In part this

resulted from a more or less invincible prejudice in regard to the quality of the French military, a prejudice reinforced by repeated requests from French generals for assistance from British troops. The French of course, at almost every stage in the war, bore a far greater burden than Britain, and, like most military partners, thought that their allies were not doing their bit. At any rate, Haig was not greatly surprised by the mutinies, though what he learned about them came to him in confidence: a decade later he told Charteris that he had not been able to share with him what he had known. The quality of Charteris' intelligence was not enhanced by this enforced ignorance. It is not clear that the Cabinet, either, wholly understood the extent of the mutinies.

Spears returned from France after Arras, and reported the crisis within the French armies to Robertson, who told him that he had heard nothing from the other British military liaison officers. He was sent back to the front to investigate further and to return to report, which he did to the War Policy Committee on 11 June. Lloyd George took the young Spears away from the others, towards the window and asked him 'Is the French army going to recover?' Spears said that it would and gave a detailed report. Lloyd George now put a wholly unfair question to him: 'Will you give me your word of honour as an officer and a gentleman that the French Army will recover?' Spears was being asked for an impossible answer. He retorted that he could not give his word of honour but would stake his life on his conviction. He pointed to Hankey, the Cabinet Secretary, and said 'You can get him to put down that you can shoot me if I'm wrong – I know how important it is and will stake my life on it'.[30] This bizarre little episode points up how great issues in war are frequently decided on the basis of the most unscientific enquiry.

THE ABANDONMENT OF ATTRITION.
THIRD YPRES

What followed Arras was the Third Battle of Ypres, of which the final phase is usually referred to as Passchendaele, a name that, ninety years later, continues to distil the horrors of the war which it seems to symbolise. It was the prolongation of that last phase, in the flooded, swampy conditions of a torrential autumn, that attracted most criticism of Haig in his lifetime.

Other operations on the Western Front, including the Somme, had been attacked for their lack of strategical objective. This was not the case with the Flanders campaign. The Admiralty had been in favour of driving Germany from Ostend and Zeebrugge as early as January 1915, and by 1917 the naval situation had become serious. German submarines threatened to bring Britain to her knees through starvation, and a number – but not a huge number – of submarines operated from the Flanders coastline. More significantly, there was important destroyer action from the same area. As well as conducting raiding operations, these German naval operations made it necessary to supply convoys to bring food from the neutral Netherlands. The Admiralty argued that unless the Belgian coast were occupied, the strength of the Dover flotillas would require to be increased at the expense of other units. Jellicoe said that unless Haig's plan were executed successfully, Britain would be unable to continue the war into 1918 because of lack of shipping. The naval imperative was, however, exaggerated. Despite his dramatic language at the War

Policy Committee meeting on 20 June 1917 ('There is no good discussing plans for next spring. We cannot go on.'), Jellicoe's assertion had no real impact on planning. Even Haig, who could have used it to support a project which he had long hankered after, dismissed it: 'No one present shared Jellicoe's view, and all seemed satisfied that the food reserves in Great Britain are adequate.'

But Haig had a much freer hand now. Since Calais the Prime Minister had lost the power to check him. The French were without any grand plans in the wake of the Aisne and the mutinies. At Third Ypres, therefore, Haig was more able to elaborate his own policy than ever before. What he promoted was what he had always wanted, an operation on the Channel seaboard, and it was for him a congenial alternative to a War Cabinet request that troops be moved from the Western Front to Italy, Palestine or Alexandretta.

The coastal strategy which had so long appealed to Haig did indeed have its attractions. It was the one way of turning the German flank, it could be supported easily because of the proximity of the Channel ports, and it offered the chance of clearing enemy shipping from the Straits and enemy aircraft from bases which were threatening the south-east of England. But all these desiderata only came together in the event of success on a huge scale in the early, land-based phase of the campaign, so that the naval element was an add-on, rather than a central component.

One of the earliest mentions of the Flanders campaign is in a message marked 'secret' to Kiggell from Haig of 10 December 1916: 'I send here with my special messenger a plan of operations with a view to capturing the Belgium coast . . . [T]here is enough sufficiently settled for you to tell (very secretly) the CIGS, the Head of the Admiralty War Staff and Admiral Bacon that the operation will take place, and to begin to prepare for it'.[1]

Haig and Robertson pressed the policy strongly, as an alternative to plans for action in Italy, which Lloyd George favoured. They were assisted by a resolution of the War Committee in November 1916 which acknowledged that there was no operation of war to which they would attach greater importance than the successful occupation, or at least the deprivation to the enemy, of Ostend and Zeebrugge.[2] Thereafter, for a time Haig had been obliged to shelve his plan to fit in with French requirements, but now, following the failure of the Nivelle offensive, Britain was contributing a much more important element to the Allied campaign, and he was able to see his plan adopted.

At the same time, the Allies at the Paris conference in early May 1917 agreed an important change in their philosophy:

> It is no longer a question of aiming at breaking through the enemy's front and aiming at distant objectives. It is now a question of wearing down and exhausting the enemy's resistance and if and when this is achieved, to exploit it to the fullest possible extent.

Haig of course had always thought in terms of wearing down, but wearing down with breaking through at the back of his mind. The government now appeared to be accepting attrition pure and simple, at the very moment when Haig was succumbing to the attractions of a much bolder vision.

'Attrition', 'wearing-down' and 'bite-and-hold' are distinguished one from another by fairly subtle nuances, and they are not precise military terms of art, in the sense that they are used differently by different men at different times. Attrition in its military sense was first used in relation to the American Civil War, but it is with the First World War that the word is now forever associated. It came into common currency in describing the tactics of that war. When Kitchener told Lloyd George that 'the end of the War must come through one of the two following causes: (1) by a decisive victory . . . or (2) by attrition', he was pointing to simple alternatives, without attaching qualitative values to them. The word did not then have the pejorative sense from which it now cannot escape. That said, when Churchill, for example, used the word in the immediate aftermath of the war, he did so to refer to tactics that he thought woefully lacking in the flashes of military inspiration for which he craved. For most military theorists 'attrition' had a function that was more than the straightforward etymological root of the word would suggest. In 1918, in Farrow's *Dictionary of Military Terms*, 'attrition' is defined as 'in a military sense, the act of wearing away the enemy's strength, increasing his mortality list, *and lowering his morale*'. Haig's preferred usage was 'wearing-down', but he used 'attrition' synonymously. For him the morale aspect was critical. Just as the justification of cavalry was its effect on morale, so 'wearing-down' had a more than physical role, and wearing-down had to precede victory. One suspects that if Haig's armies had broken through the German lines on the Somme and gone straight over the German frontier, his delight would have been seriously qualified by the fact that the wearing-down phase had never taken place. In the event, when his armies were indeed routing the enemy in the Hundred Days, he was very slow to recognise that wearing-down had turned into something else. In his *Final Despatch* he was at pains to say that '[t]he rapid collapse of Germany's military powers . . . would not have taken place but for that period of ceaseless attrition', and he was not simply attempting to justify the sacrifices of 1916 and 1917.

'Bite-and-hold' was different. Observation of the battles of the early years of the war showed that the Allies frequently made gains on the first day, but that thereafter the Germans were able to throw in reserves and recover all that had been lost, and sometimes more. It was a reasonably intelligent response to say that the assault should be closed down at the end of the first day, and objectives be limited to securing what had been captured. This was notably the approach of Plumer at Third Ypres, in a series of discrete operations, each of limited ambition.

What makes Haig difficult – and interesting – to assess is that for all his insistence on a structured war and the necessity of the wearing-down phase as a preliminary to breakthrough, he was carried away so often by the prospect of imminent and dramatic success.

'Attrition' for all its horrible connotations should not be dismissed as a concept of warfare. It was not a theory that was peculiar to British generals. Attrition was debated before and during the war by the

German High Command, in a dialogue between proponents of attrition and annihilation strategies. It can be argued that their training told them that attrition would be decisive in a war between nations in arms, but that they ignored this in two World Wars to their great cost. In the absence of a critical technological or other advantage, modern wars may only be capable of being won by attrition. That was how the First Word War was won, and also the Second World War (in Europe). Haig can be criticised not because he was committed to attrition, but because he was not. Sometimes he was misled by unreliable intelligence, but more often by, and *always* essentially because of, his own optimism. It was for this reason that he made the serious mistake of prolonging both the Somme and Third Ypres, with the most terrible of consequences. But the character flaw that led to these errors of judgement perhaps led also to ultimate victory. Wars are not won by nibbling away at the enemy, by biting and holding. Finally a more full-blooded approach is needed, and risks have to be taken, and if Haig had been a more logical, calculating general, he would not have recognised the opportunity that was to present itself in August 1918. He alone did.

His vision for the campaign is contained in an Appreciation dated 12 June 1917 to Robertson. It argued, above anything else, for pressing on with the war in the west:

It is my considered opinion, based not on mere optimism but on a thorough study of the situation, guided by experience which I may claim to be considerable, that if our resources are con-centrated in France to the fullest possible extent, the British Armies are capable and can be relied on to effect great results this summer – results which will make final victory more assured and which may even bring it within reach this year.

The Appreciation, which is written in the tone of a CIGS rather than a theatre commander, reflects the ambivalent position that Haig occupied. To the Appreciation was attached an intelligence appen-dix. Robertson accepted the Appreciation itself but persuaded Haig to withdraw the appendix, which was Charteris' work and completely at odds in its assessment of Germany's situation with the views of the Director of Military Intelligence at the War Office, Macdonogh (Charteris' predecessor). Robertson also coached Haig on presentation:

> [W]hat I do want to impress on you is this:- Don't argue that you can finish the war this year, or that the German is already beaten. Argue that your plan is the best plan – as it is – that no other would even be *safe* let alone decisive, and then leave them to reject your advice and mine. They dare not do that.

The War Policy Committee (which had been set up on 8 June 1917 to review policy) was not hostile to the Flanders campaign, but they did require to assess its chances of success. In 1915 the Cabinet and even the CIGS had been unaware that a battle was going to be fought at Loos. The intermingling of the political and military control of war-making had changed by 1917 to the extent that Haig could not open this offensive without detailed probing and the eventual agreement of the government.

The tragedy of Third Ypres is twofold. Haig was tempted away from attrition and wearing down, and he fixed, instead, on a hugely ambitious concept of a campaign which could win the war by smashing through a dispirited German army, linking up with a coastal attack and a naval landing, and driving through to Belgium. The naval dimension of the campaign was not negligible. Haig worked with Admiral Bacon, and was closely involved in detailed planning for landings along the lines of 1944, with flat-bottomed landing craft and tanks. Rehearsals took place on beaches with suitable configurations, and all was ready for landings in the area of Middelkerke. Aerial photographs and submarine reconnoitring took place, and Rawlinson was put in charge of the forces to be deployed in the landing and the coastal assault. All the elements of the later war were there: a division would land at dawn, under cover of a naval bombardment, and of a smoke screen laid down by a flotilla of small vessels; trawlers were to carry telephone cables to allow Rawlinson to remain in contact; in addition to their tanks, the landing force carried its own artillery support and motorised machine-gun batteries. Additional transport would be provided by the coastal assault, to be carried out by the land-based XV Corps.

Although it became abundantly clear that his grand vision would not be realised, he persisted in the battle, wearing down the Germans only at a greater cost to his own forces.

The second tragic element was the government's abdication of its responsibilities. It agonised over its decision to authorise the campaign, but then relinquished its control of the operation and even lost interest in it. The War Policy Committee stopped meeting, and though essentially the same men sat in the War Cabinet, they lacked the nerve and perhaps the strength to end the campaign, and contented themselves with criticising Haig behind his back.

The first step of the operations was the capture of Messines Ridge to protect the British right flank and dislodge the Germans from an important elevated position. The origins of Messines went back to January 1916, when Haig had asked Plumer to formulate plans for an attack at Ypres. Messines is important not simply as an isolated big bang, but as an essential prerequisite to the larger plans which Plumer formulated for Third Ypres. Work had been begun in July 1915 on French's orders on the tunnelling of nineteen mines, and at an army commanders' conference on 13 January 1916, Plumer was able to report that preparations for the capture of the Messines–Wytschaete Ridge were underway. The Ridge formed the southern edge of the Salient, and dominated the Gheluvelt Plateau. After the Chantilly conference, in November 1916, Haig asked for fresh plans for the Flanders operation and Plumer returned to what he had formerly envisaged, with the addition that he now considered that the Pilckem Ridge, to the north of Ypres, should, like Messines, be captured as a preliminary. He considered that two armies would be necessary. Haig was critical of what he regarded as Plumer's excessive caution. One of his criticisms is interesting. It demonstrates how different from the Somme Third Ypres was meant to be; it also points to the weakness of the tactics of the Somme:

> The plan, as submitted by you, indicates a sustained and deliberate offensive such as been carried out recently on the Somme front. In these circumstances the enemy will have time to bring up fresh reinforcements and construct new lines of defence.

Plumer was planning for a series of discrete, achievable advances. His proposal for the follow-up to the assault on the Ridge, for instance, was the capture of the remaining high ground and Wytschaete village, an advance of only some 1,500 yards in all. Haig, by contrast, was thinking in much more ambitious terms: in the days following the Ridge attack he wanted an advance extending to between twenty and thirty miles.

Plumer paid little attention to most of Haig's strictures, and produced fresh proposals that were little altered. His proposals were endorsed by Rawlinson who, if anything, was even more insistent on controlling the Gheluvelt Plateau before advancing beyond the Pilckem Ridge. The Plateau, as events were to show, was a critically important raised area which had to be cleared of Germans if the British were to advance on the lower ground to its left. Haig was unhappy: he saw the Ypres campaign as containing a real chance of a breakthrough opportunity, and not bite-and-hold. He turned from Rawlinson and Plumer to someone whom he found more temperamentally sympathetic, and on 30 April told Gough that he had decided to use him.

But Plumer remained in charge of the preliminary operation at Messines. On 6 May Haig told his army commanders that now Nivelle's offensive had been halted, the allies would 'exhaust the enemy's resistance by systematically attacking him by surprise'. Then an attack would take place on the Ypres front 'with the eventual object of securing the Belgian coast and connecting with the Dutch frontier'. Second Army was to capture the Messines–Wytschaete

Ridge, with the operations to the north and beyond some weeks later. Haig asked Plumer when he would be ready to launch his part of the operation. He replied, 'Today, one month, Sir.'

The army commanders during Third Ypres were Plumer, in charge of Second Army with Major-General C.H. 'Tim' Harington as his Chief of Staff, and Fifth Army under Gough. Plumer and Gough were alternately given responsibility for the main thrust of the offensive as Haig's confidence in their respective abilities waxed and waned.

Harington had been appointed earlier in the year as Plumer's Chief of Staff at Haig's instigation. He and Plumer worked as an exceptional team, on a basis of the most meticulous planning and the philosophy of, in Harington's words, 'Trust, Training and Thoroughness'. Just to give two instances of the detail and preparation which were required, water pipes were laid to supply 600,000 gallons a day for the Messines attack, and light railways constructed to bring forward 144,000 tons of ammunition. Gibbs described Harington very favourably in his *Realities of War,* which had as its general theme the incompetence of generals and the staff. Plumer, he said

had for his Chief of Staff Sir John [*sic*] Harington, and beyond all doubt this general was the organising brain of the Second Army, though with punctilious chivalry he gave, always, the credit of all his work to the army commander. A thin, nervous, highly-strung man, with extreme simplicity of manner and clarity of intelligence, he impressed me as a brain of the highest temper and quality in Staff work. His memory for detail was like a card index system, yet his mind was not clogged with detail, but he saw the wood as well as the trees. There was something fascinating as well as terrible in his exposition of the battle he was planning. For the first time, in his presence and over his maps, I saw that, after all, there was such a thing as the science of war, and that it was not always a fetish of elementary ideas raised to the nth degree of pomposity, as I had been led to believe by contact with other generals and staff officers.

There was a thoroughness of method, a minute attention to detail, a care for the comfort and spirit of the men, throughout the Second Army Staff which did at least inspire the troops with the belief that whatever they did in the fighting lines had been prepared for, and would be supported, with every possible help that organisation could provide. That belief was founded not upon fine words spoken on parade, but by strenuous work, a driving zeal, and the fine intelligence of a Chief of Staff whose brain was like a high power engine.[3]

Gibbs was unfair to Plumer. He and Harington worked as an inseparable team, but Plumer was the leader of that team. As Harington makes very clear in his biography of his Chief, *Plumer of Messines*, the methods that he followed were learned from his commander. (But the book requires to be read with caution. Plumer's widow, who during his lifetime had assiduously sought to promote his career, had a hand in it, and may have supplied Harington with suspect information to portray Plumer uncritically as the soldierly ideal.) Before Harington had joined him, Plumer already held a daily conference at which the heads of the various branches of the Staff and of the services and arms appeared. A report was given by each on the events of the last twenty-four hours and Plumer then issued his orders. After the daily conference, the participants went out to the units for which they were responsible and which they existed, as Plumer emphasised, to help. Plumer had been a regimental officer and he impressed on new staff officers that they were the servants of the infantry. To maintain a real link between headquarters and the troops within the different corps, a team of liaison officers established close links with individual units. Plumer's whole purpose was to use the most meticulous planning to achieve results with the minimum of losses. His troops knew that, and he was popular for it: units were always pleased to know that they were to be attached to his army. (It is interesting that the future Field-Marshal Montgomery was one of his staff officers and applied many of Plumer's methods in the Second World War.) But although he was good humoured and scrupulously fair, he tolerated no slackness in regard to discipline.

Plumer, almost certainly the ablest of the army commanders, had been a possible alternative to Haig when the latter succeeded French, and by 1918, with his reputation substantially enhanced, particularly by Messines, he would almost certainly have been Haig's successor if the latter had been deposed in the last year of the war. He was a loyal supporter of Haig – and of Robertson – whom he declined to succeed when Wully was dismissed as CIGS in February 1918. His loyalty, and complete failure to intrigue for promotion, constituted the second reason for his failure to achieve the supreme command. The first and very unfair reason was his physical appearance. In this war (things were slightly different by the Second World War) undue significance was attached to a commander's appearance. Haig was on the short side, and no one suggested that he exuded charisma, but he did look very much a general. Plumer did not. The significance is on the face of it surprising, given the lack of television and comparative lack of film, but the interest of the public and of the popular press in the nation's warriors was intense. As early as 1903, after Plumer had given evidence to the Royal Commission on the South African war ('The Elgin Committee') Esher wrote a note to the King: 'Lord Esher presents his humble duty and begs to inform Your Majesty that General Plumer was examined today, an officer of curious physique but evidently full of intelligence.'[4]

To the army Plumer was 'old Plum and Apple', a description that referred to the ubiquitous plum and apple jam which appears so much in the argot of the Western Front. Anthony Eden (later, as Prime Minister, Sir Anthony Eden, and latterly Earl of Avon) who fought under Plumer's command, described the army commander:

> At a superficial glance, Plumer with his eye-glass, medium height, somewhat portly figure and run-away chin, might not be impressive, but watch his methods for a while or hear him speak and you soon knew that here was a skilled and painstak-

ing commander who was a master of every detail of his job. A man to be trusted.[5]

Sir Philip Gibbs, writing after the war, and still bitter about the products of Staff College whom he described as having 'the brains of canaries', when thinking in particular of Gough's Fifth Army, made exceptions from his criticisms:

> As there are exceptions to every rule, so harsh criticism must be modified in favour of the generalship of II Army – of rare efficiency under the restriction and authority of the general staff. I often used to wonder what qualities belong to Sir Herbert Plumer, the Army Commander. In appearance he was almost a caricature of an old-time British general, with his ruddy, pippin-cheeked face, with white hair and a fierce little white moustache, and blue, watery eyes, and a little pot-belly and short legs. He puffed and panted when he walked . . .[6]

The preparation for Messines shows just how much the army, and the science of war, had advanced since 1914. Major J. Norton Griffiths, for example, who had been with Plumer in Matabeleland and South Africa, raised a unit of 'clay-kickers' direct from civilian life. They dug tunnels lying on their backs, kicking out the clay with a special shovel. Many other methods were used. On the Messines front, 5,000 yards of passageways were excavated by pick and shovel. Norton Griffiths, a larger than life soldier, was conveyed through France in a two and a half tons Rolls Royce Landaulette and supervised an immense mining operation that consisted of no less than nineteen separate mines and one million tons of explosive. There was huge artillery support, and by now the whole of that artillery could be concentrated under a single commander whereas in 1914 even two batteries could scarcely have their fire concentrated. Air power was employed, with continuous daylight patrols on the front and additional planes over the assault area. Eight balloons were used to assist the artillery observation aircraft. Four training manuals were published by Plumer for his corps, so up to the minute that they included not only analysis of the lessons on the Somme, but also those of Arras. A model of the Ridge, the size of two croquet lawns, was built, with scaffolding surrounding it to enable the officers who were to take part in the battle to study the terrain. Rehearsals took place on ground resembling the actual landscape that was to be attacked. Flags were used to show the progress of the creeping barrage, and the exercise was repeated until men automatically moved forward at the required speed.

Although their personal relationship was distant, Haig and Plumer understood each other. On 20 May, Haig had posed a typical, Socratic series of questions to the Corps Commanders:

Have you got the enemy's batteries accurately located, are changes of position occurring, and, if so, in what manner? For example, is the enemy occupying alternative positions near vacated ones; is he re-occupying his old ones after a certain lapse of time, or do you see a general tendency to move his batteries back? Have you discovered any new positions in course of construction, and are they being camouflaged as they are made . . . ? Have your intelligence and artillery reconnaissance officers detailed information as to where he is placing his machine-guns etc.? How do you propose forming up the troops for the attack? Have you a detailed plan for stopping the bridges over the River Lys or Canal D'Ypres, as the case may be . . . ? Are your infantry trained to deal with low-flying hostile aeroplanes by Lewis Gun and rifle fire? Are you satisfied that the Inter-Corps and Inter-Division barrages are all co-ordinated and that, as far as possible, they meet with the views of the Divisional Commanders?

And so on at huge length. Such a degree of involvement (some would say interference) in the planning of an army commander's planning would have been unthinkable in normal times.

The formidable written cross-examination was followed up with even more intensive oral questioning. As a result, and with Plumer's agreement, Haig sacked one of the divisional commanders. Plumer could have been resentful, but he does not appear to have been. Both men knew that victory would not be achieved by accident. Plumer refined and fine-tuned his plans till the last minute, sometimes to the irritation of subordinate commanders. He, no more than Haig, would leave anything to chance. The battle of Messines Ridge was the best-executed and most successful operation since 1914.

The mines were to be exploded at 3.10 a.m. on 7 June. Harington went to bed at 9 o'clock on the previous evening. He breakfasted with Plumer at 2.30 a.m. and then walked to the top of Cassel Hill to watch the proceedings. 'Not so the Army Commander. He was kneeling by his bedside, praying for those gallant officers and men who were at that moment attacking.'

From his vantage point, Harington heard Norton Phillips' million tons of explosive detonate on time in an explosion which was heard in London, and the Ridge had been neutralised before that day's War Policy Committee meeting. Plumer followed up the explosion with a huge barrage. Hankey recalled that 'the roar of guns at dawn on that still summer morning was louder in my Surrey garden than on any occasion in the war.' Above what had been the Ridge rose two plumes, like giant cypress trees, which slowly coalesced into what was to be the twentieth-century symbol of the perversion of science, a mushroom cloud. German counter-attacks were repulsed, and the operation was a success – although a costly one, with 25,000 casualties. 'I wish [Plumer] were C-in-C,' wrote Wilson. 'He has twice Haig's brains, and just as much character.'[7]

Haig had returned to Plumer's headquarters from his own forward headquarters, his command train. He followed the progress of the battle with a telescope from a hut specially built on the top of Mont Rouge, two miles behind the battlefield. He congratulated Plumer on his success. 'The old man deserves the highest praise for he has patiently defended the Ypres Salient for two and a half years.' He told Charteris that Plumer had become 'his most reliable Army Commander'.[8]

Some seven weeks passed before the success was followed up. Although there was an immense amount of planning to complete, and the War Policy Committee required to give its consent, the delay was regrettable. Terraine says that some responsibility for the delay lies with Haig who, as early as 7 May, had envisaged a delay between these two phases of the battle of six weeks,[9] but the delay was in truth not entirely or even principally of Haig's making. It was only on 14 March that Haig was authorized to prepare for Flanders, and then only in the event of the failure of Nivelle's campaign. Calais and the government's involvement of the British army in Nivelle's offensive did not help, but analysis of the logistic problems involved shows that the next phase of Third Ypres simply could not have been launched earlier. There was much to do, in terms of redeployment to the north and creation of road and rail links to move men and supplies.[10] The succeeding moves were planned sequentially, to secure Passchendaele Ridge, Klerken Ridge and the other rises in the land, until Ostend itself was under fire. This sequential approach was not what Haig had originally wanted: he planned simultaneous attacks at Pilckem, Gheluvelt and Messines. Rawlinson saw a need for a delay of forty-eight to seventy-two hours between Messines and the next stage of the advance. Plumer wanted three days to shift his artillery. Haig thought this excessive, transferred two corps to Gough, and tasked him with capturing the Plateau. Instead of three days' 'delay', Gough proposed, after six days' consideration, that Gheluvelt should be part of his wider operations, which would not begin for six weeks. Haig agreed. He has rightly been criticised for retaining Gough, and even for appointing him in the first place, which he may have done because of his regard for his brother, killed by that sniper earlier in the war. Not just for solid logistical reasons but also because as late as 30 April Haig chose to take the command away from Plumer, who had studied the ground intimately, and give it to Gough, who was still engaged in the Arras sector, there was a gap not of three days, but of more than seven weeks. Even if the main campaign could not have been advanced, would it not have been better planning to delay Messines? Haig's turn-arounds on timing and his changes of command do not speak of a confident, well thought-through policy at this stage.

Planning for the follow-up to Messines followed an orderly and logical process, with each stage in the operation unrolling when the previous stage was completed. The War Policy Committee, which did not minute the naval element for reasons of security, was extraordinarily cautious, weighing up the relative strengths of the Allies against the enemy, in terms of both numbers and armaments, and then went on to question whether the advance – thirty miles just to bring Ostend within gunfire, and more before Zeebrugge would be reached – was realistic. On the Somme the advance had been seven miles, and at Arras six, and circumstances were now possibly less propitious, given the reduced German activity on the eastern front. Haig and Robertson were adamant that the plan was worth essaying. They did not guarantee success, but they advised that the plan should be adopted. Ultimately, said Hankey, who was intimately involved in the deliberations in London, and who had first suggested the massive mining operation at Messines:

> [t]he decision to allow Haig to undertake the Flanders offensive was taken by Lloyd George and by most of his colleagues with reluctance and misgiving. No one believed that a strategical result could be achieved, all shrank from the terrible losses which they knew it must involve. But the consensus of naval and military opinion was so overwhelming that the War Cabinet could not take the responsibility of rejecting the advice thrust upon them with so much cogency.[11]

At the meeting of the War Policy Committee on 11 June, Robertson, who had already been hinting that the days of dramatic breakthroughs of the kind promised by Nivelle were past, returned to that theme. He did not believe that 'great attacks against a distant objective were at present practicable'. When Haig came to London in a few days it might 'be desirable to modify [Haig's] orders to a certain extent, owing to the changed situation'. What interested Lloyd George more was however the question of moving resources to the Italian front. Accordingly, before Haig's return to London, Robertson wrote to him:

> to forewarn you of what is in the air so that you may be ready for them next week. The LG idea is to settle the war from Italy and today the railway people have been asked for figures regarding the rapid transfer of 12 divisions and 300 heavy guns to Italy! They will never go while I am CIGS, but all that will come later.

It was during this session that Haig presented the Appreciation from which Robertson had persuaded him to excise Charteris' intelligence appendix. Robertson himself presented a note that referred not only to Admiralty pressure for operations in Flanders but also to the fact that:

> we must give the French the opportunity to fight. If they do not fight we must act accordingly and the plan will permit of this. In any case, French defection is not a good reason for sending British troops to another theatre for Germany may counter us by heavily attacking the French, and under the assumption that they will not fight, this attack might be disastrous to the Entente.[12]

In view of the argument that the French did not want the British to fight at Ypres, and that Haig's subsequent justification of the continuation of the battle was falsely based on France's weakness, it is interesting to note that the French element is not at least entirely *ex post facto.*

Haig returned for a further meeting of the War Policy Committee on 19 June. Lloyd George described Haig's performance in his *War Memoirs:*

> When Sir Douglas Haig explained his projects to the civilians, he spread on a table or desk a large map and made a dramatic

use of both his hands to demonstrate how he proposed to sweep up the enemy – first the right hand brushing along the surface irresistibly, and then came the left, his outer finger ultimately touching the German frontier with the nail across . . .

The War Policy Committee were then taken up into an aerial tower built during the past six months or more by the industry and imagination of GHQ to view this thrilling prospect. It is not surprising that some of us were so captivated by the splendour of the landscape . . . that their critical faculties were overwhelmed. Mr. Bonar Law, Lord Milner and I remained sceptical.[13]

Sceptical though he may have been, the minutes of the meeting record that he complimented Haig on his 'very powerful' presentation of what was indeed no attritional nibble, but a daring grand design.

The deliberations of the War Policy Committee continued for several days. On the second day that Haig was present, he gave the Committee something to hang on to, he was:

fully in agreement with the Committee that we ought not to push in attacks that had not a reasonable chance of success, and that we ought to proceed step by step. He himself had no intention of entering into a tremendous offensive involving heavy losses. His plan was aggressive without committing us too far.

At a further meeting on the next day, Lloyd George said that he had 'devoted many hours of anxious consideration' to Haig's proposals:

He considered it would be too great a responsibility for [the Committee] to take the strategy of the war out of the hands of their military advisers. [But that] made it all the more important that the military advisers . . . should carefully weigh his misgivings in regard to the advice they had tendered. If after

hearing his views, and after taking time to consider them, they
still adhered to their previous opinion, then the responsibility
for their advice must rest with them.

The formula is rather strange: Lloyd George was going as far as he
could to dump the responsibility for the decision of the Committee
on the soldiers and to overturn the principle that the military were
responsible for their advice and the War Committee responsible for
their decision. Haig declined to guarantee success and commented
that 'during nearly three years of war he had never known an offensive
to be undertaken with sure predictions of success.' The Prime
Minister suggested as an alternative to Flanders, either a concentration of effort on Austria or following the style of Pétain with 'a punch
here or there, and a process of wearing down the enemy.' There was
never, however, any real doubt that Haig would get his way,
particularly as Lloyd George said not once but twice in the course
of the meetings with Haig that the Committee would not overturn
the strategy which their military advisers recommended. All the
same, the War Policy Committee met no less than sixteen times
before 18 July and the War Cabinet itself only formally endorsed the
campaign on 25 July, by which time the battle had effectively begun.

After Haig's difficult series of meetings with hostile politicians,
who seemed, he thought, to vie with each other in pessimism, he had
a more pleasant visit from Derby, the soldiers' friend. Derby said, 'I
am anxious to see you fully rewarded.' Haig said that as a field-
marshal he was fully rewarded. Derby, who had pulled a piece of
paper with notes on it from his pocket, said he wished to recommend
Haig for a peerage. 'I thanked him most warmly but pointed out that
I and my wife were thoroughly happy in our present position. If I were
made a Peer, I would at once have to live beyond my means and so get
into debt. Again I did not wish to found a dynasty. [Difficult,
anyway, as he had no son at this stage.] The Haigs of Bemersyde were
now the oldest family in Scotland, etc.'. Not long afterwards he was
however offered a distinction which he was pleased to accept when,
visiting the King at Cassell, he was presented with the insignia of a

Knight of the Thistle. The King told Haig that this was the finest decoration that was within his power to bestow. The Duke of Buccleuch had declined to accept the award as long as 'the greatest living Scotsman' was without it.

Haig reported the attitude of the Cabinet when he came back to his Headquarters on 28 June. Charteris records 'He has had great difficulties. He tells me that every one of the Cabinet, Lloyd George, Bonar Law, Curzon, Milner and even Smuts, vies with the other in pessimism. They all, headed by the PM, wanted to stop offensives operations for this year and save up our men and resources for 1918'. Charteris went on to say that Haig had given it as his opinion that if the fighting were kept up for six months, Germany would be at the end of her manpower: this, he said, was going further than he had briefed Haig. Charteris was particularly intrigued by the news from Haig that Lloyd George was thinking of making Robertson First Lord of the Admiralty: 'that would fairly put the Naval fat in the fire, and probably bring Nelson toppling off his Trafalgar Square perch.'[14]

The reality of the situation was, however, that Haig was stronger, and not weaker, as a result of the Calais débacle, a situation which had been compounded when Lloyd George spoke at the Guildhall on 27 April, accepting the freedom of the city of London. He had spoken in the warmest terms of the nation's gratitude to the troops and, very strangely, not to the Commander-in-Chief, but to 'that brave little man who led them through all those trying months under very great difficulties, and was never beaten, and never lost heart – Lord French.' No mention whatsoever was made of Haig or his commanders. The slight to Haig was ill-judged. His tribute to the troops received loud cheers, but none were recorded at the mention of Lord French. Lloyd George was well aware that Calais had been a personal disaster: he said he did not want 'another Calais'. He was now committed to trying to repair the breach with Haig. When he was in Paris on 4 May he lunched at the Crillon with Esher, who reported to Haig (as Lloyd George knew he would do): 'He has entirely changed his point of view as to the respective merits of the chiefs of the allied armies, their staffs and the powers of offence. For the moment I do not think *you* could do wrong'.

The Prime Minister's misgivings about an offensive in the west were not echoed by Smuts, whom he had sent out to France to make an assessment; and Hankey also reported positively on a Flanders attack. Hankey's views, in particular, must have been anathema to Lloyd George. He considered that not only was action essential, or the Germans would win the war before the Americans had come on the scene, but that 'even a battle of the Somme type . . . might produce great results'. This attritional warfare, a continuation of the Somme strategy, was precisely what Lloyd George was desperate to avoid. In his Mansion House speech he had given hostages to fortune, in saying now that the army had the weapons and ammunition it needed.

Wilson, writing from French GHQ to Robertson on 2 June put a powerful case against waiting for 1918:

Dear Robertson

There is so much talk now of the plan of waiting for the Americans before putting in another great attack that I think I had better let you know what I think of it from the French point of view. I am not concerned, for the moment, with the wisdom of postponing, for 12 or 18 months, any serious attempt at a final military decision, but, should this plan be adopted, I am very clear, in my own mind, that neither the French Army, nor the French people, nor even the French women, will continue in the war.[15]

19

THIRD YPRES. PASSCHENDAELE. CAMBRAI

Douglas Haig has been characterised, above all, as an unimaginative tactician, stubborn and even stupid, doggedly persisting in a discredited and blinkered commitment to attrition. He was not stupid and far from committed to attrition, and Third Ypres, the only phase of the Great War that was wholly his concept, was imaginative. It failed precisely because it was *too* bold and imaginative, a flamboyant project in the tradition of continental wars of another century, but fatally flawed because it rested on a determined belief that Germany was about to crack. The objective of pushing through to the Belgian coast in a dash of combined operations was never remotely possible, and it was in the light of that impossibility that Churchill, who had rejoined the government after his Dardanelles humiliation, painted this dark and brooding picture in *The World Crisis*:

Meanwhile the British offensive against Passchendaele unrolled its sombre fate. The terrific artillery pulverised the ground, smashing simultaneously the German trenches and the ordinary drainage. By sublime devotion and frightful losses small indentations were made upon the German front. In six weeks at the furthest point we had advanced four miles. Soon the rain descended and the vast crater fields became a sea of choking fetid mud in which men, animals and tanks floundered and perished hopelessly. The few tracks which alone could be preserved across this morass were swept with ceaseless shellfire, through which endless columns of transport marched with fortitude all night long.[1]

The preliminary bombardment began on 15 July and continued until 31 July. Even ten days earlier, Charteris had wondered whether the season was too late to advance to achieve their objective. The choice of Gough for a pivotal role in the battle was criticised by Terraine: 'Haig's greatest and most fatal error.'[2] Gough himself said that Plumer, with his far greater knowledge of the Ypres Salient, would have been a better choice for the campaign. Gough's problems were, first, that he did not understand the strategic purpose of the battle, and secondly, the quality of the staff he had assembled under Major-General Neill Malcolm. There was poor communication of orders within Fifth Army, as there was between the Commander-in-Chief and the Army Commander.

Gough planned a frontal attack on Ostend and Zeebrugge, whereas Haig had envisaged the severing of the German line of communication and *then* a frontal attack. Haig had planned that the right flank would be secured by occupying the Gheluvelt Ridge and pushing along it to Broodseinde; Gough wanted to advance on a broader front, so that his troops would not filter into 'a very pronounced salient'. The high ground of the Ridge had always been considered by Haig and Plumer to be critical: indeed Plumer's II and VIII Corps had been transferred to Gough specifically for the purpose of clearing the Ridge. Gough appears to have thought that Haig agreed to a change of plan, although that was not the case. Haig vacillated between leaving his commander to his own initiative and interfering on points of detail and failed to satisfy himself that his orders were being followed or indeed understood, although he continued to emphasise the importance of securing the Gheluvelt Ridge. Again, while he advised Gough to concentrate his attack, he allowed him to persist on a wide front. His failure to impose his will on Gough was a serious mistake. For the following four weeks things continued in this way, with the army pointing away from its original objective. After the war, Gough complained that there had been insufficient discussion at Haig's army commanders' conferences. It does not appear that Haig or Gough understood each other on what was to happen in relation to the Ridge, and their failure to do so meant that Gough's initial attack was fundamentally at variance with what Haig wanted.

The flaw was compounded by the fact that Gough had to ask Haig for repeated delays, at one stage because of artillery losses, at another because the French on the left were not yet ready. The latter delay Gough considered fatal. But there were many problems within Fifth Army. The relationship between Gough and Malcolm, on the one hand, and the subordinate commanders, on the other, was poor. Gough was frequently overambitious. On occasion Haig counselled patience. On 3 August he advised waiting for better weather conditions. On 16 August he argued that the attack Gough planned was on too wide a front. But in these instances and others, Gough was allowed to do what he, and not the Commander-in-Chief, wanted. Throughout the operations, Haig himself was not consistent, veering from considered realism to over-optimism that envisaged a huge advance in the face of collapsing German morale.

Since the Somme there had been great tactical advances. In general, linear advances had given way to looser formations on the multi-weapon model, with light machine-guns and rifle grenades. Artillery, crucial at Third Ypres, had also evolved and become highly sophisticated. But these innovations appear to have been less favoured in this battle and this army than on other occasions.

Gough was gradually modifying Plumer's original plan, and what Fifth Army was coming to adopt was a move away from a series of discrete, planned and manageable operations, each flowing into the next, in favour of a more ambitious advance, without fixed pauses, and with discretion to commanders as to how far to go, but with Passchendaele and Poelcapelle within the planned advance. Haig's Head of Operations Branch, Brigadier-General Davidson, argued against Fifth Army's plans, advocating a series of separate and limited attacks. But despite instinctively agreeing with him, Haig capitulated to Gough, merely stressing the vital importance of securing Gheluvelt Ridge to cover his right flank and of pushing along it to Broodseinde.

Ahead of the major assault on 31 July there was a fierce artillery battle which cost a large number of lives and which did not go as well for the British as had been hoped. What the shelling did achieve was to make the 'Swamp Map' bluer and bluer, blue being the colour used to show the bogs created by the destruction of drainage dykes. The Swamp Map was sent daily to GHQ until Tank Corps HQ was instructed to stop sending them. Whether or not Haig saw the Swamp Maps, GHQ's liaison officers did report continuously on the state of the ground. Even so, did GHQ appreciate just how bad conditions were?

At this time, and against the background of his preparations for the biggest offensive for which he had been personally responsible, Haig strangely found time write to Lady Haig, suggesting that she write his biography. 'It was just five days before the beginning of the most talked of part of the war, the operations in the region of Passchendaele, that my husband wrote to me about the writing of his life'.[3] It is unsettling to observe Haig's ability to turn his mind from the certainty of the long and bloody offensive which he envisaged to study the means of promoting his place in history.

At a conference of army commanders a few days before the attack Haig was, very unusually, unsure of his position. He referred to Napoleon's remark to his Marshals: 'Ask me for anything but time.' According to Charteris, once a decision was taken his principle was to support the army commanders in their opinions on its execution. But 'as he came away from the conference, Haig, for almost the only time in the war, expressed doubt of the wisdom of his decision.'[4]

And yet the main attack on 31 July was an example of the learning curve beginning to deliver. There was cooperation between all arms, engineers, artillery and infantry. The artillery tactics were by now elaborate. There was a creeping barrage, plus a standing barrage which lifted to fit in with the advances of the creeping barrage. But the British army was not the only army which was learning. The

Germans, after the Somme, had abandoned linear defence in favour of
defence in depth, which involved the use of counter-attack formations, and at this stage there was not a proper British appreciation of
these tactics.[5]

This is not the place for a detailed account of the intricate mosaic
of fighting that took place over the next three and a half months and
which make up, according to the Official History, nine separate
battles collectively known as Third Ypres. The designation of the
different battles shows the nature of these engagements. For Ludendorff, there were five stages to the conflict, whereas Terraine
thinks it helpful to regard it as consisting of an initial three (Pilckem
Ridge on 31 July, Gheluvelt Plateau on 10 August and Langemark
on 16 August) followed by a pause before a series of victories by
Second Army (Menin Road Ridge on 20 September, Polygon Wood
on 26 September and Broodseinde on 4 October). There was then a
final phase when Second Army attempted to exploit these victories as
the weather got even worse, and a struggle for a line to hold through
the winter (Poelcapelle on 9 October, Passchendaele I on 12 October
and Passchendaele II on 26 October). Passchendaele was captured by
the Canadians on 6 November and the battle was closed down on 12
November.

The advance on 31 July was to be of some 4,000 to 5,000 yards,
much more than commanders had found from experience to be
achievable. Davidson urged on Gough a target of 1,500 yards, the
sort of bite that Plumer would take in the later stages of the battle.

Very heavy rain started to fall on the afternoon of 31 July and with
only short breaks it continued for a whole month. From the start, the
weather hindered operations. In contrast to Messines, seven weeks
earlier, it was not possible to make use of aircraft. At Messines aerial
observation had identified fresh objectives which were then targeted
by artillery under direction from the air: an example of new
technology grasped since the outset of the war. The weather got
steadily worse as the days followed. By 4 August Charteris wrote: 'All
my fears about the weather have been realised. It has killed this
attack. Every day's delay tells against us. We lose, hour by hour, the

advantage of attack. The Germans can reorganise and reinforce. We can do nothing but wait.'[6] The weather was the result of bad luck and not bad planning. Captain Gold, who had advised about the wind direction before the Battle of Loos, was now Commandant of the Meteorological Section, and in 1958 he pointed out in a letter in the *Spectator* that 'the rainfall directly affecting the first months of the offensive was more than double the average; it was over five times the amount for the same period in 1915 and in 1916.'[7] Haig was advised that the weather would generally be favourable, and indeed Plumer's September battles were fought in hot, dusty conditions. The wet conditions in August were unusual.[8] But the fact remains that heavy bombardment of an area that famously needed a sophisticated drainage system was always going to militate against success for the ambitious objectives of the campaign.

Haig restrained Gough from further attacks until the weather improved. In the meantime, he made an intelligent response to the experience of 31 July, considering whether the infantry was being asked to do too much, particularly in view of the necessity of repelling the German counter-attacks, which were now an essential part of their defensive method. He also required corps and divisional commanders to be sure that the tactics that had evolved at the machine-gun schools were being applied. Indeed, within a few days he was at the main machine-gun school, studying a demonstration of these new tactics. As usual he wanted to be as near to the fighting as practicable and his advanced headquarters were in his railway train near Ypres when the attack began.

By now concerns were being expressed about lack of progress. Hankey agreed with Lloyd George 'that rain had spoiled Haig's Flanders plan & that we ought to do something else.'[9] Three days later he wrote: 'The days are slipping by, it is time to reconsider whether Haig's offensive should be permitted to continue in the bad weather conditions, and whether the alternative for a great offensive on the Italian front should not be adopted.' That alternative had Lloyd George's strong support but not, at this point, the support of the French; and the succession of offensives continued. Just as he alternated in favouring Plumer and Gough, so Haig oscillated wildly in his appraisal of events and predictions for the future. Thus, on 16 August, appalled by Gough's lack of artillery planning, he stressed that nothing could be done until defensive posts had been knocked out, and that commanders were wrong to act 'in too great a hurry!!' But just three days later, his confidence reinforced by optimistic reports from Charteris or elsewhere, he told his Commanders that 'our armies' efforts this year have brought final victory near. Indeed, I think that, if we can keep up our effort, final victory may be won in December.' On the whole optimism greatly exceeded pessimism and characterised and flawed his conduct of the battle. For example, on 27 August, 'The state of the enemy's reserves is today the most favourable for us since the war began!' The intelligence branch at the War Office was much less optimistic and on 9 August the Prime Minister said to a conference of allied representatives that he had no confidence in the General Staff or their plans, and that he had known all along that this latest offensive was doomed to failure.

On the Italian Front, by contrast, an offensive on 19 August opened well, and Lloyd George argued strongly for the transfer of resources from Flanders to Italy. Foch was now similarly minded, and was pressing the British War Cabinet to allow him to send 100 guns to Italy without delay. Haig went to London and was allowed to have the final decision: he agreed to the transfer of 100 guns from the French 1st Army, providing Pétain replaced them in time for the next attack, which he agreed to do.

The flavour of venom in which the debate between the politicians and the soldiers was conducted is contained in a note from Robertson to Kiggell dated 9 August 1917. '[Y]ou can imagine what passed when I say that the Prime Minister was about twice as bad as on the morning you had a discussion with him in the train.' The letter is dictated and typed, but continues in manuscript: 'He is an under-bred Swine.'[10]

In the second phase of Third Ypres, Plumer carried the main burden of the attack. Gough had already lost confidence in the feasibility of the whole scheme. When Haig declined to allow him to call off operations, Gough asked that Plumer's Second Army should also be thrown into the offensive. Plumer declined and the result of Haig's adjudication between the two commanders was to ask Plumer to take over the main responsibility. That responsibility consisted in clearing the Germans from the Gheluvelt Plateau which Gough had neglected. Gough's Fifth Army was to support on the north.

Plumer had been ready to attack Polygon Wood and Broodseinde Ridge immediately after Messines, if Haig had been prepared to give him three days to move his artillery. Ten weeks had passed before he was given the opportunity once more. He was not prepared to move until his preparations were complete, and this time he required a delay of three weeks before launching his attack. His advances were planned as 'bite-and-hold' set pieces, a series of steps of 1,500 yards. At the Battle of the Menin Road Ridge on 20 September he had 1,295 artillery pieces, the densest concentration of the war. Haig was delighted by the thorough preparations he found within Second Army. Plumer's planning, helped by more favourable weather, made the first day of the Battle of the Menin Road Ridge an unqualified success. After early doubts about him, perhaps even fear of him as a potential successor, Haig had come to have great respect for 'Daddy' Plumer (and Harington). When he described Plumer as his most reliable army commander, Charteris said that was great praise for both Plumer and Harington, 'for nobody knows where Plumer ends and Harington begins'.

Plumer was very different from Gough. In the Menin Road Battle, there was an infantry advance with bomb throwers, Lewis gunners and rifle grenadiers. In tactics that presaged those of 1918, the first assault would consist of skirmishes designed to identify unknown defended positions; these were then attacked by small, multi-weapon units. The problem of destruction of telephone cables was addressed by a whole range of devices: lucas lamps, flags, fireworks, pigeons, runners, message-carrying dogs and wireless. Haig noticed all the evidence of preparation, and the confidence it engendered, when he visited Second Army Headquarters ahead of the Battle of Menin Road:

In every case, I found the officers full of confidence as to the
result of the forthcoming attack. Every detail had been gone
into most thoroughly and the troops most carefully trained . . .
Altogether I felt it was most exhilarating to go round such a
very knowledgeable and confident body of leaders.

He returned two days later:

General Plumer was in great spirits. I told him I had only small
suggestions to offer as a result of my visit to his corps and
divisions yesterday. Everything was quite satisfactory. I could
only wish him great success and good luck. The old man was
full of good spirits and confident.

Plumer limited the advance to 600 yards and then consolidated
within range of artillery and machine gun support. These were the
tactics that would eventually win the war. But Plumer's successes
did cost lives. In fact, just in terms of ground gained (excluding the
nature of objectives) against casualties, Plumer gained less ground
than Gough at a greater cost.[11] And although Plumer's attacks at
the Menin Road, Polygon Wood and Broodseinde were accounted
great successes, the losses were, respectively 21,000, 15,000 and
20,000: the scale of casualties in relation to ground gained was
more than twice that of the first day of the Somme (3,800 casualties
per square mile, as against 1,500).[12] History has been slightly
unkind in its relative assessments of Gough and Plumer. Gough
was not all bad. Training in his army was good, and under Maxse
was indeed very good. Plumer was not the only one to have troops
train on modelled landscapes until they could find their way
around the real battlefield blindfolded. Although he had more
guns than Gough, Plumer was not able to neutralise German
artillery, and suffered more losses. But Gough's reputation suffered
from his poor performance in August, and from the fact that so
much had been expected of the 31 July attack. The great difference
between Plumer and Gough was that although Gough did gain

ground at lower cost than Plumer at Menin Road, he gained much less than had been hoped for. Plumer, by contrast tended to achieve exactly what he planned for.

The next stage was the Battle of Polygon Wood on 26 September. It did not go quite as well, but all the same resulted in an advance of 1,200 yards, with significant success by I Anzac Corps. By now the Germans were seriously concerned.

The Cabinet was also concerned. Its concern related to the length of the Flanders operations and the scale of the losses. Haig was increasingly disturbed by suspicions about the degree of Robertson's commitment to the enterprise, suspicions which remained with him for the rest of Robertson's time as CIGS: 'R[obertson] comes badly out of this, in my opinion, especially as *it was definitely stated (with the War Cabinet's approval) that no discussion re operations on the Western Front would be held with the French without my being present.*' A *froideur* was developing between them. Intelligence at the War Office was not saying what Charteris was saying at GHQ. But although Robertson said that he was sticking to Flanders only because he could see nothing better and despite his own instincts and feelings, he tried to reassure Haig: 'You must let me do my job in my own way. I have never yet given in on important matters and never shall. In any case, whatever happens, you and I must stand solid together.' Robertson was coming close to resignation in the face of Lloyd George's antagonism, but Haig urged him not to do so. The Cabinet were well aware that they risked precipitating Robertson's resignation, and indeed would probably have been delighted to receive it. Churchill recorded that:

Informally consulting outside advisers the Prime Minister obviously courted the resignation of the Chief of the Imperial General Staff. It was not forthcoming. The Cabinet were not prepared to demand it; and nothing but mutual distrust resulted.

Accordingly in Flanders the struggle went on. New divisions continued to replace those that were shattered. The rain

descended and the mud sea spread. Still the will-power of the
Commander and the disciplines of the army remained invincible. By measureless sacrifices Passchendaele was won. But
beyond, far beyond, still rose intact and unapproachable the
fortifications of Klerken. August had passed away; September
was gone; October was far spent. The full severity of a Flanders
winter gripped the ghastly battlefield. Ceaselessly the Menin
Gate of Ypres disgorged its stream of manhood . . .

It cannot be said that 'the soldiers,' that is to say the Staff, did
not have their way. They tried their sombre experiment to its
conclusion . . . Sir Douglas Haig acted from convictions; but Sir
William Robertson drifted ponderously. He has accepted the
main responsibility. He could not well avoid it.[13]

What prompted Robertson's thoughts of resignation was a request
from Lloyd George to Johnnie French and Henry Wilson to submit
written advice on the conduct of the war. Haig too was of course
disturbed and wanted to return to London. Derby dissuaded him and
within a few days Haig received a telegram from Lloyd George
conveying the congratulations of the Cabinet on the success that had
been achieved by his leadership in the face of difficulties due to the
unfavourable weather conditions, and renewing his personal assurance of confidence in Haig. The telegram was strange: it was the first
time he had received any congratulatory message from the Cabinet
since the beginning of the war. It was all the more remarkable for the
circumstances in which it was sent.

Wilson, too, did his best to assuage Haig's concerns, explaining to
Kiggell that the papers that he and French had been requested by the
War Council to write about the present situation and the future of
the war were not designed to be critical of Haig:

It is not part of my duty, nor any part of my wish, to criticize my
superiors. In the end, I wrote a paper on the machinery for
conducting the war, and not on the people who conduct it . . .

I see no hostility to Sir Douglas Haig over here no matter

what anyone says to the contrary, and I have some opportunities of judging.

I hope he is well. I write to you as I know how burdened he must be with work and responsibility.[14]

Plumer launched his attack at Broodseinde on 4 October, following the same tactics as before: limited objectives and an enormous artillery barrage. Australians, as in the earlier operations, played a critical role and again there was a huge success. The German Official History described 4 October as 'a black day'. The Australian Official History described it as 'an overwhelming blow', and imagined the student of history saying to himself, 'In view of three step-by-step blows, all successful, what will be the result of three more in the next fortnight?' Prince Rupprecht began to prepare for a withdrawal which involved abandoning the Channel Ports. Up to this point Third Ypres had been a series of successful operations that were coming close to achieving their object. Plumer's victories created a feeling of euphoria and Haig was particularly elated by Broodseinde, which came close to clearing the Germans off the Gheluvelt Plateau. He was so optimistic that after an advance of three and a half miles in seven weeks, he now felt able to contemplate a further advance of the same distance in just some ten days, followed by a drive of forty-five miles to the Belgian coast.

The reason that Third Ypres is not remembered in that euphoric light lies in what followed. A conference of Haig, Plumer and Gough took place on the afternoon of 4 October. Charteris recorded that most of those present were willing to go on but would have preferred to stop. He refers to 'reasons far more vital than our own interests' which left 'no option' but to continue. The idea that these 'vital interests' related to the weak state of the French Army has been largely discredited,[15] and probably 'the vital reasons' related to the fact that by the following year Germany would have withdrawn her troops from the Eastern Front.

This last phase of the battle, now unrolling, was the source of most contemporary criticism of Haig. After the better weather of September, rain had started falling on the afternoon of the 4 October attack and continued. Even if the rainfall in Flanders that summer and autumn was exceptional, October was always a wet month. Five millimetres of rain were enough to turn the Menin road battlefield into a quagmire, and the October average was 75 millimetres. Yet Haig does not seem to have been deterred. He remained invincibly optimistic, and his attitude predicated an imminent German collapse. The army commanders did not do much to disabuse him. Plumer told him that although a collapse on his front would not take place by 10 October, things might be different if the Germans were driven off Passchendaele Ridge, which he thought might happen by the middle of the month. Gough agreed, but thought that cavalry could only operate after 16 October, as opposed to Plumer's estimate of a few days earlier. Haig called a further conference, and told his commanders that they were too pessimistic, that German morale had declined dramatically, and that reserves of infantry with supporting arms must be made ready. Plumer and Gough did not protest. Edmonds alleged that they did do so at a further conference on 7 October, but the evidence for this Conference's having taken place is highly suspect.[16] The '7 October' conference is almost certainly that of 4 October.

Charteris watched the attack on 9 October, the Battle of Poelcapelle: 'It was the saddest day of this year . . . It was not the enemy but mud that prevented us from doing better. There is now no chance of complete success this year. We must still fight on for a few more weeks, but there is no purpose in it now, so far as Flanders is concerned.' Despite this, Charteris, who felt, according to General Sir James Marshall-Cornwall, who served under him, 'that it was his duty to keep up Douglas Haig's morale', continued to tell his Chief what he wanted to hear. He talked things over with Haig that evening, but clearly did not communicate his doubts: when he left, Haig wrote up his diary. 'The enemy is now much weakened in moral and lacks the desire to fight.'

One practical reason for continuing the fight was that the army had to find ground on which it could stand through the winter and the Passchendaele Ridge was thought to fulfil that purpose, if nothing else. The Ridge was captured by the Canadian Corps on 6 November.

When Currie's Canadian Corps launched what is called the Second Battle of Passchendaele, Currie was taking bites of just 500 yards. The first such bite cost 3,400 casualties. On 12 November the battle was at an end. It was lost in the German spring offensive in the following year.

The furthest extent of the advance had been 10,000 yards and not even the first objective had been reached. The British Army had fought an infinitely more skilful war than on the Somme, but their morale had probably suffered even more. There is controversy about the figures, but the Official History figure of 244,897 casualties is probably about right, possibly understated by about 30,000. The War Cabinet did not even enquire about losses until 11 October. When it received them it was not upset, and indeed noted that rumours of exaggerated figures and public concern about stories of disproportionate Colonial losses could be dispelled if the true figures were made known in 'an occasional statement by the Prime Minister'. No one knows what the German casualties were, probably about 200,000 – less, that is than the British. Between 22 and 26 October the French captured seven miles of enemy front, to a depth of three miles, pretty much what the British had gained at infinitely greater cost.

Nothing can be said to suggest that the loss of a quarter of a million men was not an unqualified tragedy, but in a similar period in 1916, the Somme losses had been 400,000. The daily loss at Third Ypres was 2,121, as opposed to 3,552 in Normandy in 1944. The reason that Third Ypres and Passchendaele live on in notoriety is not just the tragedy of the deaths and injuries, but the unimaginable conditions in which men fought: the rain, the flooding, the mud, the incessant shelling which assailed units as they moved up on the few routes that led through the swamp to the front. Any representation of Flanders in the autumn of 1917 is an allegory of hell.

Haig was disappointed by the lack of support he received from the French in these months. He considered that France had fought unimaginatively in 1915, incurring huge losses in attacks that could not lead anywhere: 'This was fighting the enemy without intelligence . . . I began', said Haig, 'with a readiness to believe the best of the French – as was only natural for a Scot, with memories of the Old Alliance; but events were too much for me.'[17]

The debate about whether the last phase of the battle was worthwhile continues, and most would find against Haig. By the very end, however, Passchendaele Ridge had to be taken: having advanced towards it, the British troops could not camp for the winter in the swamps that had been created, overlooked by German artillery. After the war, Harington put the question, 'I still ask the critics where our advanced troops could have spent the winter of 1917.' But that is hardly a justification for the campaign or its undue prolongation. Possession of the Ridge did allow reinforcement and supply in the Salient, but a halt after Broodseinde might have been an alternative. In any event, behind the now slightly elevated British front line lay an area of sodden devastation. The Germans did not attempt a frontal attack on the Ridge in 1918: Plumer had to abandon it when Ypres was threatened from the south in the course of Ludendorff's spring offensive. Haig's motive for continuing the battle did not relate just to this tactical consideration and was obscure. There was a strategical justification, of sorts at least, for Third Ypres in its original conception as a means of cutting Germany's links with the Channel ports, turning her flank and eliminating the U-boat bases. Planning for the great amphibious combined operation was impressive, and Rawlinson was enthusiastic about prospects, but it became clearer and clearer that the battles in the Salient were never going to result in the planned combined operations. Rawlinson repeatedly asked that the landing and coastal assault should proceed independently of the main advance, but Haig, deluded by his persistent belief in imminent German collapse, refused the request, and postponed the landings from date to date, until finally cancelling this great imaginative innovation on 12 October.[18]

Haig thought that continuing the battle was wearing down the Germans. It did fulfil that purpose, in the same way as the continuation of the Somme had done, but at an unreasonable cost, both in morale and in terms of lives. In both years, Haig managed to convince himself that Germany was nearer collapse than was the case, and the true criticism of Haig at Passchendaele is that he allowed himself to be carried away by the prospect of immediate victory, and did not fight a step-by-step battle of attrition, which could have been brought to an end whenever it was no longer justified by numerical results. Rather, he pressed on in expectation of a dramatic victory which was never remotely available. Subsequently he justified the campaign by the support which he was giving to the French. But on 15 December Foch told Edward Spears that he was 'furious with Haig', and that the British campaigns of 1917 had been 'a complete failure'.[19] Foch had never viewed the Flanders campaign with any optimism. 'Who is the fool who wants Haig to go on a ducks' march through the inundations to Ostend and Zeebrugge?'[20] Even at GHQ there had been dissentient voices. Colonel A.W. Rawlins, an artillery adviser, told Haig that if the Third Ypres offensive continued, no artillery would be available for the 1918 spring offensive: the guns would be blown out or worn out. Haig became white with rage: 'Colonel R, leave the room!' Edmonds agreed. 'You go too!'

After the war, when Churchill, in *The World Crisis,* argued that the prolongation of Third Ypres had been a mistake, Haig said that Churchill had failed to understand that in prolonging Third Ypres he was providing essential relief for Pétain. Haig wrote to Charteris in March 1927: 'It is impossible for Winston to know how the possibility of the French Army breaking up in 1917 compelled me to go on *attacking*. It was impossible to change sooner from the Ypres front to Cambrai with Pétain coming to press me not to leave the Germans alone for a week, on account of the *awful* state of the French troops!' Terraine explores this issue in some depth, and concludes, probably correctly, that Haig was probably mixing up Flanders with Arras and Pétain with Nivelle.[21]

That is not to say that Haig did not, in part at least, continue at Passchendaele because of apprehensions, real or nugatory, about the French, just as he had continued at the Somme and at Arras. He fought on the Somme earlier than he would have chosen to, entirely at the instigation of Joffre, aghast at the losses suffered at Verdun. Similarly, Arras was fought at the behest of Nivelle, and was continued in the light of Nivelle's losses on the Aisne. Even if the letter to Charteris, written ten years after the event, refers to Arras rather than Third Ypres, that is no basis for suggesting, as some have done, that Haig was making up an excuse for Third Ypres after the event. The justification for initiating Third Ypres lay in the strategic vision of naval and military operations, supported by amphibious landings on the channel ports, but it was supported also by political considerations. The background is examined in the *Memorandum & Operations on the Western Front 1916–1918* written at Haig's request by his Chiefs of Staff, Lieutenant-General Kiggell and General Lawrence, and deposited in the British Museum to be left unopened until 1940 (in the event unopened until the end of the Second World War). Pétain is recorded as doubting the advisability of a full-scale attack rather than limited, local offensives, but there is no evidence that he was unhappy that Haig did take on the Germans for him. He had been, after all, 'especially desirous that the British should in no way relax their activity, in order to attack and hold the German reserves and prevent them from attacking the French.' When Churchill lunched with Haig at GHQ on 2 June 1917, Haig recorded that he 'urged the necessity of dealing a powerful blow at the present time and . . . I doubted whether our French Allies would quietly wait and suffer for another year.' And that was before, that very evening, he heard from Pétain's Chief of Staff of the mutinies in the French Army. That information was given to him in confidence: he did not pass it on to the Cabinet or even to his staff. Indeed even the French Minister of War was not told at first and the French government was never told of the full extent of the mutinies.

Haig not only thought that the Flanders offensive *would* assist the French: in the event he thought that it *did*. On 1 September 1917 he wrote: 'The result of our pressure on Ypres is shown by the slackening of the German efforts on the Chemin des Dames and the comparatively weak resistance they have made to the French attack at Verdun.

The French Army has consequently had the quiet time desired by General Pétain in which to recover from the Nivelle offensive.' On 19 September: 'The French Army has not only ceased to be able to take the offensive on a large-scale, but according to Pétain's opinions its discipline is so bad that it could not resist a determined German offensive.'

Haig's attitude throughout his time as Commander-in-Chief (indeed even before it) was conditioned by the view that the French needed to be nursed and sustained if they were to remain in the war. Part of the reason for this view lay, no doubt, in a narrow chauvinism, and part in what was regarded as the ineptitude of the French command in the early part of the war. Differing views can be taken of these factors, but the third basis for his scepticism about the French ability to continue to resist lay, quite simply, in the enormous numbers of casualties which the French had suffered, particularly in the early years of the war, casualties far greater than those of the British army. The intelligence that came to Haig told him of the effects of these casualties on morale both within the army and amongst the civilian population of France. The fact that collapse did not follow in the course of the war does not mean that Haig was wrong in feeling that it was close. In 1940 collapse could no longer be avoided.

France's closeness to cracking, at a political and social level, as well as militarily, was not a figment of Haig's imagination. From Paris, Esher reported to Derby on 'the growing reluctance of the French soldier to go over the parapet . . . We have arrived at a psychological moment when discouragement may lead to any sort of acquiescence in any sort of peace rather than continue the war . . . France is very, very tired.' On 24 May 1917 he wrote to Robertson, 'In every quarter, in every town and country, you find symptoms of fatigue, of war-weariness, of discontent . . . [T]hose who have large knowledge and insight into the secret heart of France tell you that the unconscious purpose of the nation is moving away from absolute to qualified victory.' A month later he wrote again to Derby, 'Revolution is never very deep under the surface in France. The crust is very thin just now.'[22]

The political cohesion of France in 1914 was long gone. Laval was urging negotiation. Caillaux of the Radical-Socialist Party was ready for peace. Nivelle's failure did nothing to encourage a nation that had suffered so much from war, or its soldiers, denied leave and demoralised by their sacrifices.

But even if Haig could reasonably convince himself that there were reasons for continuing, in 1916 and again in 1917, was he right to do so? He had little choice at Arras, but in the much more prolonged aftermaths of the Somme and Third Ypres he was wrong. The heavy losses at the end of the Somme campaign were not justified by its results, and the prolongation of Third Ypres, particularly in the face of the appalling weather conditions that were being encountered, was wrong-headed and a repudiation of the bite-and-hold doctrine whose value had by now been well demonstrated. Of course, choosing the moment to close down campaigns such as these is an art rather than a science and without hindsight it is impossible to know that a breakthrough is not round the corner. But in both cases, the consolidation of German defences had been so well established that breakthroughs were not going to happen. In each year, the hope remained that one final push might achieve results that would justify the months of sacrifice, and army commanders in conference with Haig tended to remain optimistic. Even in the last stages of Passchendaele, Plumer and Gough were making encouraging noises. Even without that encouragement, Haig was ready to dream. In 1916 and again in 1917 the underlying reason for unjustified persistence lay in the fact that the cavalier in the man was dominant.

Lloyd George's telegram of 16 October read:

The War Cabinet desire to congratulate you and the troops under your command upon the achievements of the British Armies in Flanders in the great battle which has been raging since July 31st. Starting from positions in which every advantage rested with the enemy and, hampered and delayed from time to time by most unfavourable weather, you and your men have nevertheless continuously driven the enemy back with such skill, courage and pertinacity as have commanded the grateful admiration of the peoples of the British Empire and filled the enemy with alarm. I am personally glad to be the means of transmitting this message to you, and to your gallant troops, and desire to take this opportunity of renewing my assurance of confidence in your leadership and in the devotion of those whom you command.

Haig's comment was, 'This is the first message of congratulation on any operation by the War Cabinet which has reached me since the war began! I wonder why the Prime Minister should have sent this message.' He might well wonder. Two weeks later, Lloyd George moved a resolution of thanks to the armed forces in the House of Commons, in terms which more accurately represented his views of Haig and what Haig was doing in Flanders. Of the campaign he said:

The campaigns of Stonewall Jackson fill us with admiration and wonder. How that man led his troops through the mire and swamps of Virginia! But his troops were never called upon to lie for days and nights in morasses, and then march into battle through an engulfing quagmire, under a hail storm of machine-gun fire. That is what our troops have gone through.

So far as Haig was concerned, the Prime Minister started by saying that it was invidious to single out individuals. He then made a bizarre reference to 'the name, the great name of Kitchener'. Finally, he lumped Haig together with French and Maude, juxtapositions that would afford little delight to Haig: the former his disgraced rival, and the latter a junior commander whose achievements had not been on the Western Front.

The outcome of the Prime Minister's request to Wilson to suggest a new way of winning the war was an acknowledgement that some sort of organisation between the Allies was needed in order to direct the war effort. Haig: 'H. Wilson . . . advises an "inter-allied council" being formed with (presumably) himself as head of the British Staff

Section.' At the Allied conference at Rapallo in November a Supreme War Council was indeed set up. Robertson was expressing Haig's views, as well as his own, when he said that it was clear that the real purpose of British Ministers was 'not so much to provide effective unity of military command as to acquire for themselves a greater control over the military chiefs'.[23] The Supreme War Council never did achieve proper unity of command: that was only done when Foch was given supreme allied command. Foch's appointment, as we shall see, was made on Haig's initiative. At the time of the establishment of the Supreme War Council, Lloyd George said in the House of Commons that he was 'utterly opposed' to the appointment of an allied Commander-in-Chief, as it 'would produce real friction and might create prejudice not merely between the armies but between the nations and governments.' He made another speech at the Council on 11 November. Referring to the 'victories' on the Western Front, he said that 'the appalling casualty list' made him wish that 'it had not been necessary to win so many.' This was a disgraceful public statement, destined to erode public support for the war as well as for the military leadership, and to supply encouragement to Germany. Many of the Cabinet shared Haig's dismay, but 'whatever happens won't make me modify the way in which I carry out my duties here.' Pétain told Haig that since Britain and France were now in his view on terms of equality so far as their armies were concerned, the two of them had to exercise command jointly, with their governments settling any points of disagreement. Haig was against the Council, but Lloyd George told him that the two governments had made their minds up; 'So I said, there is no need to say any more then!' Haig was right: Wilson became the British military representative on the Supreme War Council.

Before the end of the year, after an attack at Lens in August, the second of the two satellite operations ancillary to the Flanders campaign took place, at Cambrai. The attacks on Passchendaele Ridge were in their last throes, troops advancing at times on all fours to avoid the bullets that flew around them, the Royal Munster Fusiliers, weapons unusable in the wet, reduced to pelting the

Germans with handfuls of mud (which were fortunately mistaken for grenades). But already Haig had implicitly given up hope of achieving anything more than a symbolic achievement in Flanders, as he diverted the troops that would have been needed to make it something more. It was to Cambrai that they were sent.

Cambrai was the first tank battle: Britain deployed 476 tanks, and Mark IVs, rather than the earlier Mark Is and Mark IIs. The battle was an initial success, with an advance through two lines of the Hindenburg defences, on a front of six miles. Over 100 guns and 6,000 prisoners were seized and the news was received in Britain with hysterical delight and fulsome press reports. But a ridge overlooking the British left flank was never cleared, and after ten days Germany counter-attacked and recovered most of the British gains on the first day, plus some parts of the British line.

Cambrai was the first modern battle in the First World War. The British Army opened up with its first *predicted* bombardment: no ranging shots, each gun calibrated to take account of its peculiarities and those of different batches of ammunition. Gary Sheffield has pointed out that the approach was no longer that of 'artillery conquers, infantry occupies': the guns were part of an all-arms effort. As in the Second World War, the guns were extensively camouflaged. From the other side, in the German counter-attack, use was made of low-flying aircraft, storm troops and a short bombardment. This was to be the warfare of 1918 and of the Blitzkrieg of 1940. Churchill asked himself the question that anyone who criticises the generalship of the First World War must ask themselves: What else should have been done? The answer he gave was, more battles like Cambrai.[24] Of course, as Churchill knew, Haig was never in a position to launch a series of 400-plus tank battles. What he may have been referring to was the imaginative use of multi-weapon tactics. There *were* many more Cambrais in this sense in 1918. The technology and trained troops to use it had not existed in the early part of the war.

The use of aircraft by this stage in the war was not confined to the Germans. After his failure to use aircraft in the pre-war manoeuvres –

perhaps because of it – Haig had become one of the most enthusiastic supporters of the Royal Flying Corps. The Corps had been created in April 1912 and in August 1914 860 men and sixty-three aeroplanes went to France. When the Royal Air Force was formed out of an amalgamation of the Royal Flying Corps and the Royal Naval Air Squadron on 1 April 1918, it consisted of 291,748 men, with 22,171 aircraft. Aeroplanes had initially been used simply for reconnaissance purposes, but in the course of 1915, air-to-air fighting developed. Major-General Trenchard commanded the RFC from August 1915 onwards, and his policy was to carry the war over the German lines in the air, even if it could not be carried through their lines on the ground. In 1917 air power was deployed for ground attack, as well as air-to-air combat and bombing. Aircraft were integrated as part of the all-arms revolution with artillery and other units, as Haig noted in his *Final Despatch*.

Haig was fully aware of the importance of air power. In 1915, he told his artillery commanders that he was not prepared to tolerate 'early Victorian methods' at the imminent Battle of Neuve Chapelle: he was going to use the air. In his first despatch as Commander-in-Chief, in May 1916, he specifically referred to 'the admirable work' of the Royal Flying Corps in photo-reconnaissance and 'assisting the work of our artillery by registering targets and locating hostile batteries.'

In the course of the war, the role of military aircraft extended to embrace interdiction, close air support, strategic bombing and the aim of achieving air superiority. Haig gave his full support to Trenchard, who wrote that 'Haig made me all I rose to in France.'[25]

As one of those who had advocated its development at an early stage when he was still at the Admiralty, Churchill had a particular affection for the tank, as he was indeed enthusiastic about almost any technological advance. But the tank, even at the peak of its development by the end of the war, was still a very different affair from the weapon that the Germans would use in 1940. Even in the open warfare of the last few months of the war, although tanks were certainly used, they were not a magic solution to the problems of the

Western Front. Cavalry, the derided arm, probably performed a more important role in the battles of 1918 than the tanks. Although horses would ultimately prove to have no place on a modern battlefield, it is facile to argue that Haig and others who thought there was still a role for cavalry in the First World War were wrong. The truth is that until fast and reliable armoured vehicles were available (which they were not even by 1918) there was *no* means of effectively exploiting a rapid breakthrough. Cavalry was as good as anything else that was available. Even before the war, cavalry commanders had been giving thought to the problems they would face on a modern battlefield and had, for instance, been experimenting with radio. Cavalry was now, in reality even if the term was avoided, mounted infantry.

After the initial rejoicings, the setback at Cambrai was received very badly and there were bitter attacks on Haig. Many enquiries were carried out into the handling of the battle and it is fairly clear that Third Army under Byng had not thought through what it was trying to do, other than achieve surprise on the first day. The significance of the ridge had not been apprehended; there was no means of exploiting the tanks' wire cutting and clearing when cavalry could not operate effectively and infantry was exhausted. When mounted troops did try to follow up the initial success they were held up by machine-gun fire from the second German line. Another division had not advanced because of the inadvertent destruction of a bridge by a tank. Haig had lost Plumer and five divisions to Italy, and he undertook Cambrai with inadequate resources, fortified by intelligence from Charteris which conflicted starkly with what the latter was recording in his own diary. In particular he had concealed from Haig the strength of German reinforcements from the Russian Front.

Cambrai was not planned well by Byng, and would have had a better chance of success if it had been fought earlier, as Ellis, in charge of the Tank Corps, had wished, at a time when infantry reserves had been available. But Cambrai was bad for Haig not because the battle was not a victory, but because the public had been told it *was* a victory. *The Times* had printed an edition with the simple headline, 'The Victory', and other papers splashed the news in similar ways. For the first time since the war began, the church bells rang to mark a victory. The bells of St Paul's began to toll and they were followed throughout London and into the country at large.

Now the press as well as the public felt they had been cheated, and Northcliffe led the attack against Haig. Northcliffe had been sent to America by the Prime Minister, probably to keep him out of mischief at home. He had left instructions with his editors to 'back the soldiers' and that they did. When he returned in November 1917 he found himself increasingly disillusioned with the failure of western strategy. He may have thought that the premiership was within his grasp. Neither his ambition nor his potential should be underrated. The power that his papers gave him was immense and talk of him as Prime Minister or dictator was not entirely fanciful. On his return from America, Lloyd George had intended to put him at the head of the new air ministry (thus displacing another press lord, Lord Cowdray, who expected the post). Lloyd George asked Northcliffe whether he would be prepared to join the government. Such was Northcliffe's confidence that he not only said no, but published his letter of refusal in *The Times.* This precipitated Cowdray's resignation from the now obsolescent Air Board. Cowdray was now Lloyd George's enemy, and Lloyd George more than ever Northcliffe's client. Although Haig increasingly came under attack from the Northcliffe press, the strongest criticism was directed against Robertson.

Charteris thought that Northcliffe might have been motivated not only by professional pique, but also personal resentment: 'Northcliffe was here today very strong in his condemnation of the government, much impressed with American methods as opposed to ours, and bubbling over with importance of his own mission and of himself. Unfortunately DH was too preoccupied to respond and Northcliffe was rather wounded in his self esteem.'[26] To those who witnessed the episode it was obvious that Northcliffe's vanity was wounded; and as he left Haig's château Northcliffe remarked that he thought Haig's grasp of affairs was weakening, and that he doubted whether he could continue to support him. Yet only a short time before he had said: 'Tell the Chief that if "George" ventures to do anything against him, I will put him out of office.'[27]

Northcliffe was not the only critic. Robertson wrote a revealing letter to Plumer at this time:

> The Germans have brought down 19 Divisions to the Cambrai front line since Haig attacked and as you know *his troops were pretty well used up in the Ypres salient and therefore he is rather hard put to it to hold his own.* As a matter of fact the incident is not altogether without *value for I think it has taught the people in France that the German still has a good deal of fight in him. The diminution of German morale has been greatly overdone at general headquarters.*

Repington, although a *Times* journalist, refused to allow his copy to be cut to Haig's disadvantage. Throughout the war Haig had regarded Repington with little more than contempt, but the latter now had the courage to resign from Northcliffe's employment and moved to the *Morning Post*, where he defended Haig against the Prime Minister. Another example of Haig's poor judgement of people. Charteris too had underrated Repington in his diary entry of 25 May 1915: 'Repington is a law unto himself, overweeningly conceited, and with a dulled sense of honour.'[28] Northcliffe received a Viscountcy in the New Year's Honours List.

The year was ending dismally. Confidence in Haig had been eroded massively by Flanders and Cambrai, both battles of his choosing, and not dictated by the French. As the year came to a close he knew that both he and Robertson were vulnerable. He had however a welcome domestic interlude, when he returned to London on 28 December. He went to the pantomime at Drury Lane with the children and Lady Haig: 'I think Douglas enjoyed the performance as much as the children.' The King presented him with his field-marshal's baton at Buckingham Palace. It was appropriate, after the pantomime performance, that the cost of the baton had been met by his army commanders, 'the Wicked Barons'. He had a lunch at 10

Downing Street, when the probable duration of the war was discussed. In a moment of levity that sits uneasily with the tragedy of the times, Derby bet Lloyd George 100 cigars to 100 cigarettes that the war would be over by the next New Year. It is interesting that even at this stage Haig's opinion, over the table, was:

> that the war would be over by the autumn because, judging from the internal state of Germany, she could continue no longer. There were only a million men as reserve for the whole of the coming year's fighting, and if these were all used up there would be none left to develop the country afterwards even if Germany won . . . They might, of course, try and break through our defences by sheer pressure of numbers, but such action will be taken as a last possible chance of victory.[29]

One of the conclusions from the series of enquiries that the War Cabinet set in train into Cambrai was that Charteris had been responsible for much of the failure by reason of the faulty intelligence he had supplied. Derby told Haig that the War Cabinet considered Charteris quite unfit for his intelligence post. Haig reassured Charteris and told him that he had relied on sources of information other than the intelligence he had supplied. Even when Kiggell reported that Charteris was extremely unpopular with a wide range of officers, Haig continued to support his protégé. When he did let him go, as he soon had to, his choice of replacement showed equally questionable judgement: Herbert Lawrence (the officer who had resigned from the 17th Lancers when Haig was given its command in 1903). Charteris remained at GHQ as Deputy Inspector-General of Transportation and Haig continued to rely on him. Haig's loyalty to his subordinates and his efforts to retain them can be seen as admirable traits or as misguided stubbornness. He wrote to Derby, 'I cannot agree that Charteris should be made "whipping-boy" for the charge of undue optimism brought against myself . . . If the War Cabinet are not satisfied with the views put forward by me, it is I, and not Charteris, who must answer for those views.' He had told Lloyd

George to his face that if Gough were to be recalled to England, the government must send a specific order to that effect.

Kiggell had not been Haig's first choice as Chief of Staff. He had wanted Butler, but acquiesced in Kiggell's appointment – a poor choice. Kiggell had been a devoted supporter of Haig for a long time and worked hard – indeed too hard – for his Chief, but he had no experience of anything other than staff work and at Third Ypres he had not really understood how bad the conditions were at the front, sometimes tasking troops with objectives that were quite unrealistic. It is said (though the veracity of the story is very doubtful because it came from Edmonds and was told to Liddell Hart: Edmonds can never be regarded as safe, and the anecdotes he shared with Liddell Hart are especially suspect) that when later he did go by car towards the front he burst into tears and said 'Did we really send men to fight in this?' He was told, 'It's worse further in.'

Almost certainly Kiggell never said anything of the sort, unless, just possibly, by way of a rhetorical question. Even if the story is true, it should not be taken quite at face value: Kiggell was under horrible strain and soon afterwards his health broke down and he was sent to Guernsey, when Lawrence ended his short period in intelligence, and replaced Kiggell as Chief of Staff. Lawrence, who had not been ideal at intelligence, proved an excellent Chief of Staff, and he and Haig worked well together for the rest of the war.

Edmonds, telling the story of Kiggell's response to the conditions he saw to Liddell Hart added 'Haig of course knew but did not flinch or care.' He certainly would not have flinched, but equally certainly he did care, and it is necessary to consider Haig's reaction to his men's suffering. It is true that he did not show his emotions, either of happiness or of heartbreak. The culture of his background and the ethos of his class was to maintain an aspect of imperturbability; and he undoubtedly saw it as part of the equipment of a military leader to convey quiet confidence. Even in a social and family setting he deprecated displays of alarm. His whole character was permeated by restraint and self-control. Regrettable though it may have been, any general appointed as a Commander-in-Chief in the 1914–18 war had to look like one. Plumer did not look like one. Charteris described him rather nicely as 'placid and peaceful-looking, rather like an elderly grey-haired Cupid'. If, in those days before the internet, one had sent to Harrods for a Commander-in-Chief, Haig is exactly what would have been sent round. His demeanour had to be as it was. Wellington famously said that now that he was the Duke of Wellington, he had to behave like the Duke of Wellington; Haig only had to be Haig to behave like Haig. Churchill described him 'as a great surgeon before the days of anaesthetics . . . entirely removed in his professional capacity from the agony of the patient . . . he would operate without excitement . . . and if the patient died, he would not reproach himself.' He was a professional, and he would no more have thought of displaying his feelings in a military reverse than a distinguished Queen's Counsel would break down in tears when he lost a case. But he did have feelings. Churchill again:

> [H]e endured it all; and with such impassivity and matter of fact day-to-day routine that I who saw him on plenty of occasions – some of them potentially fatal – doubted whether he was not insensitive and indurated to the torment and drama in the shadow of which he dwelt. But when I saw after the war was over, for the first time, the historic 'Backs to the Wall' document written before sunrise on that fateful April morning in 1918, and that it was no product of some able staff officer in the bureau, but written with his own precise hand, pouring out without a check or correction the pent-up passion of his heart, my vision of the man assumed a new scale and colour. The Furies indeed contended in his soul; and that arena was large enough to contain their strife.[30]

On many occasions he deprecated praise directed at him and would indicate a soldier who had served throughout the war and say that it was men like that soldier who deserved the praise. His expressions on such occasions are so formulaic and hackneyed that they invite sceptical disbelief, but there is no reason to doubt that he meant what he said. He stated that he did not visit wounded troops in hospital or he would have broken down, and he gave a similar reason to his friend Lord Askwith after the war, when Askwith noted that he was not talking to a group of wounded ex-servicemen at a gathering they were attending. But Askwith saw that Haig looked ill at the sight of the men, and his staff had discouraged him from hospital visits when they observed the effect they had on him. Despite their efforts, he *did* continue to visit military hospitals and inspect convalescent soldiers, though on a reduced scale. He was to decline honours until pensions were settled for wounded officers, and he devoted the whole of his life after the war to the cause of the men of the British Legion. He was interested in the backgrounds and circumstances of individual soldiers and had a remarkable memory for them when they recrossed his path. He made the mistake of downplaying his humanity. He wrote to his wife in 1917:

I am very glad to hear from you that those serving under me have an affection for me. As you know, I don't go out of my way to make myself popular, either by doing showy things or by being slack in the matter of discipline. I never hesitate to find fault, but I have myself a tremendous affection for those fine fellows who are ready to give their lives for the Old Country at any moment. I feel quite sad at times when I see them march past me, knowing as I do how many must pay the full penalty before we can have peace.

If he had been more of a showman, less buttoned-up and readier to do 'showy things', he would have been a better commander and would have been better served by history, but that could not be his way.

20

The Enemy in Whitehall

On the interpretation of the events of 1918 a final assessment of Haig's leadership depends. The months until the Armistice divide into two clear parts. In the first part he faced the onslaught of the German spring offensive, displaying strength and resolve in defence. In the second part he was required to recognise the opportunity for moving on to the attack, and then to drive forward a British-led attack, sweeping the Germans back to their own frontier in a war, at last, of open advance.

By 1918 America was in the war and Russia was out. But it was not an equal equation, as Russia went out faster than America came in. On 26 October 1917 Lenin seized power and declared a three-months' armistice. The Russian army immediately melted away: when the armistice ended without signature of a peace treaty and Germany renewed the offensive on 17 February 1918 she was able to advance 150 miles within a week. A peace treaty was rapidly signed at Brest-Litovsk. But even before then Germany had been able to transfer much of her Eastern army to the Western Front (though not as much she could and should have moved). In November 1917 there were 147 German divisions on the Western Front, but by March 1918 192. Effective American deployment was much slower. In April 1917 when America entered the war, its army numbered only a little over 100,000 men: it was the seventeenth army in the world in terms of size. It was self-evident that in terms of both manpower and *matériel* the American contribution to the war would be irresistible, but it was equally clear that time would be needed before the American economy was properly on a war footing and she had trained sufficient troops to make a significant contribution. Intelligence reports confirmed the logic of these facts and indicated that Germany was preparing to make a major offensive on the Western Front early in 1918, before the full effect of America's involvement could be felt. Haig was very well aware of this, and was entirely confident that such an offensive would destroy Germany if it could be resisted. He said that 'If you set the problem to any Staff College student you would get the same answer: "An all-out attack by the Germans must end in ultimate disaster for them." '[1]

Haig asked Charteris, before the latter was deposed by the Prime Minister in December 1917, for two important appreciations, one *A Note on German Intentions* and one *A Note on the Situation from the German Point of View*. Both documents are intelligent and sophisticated and are worth perusal. The first concluded, amongst other things, that Germany would be likely, not later than the beginning of March, to 'deliver such a blow on the Western Front as would force a decisive battle which she could fight to a finish before the American forces could take an active part, i.e. before mid-summer.' The second paper, which considered very fully the German economic position and her internal politics as well as the military situation, was much less clear cut, and logic appeared to suggest either a speedy offensive or a quick peace by negotiation which might avoid an economic war after the peace.

Pétain, from the French perspective, foresaw 200 German divisions on the Western Front, where generally only 100 were needed to hold the line. In Germany, Hindenburg was looking to the arrival of the Americans:

We now had a new enemy, the most powerful in the world, an enemy possessing everything required for hostile operations, reviving the hopes of all our foes and saving them from collapse while preparing mighty forces. It was the United States of

America, and her advent was dangerously near. Would she
appear in time to snatch the victor's laurels from our brows?
That, and that only, was the decisive question.

The result of the Russian collapse was to strengthen the hands of
Hindenburg and Ludendorff, and increase their expansionist influence on the Kaiser. The immediate effect of access to the resources of
eastern Europe (which undermined the effect of the blockade) and the
availability of troops hitherto stationed on the eastern Front, cannot
be overstated, so far as German morale is concerned.

Haig's reading of the situation was not the same as the government's. Lloyd George and Hankey had an important discussion on 15
October 1917 regarding plans for 1918. Three alternative suggestions had been made:

1. To continue Haig's plan of remorselessly hammering the
   enemy.
2. To adopt Pétain's tactics of striking here and striking there,
   always carrying out the first and successful stage of an attack,
   but never carrying it through to a prolonged offensive.
3. To carry out (2) in conjunction with a great offensive
   elsewhere, for instance in Turkey.

Interestingly, the Prime Minister and Hankey agreed that whereas
the French frankly admitted that they had no underlying strategical
idea and indeed that their plans were based on 'the theory that big
operations with strategical objectives were mistaking existing conditions', Haig's operations had objectives which were grounded in
strategical logic. His operations would react 'upon the naval and
aerial situations by ultimately achieving the command of the coast,
and when advanced to a certain point they would threaten the
German lines of communication, and perhaps bring about a great
retirement'. That is an important acknowledgement of the soundness
of Haig's strategy. What Lloyd George was saying was that Haig's
policy was sound and would result in victory, but that for political

reasons he wanted that victory to be won at the cost of American rather than British lives. It was for the politicians to take political decisions; what is important from the military point of view is this vindication of what Haig had been doing in 1917. But Lloyd George's preoccupation was to avoid huge losses in 1918.

> He admitted that a continuance of Haig's attacks might conceivably result in bringing Germany to terms in 1919. But in that case it would be the US who would deal the blow and not we ourselves. If our army was spent in a succession of shattering attacks during 1918, it would, indeed, be in exactly the condition that the French army was in at this moment, with its numbers reduced and its morale weakened. He was particularly anxious to avoid a situation at the end of the war in which our army would no longer be a first class one.[2]

The conclusion of this discussion, which Hankey was asked to communicate to Balfour, Curzon and Milner, was

1. That [Lloyd George's] plan was to make the main attack in 1919, and for the Allies to conserve their strength for this tremendous blow.
2. That it was vital to our national policy that, at the end of the war, our armies should not be exhausted and demoralised.

The attitudes of Lloyd George and the Cabinet throughout most of the remainder of the war were conditioned by the thinking that lay behind this appreciation of events, reinforced by a severe manpower crisis: during the last year of the war the needs of the armies in the field and those of production and transport could no longer be met. The Ministry of National Service produced two figures, based on assumptions of different periods of 'hard fighting' and 'light fighting', which produced respectively three quarters of deficit of manpower supply in the year and one quarter. The War Office did not accept these figures and projected nothing but deficits. It is interesting that there was *décalage* even between the War Office and Haig. The War Office concluded:

> that if large numbers of men are not recruited and sent out at once, Haig's army would not be able to hold the line and that the gunners are so tired that they can scarcely hold the line.
>
> This is inconsistent with Haig's continual reports of bad German morale and that the German divisions had been put through the mill in Flanders and knocked out one by one.[3]

From the outset therefore it was clear that Haig was going to have to fight his corner in 1918 not just against the Germans.

And he had to conduct the fight against the Germans with reduced numbers. Frustrated by Haig's continued independence, Lloyd George sought to limit his freedom of action by withholding manpower. That this was his deliberate policy is not a matter of surmise: a Memorandum written for him by Hankey in April 1917 is quite explicit.

> Although it has never been formulated in the War Cabinet Minutes it is understood that the policy of the Government is first, by keeping the War Office short to compel the soldiers to adopt tactics that will reduce the waste of man-power . . . The War Cabinet, it is understood, intend to force this fact on the Higher Command . . . The Government would also like to see the adoption of reduced numbers of battalions in divisions. Although this would undoubtedly reduce the total numerical strength of the army, it would not reduce the total effective strength in anything like the same proportion.[4]

The plan had been formulated early in 1917, and was implemented a year later. What was happening was disguised somewhat by the fact that the number of divisions was not reduced: the battalions of which they were composed were now nine and not twelve (though Haig would have preferred to see some divisions disbanded rather than break up the cohesion of units that worked well together when brigades were reduced from four battalions to three.[5] The move mirrored a similar change in the German Army; it recognised a compensating increase in the mechanisation of the army, and there *was* a genuine manpower shortage. But the sad fact is that at the end of the day the real motive for a reduction in the strength of a division from 10,000 or 12,000 men to 6,000 was that the civilian and military powers were not able to agree on the war they were fighting.

Haig attended a meeting with the War Cabinet on 7 January when he 'stated that I thought that the coming four months would be the *critical period of the war.* Also that it seemed to me possible that the enemy would attack both the French and ourselves, and that he would hold reserves on hand ready to exploit wherever he might have gained a success.' Robertson says that Haig did not convey at all the impression he intended. He was asked by some members of the Cabinet whether if he were Commander-in-Chief of the German army he would think it worth incurring the losses that an offensive would produce. Here Haig had difficulties. He failed to distinguish effectively between what he himself would do if he were the German Commander-in-Chief, and what he thought the Germans would actually do in practice. He thought that the effect of the German offensive in the spring would be German defeat in the autumn, and he therefore replied that 'If the Germans were wise, they would think twice before making the attempt, because if they failed their position would be critical.' Robertson realised that to the Cabinet Haig appeared to be saying that it was unlikely that an offensive would take place and when he left the meeting he said so to Haig. Haig denied that he had said anything that would bear such an interpretation: his poor powers of oral presentation were to starve him of drafts for many months.[6] A paper Haig had prepared in relation to the need for reinforcements came before the War Cabinet on the following day. Lloyd George threw it aside, saying that it was inconsistent with what the field-marshal had said orally. Haig's official biographer said that he had been tricked into giving the opinion that the Cabinet wanted to hear, but the fault was his own as much as anyone else's.

At the lunch at Downing Street when Derby and Lloyd George bet on the length of the war Haig hardly improved his position:

> I said I thought the war would be over [before the next New Year], because of the internal state of Germany . . . Germany having only one million men as reserves for this year's fighting, I doubted whether they would risk them in an attempt to 'break through.' If the Germans did attack it would be a gambler's throw . . . The Prime Minister by cunning argument tried to get me to commit myself to an opinion that there would be 'no German offensive' that 'the German Army was done', but I refused to agree to his suggestions.

He may not have agreed with Lloyd George's suggestions, but he had done damage enough by saying that if the Germans did attack it would be a gambler's throw. His difficulty was that as a creature of logic, he found it difficult to say that he thought that the Germans *would* attack, when logic showed that such an attack would in all probability be fatal to them.

As we look back now at 1918 we tend to see the German requirement for an immediate offensive (based on the prospect of America's future contribution to the war allied to the present availability of troops from the Eastern Front) as inescapable. At the time it was not so evident. Reinforced by the accession of troops from the east, the Western Front might well have been impenetrable, even with American help, and the resources now open from the huge tracts acquired from Russia could have sustained Germany indefinitely. Lloyd George thought there good reasons for thinking that Germany would not attack in 1918, and even Haig tended to that view from time to time. In February he told H.A.L. Fisher that the Germans had 'nothing to gain by trying the offensive' in 1918.

The lunch in Downing Street had been 'a cheery one', and Haig always found it very difficult to reconcile Lloyd George's personal warmth with what he regarded as his duplicity. The Prime Minister's skill was in understanding, adapting to and manipulating all with whom he came into contact. It was said of him that a room with only Lloyd George in it would be an empty room. He was essentially reactive. He could perceive instantly the arguments that would appeal to his interlocutor and by deploying these arguments in combination with his personal charm he obtained whatever he wanted. Haig succumbed to that charm as much as anyone else. But behind the brilliance, Lloyd George was serious enough, and his aim was to win the war, and win it without the terrible losses which affronted him. There was no personal animus against Haig, but his inventive, imaginative mind was frustrated by Haig's unimaginative logic. Lloyd George was Glendower to Haig's Hotspur. And cheery lunches or no, he continued to look for a quicker, better, more inspired way of waging war.

On 21 January 1918 General Smuts and Hankey visited the Western Front. At the time Haig understood that they were simply visiting different commands to see what their needs were; in reality, they were seeking out an alternative Commander-in-Chief. In an unconscious tribute to Haig, Lloyd George acknowledged in his *Memoirs* that they found no one who would be as good. This is a finding which Haig's detractors have chosen not to address. Lloyd George said, 'It is now easy to say "you ought to have sacked him" . . . Who could we put in his place? It is a sad reflection that not one amongst the visible military leaders would have been any better. There were among them plenty of good soldiers who knew their profession and possessed intelligence up to a point. But Haig was all that and probably better within those limits than any others within sight . . . Had we removed Haig, we might have set up in his place a man who had not his mastery of the profession, and with no other greater gifts to make up for that deficiency.' A remarkable tribute from the man who was Haig's bitterest contemporary critic. Churchill was more generous:

[Haig] had no professional rivals . . . [when appointed as Commander-in-Chief] and none appeared thereafter during the struggle. The realisation of this was a strong prop to

him in the many ordeals, disappointments, and terrible disasters
which he had to face and endure. He might be, he surely was,
unequal to the prodigious scale of events; but no one else was
discerned as his equal or better.[7]

Churchill's even-handedness is appealing: 'Neither Haig's view of
Lloyd George nor Lloyd George's view of Haig is likely to be
accepted by history. They will both be deemed much better men
than they deemed each other.'[8]

There is indeed an element of tragedy in the hostility between
Lloyd George and Haig. Haig had little time for any politicians
(although Charteris could bring him up short on the issue, by
reminding him of Haldane, whom he greatly admired; and he could
tolerate a few others, like Asquith, Milner and Austen Chamberlain,
the last two a significantly bloodless pair). Yet, initially, he had as
much regard for Lloyd George as he had for any. The canker that
destroyed their relationship was that each of them passionately
wanted to win the war and saw the other as an obstacle to that
process. Lloyd George's fertile and nimble imagination could not
accept that there was no better way to win the war than acquiescing
in the terrible carnage of the Western Front. For Haig, the Germans
were on the Western Front and had to be beaten there: if Allied
resources were moved elsewhere, the Germans would destroy the
Franco-British line. Most historians today consider that Haig and the
Westerners were correct. Germany's interior lines of communication
enabled them to throw forces quickly from one front to another, but
an Allied move from the west could not be redressed speedily.

It is not to Lloyd George's discredit that he found the warfare of
attrition intolerable, and even if the war *could* only be won on the
Western Front, that does not mean that Haig was not unimaginative
and unduly sensitive to what he regarded as 'interference' by civilians
in the professional matter of fighting a war. By the time Lloyd
George became Prime Minister there had already been very high
losses and he had no choice about being economical with manpower.
He was far less secure than Churchill in the Second World War: the

Irish National Party and half of his own Liberals did not support him. He depended on the Conservatives, who never wholly trusted him. He had to face a major political challenge in May 1918. His position in relation to Haig and Robertson was particularly invidious, as he had more or less guaranteed their positions to the Conservatives when the coalition was formed, and 'the Prime Minister's self-confidence, although certainly great, was not "unlimited". In particular, it tended to fail him – after Calais – in his dealings with Haig.'[9] A modern war is never going to be 'won' by one man (except Churchill?), but Lloyd George, certainly as much as, probably more than, Haig, was the man who came closest to doing so. As Minister of Munitions he addressed the munitions crisis with vigour, though increasing the volume, rather than the quality of what was available. As Prime Minister he engendered in government and in the conduct of the war an urgency and cohesiveness that had been entirely lacking under Asquith. He did his best to create the machinery of supreme command appropriate to a total war. The structure of government was modernised and streamlined and the resources of the state were directed to the prosecution of the war. Civilians and strangers to government were brought into key posts, bringing with them energy and expertise. Sir Joseph Maclay in shipping and Sir Eric Geddes in transport were examples of these men of 'push and go'.

A glimpse of the chasm between the soldier and the politician is given in Haig's account of his meeting with the new Secretary of State for War, Lord Milner, just before the end of 1917:

> I assured Milner that I as C-in-C in France considered it my duty to assist the Prime Minister to the fullest extent of my power and not to countenance any criticism of the PM's actions. All this I had done and in fact had stopped criticism in the Army. On the other hand LG had warned me at my last meeting in Paris (end of October last) that he was going to 'retaliate on the soldiers' as he put it, because of the attacks made in the Press on him and which he thought were organised by the Military. LG had asked me what my feelings would be 'if

the men were told that the attacks in Flanders were useless loss
of life, and that all the suffering and hardship which they had
endured were unnecessary!' I said such action would be most
unpatriotic, yet the LG Press at once commenced their attack on
me and other Commanders.

Milner admitted this and said he had spoken to LG on the
subject.

Part of the problem lay in the fact that the two men held quite
different views on the proper relationship between the government
and its military advisers. This lack of common ground was well
illustrated in relation to a fairly minor issue in May 1916, when the
War Committee briefly interested itself (though characteristically
failing to follow the matter through) in the question of horses and
their fodder in France. Haig told the War Council, in Lloyd George's
words, 'to mind their own business'. Curzon regarded his letter as
'absolutely astonishing'. What Lloyd George went on to say Haig
would have regarded as constitutionally flawed, but it was not an
unreasonable statement of the realities of modern warfare:

> [Haig] talked about his responsibility – to whom was he
> responsible? He was responsible to the Government, and
> through the Government to Parliament, and through Parlia-
> ment to the people . . . He thought that the documents of the
> Army Council and of Sir D. Haig were most improper . . . they
> could not say 'hands off' to the War Committee, who were the
> real responsible body.[10]

The necessity for doing away with arcane military conceptions, which
elevated senior officers into something akin to a self-regulating
profession instead of the instruments of the civil society was self-
evident to Lloyd George, as it was to Churchill, and he was frustrated
by the failure of the army to accept his views. Robertson's conception
of his role was even more difficult to justify than Haig's. In October
1916 when Lloyd George was canvassing a direction of resources to

Salonika, contrary to the views of the War Committee and the advice of the CIGS, Robertson exploded. He complained that the Secretary of State 'felt it your duty to disagree with this advice and recommended certain action being taken by the Committee with the object of inducing France and Italy to combine with us in sending to Salonika some 8 additional divisions.' Worse, Joffre had been asked for his view 'on certain points on which I had already given my opinion.' He threatened resignation. But he had distorted his constitutional role and importance beyond recognition, as Lloyd George demonstrated in his reply. The Secretary of State said that he had the right to express his own views, rather than simply being 'a dummy or a pure advocate of all opinions expressed by my military advisers.' He ended with amused menace: 'You must not ask me to play the part of a mere dummy. I am not in the least suited for the part.'[11]

The irritation that Haig and Lloyd George felt for the other first blinded each to the other's strengths and as the years passed they came to exaggerate faults both real and imagined. Lloyd George never succeeded in bending Haig to his will or in disposing of him. The army proved more resistant to his wishes than the navy. His resentment was expressed in repeated petty gestures and was finally distilled into the bitter and unjustified assertions in his *Memoirs*. For Haig, Lloyd George was a Bolshevik, intent on destroying army and the state, and overturning the existing social order.

It does not need saying that Lloyd George was not that. Because his performance as a war leader was to be eclipsed by that of Churchill, what deserves remembering is that his commitment to winning the war was total and dynamic. He did not have the organisational gifts of Churchill, he could be inconsistent, his record in relation to agricultural production and food control can be criticised, and even his achievements at Munitions may have been exaggerated. But without his energising contribution to the war effort it is difficult to imagine victory in 1918. His work on the war was continuous, beginning before breakfast and continuing till after dinner (when, unlike Churchill he did switch off – but then he had not the advantage of an afternoon nap). His official papers were placed by his bed overnight and by breakfast they and the whole of the London press had been devoured. Thereafter, at meals and between meals, his visitors were squeezed dry of information that could assist the promotion of the war effort. Social meetings frequently transformed themselves into conferences. Notes were recorded throughout the course of meals. His regime contrasted dramatically with the Edwardian twilight of Asquith's leisured days and brandy-fuelled evenings (though Haig said that 'Squiff', even when 'exhilarated', had a better brain than any of the others), the Cabinet meetings at which he dreamed of Venetia Stanley and the paralysing enmity of hostile members of the coalition. Robert Blake described Asquith's war direction as 'a system of aristocratic anarchy reminiscent rather of government in the 18th century than of the smoothly working machine with which we are familiar today.'[12]

Lloyd George had entered politics with no interest in war, indeed with some sympathy for pacifism, but after 4 August 1914 he made it his business to learn: by visits to the Front, by listening and questioning, and by the application of his powerful intellect. Hankey worked closely with him throughout the war:

> [F]rom the man there emanated an extraordinary sense of power and strength, such as I have never encountered in any other. Hundreds of times I have watched him listening quietly while some seemingly insoluble problem was debated. One view after another would be expressed; one solution after another proposed and rejected. When all had spoken, Lloyd George would often intervene with some novel and ingenious proposal, which his fertile mind had thrown up, and which he would urge with such logic, conviction and conscious power that opposition would cease and his decision would be accepted in silence or with a few muttered words of assent.[13]

Hankey was a little dazzled by proximity to Lloyd George's brilliance, but he was not remotely alone in his admiration of Lloyd

George's gifts. From Haig's perspective, Lloyd George was inherently hostile to the crown, and the King should have been his severest critic. In fact, King George's official biographer says that was not the case. Writing about the critical time when Ludendorff's offensive threatened to break the allied line, Harold Nicolson records:

> During those four months of repeated anxiety the King's resolution was fortified by the indomitable confidence of his Prime Minister. Only those who served with or under Mr. Lloyd George throughout that dire ordeal can rightly appreciate and remember how much the State then owed to his vitality, resource and unflinching moral courage. Others flagged or wavered: Mr. Lloyd George, at the very moment of defeat, remained exuberantly sure.[14]

Beaverbrook, certainly not an unwavering supporter, wrote later:

> The war was over. Lloyd George was now the most powerful man in Europe. His fame would endure for ever. He was admired and praised in all countries. His prestige in the United States was so high that men said that he would be elected as their President if he could run for office there.
>
> He had beaten his German enemies in the war. He had scattered and destroyed his British enemies at the polls in the course of a General Election which disclosed an overwhelming popular judgement in his favour. Hardly any political opponent escaped. They had fallen like autumn leaves.
>
> It is not now possible to realise the immense position of this man Lloyd George. He had risen to such heights that only his contemporaries can understand the pre-eminence he enjoyed.[15]

Austen Chamberlain, in a wildly inaccurate but very understandable prediction, said in 1918 that if Lloyd George chose to do so he could remain Prime Minister for life.

In addition to Haig's professional 'mastery', which he acknowledged, Lloyd George also faced the difficulty that Haig would have been defended by the Conservatives, and indeed by many Liberals as well. Robertson was not so fortunate, and his days were numbered. In December, Esher had written to Haig, telling him that Charteris should have gone earlier than he did and that indeed Haig should not have admitted that he had been at fault in keeping him on. He reports that now 'Robertson is having the wind knocked out of him . . . these fellows will beat him black and blue, until he has not a breath in his body'.[16] Gough, too, was under attack in London. Kiggell had gone, with a kind letter from Haig, written later, in the heat of the events of May 1918:

> My Dear Kigge
> I am delighted to hear that you have accepted the Guernsey Command, but there is to be no idea of 'resigning yourself to the shelf' or any nonsense of that sort. You go to Guernsey to pick up your health after many <u>years</u> of <u>overwork</u>, and when you have had a rest, there will be lots of active work for you in connection with this Great Army. Even if I am moved out of the way, there are <u>many</u> in high places who know your worth and will not fail, I know, to make use of you. So make up your mind to get strong and don't talk rubbish about 'shelves'!!
>
> We have had anxious times here, and you can imagine that your old French friends did not diminish the causes for these feelings.[17]

As early as 1 January Derby told Haig that he had only been able to keep Robertson in place by threatening to resign if he or Haig were removed.

When Hankey, with Smuts, visited Haig on 22 January, Haig made two points to him. First, if the government accepted the French proposal that Britain should take over more of their line, he would resign. Secondly he outlined his extensive defensive policy, which was to consist of a front line, which would be given up if heavily attacked, then a battle zone, which would be close to the front line where there were important tactical points; and then a reserve line. The battle zone was between two and three thousand yards deep and covered the ground that was most favourable to defensive operations. This was a new and effective device, which was to work in the months to come.

The third session of the Supreme War Council opened at Versailles on 30 January. There was a sharp clash between Robertson and Lloyd George, when the former spoke against an attack on Turkey. Lloyd George, who had already received this advice in London, told Robertson that he need not repeat it at Versailles. Hankey, always tending to a Georgian perspective, told Esher that 'the incompatibility of temper between the two men and the ever-recurring quarrels depreciate LG's vitality and governing power'.[18] Various ways of disposing of Robertson, who showed no wish to resign, were canvassed. It was suggested that he should be made Commander-in-Chief in India. Haig argued against this. His argument was pretty feeble: he said that the existing incumbent, General Sir Charles Monro, was doing perfectly well there and should be left alone. Lloyd George then suggested that Wilson (as permanent military representative at the Supreme War Council) should swap places with Robertson or, if Robertson remained as CIGS, he should do so with limited powers. These alternatives were put to Robertson by Balfour. The forms and proprieties of the chain of command and of the links between the civil and military power were matters of excessive sensitivity to Robertson, Haig, and many of the professional soldiers of their generation. Robertson said that if he had merely thought that the permanent military representative had now more powers than the CIGS, he might have been prepared to make the swap. But that was not his point at all: he objected to the whole new system and did not wish to be involved in it. What he wanted was that the Military Member should be subordinate to the CIGS and if that could be arranged, he would either go to Versailles or remain as CIGS. For him and others, the position of the CIGS as a filter between the military and the civil power was a crucial principle. Robertson accordingly fell, and went to the Eastern Command of Home Forces. From the start he had made it clear that he would refuse to limit himself to giving professional advice. He considered that he had a duty to the country that overrode his duty to ministers; and that he was bound to question and remonstrate: the constitutional validity for that proposition must be questionable.

In his autobiography, Robertson was philosophical about the circumstances surrounding his sacking. He enunciated the fairly strict constitutional view he took of his role as CIGS and concluded that:

> It was upon such principles as these that I endeavoured to regulate my attitude. Whether they were right or wrong the reader must judge for himself, but I have no doubt whatever in my own mind that to their cumulative effect may be attributed my removal from the post of CIGS in February 1918, and therefore from the standpoint of personal advantage they were obviously wrong.[19]

Were Wully's arguments sound? His argument was that there had to be a clear chain of command. Foch, France's military representative at the Supreme War Council, was also French Chief of Staff. In the absence of such a combined appointment, Robertson wanted the military representative to be responsible to, and to act on the orders of, the Chief of Staff. It probably was genuinely not a matter of personal ambition: he thought it impossible that the Cabinet could receive advice from two independent military advisers, advice which was already proving to be contradictory in February 1918, when Wilson was saying that the west was in balance, and that the time was right for allied action in the eastern Mediterranean, while Wully took the exactly contrary view. It is interesting that when Henry Wilson takes over as CIGS, he quickly seeks to assert his authority over his successor as military representative, Rawlinson, and when the latter returns to France, makes sure that he is succeeded by the more malleable Major-General the Hon. Sir C. Sackville-West ('Tit-Willow' to Wilson).

On an abstract basis, Robertson's position was correct in theory, but he exaggerated the practical consequences. His successor did not find the arrangement impossible to bend to his requirements, and governments can always look for alternative sources of advice if they wish. Constitutional rules develop and change all the time. The real problem was a personal one which was hindering the conduct of the war, and Wully was an unfortunate and innocent victim of this conflict. A wartime Prime Minister cannot be expected to work with a military adviser whom he does not trust. Churchill disposed of a CIGS who did not have his confidence with little ceremony, but Lloyd George did not have the political strength in 1918 that Churchill did in 1940.

There was a last-minute suggestion that Plumer, rather than Wilson, should be CIGS; but the former, loyal to Robertson and not wanting to be a potential instrument of Haig's deposition, declined. Wilson was appointed CIGS, with Rawlinson as Military Representative until he went to the Western Front to replace Gough.

The whole episode surrounding Robertson's dismissal is rather unappealing. In his *War Memoirs*, Lloyd George said, not without a hint of paranoia, 'We were about to witness a very determined effort – not the first nor the last – made by this [military] party to form a cabal which would overthrow the existing War Cabinet and especially its Chief, and enthrone a Government which would be practically the nominee and menial of this military party.' According to Beaverbrook, Lloyd George believed that Robertson was the leader of the cabal.[20] The political activity was intense. The Opposition was against Robertson's dismissal, and so was the palace. When Bonar Law told the King that he and Lloyd George considered that the war was being mismanaged, Stamfordham reports that 'The King demurred and said that the politicians should leave the conduct of the war to experts.[21] Mr. Bonar Law said that Robertson and the soldiers were all wrong, with the result that we had lost Serbia, Romania and very likely Greece. The King expressed his entire disagreement with these views.' Derby felt that he must resign and the King assured him that he had no alternative. Haig, summoned to London, decided not

to resign. Beaverbrook speculated that Haig's decision might have
been influenced by the King. 'But whatever may have been the
influences prompting Haig, it is sufficient to record that he bowed at
once to the civilian authority. He deserted his friends without an
excuse or apology. He refused Lloyd George's suggestion that
Robertson should be given command of an army in France. Lord
Derby he left stranded like a whale on a sandbank.'[22] Derby now
contacted Bonar Law to say that he wanted to withdraw his
resignation, and Lloyd George agreed, provided he promised not
to resign again. In any event, within the month Derby had gone to
become British Ambassador in Paris.

Haig's decision was straightforward enough. It was his duty to
continue to serve as Commander-in-Chief. Indeed it was his duty
not to resign. But, short of resigning, perhaps even by threatening
to resign, he could have saved Robertson, who had so loyally and so
often supported him. Far from doing that, he put no real obstacles
in the way of Robertson's departure. On 9 February, Haig, on his
way to see Lloyd George, was intercepted by Derby at Victoria
Station, and taken to Downing Street 'by a circuitous route' so that
he could explain the proposal to send Robertson, who 'had lately
become most difficult to deal with and lost his temper quickly' to
Versailles. Haig told Lloyd George that the army 'might be very
shocked' by the appointment of Wilson, but his only and slightly
petty insistence was that orders were only to be given to him by the
Army Council or a field-marshal senior to him. On 11 February,
when Haig saw Robertson at the War Office, he simply told him
that 'it was his duty to go to Versailles or anywhere else if the
government wished it.' Haig went on to the Palace, where he
encouraged the King 'to insist on R going to Versailles'. Even
Charteris commented, 'I think he should have backed up Robertson: it might have helped, and could not have made matters worse.'
Haig wrote to his wife: 'I, like you, am sorry for Robertson, but
then it seems to me (and I can write it to you privately) that he had
not resolutely adhered to the policy of "concentration on the
Western Front" – he has *said* that this is his policy but has

allowed all kinds of resources to be diverted to distant theatres at the bidding of his political masters.' Suspicions he had formed of Robertson at the Boulogne Conference in September, 1917, had continued to rankle. Robertson was suspected of being less than fully committed to the Western Front. Robertson said to Repington that 'he had found that he had more friends that he knew, but fewer on whom he could count than expected.' Churchill summed up the end of Robertson's career, only slightly unfairly:

Sir William Robertson was an outstanding military personality. His vision as a strategist was not profound, but his outlook was clear, well-drilled and practical. During his tenure he had reintroduced orderly methods of dealing with War Office problems, and had revivified the General Staff system. He had no ideas of his own, but a sensible judgement negative in bias. He represented professional formalism expressed in the plainest terms . . . I was glad, as Secretary of State for War, when after the victory he eventually retired from the Army, to submit a recommendation to the King which enabled his long and honourable career from the rank of a private soldier to end with the baton of a Field Marshal.[23]

All who observed the situation regarded the relationship between Lloyd George and Robertson at this stage as unworkable and one or other of them had to go. It could only have been Robertson. Hankey said:

Their friends did all they could to bring them together. At my suggestion a weekly breakfast was instituted. At first it was proposed that I should be present, but I felt that it would be much better for them to be alone. But it did not work. Many years after I learned from Robertson that this was due to the fact that the Prime Minister liked to remain talking for a long time after his breakfast, a habit to which Robertson's digestive apparatus could not adapt itself!'[24]

It is a little alarming that the effectiveness of the high command of the war was imperilled by Robertson's gastro-colic reflex.

In Wilson, the Cabinet obtained a very different military adviser, unwilling, according to Lloyd George, to take the responsibility of making a final decision, but infinitely more subtle in negotiation and far better adapted to dealing with politicians as well as the military. He had his own ways of doing things. On 11 January 1918, for instance, Wilson wrote to Haig saying that the British line should be extended between the River Ailette and the Soissons–Laon Road, a decision that had been reached by the combination of mathematical calculations and a 'war game' in which half of his staff played the parts of Germans, putting their hats on the wrong way round to look like the enemy. (The result of the game was to predict two alternative areas for the German attack and the time of the attack: all the predictions were wrong.) Haig did not have much patience with Wilson's methods: 'the whole position would be laughable if it were not so serious', and he had been unhappy about his appointment. He continued to regard Wilson with great suspicion, saying that he did not have the confidence of the army, which to an extent was probably true. But in the event, despite occasional disagreement on policies, the pair of them worked remarkably well, so much so that Lloyd George was soon complaining that one was Scotch, one was Irish, but they were both whiskies.

So, without the confidence of the Cabinet, publicly attacked by the Prime Minister, deprived of his closest advisers and starved of drafts, Haig prepared for the German spring onslaught. To appreciate his achievement in 1918, it is important to keep in mind that he had predicted the onslaught, and when it would take place. He had also calculated that the German attack would result in a breakthrough. In due course he was to conduct the defence against the German assaults with masterly skill, check them and then to be the first person to discern the moment at which the process of repulsing the German attacks had so weakened the enemy that it was time to go on to the offensive. He, more than any other person, then directed the Great Allied offensive, the campaign of the Hundred Days, to achieve victory in November.

But now, by mid March, the bulk of the 192 German divisions on the Western Front was opposite the British armies between the Rivers Scarpe and Oise. The total number of Allied divisions was 165. Of the German divisions, eighty were in reserve. The British and French had no shared reserve. It was indeed on the issue of the creation of an Allied reserve that the War Council negotiations in which Robertson had been involved had become most difficult. The General Allied Reserve was to be run by an Executive Committee of the Supreme War Council, which would determine when and where the reserve was to be used. It would then hand over troops to the appropriate Commander-in-Chief. Foch was to be a member of the Committee and also its President, and Haig was hostile to the proposal on the grounds that 'to some extent it makes Foch a "generalissimo".' Robertson, equally, had been against the proposal. He could see 'much to be said for a generalissimo', but there was the constitutional objection to placing troops under 'a foreign general with no responsibility to the parliament of the country to which they belonged'. None of the allied ministers except Clemenceau was favourable to the idea of appointing a generalissimo and it was clear from the attitude of the ministers that there was no general in whom they had any degree of confidence.[25]

Haig was not greatly concerned about the objections to the scheme, either in principle or in constitutional theory: he did however see practical objections. One was that the reserve could not be created without taking them from somewhere else, and neither he nor Pétain was prepared to yield any more troops. The General Reserve never came into being. Secondly, he asked the following question 'by what channel am I to receive orders from [the Supreme War Council]? . . . Finally, LG said "orders would be issued by the members of the body nominated by the Supreme Council." I asked that the exact position might be made clear to me in writing'.

KAISERSCHLACHT. THE DOULLENS CONFERENCE AND UNIFIED COMMAND. HAIG TAKES THE INITIATIVE

Ludendorff's spring offensive, the *Kaiserschlacht*, began on 21 March. The offensive consisted of five separate thrusts, *Michael* from 21 March to 5 April, *Georgette* from 9 to 11 April, *Blücher-Yorck* on 27 May, *Gneisenau* on 9 June, and *Marne-Rheims* from 15 to 17 July. *Michael* consisted of an assault by seventy-six German divisions on twenty-eight British divisions on a front between Douai in the north and the Somme on the south. The launching of the *Kaiserschlacht* was of course expected. Churchill was with Haig immediately before it began. 'The Commander-in-Chief viewed the coming shock with an anxious but resolute eye. He dwelt with insistence on the undue strain put upon his armies by the arrangement made by the War Cabinet with the French, in which he had reluctantly acquiesced.'

On the eve of the attack Haig wrote to his wife about the birth of their son, saying that he would have to postpone coming over to see her and their boy. If he came at once 'it might lead to talk . . . not that my actual presence in France at the moment of attack is necessary because all Reserves and other questions . . . have been settled . . . Everyone is in good spirits and only anxious that the enemy should attack.'

Churchill now had two days to spare before a conference at St Omer and decided to visit his old division, the 9th, now commanded by General Tudor, a friend of his since his subaltern days in India.

Before I went to bed in the ruins of Nurlu, Tudor said to me: 'It is certainly coming now. Trench raids this evening have identified no less than eight enemy battalions on a single half-mile of the front.' The night was quiet except for a rumble of artillery fire, mostly distant, and the thudding explosions of occasional aeroplane raids. I woke up in a complete silence at a few minutes past four and lay musing. Suddenly, after what seemed about half an hour, the silence was broken by six or seven very loud and very heavy explosions several miles away. I thought they were our 12-inch guns, but they were probably mines. And then, exactly as a pianist runs his hands across the keyboard from treble to bass, there rose in less than one minute the most tremendous cannonade I shall ever hear . . . Among the bursting shells there rose at intervals, but almost continually, the much larger flames of exploding magazines. The weight and intensity of the bombardment surpassed anything which anyone had ever known before.[1]

The attack began under the cover of morning mist, suffused by chlorine and phosgene and a lachrymatory chemical which forced the British soldiers to take off their gas respirators. After five hours German storm troopers had moved forward rapidly, and by the evening of 21 March great gains had been made along a front of nineteen miles. Artillery pieces were lost, some 7,000 British soldiers were killed, 10,000 wounded and some 21,000 taken prisoner. The best of Ludendorff's troops were in battalions of what were already called storm troops. They were given no limits to their objectives. 'Infantry which looks to the right or left,' they were told, 'soon comes to a stop. Touch with the enemy is the desideratum; a uniform advance must in no case be demanded. The fastest, not the slowest, must set the pace.' There was a cost: German dead and wounded exceeded the British. The fact, however, was that there had been a collapse in command and morale on the British side, and the Germans sought to capitalise on this in the succeeding days. What Ludendorff was aiming at was to separate the British from the French and force the British back towards the Channel ports, very much as happened in the Second World War.

Haig had been aware of the weakness of Fifth Army's front. Gough, who commanded the Army and who defended the southern part of the 'Michael' front, had drawn attention to the problem; Byng and Third Army were to his left, on the north.

Haig has been criticised for not strengthening Gough's Army, but he was not unduly concerned by the course of events in the first two days of Michael. In fact he did obtain one extra division for Gough (and not at Gough's request). It was Gough's choice to man his advanced areas in strength, losing many men on the first day of the attack, rather than concentrating strength in his rearward areas. Additionally, Haig required to hold the left of his front (towards Plumer) more strongly than the right, because Plumer was closer to the critical Channel ports and was also further from potential French support. Haig's resources were stretched extremely thinly. As he told the King when he came out to France towards the end of March, he now had 100,000 fewer infantry than the year before, against three times as many Germans and on a front extended by one fifth. On 23 March he became aware that some of Gough's troops had been forced behind the Somme. Fifth Army had not been adopting the tactics of fighting retreat, and they had no rear defensive positions on which to fall back.

Fifth Army defences were based on the battle zone concept. Within the battle zone a series of strongly held positions was established, supporting one another with flanking fire. What happened was that if the enemy succeeded in breaking through the front line they would be funnelled into exposed 'boxes' in which they could be raked from defended positions. Gough's problem was first that he lacked the manpower to establish the defensive positions adequately and secondly that they proved ineffective in the heavy fog of 21 March. The troops within the 'bird cages' felt themselves vulnerable to concentrated fire from the enemy. Lack of time and lack of manpower meant that the rear zones, behind the battle zones, had not been completed and consequently the forward zones, which were meant to be held only lightly, contained too much, about a third, of the infantry. If Haig was at fault, it was in failing to be sure that Gough had understood and implemented his thinking.

Haig now moved to advanced headquarters at Dury. He was assured of support by Pétain, who undertook to assist him in the Somme Valley with two French armies. Pétain was also asked for support at Amiens. Haig was well aware of the importance of keeping the two armies together: 'If . . . the enemy comes in between us, then probably the British will be rounded up and driven into the sea!' Pétain promised help but said that he expected an attack in Champagne. Returning from meeting Pétain on 23 March, Haig reported to the army commanders 'that it was essential that we keep in touch with the French.'[2] Pétain, for his part, was perfectly cordial at this time, when his front remained tranquil.

But the next day, 24 March, the German attack was stronger than ever, and now it was threatening Pétain as well as Haig. Late that night, at 11 p.m. there was a further conference at Pétain's head-quarters. Precisely what happened at this critical meeting, which brought about the establishment of a Supreme Command, will never be known. Pétain said at the time and again much later that he had held out his hand to Haig, that he had warned Haig of the dangers of separation, and that he feared he had not convinced him.[3]

According to Haig – in the revised diaries – the position was reversed: it was he who recognised the need for keeping in touch, and Pétain did not intend to do so. Haig was alarmed: '[Keeping] in touch with the British Army is no longer the basic principle of French strategy. In my opinion, our armies' existence in France depends on keeping the British and French Armies united.' According-ing to the typescript diary Pétain told Haig that he had directed Fayolle, the General commanding the French Armies on the British right, to fall back to Beauvais in order to cover Paris. Haig said that he asked Pétain if he meant to abandon his right flank. Pétain, said Haig, assented: his orders were 'to cover Paris at all costs'.

At 9 p.m. that evening he had indeed ordered that the crucial objective (*'avant tout'*) was to keep the French armies together;

distinctly subordinate to that (*'ensuite, si possible'*) was that contact with the British was to be maintained. That was not however an order to fall back. On the contrary he did say that Fayolle (who commanded all the allied forces, south of the Somme, including most of Gough's army) would be given 'all his available troops'. Later it would become an accepted truth that Fayolle had been ordered to fall back to cover Paris; in fact all Fayolle was to do – and even then only if necessary – was to retire to the line of the river Avre, to the north-east of Montdidier. This did not involve withdrawing behind Amiens. There is no mention in Pétain's orders of falling back on Beauvais.

What Pétain said to induce Haig's pessimism is not clear. There was only one interpreter present. A French witness later thought what might have been said, and misunderstood by the British, was that Pétain would be forced to fall back *if* Haig persisted in his move to the north. That is conjecture: what is clear is that Pétain, although in pessimistic mood, did not in fact give the order that he is alleged to have given.

But Haig – in the later version of the diary – certainly came to believe that Pétain was about to fall back. According to the type-script diary, as soon as he got back to his headquarters at three o'clock on the morning of 25 March, he had a telegram sent to Wilson, asking him to come over at once with Derby, 'to arrange that General Foch or some other determined general, who would fight, should be given supreme control of the operations in France.' On the basis of this narrative, Pétain was displaying the same crisis in nerve that was to occur in the following war and it was clear to Haig that he must be overruled. This could only be done by a Supreme Commander.

What actually happened? In relation to this issue there is a serious, the only serious, discrepancy between the manuscript and the typescript diaries. In the manuscript diary for 23 March there is a record of harmony between Haig and Pétain on the vital issue of keeping together: 'Pétain is most anxious to do all he can to support me.' And again on 24 March, despite the German successes of the day, at the 11 p.m. meeting Pétain is again broadly reassuring: he expected an attack in Champagne, 'but would give Fayolle (on Haig's right) all his available troops . . .' The manuscript diary entry for the day concludes without reference to the dramatic events recorded in the typescript version, which contains an additional paragraph setting out Haig's new account. It begins, 'Pétain struck me as very much upset, almost unbalanced and most anxious.' It ends, 'So I hurried back to my headquarters at Beaurepaire Château to report the serious change in *French strategy* to the CIGS and Secretary of State for War, and ask them to come to France.' It was to be very important to Haig that he be remembered for taking the initiative in recognising the need for the appointment of a Supreme Commander.[4]

No telegram requesting the presence of the CIGS and the Secretary of State to appoint a Supreme Commander can be traced. What was sent, and put in train the historic conference of 26 March, was a telegram timed 6.35 p.m. on 24 March. It merely expressed the 'hope that General Wilson will come to France to confer with me regarding situation.'[5] The typescript, but not the manuscript, diary claims the much more forward-looking vision, with its reference to 'General Foch or some other determined general, who would fight.'

Wilson's diary is to be read with the usual caution, but certainly casts doubt on the typescript account of events. Wilson heard at 5 p.m. on 24 March that Combles and Péronne had fallen and that the British troops were falling back on the Ancre. He telephoned Lloyd George, who was in the country, and summoned him to London. Half an hour later Foch was on the telephone to discuss the situation. Wilson: '[W]e are of one mind that someone must catch a hold or we are beaten. I said I would come over and see him'. An hour and a half later, Wilson was at Downing Street ('There is no mistaking the gravity of the situation, nor the entirely inadequate measures taken by Haig and Pétain in their mutual plans for assistance'), when a telephone call from Haig was received (presumably the oral content of the telegram of 6.35 p.m., which confirmed a telephone transmission timed at 6 p.m.). 'So I go by special 6.50 am tomorrow and then Destroyer.'

The record of the whole event is shrouded in doubt, not least because Haig had a significant hand in the account which Edmonds gave in the Official History. While the typescript diary does not *contradict* the manuscript version, it adds so much to it as to sound like the account of a different meeting. Pétain's account, perhaps for political reasons, received little subsequent support from the French. Haig's account is supported by the official British records, which is hardly surprising as they largely relied on what he had said. On the whole, the narrative in the revised diaries must be regarded as suspect.

Did Haig 'panic'[6] at some stage after he had written his diary, and then seek to justify what he had done by the addition to the record? There certainly is evidence of very serious worry, if not panic. Haig had awaited the German attack with confidence, almost impatience. As a result of German deceptive manoeuvres he had initially mis-understood the nature of the attack of 21 March, and he underrated its seriousness for forty-eight hours. He *may* have envisaged falling back on the Channel ports,[7] in which case it would have been he and not Pétain who would have broken contact. On 26 March Clem-enceau took the possibility seriously enough to raise it with Haig.

It would scarcely be surprising if Haig had been rattled. He cannot have felt personally secure. He is said to have told Gough in April that he expected to be dismissed within the week, and as late as June Rawlinson feared that Haig would go.[8] There was certainly an element of panic in London, where the War Cabinet on 23 March discussed falling back on the Channel ports, and evacuating the troops to England. Against this sort of backround Haig issued an Order of the Day on 24 March to be read out to all ranks. It is very different in tone from the famous 'Backs to the Wall' Order of the Day of 11 April, and is not now remembered. It has a hesitant note: 'We are again at a crisis in the war . . . I feel that everyone in the Army, fully realising how much depends on the exertions and steadfastness of each one of us, will do his utmost to prevent the enemy from attaining his object.'

Haig's concerns were very comprehensible. What is remarkable however is how very little he wavered. His instructions from Kitchener were as contradictory in relation to the Channel ports as they were in other respects. The safety of the Channel would depend not on occupying the coast, but on overthrowing Germany, and any retiral should be directed to that end and in conjunction with France, rather than to securing the Channel. But at the same time, if compelled to do so or if it were strategically necessary to do so, in cooperation with France, '[t]he requisite steps required to meet this contingency should . . . receive due attention.' Haig, unlike French in 1914, held to the view that remaining united with his allies was even more important than securing the Channel ports, important though that was. As early as 1915 he had written: 'It is obvious that the occupation of the Channel Ports cannot decide the issue of the War. On the other hand, if the enemy inflicts a decisive defeat on the French, it only remains for us to get what terms we can from Germany!' And by 1918, half the army's supplies came by way of Rouen, Le Havre and Dieppe, ports south of the Somme. Further, Colonel Payot, the French head of supply, guaranteed, if Calais and Boulogne fell, 'to feed the British Army from our southern bases and the other French ports.'

The panic argument is unconvincing, and similarly it would be simplistic to think that Haig's rewriting was a crude falsification of the record. Scope for misunderstanding may lie in the degree of emphasis given to hypotheses. Even if Pétain never intended to lose touch, he could not have excluded the possibility. Paris was to be covered 'at all costs'. Thus in the added, typescript, paragraph he is recorded as having said that he had ordered Fayolle to fall back to the south-west to Beauvais '*in the event of*' a further German advance. Thus again, when asked by Haig if he intended to abandon his right flank, '[h]e nodded assent', and added, 'It is the only thing possible, *if* the Enemy compels the Allies to fall back still further.' Haig and Lawrence may just have failed to understand what Pétain was saying; at any rate, Haig believed in what he wanted history to record, even if his recall was flawed by a desire to be seen to have been the one who directed these momentous events.

When Wilson arrived at Montreuil at 11.30 a.m. on 25 March, he scarcely rose to the level of events. He could not help pointing out that it was Haig, with Clemenceau's support, who had killed off Wilson's plan for a general reserve, and that he had warned Haig that without a general reserve he would be 'living on the charity of Pétain'. Wilson claimed that he now found Haig 'cowed', and that the initiative in calling for Foch to coordinate the action of both C-in-Cs lay with himself. 'DH said he would prefer Pétain but I simply brushed this to one side. Pétain is a very inferior person and is now proving all I have said against him. In the end DH agreed.' It is scarcely credible that Haig would have had much enthusiasm for Pétain's appointment. He was much more sympathetic to Foch; and the whole point of a Supreme Commander was to have someone who would take a wider view than Pétain was disposed to do. When Milner arrived in France that same day he was unable immediately to meet Haig and Wilson, but did have discussions with, amongst others, both Pétain and Foch. He found the latter much more conscious of the risk of separation of the two nations at Amiens. Unlike Pétain he considered this such a formidable danger that he was prepared to take risks to safeguard the position, the risks consisting essentially in deploying forces which Pétain wanted to retain against the possibility of the German attacks which he expected in Champagne.

How 'cowed' was Haig? He certainly would not have felt uplifted by Wilson's triumphant self-congratulation, but there was a little more to it than that. No-one else records him as going through a defeatist phase, but the confusion of the record over these days, the subsequent rewriting of the diary and the *ex post facto* stressing of his role in the appointment of Foch all underline the fact that for the moment he was tending to feel his way. That is hardly surprising. He was tired, baffled by events that had not developed as he had expected, and he was having to adjust to a new settlement, profoundly at odds with his conservative inclinations. After all he had said about the impossibility of British armies fighting under a French general, after all he had said indeed on the subject of French generals *per se*, after Calais, he was now faced with the fact that the continued British contribution to the alliance could only exist under a French

Supreme Commander. It was not what the British army was used to. It was not Wellington's way.

A historic series of three conferences took place in Doullens on 26 March. The setting, as well as the momentous issues at stake, made Doullens exceptional. No other conference throughout the war took place so close to the front line. Shells were falling nearby and troops fresh from the battle marched through the town. The first conference was a meeting of army commanders at 11 a.m. At 11.40 Milner and Wilson joined for the second conference, effectively a briefing for Milner, to whom full powers had been given by Derby. Haig quickly disposed of Clemenceau's fear that he was preparing to fall back on the Channel ports. The vital main conference began at 12 noon. Foch said that the armies must fight in front of Amiens; there was no question of any withdrawal at all. Haig, according to his own account, said: 'If General Foch will consent to give me his advice, I will gladly follow it.' After some discussion in corners, Clemenceau produced a draft agreement which would give to Foch 'the co-ordination of the action of the British and French armies in front of Amiens.' It may have been Haig, as he claimed, who saw that this subordinated Foch to Pétain – and indeed to Haig himself. At any rate, on someone's initiative the draft was amended to give Foch the responsibility of coordinating the action of *all* the allied armies *on the Western Front*. The amendment was critical. The neutralisation of Pétain was essential. His defeatism was dangerous. Even at the conference he told Clemenceau, 'The Germans will beat the English in the open field, after which they will beat us too.'

By the end of the conference Foch had in reality become Supreme Commander (though the title only followed some time later). Much of how that came about remains shrouded in doubt. The records of the Doullens conference, and particularly of the meetings between Haig and Pétain that led up to it, are scanty, and in the lack of other materials were largely supplied by Haig. Haig's role in convening the conference to secure Foch's appointment is based on the evidence of his own amended diary. It is not even clear what happened at Doullens itself, and who was responsible for what. Haig (in this instance in the manuscript diary) claimed the initiative for the changes to the draft Agreement, but his account conflicts with those of Milner and the French Loucheur. Edmonds had difficulties with the discrepancies, but after trying to reconcile them (ten years after the events), he fell back on an account that was largely inspired by Haig. Montgomery-Massingberd who may have drawn up the official record of the conference (though even that is not certain) was asked by Edmonds for his memories of what happened, and his reply is indicative of the realities of a critical wartime conference, taking place as history was being made. Most of the proceedings were in French, 'spoken fast', his time was taken up in trying 'to keep the hang of all that went on,' the conference broke up into small groups of people talking simultaneously. 'What you claim for D.H. may be true, but I cannot confirm from what I actually heard or saw . . . In my experience it is very hard to say who was the real originator of a proposal such as this. If you could really trace it out, you would probably find it was someone quite different . . . as the result of the obvious impossibility of any other course of action.'[9] In my opinion Haig almost certainly did everything at Doullens that he claimed to do, but the matter will never be free from doubt.

What is free from doubt is the enormous importance Haig gave to establishing his account as the historical record. It mattered hugely to him. The extensive emendations to his diary were all directed to showing that it was he who had recognised the need for Foch as Supreme Commander and that equally it was he who had secured the appointment. He even lobbied Foch on the point (and it is interesting that Foch, present at Doullens and with a pretty real interest in the events, did not know that it was Haig who had been responsible for his prestigious command). In 1919 Foch wrote to Lloyd George, saying that the appointment had been made on his (Lloyd George's) initiative. No, said Haig in a letter to Foch, 'I claim for myself that honour . . . I personally pressed for this . . . I think I can fairly claim that the *initiative* in this matter was mine! It was a privilege the credit for which I cannot abandon to anyone.' Foch had earlier written that the appointment had originated with the 'British Government'; now he accepted Haig's claim, which duly found its way into the Marshal's *Mémoires*.[10]

The reason for Haig's concern was that he wanted nothing to diminish what he saw as an outstandingly British achievement. He considered that the French armies had unwisely dissipated their strength in the early part of the war, and that thereafter French morale always remained dangerously close to cracking. It was Britain in 1916 and 1917 that kept the Allied cause going and that in 1918 played the key part in winning a dramatic and unparalleled series of victories that brought the war to a successful conclusion. Even before the end of the war, Lloyd George deliberately sought to minimise Haig's achievements – and thus Britain's – by elevating Foch's contibution. Haig did not want that. The record had to reveal that the appointment of a Supreme Commander was not imposed on him, but was of his devising.

The setting of this momentous conference has been preserved more or less unchanged. In an ante-room to the Council Chamber of the Mairie, Haig's chair still sits at the end of the table. A painting and a stained-glass window represent the scene on 26 March 1918. They reveal nothing of the turmoil of events.

The reaction of the parties varied: immediately afterwards Haig looked ten years younger. Pétain was a man who had lost his nerve. Clemenceau, who did not like Foch, patted him on the head, called him 'un bon garçon', and told him sourly: 'Well you've got the job you so much wanted.' Foch replied: 'A fine gift; you give me a lost battle and tell me to win it.'

On the face of it, Haig had got exactly what he had not wanted at Calais: but there were practical differences. The situation was desperate; Amiens had to be defended; Pétain had to be overruled. (But Pétain was still in place, not humiliated, and continuing to demonstrate his philosophy of launching, winnable, nibbling attacks. At the end of the war his standing remained high, both with the French people in general and amongst his colleagues.) There was also an important difference in principle. Haig was not fighting under the direction of a French general, but under the direction of an

Allied Commander-in-Chief (who happened to be French), who would give orders to both French and British generals. The appointment of Foch was an expedient of the times. His role was very much a personal one, an arbitrator to whom Haig could appeal. He had no proper staff, nor did he work closely with the Supreme War Council.

Haig's stock had not been improved by the events of the German March onslaught. Wilson reports a War Cabinet Meeting on 4 April, when Smuts said that Haig had proved completely unfit as Commander-in-Chief. There was talk of various possible successors. Wilson himself argued against removing Haig, saying that the government would not find anyone to fight a defensive battle better than Haig, and the time to remove him was after the German attack had concluded.[11] When the worst of the attack was over, he did once, and once only, suggest that Haig might be replaced by Plumer. This was no stab in the back: he told Haig exactly what advice he had given the government, and apart from that one suggestion, he defended Haig not only at home, but also against the French – to the extent of coming close to alienating his close friend, Foch. A couple of days later Haig, conscious of his at least nominal responsibility for a major reverse, wrote to Derby:

> It is the duty of everyone to do his utmost in his own particular line to help the State to weather the storm. Personally, I have a clear conscience, and feel that I have done the best with the means at my disposal and am prepared to continue on here as long as the government wish me to do so. But, as I have said more than once to you and others of the government, the moment they feel that they would prefer someone else to command in France, I am prepared to place my resignation in your hands. The needs of the State . . . must take first place, and the interests of individuals must be ignored. So do not consider me.

When the letter was discussed by the War Cabinet on 8 April, Lloyd George asked Wilson if he did not think that Haig should be taken at his word.

Consideration had been given to falling back behind the line of the Somme, and, while that had not been acted on, the possibility of a withdrawal in that direction in the face of attack was not eliminated. 'It may well be desirable to fall back to rearward defences of Péronne and the Somme', but Gough was to protect Péronne and the Somme itself. Derby wrote to Haig, stressing that he would be delighted to see Gough degummed: 'I will do my best to see that the man you send home is not left on the rocks.' But Haig, despite taking the trouble to inspect Gough's front carefully, concluded that he was doing all that he could do with a front without defences which he had inherited from the French. The shortage of manpower meant that the back lines were still not in place.

Gough did not last. The feeling within government against him was too strong to be resisted, although it can be argued that he had done about as well as he could, with limited resources. Haig's choice of him for command at Third Ypres was much more questionable. Gough's thrusting, slapdash methods were much less appropriate than Plumer's abilities. 'Officers who served under him formed the opinion that lives were lost in the battles he organised because he failed to co-ordinate artillery support with infantry assaults, failed to limit his objectives to attainable ends, failed to curtail operations that had patently failed and failed to meet [Plumer's] standards of administrative efficiency.'[12] The dismissal was carried out fairly clumsily. Gough was told that Rawlinson would supersede him before an order to this effect from the War Cabinet had been received. When the order did arrive, Haig recommended not Rawlinson but Cavan, from Italy, as a replacement. In the meantime Gough continued to command Fifth Army. When Haig told Gough of his dismissal, he made it clear that the order came not from him but from Derby. He reassured him: 'You will have every chance to defend yourself, Hubert. There will be a court of enquiry.' In the event there was not. In June Haig wrote to Lady Haig: 'As regards Gough, I am sorry that he is talking stupidly . . . I am doing all I can to help him, but, as a matter of fact, some orders he issued and some things he did were stupid –

and anything in the nature of an enquiry would not do him any good.' He wrote to Gough on 6 July:

My dear Hubert

I . . . am sorry that I have not been able to reply to [your letter of June 21] before now as we have been having rather busy times here . . .

I strongly recommend you to remain quiet and not stir up an agitation, because, even though an officer has right on his side, it does not mean in the least that he will get what he wants. The Government has a perfect right to send any one of us away at a moment's notice without giving us any reason beyond saying that they are not satisfied with us . . . I regard the conduct of the Government towards you in that light . . .

During the winter I was on several occasions cross-questioned as to your military qualities, and, as I told you, always replied that I was thoroughly satisfied. The failure of the Fifth Army to hold its position of 21 March, even though there are many good reasons why it was forced back, has furnished the Government with a reason for ordering me to send you home. That being the case, I strongly recommend you to remain quiet until more history is made and the events of 21 March and following days have faded somewhat from the memory of the people at home. Then, I hope, there may be a chance of getting you back to some active appointment.

With every good wish and hoping it won't be long before we are soldiering again together.

Haig said later that he had not supported Gough to the point of being prepared to resign because 'I was conceited enough to think that the Army could not spare me.' In fact, Gough's career was far from over: after the war Lloyd George found military employment for him. The two became quite close, and Lloyd George speaks favourably of Gough in the *War Memoirs*. Gough died in 1963, aged ninety-three.

The next part of the German onslaught was a fierce attack much further north, near Ypres, where Generals Horne and Plumer were attacked in the area where Britain could not afford to give ground and where First and Second Armies had been depleted when reinforcements had been moved south. Foch, faced by demands from Haig for reserves, and pleas from Pétain, who wanted to hold on to all he had, kept his nerve, but responded with niggardly generosity. For the most part he made no promises that he did not and could not implement. Haig never despaired, but equally he did not lose sight of what he had to do: 'The most important thing is to keep connection with the French . . . I must also cover Calais and Boulogne.' He sent to Foch to urge that the French should come to his assistance. 'General Foch replied that the British forces must hold on where they stood and that he could not guarantee any more reinforcements being sent north beyond the divisions already ordered.'

Thus Haig came on 11 April to draft the Order of the Day, which so moved people at the time (but civilians much more than soldiers) and which, along with Nelson's signal at Trafalgar, has become part of the lore of military history:

To all Ranks of the British Forces in France

Three weeks ago today the Enemy began his terrific attacks against us on a 50-mile front. His objects are to separate us from the French, to take the Channel ports and destroy the British Army.

In spite of throwing already 106 divisions into the battle and enduring the most reckless sacrifice of human life, he has as yet made little progress towards his goals.

We owe this to the determined fighting and self-sacrifice of our troops. Words fail me to express the admiration which I feel for the splendid resistance offered by all ranks of our Army under the most trying circumstances.

Many amongst us now are tired. To those I would say that victory will belong to the side which holds out longest. The French Army is moving rapidly and in great force to our support.

There is no other course open to us but to fight it out! Every position must be held to the last man: there must be no retirement. With our backs to the wall, and believing in the justice of our cause, each one of us must fight on to the end. The safety of our homes and the freedom of mankind alike depend on the conduct of each one of us at this critical moment.

D. Haig, F.M.

Charteris regretted that the Order had been issued. He thought that it was unnecessary and that it might give heart to the Germans, but Haig had judged the situation to be critical, and the Order did have an inspiring effect on many who read it. He drafted it himself, in his usual neat, meticulous handwriting, with only three corrections. Churchill's subsequent comments on the Order have already been noted. Ever susceptible to the power of language, even at the time he was strongly affected by what Haig had written, and sent a telegram to him on 12 April: 'I cannot resist sending you a message of sympathy and sincere admiration for the magnificent defence which you are making day after day and of profound confidence in the result'.[13] If there is doubt that Haig was a man of suppressed feelings and emotion and even poetry, the Order should dispel such doubt.

Ludendorff was deploying new tactics learned on the Eastern front: Blitzkrieg tactics involving small groups of multi-armed troops supported by sophisticated artillery methods. 'Strategic victory follows tactical success.' Again: 'I forbid myself to use the words *strategy*. We chop a hole. The rest follows. We did it that way in Russia'. Machine-gun reconnoitring units were in the front line, seeking out vulnerable enemy positions to which they called up fire using signal flares.

By the end of April the German advance had been brought to a stop, but at the cost of substantial losses, both in terms of men and in terms of ground. The first three waves, *Michael*, *Georgette* and *Blücher-Yorck*, had in forty days resulted in British casualties of 236,300, of which over 70,000 were prisoners. France had lost over 90,000 men. German losses were slightly higher that the combined losses of the allies. On the ground, the Germans had made significant advances in the north in the area between Ypres and Béthune held by Second and

First Armies. To the north and south of that stretch there had not been any change in the line, but further to the south, from Douai to the Somme, there had been a big push through the areas held by Third and particularly Fifth Army, with a bulge that threatened Compiègne, and thus ultimately Paris. Indeed on 30 March Paris had been bombarded to such an extent that Mary Borden, Edward Spears' fiancée, spent the morning of this, her wedding day, lying flat in the bath, hoping to avoid disfigurement.[14]

After *Georgette*, Ludendorff had effectively rejected bite-and-hold, and when his infiltrating storm troops had run too far ahead of his guns, gains could not be consolidated and forward movement slowed down. German casualties, too, were immense. Tim Travers and others have argued that the Germans defeated themselves in 1918. That is not the case, but their tactics were flawed by the lack of means of consolidating their fast advances.

Haig now recognised Germany's predicament, and sought to capitalise on it. In the darkest days of *Michael* he had been unperturbed, and these days were indeed dark. There is a suggestion of poor morale in Fifth Army, when on 21 March amongst 38,000 casualties 21,000 were taken prisoner. This was something approaching a huge mass surrender. Five hundred guns were lost. These hints of an army on the verge of collapse threatened a rout as well as the separation which Haig feared of the French and British armies. Duncan gives two interesting pictures of Haig at this time:

It was on the morning of Sunday, March 24th 1918, three days after the opening of the terrific German offensive designed to smash the Allied line and so end the war. I scarcely expected that in such a situation he would feel free to attend worship as usual, travelling from his château some miles away to our little church on the ramparts of Montreuil. But a few minutes before 9.30 his car appeared; and as he approached to where I awaited him I noted that there was no smile on his face this morning, only a look of calm resolution. He shook hands with me, but said nothing; and so, scarcely knowing what I said, I haltingly expressed the hope that things were not too bad. I did not know that it was a strict rule with the Chief that, when he was on his way to church, none of those who accompanied him, or whom he met, should utter a word in his presence about the war. And so, when he replied tersely that they would never be too bad, I took this to be in part no doubt a gentle rebuke, but in part also an expression of his own calm assurance. It was a solemn moment; and then, as one who understood something of what it all meant for him, I stumbled on and said: 'No! You who were through Mons and Ypres in the first year will never think anything too bad after that.' At once he followed up with a statement which lifted the whole conversation on to a higher level; and I recall how I stood transfixed as he uttered it, for I had never before heard him use language that was even remotely like this. 'This,' he said, 'is what you read to us from Second Chronicles: "Be not afraid nor dismayed by reason of this great multitude; for the battle is not yours, but God's." ' (II Chronicles XX 15.) And having said that he passed at once into the church.[15]

Three weeks later, after the 'Backs to the Wall' Order, when Haig had been unable to attend church, Duncan wrote to him with his good wishes and a blessing. Although he said he needed no reply, the following day he received a note, written in Haig's hand:

> Tuesday, April 16th 1918
>
> My Dear Duncan,
> One line to thank you most truly for your letter. I am very grateful for your thinking of me at this time, and I *know* I am sustained in my efforts by that Great Unseen Power, otherwise I could not be standing the strain as I am doing.
> Yours most truly,
> D. Haig
>
> I missed my Sunday morning greatly. But it could not be helped.

Churchill had been with Haig as *Michael* was awaited. When he reviewed this phase of the war in *The World Crisis*, he made the 'provisional judgement' that

if Haig had not consumed his armies at Passchendaele, or if at least he had been content to stop that offensive in September, he would have commanded . . . sufficient reserves on March 21st to enable him to sustain the threatened front. But for the horror which Passchendaele inspired in the minds of the Prime Minister and the War Cabinet, he would no doubt have been supplied with very much larger reinforcements. If, notwithstanding Passchendaele, the War Cabinet had reinforced him as they should have done, the front could still have been held on March 21st. The responsibility for the causes which led to the British inadequacy of numbers is shared between General Headquarters and the War Cabinet . . . In view however of the preponderance of military influence in time of war, and the serious dangers of the collision between the 'soldiers' and the politicians, a very considerable burden must be borne by the British Headquarters.'[16]

All the same:

for all the criticisms I have made and all the convictions I held about the Somme and Passchendaele, my heart went out to the Commander-in-Chief as he bore the trial with superb and invincible determination.[17]

Esher was equally impressed by Haig's bearing:

DH is behaving wonderfully. His coolness and detachment of mind under all forms of provocation are admirable, but they are only what I always knew were the qualities he would display. He trained himself in early days in self-control as part of a soldier's equipment.[18]

This was Haig at his finest, sublimely professional, effectively commanding his armies in the face of the fiercest of onslaughts, keeping his nerve so well that he could be thinking not just of controlling the retreat, but also of seeking out the moment for moving on to the offensive.

The offensive action that Haig was now planning had its origins in a meeting with Foch on 16 May, when the Generalissimo said that he wished to entrust a major project to Haig if the Germans did not attack within the next few weeks. The following day, Haig asked Rawlinson to consult with General Debeney, who commanded French First Army on Rawlinson's right, and study an attack eastwards in combination with the French. Rawlinson, who had been elsewhere, came back to command on the Western Front in 1918, apparently refreshed and invigorated and soon to distinguish himself as he had never done in the earlier stages of the war. He, like Haig and some others, recognised that the opportunity for a move to the offensive was now possible and in a paper in June 1918 he urged the use of:

all possible mechanical devices in order to increase the offensive power in other divisions. The only two directions which such developments can be reasonably expected are (1) the increase in machine guns, Lewis guns and automatic rifles, and (2) the increase of numbers and functions of tanks.[19]

In the interim, there were particularly savage attacks on the French front from Ludendorff. As a result Foch asked for the return of the French troops which had reinforced the British front. Haig protested to Foch, with copies to the War Office, and another allied crisis of command ensued, although a minor one compared to Doullens. The Doullens formula had been expanded after just a week, at Beauvais, to give Foch authority over the 'strategic direction of military operations,' with the National Commanders-in-Chief responsible for the 'tactical employment of their forces'.

After just another ten days, a further twitch to the control of the allied war effort was needed and Foch was now appointed quite simply Commander-in-Chief of the Allied Armies in France. At a meeting on 7 June, which involved Milner, Wilson, Haig, Foch and Clemenceau, Haig said that the telegram he had copied to London was intended to indicate that circumstances were close which might compel him to appeal to the British Cabinet in terms of the Beauvais Agreement of 3 April, as the order he expected from Foch, requiring a transfer of French troops from the British sector, would imperil the British Army in France. Haig was unhappy with the new reality: 'The effect of the Beauvais Agreement is now becoming clear in practice. This effect I had realised from the beginning, namely that the responsibility for the safety of the British Army in France could no longer rest with me because the "Generalissimo" can do what *he* thinks right with *my* troops.' But beyond the face-saving concession from Clemenceau that orders from Foch moving French or other units in Haig's area should go through his hands first, plus an encouragement to Haig and Foch to meet more frequently, Haig had to accept what it meant to be under an allied Commander-in-Chief. He resolved to ask the government to modify in writing his responsibility for the safety of British troops.

When the move from the defensive to the offensive was foreshadowed at the meeting between Haig and Foch on 16 May, Foch had in mind a preponderantly French project, in view of the state of the British forces. His plans were contingent on the enemy's not launching a big attack within the succeeding weeks. In the event attacks did take place on the Aisne and the Matz, and the allied offensive was delayed. France, rather than Britain, was now bearing the brunt of the German offensive, and her military vitality was sapped to an extent from which she had not recuperated by the end of the war. In the meantime the British Army recovered its strength for a more active role than it could have played in May. By the middle of July Haig sensed that the opportunity for a major offensive might be close.

The strain on the relationship between Haig and Foch increased as the Germans continued to press the French, and pushed their bulge

towards Paris. In the face of this, and expecting a further attack in
Champagne, Foch ordered four British divisions to move east. Haig
was on leave in London and in his absence Lawrence, the Chief of
Staff, courageously sent two, though delaying dispatch of the
remaining two. On his return to France, Haig arranged to meet
Foch. Before he could do so he received a message from Wilson,
pretty well telling him not to send further troops: the War Cabinet
would 'rely on the exercise of your judgement, under the Beauvais
Agreement, as to the security of the British Front after the removal of
these troops.' Haig wryly noted that he was being told 'to use my
judgement' in relation to orders from the Supreme Commander,
whereas at the 7 June conference he had been directed to obey all his
orders, notifying the War Cabinet if he took exception to any of
them. 'This is a case of "heads you win and tails I lose". If things go
well, the government would take credit to themselves and the
Generalissimo; if badly, the Field-Marshal will be blamed!' Hankey
was sent out to ask Haig if he wanted to appeal to his government, as
he was entitled to do in terms of the Doullens Agreement. Haig
declined, bravely ignoring the broad hint that the War Cabinet was
giving him. He met Foch, explained his fears of a renewed German
attack on the Lys, but accepted his assurance that the British
divisions would be returned at once in the case of necessity. He
agreed to send the outstanding two divisions without delay.

Haig's judgement that the tide was on the turn was sound: the
French attack which Foch entrusted to General Mangin in the south
went well, and meanwhile British counter-attacks in the Somme area
under Monash and the Australians were encouraging.

THE HUNDRED DAYS.
'THERE NEVER HAS BEEN SUCH A VICTORY'

We are now moving into the final section of the Great War: the battles of the Hundred Days, one of the great feats of British arms. It was indeed primarily a British achievement. During the Hundred Days Britain took 188,700 prisoners and captured 2,840 guns. France took 139,000 prisoners and seized 1,880 guns, the Americans 44,142 and 1,481, the Belgians 14,500 and 414. With an army smaller than that of France, Britain took 49 per cent of all prisoners captured by the Allies, and 43 per cent of all guns.

The victory was Britain's, and it is by far the greatest victory that Britain has ever won. But it is a victory of which most people are unaware, and Haig is not remembered as the man who delivered it. Foch acknowledged the achievement: 'Never at any time in history have the British Army achieved greater results in an attack than in this unbroken offensive.' Moreover, although Foch remained Commander-in-Chief, in many ways the direction of the campaign was Haig's, and the initiative for it lay in his recognition that there was a key change: Ludendorff's offensive had exhausted the German army. The tone of his diaries becomes confident and upbeat and on 20 July he played a game of golf at Le Touquet, the first time he had permitted himself a visit to the pleasure resort, despite its proximity to his headquarters. He had prepared for an attack by Prince Rupprecht, but when it did not materialise he was ready to deploy Rawlinson's Fourth Army east of Amiens, with diversionary operations by Byng and Horne. Haig advised Foch of his plans, rather than the other way round. But Foch was fully committed to the idea of the offensive and placed Debeney's French First Army directly under Haig.

When Haig meets his army commanders on 29 July, his remarks indicate clearly that he has sensed a different character to the war: 'Army Commanders must do their utmost to get troops out of the influence of trench methods. We are all agreed on the need for the training of Battalion Commanders, who in their turn must train their company and platoon commanders. This is really a platoon commander's war.' That remark shows just how far the nature of the war had changed from 1915 and 1916. What is called 'the learning curve', the amalgam of various trends in new tactical thinking, had come together to favour the intelligent use of small, multi-skilled units, relying far less on the rifle than before, adapting their movements to the terrain in which they found themselves, and exercising individual initiative. It has been said that now, in the Hundred Days, 'British tactics had effectively reached a pitch that would scarcely be surpassed for at least 30 years thereafter'.[1] The sheer professionalism of the army in at least the second half of the war will surprise those who still have a stereotype picture of long rows of men advancing in extended line into machine-gun fire and barbed wire, on the orders of boneheaded ninnies with red tabs. Preparation and rehearsal were meticulous and took place in full-scale training areas behind the lines. Security was strictly enforced, camouflage was used and misleading diversionary attacks took place in other areas. To many, all of this will savour much more of the Second, rather than the First, World War.

The use of the extended line (in as far as it ever really did exist) and rifle-dominated infantry advance had been greatly reduced with developments in artillery control and the introduction of the creeping barrage. Infantry units now relied less on the rifle: infantry was part of an all-arms cooperation, and its own armoury included mortars (which from 1918 were available at battalion level, rather than being retained at brigade headquarters), Lewis guns operated as co-ordinated tactical weapons (and with the Vickers machine-gun now in the hands of the machine-gun corps), trench mortars, hand grenades and rifle grenades. As early as 1916 manual SS143 advocated tactics at platoon level with a Lewis and rifle grenade section to pin down the enemy while a rifle section led a frontal attack supported by a further hand grenade section as 'moppers-uppers'. 'In essence this brought together a miniature version of all the functions of infantry, artillery and the machine-gun corps. Furthermore, since smoke and thermal grenades would also be carried, it even included an element of chemical warfare. It was a formula that would continue to be taught in the British Army, with only relatively minor modifications, for over half a century thereafter.'[2] As advocated by General Maxse, who attempted to coordinate the training through the Inspectors of Training, a battalion with each of its sixteen platoons under the command and training of a leader who remained with that unit was to be the model that dominated infantry tactics in the Second World War. Indeed platoon and sectional tactics changed little until the extensive mechanisation of the 1970s. The machine-gun corps for some time by now had been using their Vickers guns to create a massive hail of bullets over the heads of the advancing infantry in order to neutralise the enemy's rear areas. Thirty Vickers guns could direct something like a million rounds in this way. Despite concerns amongst infantry about 'drop shorts', Vickers gun barrages were used extensively in the Hundred Days, sometimes as many as a hundred guns firing together.

As early as June 1915, the Army Council authorised the formation in each battalion of a hand grenade detachment of one officer, two NCOs and fifty-six other ranks as what became called 'bombers'.[3]

The Lewis gun, which could be carried by just one man, was initially distributed in late 1915, in the ratio of eight guns per battalion. A further eight were allocated in the spring of 1916, so that by the Somme each platoon had its own gun. Trench mortars, originally called bomb-guns, or trench howitzers, developed through the Stokes mortar. The first safe grenade, depending on timing and not percussion, appeared in May 1915, in the shape of the Mills bomb. Later it was designated the No.36 grenade, and it was still in use in the 1970s.

The scale of the army which used these weapons must be kept in mind. At Staff College right up to the outbreak of the war, no thought had been given to handling anything beyond the six-division Expeditionary Force, and in August 1914 the Expeditionary Force consisted of just four divisions of infantry and one of cavalry, organised in two corps. By 1918 there were nineteen corps, sixteen British, one Australian, one Canadian and one Portuguese, in five armies, making fifty-one infantry divisions and three cavalry divisions: 118 brigades as opposed to twenty-two in 1914. In addition to these conventional corps, there was the new tank corps, machine gun corps and the expanded RAF.[4]

In 1918 five army commanders were in the age group fifty-three to sixty-one and the average age of a British corps commander was just fifty-four. At divisional level, commanders were mostly in their late forties and one (Jackson) had started the war as a captain and was still only thirty-nine. Brigadiers, as would be expected, were even younger, and battalions were frequently commanded by men in their twenties or thirties, a good decade younger than they would formerly have been.

As is now sometimes grudgingly acknowledged, the generals did not have the cushy time in their safe billets which was an essential part of 1960s prejudice. Four lieutenant-generals, twelve major-generals and eighty-one brigadier-generals died or were killed in the course of the war and 146 were wounded or taken prisoner. These figures are far higher than in the Second World War, and indeed prompt the question of whether the First World War generals were not rather too dare-devil and inclined to take risks: it is not really part of a general's job to get himself killed. At Loos, a third of the divisional commanders were killed and GHQ required to order senior officers not to become personally involved. The culture of the value of courage in the professional army had to be controlled.

When Haig took over from French, the expeditionary force totalled 600,000 men. By 1918 it contained 1,800,000 men. Its thirty miles of front in December 1915 had expanded by February 1918 to 123 miles. This was the largest army that Britain had ever put into the field, and Haig was responsible for commanding, training, feeding and managing this vast operation.

As Commander-in-Chief he had to play a role which had never existed before, administering the vast resources that made up and supported his armies in France. It was one of his great achievements that he was able to adapt to a changed situation and to responsibilities that in 1914, or even 1916, were quite beyond the bounds of imagination. That is not to say that things could not have been arranged better. Haig could have fulfilled the role of a theatre commander with Plumer, say, as an operational commander. Haig's relationship with his army commanders was not that of Eisenhower and his commanders. Haig gave general directions and not orders. His disapproval came to consist of a process of slow disillusionment. His principle was to leave much to 'the man on the spot', which was a practice appropriate to earlier wars. The principle never excluded him from interfering in 'grand tactics', and it was compromised by the fact that the inexperience of his commanders meant that he had no choice but to be involved in their plans for a considerable time. He may have extended that involvement longer than he needed, but at least by the second half of the Hundred Days he felt able to control his commanders with a loose rein. By that stage they could be allowed more or less unrestricted discretion, and when that was possible they – and GHQ – operated best.

What is really remarkable and what is possibly Haig's greatest achievement is that he was able to take control of this huge expanded force, create a system of decentralised and specialised administration (frequently against the trend of traditional military thought) and run this vast machine as an efficient engine of war.

The Staff College had closed at the outbreak of the war, but soon staff schools were established in France at Hesdin and in the UK to secure a uniformity of approach. In April 1916 Army Council Instruction 786 required all staff to be psc (to have passed the Staff College), to have held already a staff appointment, to have completed a staff course with an army in the field or to have been recommended as a result of a staff school course. Army Council Instruction 1128 scaled down these requirements. The shortage of staff officers, which was a big problem in the early years of the war, became less serious as the years passed, and a large body of planners was gradually developed.

The need for specialists was not met solely from the ranks of the military. Lloyd George, as Minister for Munitions, was instrumental in addressing the transport problems in France, and Haig was ready to accept help. In 1916 a commission visited the Western Front under Sir Eric Geddes, in peacetime the Deputy General Manager of the North Eastern Railway. Geddes was described by Lloyd George as 'one of the most remarkable products of the Great War'. He came from a solidly professional, middle-class family and attended a series of public schools from most of which he was successively expelled. Thereafter he worked as a labourer and in other ill-paid employments in the United States and subsequently created the myth that he had pulled himself up from the humblest of backgrounds. After just two years in America, he returned to the United Kingdom and to the sort of career that might have been expected for someone of his background. Then in the course of work with the British Railway Company in India he came into contact with, and greatly impressed, Kitchener. By the outbreak of war he was a highly successful executive in a railway company that was, for its time, outstandingly conscious of the role of efficient, modern management. He first crossed the path of Lloyd George when the latter became Minister of Munitions and appointed him Director-General of Munitions Supply. When Lloyd George moved to the War Office, he asked Geddes if he 'would come and put transport right in France?' Geddes went with him, and became Director-General of Military Railways. On the very next day, Haig was so impressed by Geddes that he asked to have him at his headquarters as Director-General of Transportation. Geddes combined the two posts and was given the rank of Major-General. His base at GHQ, known as Geddesburg, was resented by traditionalist army officers.

After Geddes left France, Lloyd George, now Prime Minister, appointed him Controller of the Navy with responsibility for Admiralty dock facilities and shipyards. In this role he was given the rank of Vice-Admiral and he was thus the only man, other than members of the Royal Family, to hold simultaneously the ranks of Admiral and General. His stature and the professional resentment he attracted are both reflected in an 'Action This Day' note from Churchill to the War Office in 1941: 'If you do not give me your very best man and one thoroughly capable of doing the work, I will look for a civilian of the Eric Geddes type, and have him invested with the necessary military rank.' Geddes looked at transport in France in its entirety – not separately at the road, rail and canal elements as the army was inclined to do. Haig agreed to nearly all of his proposals. For technical reasons the linkage of the French railway system to the front area worked badly, and additionally the Allies suffered from the lack of the internal rail communications that enabled Germany to swing her manpower from one front to the other. Geddes established a light rail network to deliver supplies from the conventional railheads to the front. In 1918, thanks to Geddes, Haig was able easily to vary his objectives and switch attacks. Haig was making a radical departure in appointing civilians such as Geddes to important posts in the military world. Traditionally the army used soldiers and only soldiers. He faced much opposition when he diluted the military with civilians – and in senior appointments.

There is a good deal of criticism apparently being made at the appointment of a civilian like Geddes to an important post on the Headquarters of an Army in the Field. These critics seem to fail to realise the size of this Army, and the amount of work which the Army requires of a civilian nature. The working of the railways, the upkeep of the roads, even the baking of bread and a thousand other industries go on in peace as well as war. So with the whole nation at war, our object should be to employ men on the same work in war as they are accustomed to in peace. Acting on this principle, I have got Geddes at the head of all the railways and transportation, with the best practical civil and military engineers under him. At the head of road directorate is Mr. Maybury, head of the Road Board in England. The docks, canals and inland water transport are being managed in the same way, i.e. by men of practical experience. To put soldiers who have no practical experience of these matters in such positions, merely because they are generals and colonels, must result in utter failure.

Such sentiments seem now no more than commonsense: in 1916 they were revolutionary.

What Geddes did for the railways, Maybury did for roads. Again he did it with much imported civilian assistance, quarry managers and quarrymen from England. The five quarries near Boulogne that supplied the British armies had been producing 47,000 tons of stone per month when Maybury took them over in December 1916. By August 1917 they were producing 126,132 tons a month, with a projected annual production of nearly two million tons. Haig took a keen, personal interest in all this, noting the technical aspects of the exercise, the use of air compressors and stone breakers. He also noted with irritation the price demanded by the French for the stone – 'and it all goes back on to *French* roads!!'

Geddes' work is just one example of the huge logistical exercise in which Haig, in the absence of a Theatre Commander, had to be involved. Correlli Barnett has illustrated the size of the province that Haig commanded:

For a start, we are talking about a total ration strength by late 1918 of nearly 3 million men and half a million animals. In other words, the British military presence in France was the equivalent of a conurbation six times more populous than the Birmingham of the time, and only a third less populous than London, then the largest city in Europe. To feed these huge numbers required every month some 32,000 tons of meat, 44,000 tons of bread, over 14,000 tons of forage and 13 million gallons of POL (petrol, oil, lubricant). When I say 'the equivalent of a major conurbation', I mean: complete with elaborate infrastructure and transport systems, plus comprehensive medical facilities. But I also mean, on top of all that, the purely *military* supplies, depot and services needed to keep a great army in the field, and, what is more, an army on the offensive every year.[5]

In the area of artillery the advances in the course of the war were dramatic. In 1914 most artillery shelling was directed at visible targets. The theory of aiming at unseen targets based on their position on the map was understood, but was difficult to apply in practice without the most accurate of maps. By degrees it proved possible to make this essential advance. First detailed geographical surveys were carried out, and later the enemy positions were precisely identified from the air. At the start of the war straight barrages moved over the battlefield at intervals that bore no relation to objectives. That was replaced by the 'lifting barrage', which moved from target line to target line. In 1916 and 1917 the creeping barrage was introduced, which took account of the fact that some enemy positions could not be identified in advance. There were problems with 'shortfalls' and with the psychological difficulty of inducing the advancing infantry to be as close behind the falling shells as could be: ideally only twenty metres back, although in practice usually fifty. In the early days of the creeping barrage, there were accordingly dangerous disjunctions between the rate of advance set by the guns and the rate of advance of the troops on the ground. This led to friendly fire or, alternatively, to a useless gap between the position of the barrage and the position of the infantry. The problem was imperfectly addressed by having long pauses when the stalled troops were sitting targets for enemy fire and, in the absence of effective radio communication, was never entirely resolved: the best that could be done was to set the speed of the barrage to suit the nature of the terrain that was to be crossed. In ordinary conditions, the infantry's rate of advance was 100 metres in three to four minutes, but in the mud that was so often a feature of the Western Front the rate of advance could be half that, or even slower. As the creeping barrage was increasingly adopted, the enemy response was defensive artillery fire, to which the answer proved to be counter-battery procedures. A whole range of technical procedures was used to identify the precise location of enemy batteries. Equally, scientific advances were used to avoid revealing the position of the British artillery batteries. The biggest advance was the move from using sighting shots to pre-calibration, on a complex equation that took account of the particular batch of shells and their physical character-istics and external factors such as atmospheric conditions. The result was that a gun could open accurately on to its target without any preliminary sighting shots. Together, these changes in artillery involved abandonment of the indiscriminate destruction of 1916 which hindered the progress of the advancing troops, in favour of a more selective neutralisation. Very soon after Third Ypres, this technique of eliminating specific targets, whether artillery or pockets of infantry, was being used to increase mobility.

In the advances of 1918 the new philosophy was fully applied: minimal preliminary bombardments, sometimes none at all, move-ment of batteries at night, concealment of ammunition dumps, accurate predicted fire.[6]

Many of the technical advances that were made by the army in the course of the war originated not at headquarters level or even at army level. The use, for instance, of high explosive rather than shrapnel was a device pioneered by the 9th (Scottish) Division on the Somme. High explosive kept defenders' heads down, and, in conjunction with the No.106 Fuse, which detonated on contact with the ground (unlike the earlier shells whose fuses detonated far below the ground, creating craters), it destroyed wire effectively. Haig was very approv-ing of this new tool, which assisted the advances at Amiens and Albert. 'Sound ranging, using microphones to provide data from which the position of enemy batteries could be established, made it possible to eliminate enemy artillery scientifically. The first sound range section was commanded by the Nobel Prize winner, Sir

Lawrence Bragg.'[7] Ninth (Scottish) Division were also responsible for the use of smoke shells within the creeping barrage.

Haig himself was not a specialist, but he reminds one of Churchill in the avidity with which he seized on new technology which could be applied towards winning the war. Once enthralled by a new idea, as he easily was, he pressed and pushed to make sure that it was developed. His personal intervention in relation to technological advances can be seen in securing the development of the Royal Flying Corps, gas, the Lewis machine-gun, the Mills grenade, trench mortars and tanks.[8] He has even been described as a 'gadget freak'.

J.M. Bourne summarises very well the revolution over which Haig presided:

In August 1914 the British soldier might have passed for a gamekeeper in his soft cap, puttees and pack. He walked into battle. He was armed with little more than a rifle and bayonet. For support he could call only on the shrapnel-firing field guns of the Royal Artillery. His commanders were often elderly and unfit, with little relevant pre-war experience of any level of command above the battalion. By September 1918 he was dressed like an industrial worker in a safety helmet, with a respirator protecting him against gas close to hand. He was just as likely to be armed with a Lewis gun, grenade or rifle grenade as a simple rifle. He was trucked into battle. His appearance on the battlefield was preceded by a deception campaign based on sophisticated signals intelligence. He was supported by an high explosive artillery barrage of crushing density, by tanks, armoured cars, machine-guns, smoke and gas. Enemy guns were identified and attacked using leading-edge technologies of sound-ranging and flash-spotting, in which specially-recruited scientists played a key role.[9]

On 5 August Haig told Rawlinson that his plans for the forthcoming battle were not ambitious enough, being predicated on taking the former Amiens defence line and stopping there. What Haig wanted was a rapid advance, and a push beyond the defence line, with cavalry prepared to push through and whippet tanks to be available 'for pursuit and to reap the fruits if we succeed'. The enemy was not now in a heavily defended position, and Haig was at last able to contemplate the sort of fluid war which had been planned in 1914 but had come to an end with the end of that year. The army that Rawlinson commanded, Fifth Army now reconstituted as Fourth Army, was different from those of previous years. Apart from the scaled-down size of the battalion, he had 534 tanks, including 324 of the latest Mark Vs, and 96 whippets, the fastest tanks available. He also had 800 aircraft.

A huge attack took place on 8 August, in conditions of great secrecy, protected by deceptive ruses and despite an attack on 6 August on III Corps. The Australians and the Canadians were prominent in the attack. By now Haig recognised the value of the Dominion troops. He had regarded them with scepticism earlier in the war, but now they were present in significant numbers, conspicuously well trained in the new methods of warfare, and fresh and with better morale than some of the British units that had borne the brunt of fighting since the outset.

The battle that was fought on 8 August was different from anything since 1914. There was no preliminary bombardment. Indeed the insistence on secrecy was absolute and was enforced by the most stringent orders. Information was limited in the most amazing ways. At first only corps commanders knew what was happening. Divisional commanders were allowed to share the secret on 30 July, but officers as high as brigadiers were kept in the dark until the last minute. Deceptive ruses were also employed.

In addition to the tanks there were three divisions of cavalry. Horses were being used again on the battlefield. Predictably, the horses outpaced the tanks and operated on their own, albeit incurring heavy losses where they met German machine-gun positions.

Most of the fighting was over by 1.30 p.m. Infantry had advanced well – so well that they could not be supported by artillery. An advance almost eight miles had been completed. The French component did not fare so well, but the French troops were pitifully tired, and indeed the British troops performed less well (though in less favourable terrain and with more limited resources) than the Dominion forces. All the same, 8 August was a great allied success. For Ludendorff: 'August 8 was the black day of the German Army in the history of the war. This was the worst experience I had to go through . . .'

Great as the success had been, what happened next would be critical. The fighting on 9 August stalled somewhat. The gains of the previous day could not be fully exploited. Two-thirds of the tanks were knocked out by enemy fire or mechanical breakdown, and the cavalry, as always, had proved vulnerable to machine-guns. The increasingly exhausted French element was only of limited value, until their First Army was reinforced by their Third Army. Rawlinson was apprehensive that the German reserve would counterattack and the ground gained on the previous day would be lost. Despite these factors and apprehensions, Fourth Army advanced three miles on the second day of the battle. By now the allies were approaching the solid defensive positions of the 1916 battlefields. Haig was faced by representations from the generals on the spot, the French Debeney and the British Rawlinson, who were not ready to push on. There is said to have been was a minor rebellion from Rawlinson. He was told that 'if he had any views to express [he should] come and see me in the morning.' When he did, the story goes, he asked Haig, 'Who commands the British Army, you or Foch?' No full account of the interview exists, and questions have arisen about whether it ever took place, but the episode appears to be substantially vouched by Haig's diary entry of 14 August. There is no doubt that Rawlinson and Currie (Canadian Corps) were able to induce Haig to delay the next stage of the attack. Rawlinson produced aerial photographs of the enemy defences which caused Haig to hold the attack while wire cutting and counter-battery work proceeded. This insubordination by Rawlinson would have been unthinkable in 1915 or 1916. Then Haig had been commanding a force whose generals had little or no experience of warfare. Then he had needed to interfere with his army commanders' plans, and should indeed have done so more than he did. Now, in the course of the planning for Amiens, he continued to interfere, when he should not have done so, and frequently required Rawlinson to extend his objectives too ambitiously. By 1918, the army and its commanders had learned much and matured greatly. It was a mark of Rawlinson's confidence and knowledge of his craft that he could now address Haig as he did.

Rawlinson's question about who commanded the British Army was prompted by the fact that Foch, combative as ever, 'saw no necessity for delay IV Army and 1st French Army attack.' He and Haig met, and Haig was subjected to sharp interrogation. Foch:

> wanted to know what orders I had issued for attack? When I proposed to attack? Where? And with what troops? . . . I spoke to Foch quite straightly and let him understand that *I was responsible to my government and fellow citizens for the handling of the British forces*. F's attitude at once changed and he said all he wanted was early information of my intentions so that he might co-ordinate the operations of the other armies, and that he now thought I was quite correct in my decision not to attack the enemy in his prepared position.

The pause that Rawlinson obtained marks the gap between the Battle of Amiens and the Battle of Albert, which was to open on 21 August. On that day Churchill discussed munitions for 1919. Haig 'told him we ought to do our utmost to get a decision this autumn. We are engaged in a "wearing out battle", and are outlasting and beating the enemy. If we allow the enemy a period of quiet, he will recover, and the "wearing out" process must be recommenced.' Churchill replied that the General Staff in London did not think that the 'decisive period' of the war would arise until July 1919. Haig pressed his point in a talk to his Army Commanders on 22 August which shows how much he, if not the General Staff, understood the prize that could be grasped:

I request that Army Commanders will, without delay, bring to the notice of all subordinate leaders the changed conditions under which operations are now being carried on, and the consequent necessity for all ranks to act with the utmost boldness and resolution in order to get full advantage from the present favourable situation . . .

To turn the present situation to account, the most resolute offensive is everywhere desirable. Risks which a month ago would have been criminal to incur, ought now to be incurred as a duty.

It is no longer necessary to advance in regular lines and step by step. On the contrary, each division should be given a distant objective which must be reached independently of its neighbours, and even if one's flank is thereby exposed for the time being.

There is no evidence here of the conservatism which is so often said to characterise Haig. He was urging on his commanders tactics that were radically different from those which had been appropriate earlier in the war, and his appreciation of the balance of power between the Allies and Germany was far in advance of London's view. He was reinforced in his determination by discussions on manpower with the Adjutant-General on 27 August. The manpower shortage was such that he could expect to lose nineteen British divisions. It was all the more necessary to finish the war in 1918.[10]

On the German side, Ludendorff offered his resignation, which was refused. The Kaiser noted that 'we have nearly reached the limit of our powers of resistance. The war must be ended.'[11] Haig and the Kaiser may have been as one, but Churchill was talking of 1919, Henry Wilson talked of 1919 and 1920. Lloyd George talked of 1922 and even Foch, as late as 4 September was still thinking of 1919. Haig was magnificently unmoved by their caution. When he received a War Office memorandum from Wilson in July, envisaging a protracted war, he scribbled in the margin: 'Words! Words! Words! Lots of words and little else. Theoretical rubbish! Whoever drafted this stuff could never win any campaign.' The cavalier was exhilarated by the scent of victory. His vigour and dash in 1918 give the lie to the notion that he was a cautious plodder. They also give the lie to the argument that the war, and the campaign of the Hundred Days, was won by his commanders and not by Haig. He still intervened to prod, stimulate and drive on. Freed from involvement in the detail of the operations of his armies, he was able to function truly as a Commander-in-Chief, and his Operations Staff were crucial in phasing the offensives that his armies carried out.[12]

Haig could afford to be bolder now than before. After the Battle of Amiens the Committee of Prime Ministers of the Empire, meeting at Versailles, sent their congratulations to the Field-Marshal and to the troops under his command on their brilliant success. Hankey commented: 'There was hence-forward no question of replacing him, for which I myself was glad, as I have never discovered any other officer of the calibre of Haig.'

The advance which Byng's Third Army made at Albert on 21 August went well. On 24 August Haig extended the line of attack further, and launched First Army under Horne into the battle. By 3 September First Army had caught up with Third and Fourth Armies, and the whole German line was coming apart.

In four weeks, Haig had brought the army up to the Hindenburg Line, beyond which a network of railways radiated from Namur on the edge of the Ardennes. A less important series of lines radiated from Liège to the east. Between them, Liège and Namur gave access to the lines that supplied troops and materials to the Germans on the Western Front.

There are two ways of looking at the progress that Haig made. It had taken four months to drive the Germans back sixty miles at the rate of a marching soldier or a gun dragged by a horse. And by the end of September the Germans were only back to where they had been before their March offensive. Indeed, Edmonds criticised the advance for its caution. On the other hand, the pace had very greatly increased in the last four weeks. Ludendorff's approach had been a series of opportunistic probes which might – might well – have been lucky enough to break the allied front line fatally. Haig was not attempting deep penetration, but proceeding by a series of shallow and broad advances. He was rolling up the crumbling German armies, rather than attempting a flanking operation. He was able to carry forward his armies with the support of the lines of communication that had been created by Sir Eric Geddes.

It was Haig, rather than Foch, whose mind was directing events, and Foch recognised Haig's stature, describing him as 'the greatest General in the world' – a generous tribute to a soldier from a different nation. The attack by Fourth Army under Rawlinson on 8 August was Haig's plan, pressed on Foch instead of an attack on Festubert-Robecq. He convinced Foch that the assault should rest when he thought that the appropriate moment had been reached. The attack on 21 August under Third Army was again of his devising. From now on he was in effective command of the campaign, though sustained by Foch's magnificent and belligerent resolution. Foch acknowledged as much:

My Dear Field Marshal

Your affairs are going on very well; I can only applaud the resolute manner in which you follow them up, without giving the enemy a respite and always extending the breadth of your operations. It is this increasing breadth of the offensive – an offensive fed from behind and strongly pushed forward on to carefully selected objectives, without bothering about the alignment or about keeping too closely in touch – which will produce the greatest results and the smallest casualties, as you have perfectly understood.

All this was done by an army starved of resources. Britain's reserves of men were almost exhausted and the Cabinet had failed to recognise the change that had taken place in the war. They continued to try to withhold what reserves there were.

The pace of movement throughout the Hundred Days, though slow in terms of what happened on the Eastern Front in the Second

World War, is comparable to that of Hitler's Blitzkrieg. It had proved almost impossible to capitalise on breakthroughs in the context of trench warfare. Haig was criticised for seeing cavalry as an essential part of a breakthrough. He understood perfectly well that there was no place for cavalry amidst barbed wire, trenches and machine-guns, but equally, there was nothing else that could move at any great speed. The maximum speed of the Mark IV tank (1917) was 3.7 miles per hour, and the Mark V (1918) was little faster at 4.6 miles per hour. And these were *road speeds*: on rough ground the tanks moved at 1 or 1.5 miles per hour. Even the so-called whippet tanks (1918), with a maximum road speed of 8.3 miles per hour, dashed around the *battlefield* at an average of just 2 miles per hour. The limitations of tanks must be kept in mind. They could indeed flatten barbed wire without making craters, allowing infantry to advance without difficulty, but horses could not advance over the uncut strands. This meant that wooden planks had to be laboriously brought forward before the guns (which were pulled by horses) could be advanced.

Cavalry still had its uses, and as early as the spring of 1916, Haig was using cavalry in a sophisticated way, as part of an all-arms striking force,[13] and in the looser warfare of the Hundred Days cavalry was an indispensable part of his range of resources.

Gary Sheffield quotes the advice of a brigadier in the 9th (Scottish) Division to his men at this time and one can imagine a Second World War Brigadier giving exactly the same instructions:

Keep as close as you can to 18pdrs (pipsqueak) barrage. Its their [*sic*], so don't go into it. Never mind your dressing.

Reply at once to any enemy small arm [*sic*] fire. Fire at once at any enemy you see in range – slowly and accurately from the quickest position, lying, standing or kneeling.

Don't crowd, the loose order will save you casualties if you use your wits.

Watch your flanks and draw them back if necessary.

If held up reply steadily to the fire whilst your comrades get round.

If necessary help your comrades on flank by cross fire.

Surround pill-boxes and Machine Guns. They can only fire one or two ways.

Don't have more than about 100x [yards] between sections.

Don't scatter from your sections, file is best for advancing, a few paces interval for firing.

Push steadily forward in your little groups, using slow covering fire where necessary, and stick roughly to your own line of ADVANCE.[14]

So very, very far from being the blinkered traditionalist of the caricature, Haig did not merely allow change: he was its catalyst. The professionalism that, as an 'educated' soldier, he had encouraged as a young officer, and in his years at the War Office, Aldershot and in India he applied throughout his command. Schools of instruction were set up in huge numbers. A minor example of his approach relates to the Stokes mortar, which has already been mentioned. It had been rejected by the War Office on technical grounds. General Rimington disagreed and had the mortar brought out to France for further trials. Haig, ever on the lookout for useful devices, made a point of being present at the demonstration. Although the weapon was still clearly imperfect and unreliable, Haig could see its potential and insisted on further development and trials in the United Kingdom. Ultimately the Stokes mortar became an important part of his armament. John Terraine disposes of 'the idea of the First World War as a period of almost total intellectual and imaginative stagnation' and demonstrates that the reverse is the case: 'Experiment was going on all the time in all armies. Never had the art of war undergone such intense change. This is reflected in the growth of the 'experimental section, Royal Engineers' (formerly and endearingly, the 'inventions committee'). Starting off with an establishment of 13,640, it grew by the end of the war to 237,370, conducting trials and experiments with:

hand and rifle grenades, trench mortars, flares, land-mines, delay-action fuses, catapults, smoke producers and projectors, body armour, armour-piercing bullets (to penetrate armoured loopholes), wire-destroying apparatus, aeroplane height-finders and optical instruments – and much else besides. It had to inspect and assess (often at considerable risk) all manner of amazing devices put forward by their inventors as certain war-winners: a giant hose which would wash away the German trenches, a kite to drop explosives, a grapnel to pull away the enemy's wire, a bow to shoot high-explosive arrows at machine-gun emplacements, a boomerang hand-grenade to kill Germans behind traverses, a thing like a barrel-organ which would project a stream of disc grenades when the handle was turned, igniting each one by friction as it flew out, even (one is tempted to say 'inevitably') a 'death ray'.[15]

Haig was not complicit in all the details of the technical advances which were made during the war. But equally, he did not simply preside over them. He created a culture in which boffins could flourish. It would have been easy for him to have conveyed his disapproval of the former civilians who were the mainstay of the experimental section. Desperately starved for men, as he increasingly was, he could have found places in conventional warfare for almost a quarter of a million men who were busy with their experiments and inventions. '[T]he Second World War, although it carried many aspects of technology a long way forward and produced some striking new advances (radar, penicillin, and nuclear fission spring immediately to mind as major war innovations) never faintly matched its predecessor as regards the 'white heat' of change.'[16]

These were the resources with which Haig now stood facing the Hindenburg line. But as his cavalry probed ahead, reconnoitring and harrying, he faced difficulties at home. Foch had initially been hesitant about attacking the untested fortifications which seemed almost impregnable, but he responded to Haig's encouragement. The Cabinet was more fearful. On 1 September he received a telegram from Wilson marked 'Personal': 'Just a word of caution in regard to incurring heavy losses in attacks on Hindenburg Line as opposed to losses when driving the enemy back to line. I do not mean to say that you have incurred such losses but I know the War Cabinet would become anxious if we received heavy punishment in attacking the Hindenburg Line without success.'

Haig replied that same day:

My Dear Henry

With reference to your wire re casualties in attacking the Hindenburg Line – what a wretched lot! And how well they mean to support me! What confidence! Please call their attention to my action two weeks ago when the French pressed me to attack the strong lines of defence east of the Roye-Chaulnes front. I wrote you at the time and instead of attacking south of the Somme I started Byng's attack. I assure you I watch the drafts most carefully.

Wilson's response to that ('It wasn't really want of confidence in you . . .') was pretty poor. His letter 'was only intended to convey a sort of distant warning and nothing more. All so easy to explain in talking, all so difficult to explain in writing.' It was clear that if Haig succeeded, the government would take the credit, and if he failed, he would take the blame.

Even as this correspondence was taking place, the advance was continuing. The 2nd Australian Division had had remarkable success on 31 August, and had seized Mont St Quentin in the Somme sector. Further north, the Canadians broke through the Drocourt-Quéant 'switch' line, a continuation of the Hindenburg defences. German High Command reacted dramatically by pulling back behind the Canal du Nord and the Hindenburg Line itself. Haig: 'The end cannot be far off, I think.'

But it is important not to let hindsight suggest an inevitability to German collapse, even at this stage. On the same day that Haig wrote so confidently to Wilson, he recorded in his manuscript diary that

> I told [Byng] that owing to shortage of men I was opposed to
> doing more attacking than was absolutely necessary. The object
> is to keep the battle going on as long as possible until the
> Americans can attack in force.[17] I did not agree, because our
> object at the present time is to wear out the enemy by
> continuously attacking him, and so to prevent him from
> settling into a strong position. The decisive moment will arrive
> when the Americans attack in force. The British army must still
> be able to attack then, and to have the means of exploiting the
> victory and making it decisive . . . I therefore wished the
> Cavalry Corps to be kept as strong as possible and at the
> present time merely to detach the <u>minimum</u> number of
> squadrons necessary for Divl. and Corps requirements. By this
> procedure I hoped to have the efficient Cavalry Corps ready to
> act when the decisive moment comes.[18]

In view of all that Haig said, both afterwards and at this time, about
finishing the war in 1918, it is interesting that as late as 1 September
1918 he thinks that the end will not come until the Americans could
deliver it, something they would not be in a position to do until well
into the following year. It is also interesting that Haig did not
attempt to suppress his reservations about the duration of the war:
the typed copy of the diaries reveals the same lack of confidence as the
manuscript copy.[19]

On 3 September he received a letter from Henry Wilson in which
the latter sought to place his telegram in an extenuating context:
'Police strike and cognate matters make Cabinet sensitive to heavy
losses, especially if these are incurred against old lines of
fortifications . . .' Haig's reaction was explosive: 'How ignorant
these people are of war!! In my opinion it is much less costly in
lives to press the enemy after a victorious battle than to give him time
to recover & organise afresh his defence of a position!'

Foch was kinder when he arrived the following day and spoke
warmly of British achievements in 'La Grande Bataille', and when
Churchill arrived a few days later Haig 'told him that I considered

that the allies should aim at getting a decision <u>as soon as possible</u>. This month or next, or next spring.'

The Australian Army Corps was formed in November 1917. In August 1918 its five divisions came together into a single unit and three months earlier it came under the command of Lieutenant-General John Monash, who had earlier served at Gallipoli. He was a singular individual, the son of immigrants from Poland, a handsome student who had spent much of his university life pursuing women and attending the theatre. In civilian life he was an engineer who became very rich by achieving a near monopoly in the use of reinforced concrete. His real interest, however, was in his life as what was disparagingly known as 'a Saturday-afternoon soldier' the equivalent of a British Terroritorial. In 1894, as a 29-year-old lieutenant, he set out the essence of his military views: individual effort and collective impact were now less important than 'the perfect unity' of 'forces . . . acting together as a machine'. At Gallipoli his experience of command in a situation which his superiors had not thought through briefly affected his considerable self-confidence. But others were impressed, and by the time he reached France in 1917 he was a divisional commander at Messines. Haig promoted him lieutenant-general in command of the Australian Corps, and his 'limited objective' action at Hamel on 4 July 1917 was a model of his concept of warfare:

Nothing was left to chance in an all-arms, co-ordinated effort which anticipated the warfare of 20 years later. Everyone knew his role. The German defenders were blinded by smoke. Tank crews fraternised with the infantry well beforehand, and their tanks were used in unprecedentedly close support of the infantry, not only with fire power, but also by transporting a great deal of ammunition and by crushing the wire. Aircraft masked the sound of the approaching tanks, strafed the German line, and dropped ammunition to forward positions. The artillery and machine-gun fire plans were superlative and each battalion carried 30 Lewis guns. It was all over in 93 minutes, at a cost of 1,400 casualties on each side; 1,600 German prisoners were taken and 177 German machine-guns captured.[20]

Liddell Hart wrote that Monash 'probably had the greatest capacity for command in modern war among all who held command'. He exaggerated, but Monash might not have thought so: he was confident and opinionated, and did not underestimate what his troops achieved or the importance of his own philosophy in that achievement:

> I had formed the theory that the true role of the infantry was not to expend itself upon heroic physical effort, nor to wither away under merciless machine-gun fire, nor to impale itself on hostile bayonets, nor to tear itself to pieces in hostile entanglements . . . But, on the contrary, to advance under the maximum possible array of mechanical resources, in the form of guns, machine-guns, tanks, mortars and aeroplanes; to advance with as little impediment as possible; to be relieved as far as possible of the obligation to *fight* their way forward; to march, resolutely, regardless of the din and tumult of battle, to the appointed goal; and there to hold and defend the territory gained; and to gather in the form of prisoners, guns and stores, the fruits of victory.[21]

The route towards achieving this approach lay in the most diligent preparation in detail, supported by secrecy and discipline:

> A perfected modern battle plan is like nothing so much as a score for an orchestral composition, where the various arms and units are the instruments, and the tasks they perform are their respective musical phrases. Each individual unit must make its entry precisely at the proper moment, and play its phrase in the general harmony.[22]

Monash could be critical of his British Allies:

> Some of these Tommy divisions are the absolute limit, and not
> worth the money it costs to put them into uniform . . . If we
> only had twenty divisions like the 5th Australian, 4th Canadian
> and 1st New Zealand there would have been a different tale to
> tell.[23]

Monash was not the only Dominion soldier to take this view, but he
was being unfair. The Dominion troops tended to be far fresher than
the British forces that had been involved in the war from the outset.
And extensive detailed analysis of the performance of individual
British and Dominion divisions has demonstrated that the British
contribution to the Hundred Days was crucial. *All* élite divisions
made a disproportionate contribution to victory, and the ten best
British divisions performed as well as or better than the best six or
seven Dominion divisions.[24]

For Monash, the planning of a battle was not a matter of pragmatism
or compromise: as an engineer, he formulated plans with scientific
precision. Even if he was not at his best as a front line commander (the
Australian Official History said that 'Monash often lacked knowledge
of what had happened in battle') he was a brilliant staff officer, and as
forceful as he needed to be. Thus, for example, when he learned on the
eve of the 4 July 1918 attack that he was to be deprived of American
units that had formed part of the plan, he immediately made strenuous
representations to Rawlinson. Rawlinson readily understood his concern and did his utmost to contact Haig, who was responsible for the
order, and which he had made 'in deference to the wish of General
Pershing'. Haig, no less than Rawlinson, understood the force of
Monash's arguments, and the order was rescinded.

Haig appreciated Monash's qualities. He described him as 'A
clear-headed determined commander. Every detail had been thought
of. His brigadiers were equally thorough. I was most struck by their
whole arrangements.' Perhaps he would have been less generous if he
had not been able to add: 'Every suggestion that I made was most
carefully noted for consideration.' He was less comprehending in
relation to feelings of Australian nationalism:

Mr. Murdoch, an Australian, a friend of Hughes (Prime Minister), and also a newspaperman, came to see me and lunched. He expressed a wish of Australia to have their five divisions organised as 'an army!' I pointed out the impossibility of complying with this wish, but said everything will be done to keep the Australian troops together. I could not help feeling at the back of this fellow's mind there is a desire to be independent of the old country!'

Of the fifty VCs won in the Fourth Army during the Hundred Days, twenty were won by Australians. General Monash recorded with pride the achievement of the Australian Corps:

From March 27th, when Australian troops were for the first time interposed to arrest the German advance, until October 5th, when they were finally withdrawn from the line, the total captures made by them were:

| Prisoners | 29,144 |
| Guns | 338 |

. . . During the advance, from August 8th to October 5th, the Australian Corps recaptured and released no less than 116 towns and villages. Everyone of these was defended more or less stoutly . .

For the last 60 days of this period the Corps maintained an unchecked advance of 37 miles against the powerful and determined opposition of the still formidable enemy, who employed all the mechanical and scientific resources at his disposal.

Such a result alone, considered in the abstract and quite apart from any comparison with the performances of other forces, is a testimony, on the one hand, to the pre-eminent fighting qualities of the Australian soldier considered individually, and, on the other hand, to the collective capacity and efficiency of the military effort made by the Corps. I doubt whether there is any parallel for such a performance in the whole range of military history.

Grotesque though it is to use the word 'only' in relation to casualties, on a comparative basis it has to be applied to the number of Australian deaths during a period of sixty days continuous fighting: losses of 5,000 bear no relation to the huge numbers who died in the campaigns of 1916 and 1917.

Haig did not always appreciate the Australians as Monash did. When the Australian Prime Minister said that his countrymen deserved a rest and it was reported that two divisions were likely to decline to go into the line if ordered, Haig calculated that:

The casualties since 21st March (infantry only) are:-

		average
English, Scottish, Welsh,		
Irish per Battalion	45 officers	1088 other ranks
Australian	36 officers	704 other ranks
Canadians	42 officers	956 other ranks

The Australians have the least claim of any therefore for consideration on account of losses.[25]

Considerable mention has already been made of the contribution of the Canadians. They were first commanded, and commanded well, by Lieutenant-General The Hon. Sir Julian Byng. He supported the Canadian citizen who was to succeed him as Canadian Corps Commander on 6 June 1917, Lieutenant-General Sir Arthur Currie. Currie was another part-time soldier and, at the age of forty-one, was the first non-regular officer to command a corps in the BEF. Neither his background as auctioneer, estate agent and militia officer, nor his appearance ('a very big, tall, heavy fat man') might have been thought to commend him to Haig, but he was Haig's choice for promotion to corps commander, and the Canadian government had to acquiesce in an appointment which Haig had already made.

Haig, as commander of a conscript army, involved himself in the details of what his commanders and their subordinates were doing to an extent that would have been inconceivable in a professional army.

Byng did the same thing and Currie followed his example. Currie had been sent by Byng to study French methods at Verdun. His report promoted a new approach which was adopted in the Canadian army months before it formed part of the procedures of the army as a whole. The role of the platoon was revised; training was improved for infantry and artillery.

> He summarised the primary factors behind successful French offensive operations as being 'careful staff work' thorough 'artillery preparation and support,' the 'element of surprise' and the 'high state of training in the infantry detailed for the assault.' Currie was impressed by the fact that the French were producing what he termed ' "storm" troops on a large scale.' Indeed if one looks at its subsequent adoption in the British Armies, by late 1917 every British soldier was trained in the tactical skills of fire and manoeuvre and it is this breadth of training that marks the critical difference between the allied and German approach where [in the latter case] the *Stosstruppn* or specialist storm trooper remained an élite and the German Imperial Armies suffered for it.[26]

The Canadian government insisted that Canadian Divisions should always fight together. This caused logistical problems, when smaller units could usefully have filled gaps, but it did mean that in 1918, by which time there were four Canadian divisions, these troops were fresh and strong. Their role in the Hundred Days was to be played on the Somme front, where the main advance took place, but the divisions had been placed north of that, to defend the vulnerable Flanders area. In deception tactics that presaged Second World War ruses, an immense flow of bogus radio traffic was used to suggest an imminent attack by the Canadians in Flanders. Under cover of this counter-intelligence, the Canadians were able to make their move, and although the Germans were aware that some movement was going on, they did not know where it was directed. On the Somme, complete radio silence was maintained and the Australian Front was extended to obscure the Canadian arrival. Throughout Fourth Army's area signposts said: 'KEEP YOUR MOUTH SHUT', an admonition which also appeared in every soldier's paybook. Deception tactics were elaborate: some troops were allowed to be seen moving *away* from the Front. No forward movement was normally allowed. RAF patrols monitored the maintenance of secrecy. Later, at Amiens, noisy patrols of aircraft flew up and down the Front for another deceptive purpose: to mask the din of the tanks.

On 7 September, Haig issued an Order to all ranks, very different from the 'Backs to the Wall' one:

One month has now passed since the British Armies, having successfully withstood all attacks of the enemy, once more took the offensive in their turn. In that short space of time, by a series of brilliant and skilfully executed actions, our troops have repeatedly defeated the same German Armies, whose vastly superior numbers compelled our retreat last Spring . . .

Yet more has been done. Already we have passed beyond our old battle lines of 1917, and have made a wide breach in the enemy's strongest defences . . .

In this glorious accomplishment all ranks of all arms and services of the British Armies in France have borne their part in the most worthy and honourable manner. The capture of 75,000 prisoners and 750 guns in the course of four weeks' fighting speaks for the magnitude of the efforts and for the magnificence of your achievement . . .

We have passed many dark days together. Please God, these will never return. The enemy has now spent his effort, and I rely confidently on each one of you to turn to full advantage the opportunity which your skill, courage and resolution have created.

On 9 September, Haig went to England the following day to try to impress on Milner the scale of the prize that was within his grasp:

I had specially asked for this interview, and I stated that the object of my visit was to explain how greatly the situation in the field had changed to the advantage of the Allies. I considered it to be of first importance that the Cabinet should realise how all our plans and methods are at once affected by this change.

Within the last four weeks we had captured 77,000 prisoners and nearly 600 guns! There has never been such a victory in the annals of Britain, and its effects are not yet apparent. The German prisoners now taken will not obey their officers or their NCOs. The same story of indiscipline was told me of the prisoners from our hospitals. The discipline of the German Army is quickly going, and the German officer is no longer what he was. From these and other facts I draw the conclusion that the enemy's troops will not await our attacks in even the strongest position

Briefly, in my opinion, the character of the war has changed. What is wanted now at once is to provide the means to exploit our recent great successes to the full. Reserves in England should be regarded as reserves for the French Front, and all your yeomanry, cyclists and other troops now kept for civil defence should be sent to France at once.

If we act with energy now, a decision can be obtained in the very near future . . .

Lord Milner fully agreed and said he would do his best to help.

The austere, unbending Milner, although in the main a supporter of Haig, on this occasion failed in his vision, telling Wilson, on 11 September, that Haig was 'ridiculously optimistic'. He had warned Haig that if he 'knocked the present army about, there was no other to replace it.' The advice that he had been given by the War Office was still that the decisive moment in the war would be in July 1919.[27] The government had indeed failed to grasp how things had changed. And yet, despite all his excitement, and a truer view of the historic achievements that were taking place, Haig himself, as the diary entry for 10 September went on to show, was still not certain of victory in 1918.

Even Foch, and even as late as 7 October, was as one with the British War Office in expecting the final, critical push to be in 1919: in his case he nominated April of that year.[28]

Churchill, always capable of magnanimity and of rising to the level of events, acknowledged that:

> When in the autumn of 1918, the government, often only too right before, doubted the possibility of early success, and endeavoured to dissuade him from what was feared would be a renewal of melancholy and prodigal slaughter; when in the most invidious manner they cast the direct responsibility upon him, he did not hesitate, and the war-worn, five-times decimated troops responded to the will and impulse of their leader, and marched forward answering to the awful convulsions of victory final and absolute.[29]

Haig was undismayed by the lack of enthusiasm from Lloyd George, Wilson and Milner (on whom he renewed his attack on 21 September: 'In my opinion it is possible to get a decision this year but if we do not, every blow that we deliver now will make the task next year more easy'). He continued his advance through the outlying defences and towards the core of the Hindenburg Line. The main attack began, sector by sector, on 22 September, a huge assault, with the Belgian Army and British Second Army in the north, the centre consisting of British First, Third and Fourth Armies and French Fourth Army, and the American Army under General Pershing in the south.

After the war Haig wrote to Churchill:

> [A]s for criticisms of what I did or did not do, no-one knows as well as I do how short of the ideal my command was . . . But I do take credit for this, that it was due to the decisions which I took in August and September 1918 that the war ended in November.

The Allied armies did not walk through the Hindenburg Line. The fighting was extremely fierce and there are innumerable cameos of great bravery and also of great inventiveness. The crossing of the Canal du Nord, led by the Staffordshire Brigade, is such an instance.[30]

On 28 September Ludendorff

> went down to the Field-Marshal's room, which was on the floor below mine. I explained to him my views as to a peace offer and a request for an armistice . . . The Field-Marshal [Hindenburg] listened to me with emotion. He answered that he had intended to say the same thing to me in the evening, that he had considered the whole situation carefully, and thought the step necessary . . . The Field-Marshal and I parted with a firm handshake, like men who had braved their dearest hopes, and who were resolved to hold together in the hardest hours of human life as they have held together in success. Our names were associated with the greatest victories of the World War. We now shared the conviction that it was our duty to sacrifice our names to ensure the step being taken that we had done everything humanly possible to avoid.

By 19 September, Wilson, ahead of Ludendorff, had recognised the climactic stage that had been reached:

> My General,
> Well done! You must be a famous general!
>
> Henry.

Haig's reply the following day contained a reference to Repington that has been noted already:

> My Dear Henry
> Very many thanks for your kind little note of yesterday. No, certainly not! I am not nor am I likely to be a 'famous general'.

For that must we not have pandered to Repington and the Gutter Press! But we have a surprisingly large number of *very capable* Generals. Thanks to these gentlemen and to their 'sound military knowledge built up by study and practice until it has become an instinct' and to a steady adherence to the principles of our Field Service Regulations Part I are our successes to be chiefly attributed.

In all the circumstances in which it was written, this letter may sound a trifle pedestrian (the reference to Field Service Regulations Part I certainly falls a bit short of the heroic), but it contains a distillation of Haig's greatness: his modesty and his vision of military success achieved by the capacity of his army, and not through the efforts of any one man. In the meantime, Ludendorff may have known that the war was lost, but the fighting continued.

By 30 September, Haig is certainly feeling that something critical is underway and that 1918, rather than 1919, will be the critical year:

During the month of Septr the British Army has taken 66,300 prisoners including 1,500 officers and 700 guns.
For the months of August & Septr the total is 123,618 prisoners, including 2,783 officers & 1,400 guns.
The machine guns taken are numbered by the 1,000.
During the last four days fighting – i.e. from 27th Septr we have engaged on the Cambrai – St. Quentin battlefront 36 German Divns & have defeated them with heavy loss.[31]

On the following day he met Byng and Rawlinson and it was agreed that they could now press on without further orders from Haig. Until about now, Haig had seen what was happening as part of a wearing-down process. When he spoke to Byng on 1 September about waiting for the Americans he still saw the end as being some distance away. Now, almost a month later he recognised that breakthrough had been achieved. The French on Rawlinson's right appeared to be hanging back and Lawrence telephoned Foch's headquarters to ask him to urge Debeney forward.

When Haig went to see Foch on 6 October he found him reading the Paris newspapers with the story that the Central Powers were looking for an armistice on the basis of Wilson's Fourteen Points. 'Here,' said Foch, 'there is the immediate result of the British piercing of the Hindenburg Line.' The bulk of the fighting at this stage was borne by the British army. During October Britain lost a further 121,000 men. The German army continued to defend heroically. Although tired, and moving more slowly, the five British Armies did move ahead. The Germans were driven from their positions behind the St Quentin Canal, and Lloyd George responded with the first words of congratulation from the government on the great advance: 'I have just heard from Marshal Foch of the brilliant victory won by the First, Third and Fourth Armies, and I wish to express to yourself, Generals Horne, Byng and Rawlinson, and all the officers and men under your command my sincerest congratulations on the great and significant success which the British Armies, with their American brothers-in-arms, have gained during the past two days.' Extraordinarily grudging, with reference only to 'the past two days', and the emphasis on the role of Foch was a very intentional slight that was much resented.

On 17 October Fifth Army liberated Lille (where the Germans had left six days' food supplies for the population, a fine gesture). In Paris the statue that symbolised Lille in the Place de la Concorde had been covered in black crêpe since the loss of the city to the Germans in 1870. The mourning was now removed and replaced by the Parisians with a flag of the British XI Corps. But the German Army was by no means broken. Haig reported on 25 October that he expected the Germans to shorten their line from 250 miles to 155, a length which he considered they would be able to hold[32] and the battles continued. As late as 31 October, at an army commanders' conference, Haig was told that the enemy was fighting a good rearguard action, and was not yet 'sufficiently beaten as to cause him to accept an ignominious peace.' What Ludendorff had feared (he resigned on 25 October) was not so much an attack on his Western Line as attacks on other fronts where 'the props had been kicked away'. Turkey signed an armistice on 30 October, Austria-Hungary on 3 November. On 4 November the British, Americans and French won significant gains on the west. On 10 November the Kaiser accepted Hindenburg's advice. He abdicated, and at 5 a.m. on 11 November left for the neutral Netherlands.

Five weeks earlier the Germans had asked President Wilson for an armistice. Foch submitted a paper to the Allied Conference in Paris suggesting what the requirements of a peace treaty should be: they amounted pretty well to unconditional surrender. Haig was sceptical about the reality of the proposals. At a meeting of the War Cabinet on 19 October he said that in his view the enemy was not ready for unconditional surrender and if this were demanded, 'there would be no armistice and the war would continue for at least another year!' Haig did not want the war to continue for another year. When Lloyd George asked him for his views on terms, he replied, as he so often did, with the dialectical device of putting questions to the War Cabinet:

1. Is Germany now so beaten that she will accept whatever terms the Allies may offer? i.e. unconditional surrender.
2. If he refuses to agree to our terms, can the Allies continue to press the enemy's position vigorously during the coming winter months, to cause him to withdraw so quickly that he cannot destroy the railways, roads etc?

As the answer to both questions was in the negative, the inference was clear and he recommended as the terms for an armistice:

1. Immediate evacuation of Belgium and occupied France.
2. Metz and Strasbourg to be occupied by the Allies and Alsace-Lorraine to be vacated by the Germans.
3. Belgium and French rolling stock to be returned, inhabitants restored etc.

Haig was realistic when others were carried away by a desire for revenge. Here, he dissented from Foch. He was not in favour of a punitive peace. He did not wish the war to be prolonged, as it would be if the Allies' demand were too aggressive. Already there was talk in Germany of a defensive *levée en masse*. He did not think 'the democratisation of Germany' worth a single English [*sic*] life. He saw it as 'to our interest to return to peace methods at once, to have Germany a prosperous, not an impoverished country. Furthermore we ought *not* to make Germany our enemy for many years to come'.

Some have thought that Haig's attitude at this point indicated a pessimistic assessment of the position. In fact he was no more than objective. He told the Cabinet that the French Army was 'worn out, and has not been fighting latterly'; the 'American Army is disorganised, ill-equipped and ill-trained'; the 'British Army was never more efficient but has fought hard, and it lacks reinforcements'. As for the German army, it was 'capable of retiring to its own frontier, and holding that line if there should be any attempt to touch the *honour* of the German people.' He was against 'the French entering Germany to pay off old scores' and then provoking her to sustained resistance when she would be able to make use of the 1920 class of recruits. That was a sensible enough appraisal at the time (but after the peace Germany's awareness that she had never been comprehensively defeated in the field was to be an element of the 'stab in the back' theory that nurtured the growth of the National Socialists).

At a conference with Foch and other Commanders-in-Chief on 25 October, when the armistice terms were discussed at the request of the French government, Haig repeated what he had said to the British Cabinet. He went on to argue that the enemy would not accept the terms that Foch proposed

> because of military necessity alone – and it would be very costly and take a long time (two years) to enforce them unless the internal state of Germany compels the enemy to accept them. We don't know very much about the internal state of Germany [very different from all he said in 1916 and 1917!] – and to try

to impose such terms seems to me really a gamble which may come off or it may not . . . Pétain spoke of taking a huge indemnity from Germany, so large that she will never be able to pay it – meantime French troops will hold the left bank of the Rhine as a pledge! . . .

Haig wrote to his wife on 1 November:

I am afraid the Allied Statesmen mean to exact humiliating terms from Germany. I think this is a mistake, because it is merely laying out troubles for the future, and may encourage the wish for revenge in the future. Also, I doubt if Germany is sufficiently low yet to accept such terms.

He was right both in his analysis of the current situation and, as history was to show, of the perils that might flow from imposing a harsh peace.

The terms of the armistice continued to be discussed, and delegates of both sides at last came together. At 7 a.m. on 8 November the German Armistice Commission train arrived at a siding in the Forest of Compiègne. Foch's carriages stood nearby. Talks began at nine o'clock in Foch's office on the train. The German delegates were asked by Foch the purpose of their visit. They replied that they had come to receive the Allies' proposals in regard to an armistice. Foch replied that he had no proposals to make. A German representative asked the Marshal in what form he desired that they should express themselves. He did not stand on form; he was ready to say that the German delegation asked the conditions for an armistice. Foch replied that he had no conditions to offer. The Germans then quoted from President Wilson's last note which said that Foch was authorised to make known the armistice conditions. To that Foch replied that he was indeed authorised to make them known if the Germans asked for an armistice. 'Herr Erzberger and Count Oberndorff declared that they *asked* for an armistice.' After this little gavotte, Foch announced that the armistice conditions would be read. Between 7 and 8 p.m. on 10 November, the German Government communicated that it accepted the conditions that had been put to it. The guns fell silent on the following morning at 11 a.m., French time.

In victory, Haig remained as imperturbable as in defeat. He stressed the importance of looking after the troops in their new situation: the best fighters could be the most difficult in times of quiet. They were to be kept occupied and it was the *duty* of officers to keep the men amused.

The British Commanders then went off to be filmed for the cinema newsreels, or, as Haig put it,

> Taken on the Cinema! Gen. Plumer, whom I told to 'go off and be cinema-ed' went off most obediently and stood before the camera, trying to look his best, while Byng, and others near him, were chaffing the old man and trying to make him laugh.

23

SUNSET

The war was won, but who had won it, the Commander-in-Chief or the Prime Minister? The rest of Haig's life was clouded by the government's determination to minimise the role of the military, and particularly his own role, in achieving victory. As the war receded into the past, Haig did increasingly find a new role, and fulfilment within it, but in the early years, at least, he was not accorded what he felt to be due, either to himself or to the army, which had fought so bravely and made such sacrifices for the cause in which he fervently believed. Churchill, who had argued so often against Haig in honest disagreement, recognised this rejection when he recorded that 'Early in 1919 Lord Haig walked ashore at Dover after the total defeat of Germany and disappeared into private life . . . He became one of the permanent unemployed.'[1]

Haig was in no doubt about the scale of what had been achieved, although he attributed it not to himself, but to the British Army. He acknowledged the achievement, and also the change in the army itself:

In three months of epic fighting the British Armies in France have brought to a sudden and dramatic end the great wearing-out fight of the past four years . . . In the fighting since November 1st our troops had broken the enemy's resistance beyond the possibility of recovery, and forced on him a disorderly retreat along the whole front of the British Armies. Thereafter the enemy was capable neither of accepting nor refusing battle. The utter confusion of his troops, the state of his railways congested with abandoned trains, the capture of huge quantities of rolling stock and material, all showed that our attack had been decisive . . . In the decisive moments of this period (August 8th to November 11th), the strongest and most vital parts of the enemy's front were attacked by the British, his lateral communications cut and his best divisions fought to a standstill . . .

This record is a proof also of the overwhelmingly decisive part played by the British Armies on the Western Front in bringing the enemy to his final defeat.

It would be impossible to devise a more eloquent testimony to the unequalled spirit and determination of the British soldier, of all ranks and services. We have been accustomed to be proud of the great and noble traditions handed down to us by the soldiers of bygone days. The men who form the armies of the Empire today have created new traditions which are a challenge to the highest records of the past and will be an inspiration to the generations who come after us.

The enemy had been defeated in France, not in its own country, and it was not until 1 December that the British Army passed into Germany. On 12 December Haig watched his troops crossing the Rhine.

In late November Foch was invited to a formal reception in London. Lloyd George's plan was that Haig should play a subordinate part in the ceremony. Haig was infuriated. He was to take part in the procession, but was not invited to the reception afterwards. All that was to be done for him was the provision of a car to take him off wherever he wanted to go. In the procession itself, he was to travel in 'the fifth carriage along with General Henry Wilson. I felt that this was more of an insult that I could put up with, even from the Prime Minister.' Lloyd George was clearly 'trying to belittle the British

Army', which 'might interfere with him and his schemes of revolution and bolshevism.' He had 'no intention of taking part in any triumphal ride with Foch, or with any pack of foreigners, through the streets of London, mainly in order to add to LG's importance and help him in his election campaign . . . Was there ever such an insult prepared for the welcome of a General on his return from commanding an Army in the field during 4 long years of war? Yet this is the Prime Minister of England's view of what is fitting.' Esher advised Haig to refuse point blank.

> Years ago you believed this war to be inevitable. Years ago you trained for it, and your faith in your destiny to lead our British Armies to victory was never shaken. That, and its achievement, are fine rewards and quite imperishable compared with the more material ones that must – in the end – cumber the dustbin.[2]

The crisis was resolved by the intervention of the King, and instead of playing an ignominious part in Foch's reception, Haig and his army commanders were accorded a reception in their own right in the following year, when they proceeded from Charing Cross in a Grand Victory March (sometimes 'Peace March') to Buckingham Palace. At Marlborough House, Queen Alexandra, his old protectress, with Lady Haig, her former maid of honour, waited to greet the Commander-in-Chief. The commanders were applauded as they made their way to be received by the King-Emperor. After the reception, Haig returned to his home, then at Kingston Hill. Later that evening his house was surrounded by a huge crowd of 10,000 people: 'Today, indeed, has been a red letter one in my life. To receive such a spontaneous welcome . . . shows how the people of England realise what has been accomplished by the Army and myself. This more that compensates for the . . . coldness displayed towards me by the Prime Minister since the Armistice.' As for the reception itself, it

> was essentially a welcome by the people without any official interference, and I could not help feeling how the cheering from

the great masses of all classes came from their hearts. As ADC to King Edward, I have taken part in many functions, but never before have I seen such crowds, or such wholehearted enthusiasm. It was indeed most touching to take part in such a ceremony.

Haig was not egotistical: in many ways his was a shy and retiring character. But he had been fired with honourable ambition, and he had an appropriate regard both for his achievements and for the offices he held. He could, and did, hold out for an acknowledgement of the army's achievement and of the status of Commander-in-Chief without personal vanity.

The concept of respect for an office is a difficult one today, but understanding that concept is important in arriving at an assessment of some aspects of Haig. It lies at the heart of how he could simultaneously be personally modest but concerned for the respect and recognition that he felt to due to the institutions that he venerated and the paraphernalia that surrounded them. Nowadays society is, fortunately, less deferential and hierarchical, and we do not consider that respect is automatically due to the holders of office, irrespective of their merits. For Haig and his contemporaries it was an impiety to the existing social order to fail to accord respect to the pillars on which they considered it rested.

According to Haldane's *Autobiography,* on the evening of the Grand Victory March, Haig appeared at Haldane's house, and handed him a copy of his *Despatches*, inscribed thus:

> To Viscount Haldane of Cloan – the greatest Secretary of State for War England has ever had. In grateful remembrance of his successful efforts in organising the Military Forces for a War on the Continent, notwithstanding much opposition from the Army Council and the half-hearted support of his Parliamentary friends.
>
> Haig, F.M.

The story is all the more touching for the fact that Haig had been ill on the day, and had led the march against the advice of his doctor. (His Private Secretary recorded that 'at that time the Chief was really ill. He was only able to take part in the March as a result of being gingered up in some way for the occasion by a curious medico named Gomez.') When Foch arrived at Victoria and was told that Haig might not be able to take part, he replied magnificently, 'If the Field-Marshal does not ride, nor shall I.'

Dudley Sommer has reviewed the complicated evidence relating to the incident and concludes that the story cannot be entirely accurate. There is a discrepancy between the typescript and the published version of the *Autobiography*. Haig certainly did not present Haldane with the *Despatches* on that occasion, but when he did they *were* inscribed in the way that Haldane described. Almost certainly, too, he did take the trouble, on the evening of the march, and despite his indisposition, to make a special visit to his old chief. One of his staff recorded in 1953 that he had said that 'he had one thing to do before any other – namely he was going to see Haldane on his way home, and tell him that he should have been present to share the cheers and gratitude of the people'.[3]

On 19 November 1918 he had been offered a viscountcy. This, he was very clear, was an inadequate recognition of the army's achievement. 'When FM French was *recalled* from the command of the armies in France for *incompetence*, he was made a Viscount!' He continued to dig his heels in over his peerage, but not merely in order to get the earldom which he felt was appropriate. He had become very conscious of the needs of ex-servicemen, particularly those disabled by war service, and he was determined that they should not have to rely on charity. He was adamant that the state must support those disabled in the war, and that any charitable aid should be in addition to, and not in substitution for, the government's contribution. Even before the war had ended he told his wife that he would 'give not only money, but all the energy which I may have left after the war is over, to help Disabled Officers and men who have suffered in this war.' He continued to stall whenever the peerage issue was raised, saying that he did not want a peerage or the money grant which would go with it until the Pensions Ministry had 'really accomplished something'.

The government was in some embarrassment, as they could hardly give honours to subordinate and other commanders – Admiral Sir David Beattie had indicated that he would accept a viscountcy – until Haig's position was settled. Wilson was appointed to negotiate, but ultimately Haig's tactics succeeded and he was assured that his requirement regarding ex-servicemen's pensions would be met. He was to receive an earldom and, as he had indicated that he would have to decline an honour 'unless an adequate grant is made to me to enable a suitable position to be maintained', a grant of not the £250,000 which he had requested but £100,000. 'What's the use,' he asked Sassoon, 'of being a peer and having to live in hotels?' Over a hundred years earlier, and in the middle of the Peninsular War, Wellington had been voted £2,000 a year for life. Later, but still before Waterloo, he received a dukedom and a further £400,000. After the Sudan, Kitchener was given £30,000 and after the South African War a further £50,000. He would no doubt have received more if his career had not been cut short when HMS *Hampshire* was torpedoed. Lord Roberts received a gratuity of £100,000. The disgraced French received £50,000 for his seventeen months as Commander-in-Chief.

Haig wrote to Lord Elibank:

I was induced to abandon my previous attitude because I had no wish to appear to be setting myself up as superior to all the rest, and too superior to accept reward! Nor did I wish to join the Bolshevists by refusing the title which the King proposed to give me! Moreover any further refusals to accept the reward on my part won't benefit the ex-soldier. The Govt. has promised to do its duty in the matter – indeed the whole country is now behind me in its determination to see these gallant fellows and their dependants are *properly* treated.

Wilson declined a peerage and a grant, saying that he wanted nothing, but would be glad to have promotion. Two weeks later he was a field-marshal and a few days after that he received a baronetcy and £10,000.

After giving up his command in France, Haig was appointed Commander-in-Chief, Home Forces. In his previous command, when in January 1919 there had been a riot at Calais amongst soldiers, some of them returning from leave and refusing to rejoin their units, Haig had disagreed with Churchill, now War Minister. Haig had wanted, or at least said he wanted, to shoot the ringleaders: 'I have the power, by warrant, to try by Court Martial and shoot in accordance with Army Act; and no telegram from S of S can affect my right to do what I think is necessary for the army.' But he did not shoot them. It was Churchill who appointed him to Home Forces and, in doing so referred to the 'very serious strikes' which 'seem imminent'. But if Churchill thought that he was appointing someone who would crush unrest with an iron hand, he was misled. In the context of a threatened General Strike in the autumn of 1919 Haig stressed his troops should keep a very low profile. 'It is not their duty to act as policemen.'

His political stance is reflected in the fact that in the Coupon Election of 1918 he voted for the Coalition Government even though it was led by the despised Lloyd George, 'as being better than the alternatives – *Labour* and *Liberal*.'[4]

The post of Commander-in-Chief Home Forces was abolished in January 1920 and although Haig remained on the Active List as a field-marshal, his military career had ended, although he was only fifty-eight years of age and in excellent health.

Most of the army commanders became Governors-General or High Commissioners. Haig's name was mentioned as a possible Viceroy of India, but the post was not offered to him and he may not have sought employment which would take him from his family. There was a long gap between the births of his first two children, and the birth on 15 March 1918 of his son George (known as Dawyck from the courtesy title he received when his father was ennobled) and of his youngest daughter on 7 October 1919. Dawyck was born six days before the commencement of the great German attack. Haig had been concerned about his wife's health and he was delighted that the birth went well for her – and that the baby was a boy. When he returned home his reaction was wildly out of character: he hugged the doctor and kissed him on each cheek 'like a damn foreigner' as the doctor described it. It is rather touching that alongside special friends and, of course, royalty, one of the godparents was Johnnie French.

Lloyd George, speaking on the vote on the grant of £100,000, pointedly referred to the fact that in the war Haig 'had accepted the command of FM Foch over the British Forces'. For very many people Lloyd George was 'the man who won the war'. There is no doubt that he was crucial for British victory. But the fact remained that it was Haig who had commanded the armies in France, and there was huge public acclaim for him. The only way in which Lloyd George could minimise Haig's achievement was by emphasising that of Foch. Thus the news of the advance during the Hundred Days had come to him via Foch. Thus, in his *War Memoirs*, he wrote that Haig 'did well in the concluding stages of the 1918 campaign – under Foch's supreme direction.' Statesmen enjoy fame, and are anxious to secure their place in history. Churchill, in his *War Memoirs,* minimised the role of Alanbrooke, his Chief of Staff, though without grotesquely deni- grating him as Lloyd George did Haig.

The gap between the cool regard in which Lloyd George held Haig and the warmth of appreciation for him in the country at large was enormous. As early as August 1918, congratulations poured in from every corner, from the King, from Queen Alexandra, from the Lord Mayor of London and from the leaders of communities throughout the Empire. One poignant and brief note: 'You will be tired of congratulations but just let me say that as you approach the scene of our former exploits together my heart and thoughts are with you. Don't reply. French.' Now, at home in the United Kingdom, Haig was regarded perhaps not quite with affection, but certainly with huge admiration and respect. He never won the heart of the soldiers or of the public in the way that Roberts or Kitchener or French did.

He was less of a physical presence than they were and he did not have their charisma. But the nation seemed able, all the same, to understand his steadiness and reliability. Children were named after him. There was 'a rain of golden boxes', as was said of Chatham after the Seven Years' War: he became a freeman of innumerable cities and received many honorary doctorates, including a DCL from Oxford. The students of St Andrews University had elected him as their rector in 1916 and in 1919 he gave his rectorial address. The subject he chose was 'Character'. In 1921 he became Chancellor of the University.

In 1921 too, Bemersyde, the family home of the senior branch of the Haig family in the borders, where Haig since his boyhood had dreamed of living, was bought by subscription and made over to him. Thereafter his time was divided between the border country and London. At Bemersyde, often assisted at weekends by improbably distinguished assistants, he worked on the garden with his bare hands. There was artistic ability in the family and he shared it. He was a competent topographical artist and his son was to be a professional artist of distinction. With the advice of his cousin, Rose Haig Thomas, and his friend, Lady Southampton, he designed a garden on the model of Hampton Court and planted it in place of the established Victorian flower beds. His sketch of the garden he was to create can still be seen at Bemersyde. He was an elder of the local church, as well as of St Columba's in Pont Street, London. He hunted locally, played tennis, and above all spent time with his family. In his autobiography, the present Earl describes their family life:

He was a very quiet, easy going, loving father and great fun to be with. He wasn't, I suppose, enormously communicative but he was very patient. He would love starting us off playing golf or tennis and would lob balls at us. He used to teach us to ride. He used to smarten us up somewhat rather like the rough-riding sergeant major. That was when the tough side of him came out. Clearly he wished to give us a taste of strict discipline in accordance with his own experiences in the cavalry riding school . . . Our country rides were more peaceful, and in them he explained the time and place for each pace. He always insisted that my younger sister Rene and I should never frighten our ponies, warning us that if we did we would pay for it later by being thrown off . . . When one of us did fall off cantering downhill behind his awesome back, we would be greeted by the sudden disappearance of all traces of austerity from his face and good-natured laughter shone at us instead.[5]

In the same book Haig's daughter Alexandra is quoted, recalling riding back from days out hunting: 'I can remember looking at that merciless back rising in a trot ahead of me and longing for it to stop. If I was really desperate with a stitch in my side I would call out "Daddy" and then at last he would stop.'[6] Despite the references to the 'awesome' and 'merciless back' the present Earl emphasises that it was a loving home, with indeed a 'homely' atmosphere. Haig did not overawe his wife, who was quite ready to criticise him if she thought it appropriate, for instance for spoiling his daughters. Lady Haig recalled that Haig was afraid of spoiling his son, but showered attention on his daughters. It is a reflection perhaps on the present Earl's character, rather than that of his father that he recalls that when he was taken prisoner in the Second World War 'I was able to shed the burden of the responsibility of living up to my father's great reputation as a soldier. Now suddenly fate had liberated me.'[7] Earlier, as a child:

I spent some time each morning with my mother as she lay in bed, talking about my father's life and career. Her praise and admiration were unqualified. In her eyes he was greater than Wellington, greater than Marlborough. She was determined to inspire in me some of the sense of duty and the humility which were his. The picture she painted assumed a powerful if unreal force in my life and imbued me with worship and admiration for an ideal almost saint-like father figure.[8]

It is an interesting reflection on Haig's essentially simple, down-to-earth outlook that he vetoed Eton for his son because of its association with snobbery and with toffs with whom he did not feel at home.

The grant of £100,000 had not made Haig a rich man. Of it £40,000 was required for essential repairs to Bemersyde. The house was in a very poor state when it was given to him, and it was three years before he could move in. Haig told his wife that his son would not be able to keep it on after his death, and the present Earl was only able to do so by extending the estate to supplement its income when he reached his majority. While serving in Palestine in 1940 he used £10,000 which remained from the government grant to buy two neighbouring farms from a cousin.

The recognition that Haig received from the state after the war is briefly referred to in a barbed little biographical note at the beginning of Beaverbrook's *Men and Power, 1917–1918,* which deserves to be quoted, not for its accuracy, but for the Beaver's enthusiastic malice and a literary style that is reminiscent of that of A.J.P. Taylor:

HAIG, Field-Marshal Sir Douglas
Fifty-six years of age in 1917, Haig was married, with one son and two daughters. He had been educated at Clifton and Brasenose College, Oxford, from which he went on to Sandhurst.

The war diary is a self-revealing document: frank, truthful, egotistical, self-confident and malicious. His spear knew no brother.

Careful of his health, he ate sparingly and drank with moderation, yet he died in 1928 at the age of sixty-six. With the publication of his Private Papers in 1952, he committed suicide 25 years after his death.

Throughout the war Haig held high command in France. He was Commander-in-Chief of the Expeditionary Forces in France and Flanders. In 1917 he was raised to the rank of Field-Marshal.

In 1918 he received the American Cross of Honour and the American Distinguished Service Medal. In 1918 he was offered and refused a Viscountcy. In 1919 he was offered and accepted an Earldom. The same year brought him £100,000 from Parliament and the Order of Merit. In 1920 public subscriptions provided a fund for the purchase of Bemersyde Mansion and estate.

Thereafter Lloyd George's 'War Memoirs' and Haig's own Private Papers redressed the balance of the public favour.[10]

But little criticism was made of Haig during his lifetime. French published *1914*, partly ghosted with the assistance of a well known journalist, Lovat Fraser. Edmonds said that he understood 'that the Field-Marshal sat in an armchair and talked to his ghost and was questioned by him, a shorthand writer taking down what was said'.[10] The purpose of his book was mainly to address criticisms of the retreat from Mons made by Smith-Dorrien, although it also touched on Haig's contributions to the Council of War of August 1914.

Churchill's *The World Crisis* appeared in 1927, and in it he criticised some aspects of Haig's command, including the prolongation of the Battle of the Somme and of Third Ypres. Haig was particularly annoyed, as he had assisted Churchill by lending him his diaries. The second Earl presents an intriguing picture of Haig and his chief gunner, Sir Noel Birch, driving back to Bemersyde from a Conservative rally at Floors Castle in the summer of 1927, their car explosive with criticism of Churchill and his description of Passchendaele. Churchill himself was driving along in the car behind, on his way to join them for tea at Bemersyde.[11] As soon as Haig emerged from his car, his anger was displaced by the geniality of a host; and indeed he respected Churchill as Minister for Munitions and later Secretary of State for War.

Despite the private outburst about Churchill's use of the diaries, he and Haig formed an unlikely collaboration as *The World Crisis* was written, Haig coming close to displacing Edmonds as Churchill's principal military adviser. Churchill proffered a draft of an early section, generously pointing out that later passages would not conceal his view that Haig was wrong in certain areas, such as Third Ypres. 'I need scarcely say that these criticisms are expressed in terms appropriate to the pleasant personal relations which have for so many years and in such varied circumstances existed between us.'[12] Haig acknowledged a copy of the published work: 'The book will have an honoured place in my library here . . . In order to enjoy reading your writings it is not, I find, necessary to agree with <u>all</u> the opinions which you express.' The criticisms would have been more extreme, had Churchill not been fairly ready to accept many of the amendments which Haig pressed on him. Churchill was prepared to agree that Haig had cooperated willingly with the French, to correct his account of the politics behind the Nivelle offensive and the Calais agreement, and to emphasise the British role in the Hundred Days. Indeed Beaverbrook complained to Churchill that he was taking too soft a line on Haig. Churchill replied with vigour: 'As a matter of fact my subsequent study of the war has led me to think a good deal better of Haig than I did at the time. It is absolutely certain there was no one who could have taken his place.'[13]

Haig was anxious to establish the record for history. During the war Lady Haig typed up the copies of the manuscript diaries that arrived daily by King's Messenger from Haig's carbon notepad. Haig had total confidence in his wife's discretion and through the war years had been able to cope with the stresses that he faced by pouring out his thoughts into the diaries and letters. After the war he gave her a copy of his *Despatches*, which he inscribed:

> To my wife Doris in grateful recollection of all she was to me during the Great War . . . Although she regularly received instalments to my daily diary and so knew more than those at home what was taking place at the Front, yet no one has ever been able to say 'Lady Haig told me of this'!

This typewritten series has not been preserved. Now, after the war a little cottage industry was established, as Lord and Lady Haig and Lady Haig's mother sorted through all his papers, and Lady Haig typed out the manuscript diaries in their entirety. In the process Haig made additions and deletions, a process that obviously invites suspicions that he was falsifying the record. It has even been suggested that all of the diaries was written after the war.[14] Much scholarship has been devoted to the issue, and that suggestion, along with various other attacks on the reliability of the diaries, can safely be dismissed.[15]

Haig had no correspondence secretaries after the war. He wrote all his own letters including many letters to ex-servicemen in his own meticulous handwriting and, with Lady Haig, now embarked on revising the diaries so that they were in a form which he considered appropriate. That did not involve falsification of the record. What he was particularly anxious to do was not to leave the impression of pettiness which could be created by a record of comments and criticisms made in the heat of the moment. Brought up, as his son described it, 'in a simple Scottish way intent on doing his duty', he disliked personal vituperation. He eschewed undignified dispute. He had an elevated, perhaps unrealistic, notion of duty and public life, and he did not wish the moments when he had used the diaries as a means of letting off steam to compromise these principles. The other purpose of his revisions was an attempt to clarify incidents in the light of any controversy that surrounded them. He did not in any meaningful sense falsify the record, and would not have regarded himself as doing so: what he was doing was not unusual in an age in which dignity was expected of its public men; Wilson's diaries, and later Alanbrooke's diaries, were not so sanitised, and were both criticised by some for being too speedy a publication of private thoughts composed when feelings were high.

The manuscript diaries, as well as the typescript, are in the public domain in the National Library of Scotland and can be compared. That anyone has undertaken the Stakhanovite task of comparing them in their totality seems unlikely, but many partial exercises have been carried out and no dramatic discrepancies have been discovered. One or two interesting divergences (already noted in this narrative) have been found, but otherwise only minor amendments and additions, with very few alterations. He decided not to publish the diaries, though he made them available to scholars.

The preparation of the diaries was part of his wider approach to the history of the war: he wanted to stand aloof from criticism and self-justification, and let an objective study of the facts speak for itself. He published a long *Final Despatch* in 1919. This document does, it deserves to be noticed, acknowledge the use of technology and the movement to all-arms warfare, but for the most part it is a recapitulation of his long-held and frequently expressed views about wearing-down before breaking through:

Neither the course of the war itself nor the military lessons to be drawn therefrom can properly be comprehended, unless the long succession of battles commenced on the Somme in 1916 and ended in November of last year on the Sambre are viewed as forming part of one great and continuous engagement . . .

If the views set out by me . . . are accepted, it will be recognised that the war did not follow any unprecedented course, and that its end was neither sudden nor should it have been unexpected. The rapid collapse of Germany's military powers in the latter half of 1918 was the logical outcome of the fighting of the previous two years . . .

It would not have taken place but for the period of ceaseless attrition which used up the reserves of the German Armies, while the constant and growing pressure of the blockade sapped with more deadly insistence from year to year at the strength and resolution of the German people. It is in the great battles of 1916 and 1917 that we have to seek for the secret of our victory in 1918.

The content of the *Final Despatch* was predictable, but unfortunate. He could have said, and for the sake of his position in history should have said, that he had presided over the biggest and most sudden change that had ever taken place in British military history, and in doing so had shortened the war by at least one year, perhaps considerably more. He could have explained that he had stimulated and encouraged the adoption of totally new tactics, weapons and technology, harnessing the results of research and experiment in order to make warfare infinitely more scientific that it had been before. He could have predicted that warfare would never be the same again. Instead of all that, he remembered what he had been taught at Staff College about the structured nature of warfare, and he distorted what had happened in France to make it conform to that structure. In truth, the battles of the latter half of the Hundred Days, to take the most obvious example, were not 'wearing-down' battles, except in the sense that an enemy would be worn down by any defeat. In practice, Haig had proved innovative, flexible and imaginative; as to the theory of warfare, he remained rigidly conservative. His portrayal of his war as one fought in the traditional way tends to reinforce the idea that he was a blinkered traditionalist.

The backward-looking aspects to the *Final Despatch* point to the ambivalence and confusion that existed in Haig's mind throughout the war, ambivalence and confusion which largely resulted from the collision of his views with events, compounded by his inherent optimism.

Conversely, even in the excitement and drive of the Hundred Days, he failed to recognise that this *was* breakthrough: he saw his operations still as a prelude to breakthrough that had not occurred and which, as late as October 1918, he thought might not occur for another year.

Another literary exercise at Bemersyde was to copy a number of quotations into his notebook. His favourite, according to Lady Haig, was from a poem by Adam Lindsay Gordon:

> Question not, but live and labour
>   Till the good is won,
> Helping every feeble neighbour,
>   Seeking help from none.
> Life is mostly froth and bubble.
>   Two things stand like stone;
> Kindness in another's trouble,
>   Courage in your own.

He read and approved of many of Edmonds' chapters of the *Official History*. Edmonds, his old colleague at Staff College, was in correspondence always 'Archimedes.':

6th Augt. 1925
My Dear Archimedes
I am returning with this the chapters on Neuve Chapelle. I think that they are all very excellent and I congratulate you on the way in which you have told the story so <u>accurately</u>, and yet without attaching blame to anyone . . . There is no doubt that for fully five hours our troops were walking about in the village of Neuve Chapelle without being fired at from anywhere! . . . [S]tories round it reached the CinC at Hazebroucke, and it took all my influence to stop him from sending Rawley home . . .

In judging our attitude at Neuve Chapelle, it should always be remembered that until that action was fought the French were of an opinion that the British might be helpful to hold and act defensively ('comme à Waterloo, Ypres etc.') but that they would be of little help to <u>drive</u> the Germans from France.[16]

In the same letter he goes on to say that in 1917 after taking Vimy and Monchy-le-Preux he had to go on attacking to prevent 'Nivelle and co. from saying that the British had not held the German Reserves, and so the French attack was not successful'.[17]

To finish the story of the diaries, we move to the period shortly after Haig's death. His trustees, who were General Hugo du Pree and Brigadier Fisher along with Lady Haig entrusted to Duff Cooper the task of writing the official biography. Lady Haig's health, both physical and mental, was now suffering and her attitude to Haig, whom she 'regarded as greater than Wellington, greater than Marlborough', was unbalanced. She had been greatly upset by early criticisms of her husband, particularly Lloyd George's. Despite her financial worries (she received no widow's pension), she had thrown herself into a continuation of her husband's work. She travelled widely to support his interests and in particular worked hard for the welfare of ex-servicemen. These burdens were too great, and she found any criticism of the Commander-in-Chief unacceptable. She took exception to Duff Cooper's biography despite the fact that it is a fulsome tribute almost in the Victorian tradition. She was also horrified to know that Duff Cooper, who was writing the biography amidst his responsibilities at the Treasury and the War Office, had temporarily mislaid the Atbara print and several photographs she had entrusted to him. In response to the criticisms that she found so distressing, she planned to bring out her own biography, making use of the diaries, despite the fact that Duff Cooper had been granted sole access to them. She was stopped by the Scottish court action of Interdict, and was therefore in the invidious position of being sued by her fellow trustees.

She did then write (but without making use of the diaries) her own biography called, tellingly, *The Man I Knew:* a well-written book, not without humour and insight, which supplies a useful, intimate picture of Haig to supplement the more formal studies. It is of course uncritically loyal and supportive. The first volume of the planned life that did make use of extracts from the diaries, and which could not therefore be published, covering the years up to the First World War, was written and provides the student with a valuable picture of Haig's pre-war military career. In 1930 she was in correspondence with Edmonds regarding General Charteris' *Field-Marshal Earl Haig*: 'What a cruel description of my husband's childhood General Charteris gave and without knowledge!'[18] Edmonds had been lent the diaries in connection with the Official History, and he was bombarded with concerned letters and telegrams from Lady Haig despite his assurances that he would keep the diaries safe. She talks of wanting to write a short book 'to clear away the mischief made by General Charteris's book and rumours floating everywhere that Douglas was so antagonistic to the French . . .'[19] Haig had 'deplored the books that came out' but intended his diaries, shorn of contemporary, heated criticism, notably of French, to set the record straight. The other parts to be excised were comments regarding the prelude to the war, Wilson's intrigues, the King's criticism to Haig of 'his Commanding Officer, French', Sir Clive Wigram's attempts to bring him into an intrigue and Sir Clive's naming all French's staff in an intrigue against Kitchener. 'About Duff Cooper, I shall not dare – to a great man, like you, to say, "Shut up", but please do not make my task so difficult is all I ask.'[20]

Edmonds wrote to Charteris on 10 December 1928:

My Dear Charteris,

I was summoned by Lady Haig to tea. She is much displeased with you about the Life of D.H. of which you told her in a letter. Incidentally she expressed annoyance that I had read your proofs – I could of course say that I hadn't seen them – and had given you a letter of D.H.'s. I can't remember that I did, at any rate it could not have been an important one. *"Eine Frau muss Man so zart behandeln wie ein Pferd."* ['A woman must be handled as carefully as a horse."], so don't mention things . . .[21]

Haig wanted his wife to write his biography, but intended that the full diaries should not be published for two generations. In the event his son made them available to Robert Blake for the purpose of publishing substantial extracts, edited only 'in order to make them more accessible', and then put them into the public domain by depositing them in the National Library of Scotland.

To return to the chronology of the narrative, and Haig's later years, Charteris noticed a change in him at this time:

Though the years had dealt kindly with him physically, and though he himself was unconscious of any change, those who knew him best, and who saw him only at intervals, noticed the marks that the passage of time was leaving on him. He was less alert, less abrupt. The barrier of reserve was still there, but it was markedly less pronounced than when he was still in office. His criticism was more kindly, and his toleration broader and more sympathetic. His mind turned more to events of the past; at times he appeared to brood and commune with himself, and it seemed as if it was only by a conscious effort that he could recall his mind to the present day. He had lost much of his dislike of old age, and would talk of what he would be able to do if and when infirmity came to him. There was still that almost pathetic confidence in special diets. Sanatogen had given place to oranges. There was still that complete indifference to affairs that not immediately concerned him . . . His thoughtfulness for others became very noticeable.[22]

His struggle for achievement was over. He had succeeded. He could relax and, perhaps for the first time, be himself.

His views on public affairs were essentially those of a man of his time. He was, like so many of the middle and upper classes, pathologically afraid of what he called Bolshevism. He did not question for a moment the permanence, for the foreseeable future, of the British Empire, and he remained committed to its values. In a speech at Clifton in June 1922, for instance, he told the boys that:

> Only by work and worth can a man attain true eminence or a nation remain great. We have received from the hands of our forefathers an Empire that is yet greater in ideals and qualities for which it stands than in the wide territories of which it is composed. It is for us to preserve these qualities and seek after these ideals, no less than to keep these territories free from the foot of the invader. Courage, manliness, truth, clean-living and honest dealing are the qualities that have made our nation great and must be preserved if that greatness is to last.

Again like many of his contemporaries, he regarded Mussolini, whom he met in Italy in 1926, with some admiration, in contrast to the lack of leadership he observed in Britain:

> Yesterday evening I had an interview with Mussolini. I found him most pleasant. There is no doubt that he has already done much good in this country. His view is, that everyone is a

servant of the State and must honestly do his best to serve the State. If anyone fails he is punished. We want someone like that at home at the present time.

But his preoccupation in the post-war years, the cause for which he sacrificed his health, ignoring his doctors' advice and probably shortening his life, was the promotion of the interests of his ex-servicemen, particularly through the British Legion. Norman Dixon has said that Haig's work with the British Legion was deliberately intended to supplant a picture of a callous, uncaring leader.[23] But Haig's mind simply did not work in that way. He was never callous or uncaring, but as Commander-in-Chief he had applied himself to the practical task of winning the war; now he applied himself to the practical task of doing what he could for those who had fought in the war. Haig was of course a product of his times and his background. His childhood, with an alcoholic and ill-tempered father in the background, was singular, and according to conventional Freudian theory, a close relationship with a doting mother will tend to produce an uncheckable confidence on the part of the grown boy in his own abilities and capacity to flourish: 'The young man who is his mother's unquestioned favourite will develop a triumphant sense of self-esteem and, with that the strength for success in later life.' Some doctors also hold that those who suffer from asthma are likely to throw themselves into a determined bid for achievement. Not everything about Haig was attractive. In many but not all matters he *was* unimaginative and profoundly conservative. He would not have been much fun as a dinner companion – at least in his early and middle years. Later he was more reflective and might have been interesting, although he would be unlikely to say that he had made any serious mistakes, and he would not be someone with whom to have an approving discussion of radical politics. But he had strengths and weaknesses, just as he had in his career successes and failures, and it is unproductive to try to force him into caricatured attitudes so as to obscure reality, rather than to illuminate it. Dixon's commitment to an extreme and predetermined behavioural type sheds little light on the real Haig.

It is a widely accepted myth that he was the founder of the Legion, just as it is a myth that it was he was solely responsible for bringing together all the ex-servicemen's organisations that were established after the war. Niall Barr and Gary Sheffield have traced the true origins of the Legion and have also shown that Generals Smith-Dorrien and Hamilton successively explored the amalgamation of the rival organisations.[24] He did, however, *encourage* the idea of unity amongst the different groups, and once the Legion was formed as its National President he gave it immense support. The first request that came to Haig to lead the Legion was met with a categorical refusal. He said that the ex-service organisations had no business to be quarrelling amongst themselves and that he would only come in as President when unity had been achieved. At that stage, one of the two other principal ex-service organisations did not accept former officers and the other, although it accepted them, directed its main work to former other ranks. Even as the war was ending, Haig – and Lady Haig – had been particularly concerned about the plight of ex-officers and their dependants, and before coming to the Legion, Haig was involved in forming an Officers' Association and raising funds in that connection. The establishment of the Officers' Association acted as a catalyst to the process of unification, a process to which Haig contributed. He wrote to the Chairman of the Legion on 9 February 1920: 'I am doing all I can to get the ex-officer to take an interest in ex-service organisations generally.'[25] Although his concern for former officers pre-dated his involvement in the Legion, once that involvement was established it was his fundamental principle that no distinction amongst members should depend on the ranks that they had held.

He was not involved in the detailed, day-to-day work of the Legion, but he tirelessly did what he could, making speeches, inspecting parades, and giving the Legion the benefit of his prestige. Some left-wing ex-servicemen took the cynical view that the purpose of the Legion was to act as a paramilitary force, 'Haig's White

Guard'. The government was also concerned that the Legion might come to resemble the Grand Army of the Republic in the United States after the Civil War, which had become a powerful interest group with close links to the Republican Party. But the reality was that the Legion proudly kept apart from government influence, so that they could argue more strongly for pensions. The Legion was never identified, as were some continental ex-servicemen's associations, with reactionary politics or direct action. His essentially non-political view of the Legion's activities is stressed in an article he wrote for *John Bull* in 1922 in which he dwelt also on the importance of recruiting new members: Don't go off with the idea that it is no good asking so-and-so, because he is doing very well and does not need help. He is the very man we want! Ask him to join. Tell him it is his duty, and see that he does his duty.[26]

His commitment was practical and not sentimental. When a committee member pointed out that a member who was working unsatisfactorily was nonetheless a volunteer, Haig responded: 'But there is no reason we should trust a voluntary fool.'[27] Although the British Legion was not his own creation, the 'Annual Poppy Day' was, and indeed he privately guaranteed the first, 1921, Poppy Day against financial loss.

Haig travelled extensively, both to visit overseas ex-servicemen's organisations, and to found the British Empire Services League, which he described as 'a mighty federation to bind together all who served in the forces of the Empire during the Great War'. The Empire Service League was very much in line with Haig's views. Its policy was 'Loyalty to King and Empire', and 'Unity and development of the British Commonwealth'. Its objects were 'to further and maintain the spirit of self-sacrifice which inspired all ranks in the War, to subordinate their individual welfare to the interests of the common weal, and to perpetuate a spirit of comradeship and patriotism throughout the Empire.'

He continued to press the case for the united National Church. Although a member of the Church of Scotland and an elder both at St Columba's, Pont Street, and at the little church near Bemersyde, where he regularly carried out his duties, he took no narrow, sectarian view of religion. In 1927 he attended the House of Lords debates on the Prayer Book, ultimately voting in favour of the Revised Book.

On 28 January 1928 Haig attended the enrolment ceremony of the 20th Richmond (Earl Haig's Own) Boy Scouts, the sons of disabled ex-servicemen employed at the local British Legion poppy factory. He told them that:

> I have come to the enrolment ceremony, and have become patron of the troop, because I wish to encourage the British Legion spirit in the rising generation . . . It is essential that the young should be taught the meaning of Empire and the sacrifices that their fathers have made for it . . . I ask you boys always to play the game and to try and realise what citizenship and public spirit really means. When you grow up always remember that you belong to a great Empire, and when people speak disrespectfully of England always stand up and defend your country.

While in London for this engagement he stayed with Henrietta, as did his brother John. Two days later, on Sunday 30 January, he played cards after dinner. At 10 o'clock in the evening he said goodnight and went to his room. A few minutes later John heard sounds and went to his brother's room to find him in distress. He died almost immediately. Fortunately Henrietta, who had done so much for her brother throughout her life, was now so frail that she was unaware of his death.

In the days, weeks and months that followed, Lady Haig received countless letters of condolence. The letter from the King was in his own hand, and was addressed to

> My Dear Doris . . .
> You know how fond I have always been of Douglas & I had absolute confidence in him & knew that if he was given the chance and not interfered with, that he would win.[28]

Haig's son, the young new Earl, received a letter from Dr Charles Warr, Dean of the Thistle:

You have had such a wonderful Father – one of the greatest Scotsmen that ever lived – and he has left you with a name which will always be held in honour not only in this country but throughout the whole world. And I am sure that you will always try to remember that the reason he was so <u>truly</u> great, was because in his character he was so simple and so good'.[27]

'It is hard to convey to a later generation', wrote George Duncan,

the emotion that swept the country when the news went out that Haig was dead. Not within living memory had the nation accorded to any of its sons such a demonstration of loyalty, gratitude and affection. Day after day thousands filed reverently past the body as it lay in state, first in London and then in Edinburgh. Vast crowds lined the London streets as the procession went on its way from St. Columba's (Church of Scotland) in Kensington to the National Service in Westminster Abbey, and then to Waterloo Station, from which the body was now to go by train to Edinburgh.[30]

After the ceremony in St Giles' Cathedral, Haig's body was taken by train down to the Borders. Then, in accordance with his wishes, and in an expression of the poetry and simplicity that lay at his heart, the coffin was placed on a plain farm cart, and, drawn by four farm horses, it was taken to be buried in the grounds of the ruined Dryburgh Abbey, near Bemersyde. The grave was marked, again in accordance with the field-marshal's wishes, with the same simple headstone as marks the grave of every soldier who lies in France.

Haig lies where he should. The fierce feuds of the Borders are long past. The landscape is beautiful, quiet and pastoral. Not far away is

the view of the Eildon Hills which Sir Walter Scott so loved. The
people that inhabit that landscape are quiet and peaceful too, but
conscious of their worth and of their history. They are decent, reticent
countrymen, straightforward and honourable. Far from Westminster
and Whitehall, Haig is amongst his own.

Notes

I have tried to avoid references where the source of a quotation is clear from its context, or where it is of an uncontentious nature. In particular, except where I thought them particularly important or they are hitherto unnoticed, I have refrained from giving references for what are obviously quotations from Haig's diaries and correspondence. Haig's papers have been published in part in Lord Blake's edition of 1952 and in the edition published by Gary Sheffield and John Bourne in 2005. They are also available for consultation in the National Library of Scotland, at length and accompanied by tantalising ephemera that interested the Field-Marshal, like a brochure on *Profitable Poultry Keeping*.

Abbreviation used

DHF Douglas Haig Fellowship
NLS acc. National Library of Scotland accession
LHCMA Basic Liddell Hart Centre for Military Archives, King's College, London

Chapter 1

1. See Daniel Todman, 'Sans Peur et Sans Reproche', in *The Journal of Military History* 67 (October 2003), p. 1083ff.

2. Parliamentary Debates House of Lords 8 February 1928, Col. 45ff.

3. Parliamentary Debates House of Lords 8 February 1928, Col. 50ff.

4. Parliamentary Debates House of Lords 8 February 1928, Col. 100.

5. Parliamentary Debates House of Lords 8 February 1928, Col. 107.

6. For an extensive study of the background to the erection of the statue, see Stephen Heathorn, 'A "matter for artists, and not for soldiers"? The Cultural Politics of the Earl Haig National Memorial, 1928–1937', *Journal of British Studies* 44 (July 2005), p. 536ff.

7. *Express*, 6 November 1998.

8. A.N. Wilson, *Sunday Telegraph*, 7 May 2000.

9. LHCMA, Edmonds II/III/16, WSC to Edmonds 7/7/26.

10. Churchill, *Great Contemporaries* (1941 edition), p. 192.

11. Powell, *Plumer, The Soldiers' General*, p. 252.

12. Gary Sheffield & John Bourne, *Douglas Haig. War Diaries and Letters 1914–1918* (London, Weidenfield & Nicolson, 2005).

13. *The Listener*, 3 August 1961.

14. Robert Gore-Langton, 'Truth from the Trenches', *The Spectator*, 15 January 2005.

15. *Daily Mail*, 20 March 1963.

16. See Brian Bond, *The Unquiet Western Front, Britain's Role in Literature and History*, p. 79 – and generally, for an excellent study of the clash of literature and history in relation to the war.

17. See Brian Bond, *The Unquiet Western Front*, and BLHCMA Lecture, 'A Victory worse than a Defeat? British Interpretations of the First World War', 20 November 1997.

18. Hugh Cecil, 'British War Novelists', in Hugh Cecil & Peter H. Liddle (eds), *Facing Armageddon: The First World War Experienced*, 1996, p. 801ff. See also an interesting article: Emma Mahoney: 'The Worst Donkey: representations of F.M. Sir Douglas Haig in Great War Television Documentaries', in *Stand To!* The Journal of the Western Front Association No. 73, April 2005, p. 11ff.

19. John Terraine, DHF *Records*, Issue No. 3.

20. DHF *Records*, Issue No. 10.

21. Hew Strachan, reviewing *The Smoke and the Fire* in *Journal of the Society for Army Historical Research* 59 (1981), p. 177.

22. Gary Sheffield and John Bourne, 'Dropping the Donkey Epithet', in BBC *History*, March 2005, Vol. 6, no. 3, pp. 12–16.

23. Dr N. Faulkner, 'Haig's Reputation', in BBC *History*, April 2005, Vol. 6, no.4, p. 104.

24. Note to Address by Gary Sheffield, DHF *Records* Issue No. 7.

Chapter 2

1. John Russell, *The Haigs of Bemersyde*.

2. Robertson, *From Private to Field-Marshal*, p. 175.

3. National Library of Scotland acc.3155/324(a).

4. Quoted Lady Haig, *The Man I Knew*, p. 13.

5. Quoted Lady Haig, *The Man I Knew*, p. 14.
6. Warner, *Field Marshal Earl Haig*, p. 14.
7. Derek Winterbottom, *John Percival, The Great Educator*, p. 1.
8. See Derek Winterbottom, *Henry Newbolt and the Spirit of Clifton*, Bristol, 1986.
9. Sir George Arthur, *Lord Haig*, pp. 3–4.
10. Lady Haig, *The Man I Knew*, p. 15.
11. Family communication.
12. Memorial Issue, British Legion *Journal*, March 1928, p. 280.
13. Huntly House 4303/820/81.
14. Charteris, *Field-Marshal Earl Haig*, p. 145.

Chapter 3

1. See M.G. Brock & M.C. Curthoys (eds), *The History of the University of Oxford*, for an extensive account of Oxford in Haig's time.
2. F. Madan, 'Brasenose' in A. Clark (ed.), *The Colleges of Oxford: Their History & Traditions* (1891), p. 265.
3. G.S. Duncan, *Douglas Haig As I Knew Him*, p. 101.
4. Duncan, *Douglas Haig As I Knew Him*, pp. 102–3.
5. Duncan, *Douglas Haig As I Knew Him*, p. 27.
6. Unpublished autobiography of Brigadier-General Sir James Edmonds, LHCMA, Edmonds MSS, III/2/10.
7. John Terraine, *Douglas Haig, The Educated Soldier*, p. 5.

Chapter 4

1. Arthur, *Lord Haig*, p. 93.
2. Gerald J. De Groot, *Douglas Haig 1861–1928*.
3. Quoted De Groot, *Douglas Haig 1861–1928*, p. 32.
4. See 'Douglas Haig, Adjutant: Recollections by Veterans of the 7th Hussars' in *Journal of the Society for Army Historical Research*, Vol. LXX111 No. 294 (Summer 1995), p. 124.
5. Quoted Richard Holmes, *The Little Field-Marshal*, p. 278.
6. Holmes, *The Little Field-Marshal*, p. 48.
7. Quoted Holmes, *The Little Field-Marshal*, p. 3.

Chapter 5

1. Interview with Lord Haig, October 2003.
2. Quoted Farrar-Hockley (ed.), *The Commanders*, p. 50.
3. Bond *The Victorian Army & the Staff College*, London, 1972, pp. 301, 313.
4. LHCMA, letter to Kiggell 27/4/11, Kiggell 1/10.
5. See a most interesting study of Haig's Staff College examination history: John Hussey, ' "A Very Substantial Grievance", said the Secretary of State: Douglas

Haig's Examination Troubles 1893' in *Journal of the Society for Army Historical Research*, Vol. LXXIV No. 299 (Autumn 1896), p. 169.

6. See Gerald De Groot, *Douglas Haig*, p. 39.
7. DHF *Records*, December 2002, p. 14ff.
8. NLS acc.3155/6(e).
9. Arthur, *Lord Haig*, p. 11.
10. Quoted by Terraine, *Douglas Haig*, p. 10.
11. See Bond, *Victorian Army*, p. 164, quoting correspondence from Creedy to Duff Cooper, 21 May 1935. See also John Hussey 'A Very Substantial Grievance', quoted above. See also H.J. Creedy, 'H.J. Creedy to Duff Cooper 21/5/35', copied to Brig.-Gnl Edmonds LHCMA I/2B118G.
12. George Barrow, *The Fire of Life*, Hutchinson, 1941, pp. 43–4.
13. Field-Marshal Lord Wavell, *Reminiscences* Chap. XIV, pp. 266–8.
14. Quoted De Groot, *Douglas Haig*, p. 48.
15. See Brian Bond, *The Victorian Army & The Staff College 1854–1914*, p. 163.
16. Edmonds Memoirs, quoted Bond, *The Victorian Army*, p. 154.
17. For a study of the Staff College in Haig's time, and indeed before and after, see Brian Bond, *The Victorian Army*.
18. Stephen Badsey, 'Cavalry and the Development of Breakthrough Doctrine', in Griffith (ed.), *British Fighting Methods in the Great War*, p. 141.
19. *Military Operations 1915* Vol. I I, p. 152.
20. LHCMA, Edmonds 1/2B/5a.
21. Quoted Laffin, *British Butchers and Bunglers of World War I*, p. 161.
22. Tim Travers, *The Killing Ground*.
23. British Legion *Journal*, Memorial Issue, p. 258.
24. Charteris, *Field-Marshal Earl Haig*, p. 14.
25. Personal communication.
26. E.K.G. Sixsmith, *Douglas Haig*, pp. 9, 10.

Chapter 6

1. Bond, *Victorian Army*, p. 167.
2. Warner, *Field Marshal Earl Haig*, p. 17.
3. Haig's emphases.
4. Quoted Sixsmith, *Douglas Haig*, p. 26.
5. Terraine, *Douglas Haig*, p. 19.
6. See Duff Cooper, *Haig*, p. 13.
7. Quoted Sixsmith, *Douglas Haig*, p. 25.
8. Quoted Terraine, *Douglas Haig*, p. 20.
9. Quoted Charteris, *Field-Marshal Earl Haig*, p. 17.

Chapter 7

1. Charteris, *Field-Marshal Earl Haig*, pp. 17–18.
2. John Hussey, 'Saving Johnnie French: Douglas Haig's Loan: May

1899', *Army Quarterly and Defence Journal*, Vol. 121, No. 3 (July 1991), p. 318.

3. Holmes, *The Little Field-Marshal*, pp. 50–1.
4. Holmes, *The Little Field-Marshal*, p, 80.
5. Quoted Warner, *Field Marshal Earl Haig*, p. 71.
6. *The Times History*, III, pp. 394–5.
7. See De Groot, 'Ambition, Duty and Doctrine: Douglas Haig's Rise to Command', in B. Bond & N. Cave (eds), *Haig: A Reappraisal 70 Years On*.
8. Sixsmith, *Douglas Haig*, p. 39–40.
9. Tim Travers, *The Killing Ground*, p. 9.
10. Arthur, *Lord Haig*, p. 34.
11. Quoted in Beckett in J. Gooch (ed.) *The Boer War*, 2000, p. 45.
12. Charteris, *Field-Marshal Earl Haig*, p. 21.
13. Quoted by Liddell Hart, *Through the Fog of War*, p. 47.
14. Sixsmith, *Douglas Haig*, p. 36.
15. *Report on the Imperial Yeomanry*, W.O. 108/263.
16. Quoted Terraine, *Douglas Haig*, p. 32.
17. De Groot, 'Ambition, Duty and Doctrine', pp. 99–100.
18. Quoted Warner, *Field Marshal Earl Haig*, pp. 87–8.
19. Henderson, *The Science of War*, p. 371.
20. Arthur, *Lord Haig*, p. 38.
21. Arthur, *Lord Haig*, p. 41.
22. Arthur, *Lord Haig*, p. 50–1.
23. Quoted De Groot, 'Ambition, Duty and Doctrine', p. 98.
24. Philip Warner, *Kitchener, the Man behind the Legend*, p. 145.

Chapter 8

1. Family tradition, communicated to the author by the present Earl Haig.
2. See Second Earl Haig, *My Father's Son,* p. 4ff.
3. Terraine, *Douglas Haig*, p. 37.
4. DHF *Records*, December 2002, p. 17.
5. DHF *Records*, December 2002, p. 18.
6. Lady Haig, *The Man I Knew*, p. 38.
7. French to Haig, 6 August 1905 NLS acc.3155/334(e).

Chapter 9

1. Lady Haig, *The Man I Knew*, p. 73.
2. Esher, Journal, 11 August 1916, quoted James Lees-Milne *The Life of Reginald Second Viscount Esher, the Enigmatic Edwardian,* p. 261.
3. Quoted Arthur, *Lord Haig*, p. 56.
4. Dudley Sommer, *Haldane of Cloan*, pp. 192–3.
5. J.A. Spender, *Men & Things.*
6. Sommer, *Haldane*, pp. 318–19.

7. LHCMA, Report of the Committee appointed to consider the Education and Training of Officers of the Army Cd982.

8. Terraine, *Douglas Haig*, p. 38.

9. H.C.G. Matthew, *Oxford DNB*.

10. A.J.P. Taylor, *The Struggle for the Mastery in Europe, 1848–1918,* Table VI, p. xxix. And see John Hussey, 'Without an Army and Without any Preparation to Equip One' in *The British Army Review*, no. 109.

11. Cd. 7523, *Memorandum by the Secretary of State for War*, p. 2.

12. Quoted, Sir George Arthur, *Life of Lord Kitchener*, iii, p. 265fn.

13. Quoted Robertson, *From Private to Field-marshal*, p. 93.

14. Sixsmith, *Douglas Haig*, p. 57.

15. Quoted in British Legion *Journal*, Memorial Issue.

16. Private communication, Lord Haig, 30 June 2005.

17. Charteris, *Field-Marshal Earl Haig*, pp. 44–5.

18. Charteris, *Field-Marshal Earl Haig*, p. 389.

19. See Duff Cooper, *Haig*,

20. Quoted De Groot, 'Ambition, Duty and Doctrine', p. 123.

21. Quoted Terraine, *Douglas Haig*, p. 45.

22. Lady Haig, *The Man I Knew*, p. 55.

23. Lady Haig, *The Man I Knew*, pp. 70,72.

24. LHCMA, Kiggell 1/1.

25. LHCMA, Kiggell 1/4.

26. LHCMA, Kiggell 1/5.

27. LHCMA. Kiggell 1/8.

28. Charteris, *Field-Marshal Earl Haig*, p. 49.

29. LHCMA, Kiggell 1/2.

30. Quoted Charteris, *Field-Marshal Earl Haig*, p. 57.

31. LHCMA, Kiggell 1/18.

32. LHCMA, Kiggell 1/2.

33. Lady Haig, *The Man I Knew*, p. 46.

34. Lady Haig, *The Man I Knew*, pp. 48–50.

35. Lady Haig, *The Man I Knew*, p. 85.

36. Charteris, *Field-Marshal Earl Haig*, p. 60.

37. Charteris, *Field-Marshal Earl Haig*, p. 59.

38. LHCMA, Kiggell 1/18.

39. Lady Haig, *The Man I Knew*, pp. 93–4.

Chapter 10

1. Lady Haig, *The Man I Knew*, pp. 102–3.

2. Duncan, *Douglas Haig as I Knew Him*, p. 68.

3. Charteris *At GHQ*, p. 151.

4. LHCMA, Charteris 2/2.

5. LHCMA, Charteris 2/2.

6. LHCMA, Charteris 2/2.

7. Collier, *Brasshat*.

8. Charteris, *Field-Marshal Earl Haig*, p. 66.
9. Charteris, *Field-Marshal Earl Haig*, pp. 64, 68.
10. Charteris, *At GHQ*, p. 11.
11. Duff Cooper, *Haig*, p. 143.
12. Charteris, *At GHQ*, p. 203.
13. Quoted Collier, *Brasshat*, p. 240.
14. See Sir Sam Fay, *The War Office at War*.
15. Spears, Churchill College, 1/20. 2 July 1968. Quoted, Max Egremont, *Under Two Flags*, p. 11, paperback edition.
16. Churchill, *The World Crisis* II, p. 1264. NB All references to *The World Crisis* are to the two-volume edition.
17. LHCMA, Kiggell 2/1–7.
18. Charteris, *Field-Marshal Earl Haig,* p. 82.
19. Quoted Terraine, *Douglas Haig*, pp. 59–60.
20. Hankey, *The Supreme Command*, p. 80.
21. Terraine, *Douglas Haig*, p. 60–1.
22. Quoted Holmes, *The Little Field-Marshal*, p. 148.

Chapter 11

1. Charteris, *At GHQ*, p. 3.
2. Hankey, *The Supreme Command*, pp. 161–2.
3. Egremont, *Under Two Flags*, p. 14.
4. Quoted Charteris, *Field-Marshal Earl Haig*, p. 80.
5. NLS acc 3155/131.
6. Haig to Major Philip Howell, LHMCA: Howell Papers, 6/12/14.
7. Sir C.E. Callwell, *Field-Marshal Sir Henry Wilson: His Life and Diaries* (London: Cassell, 1927), I, pp. 157–8.
8. Holmes, *The Little Field-Marshal*, pp. 200–3.
9. Quoted Holmes, *The Little Field-Marshal*, p. 233.
10. Quoted Holmes, *The Little Field-Marshal*, p. 234.
11. Charteris, *Field-Marshal Earl Haig*, p. 91.
12. Collier, *Brasshat*, p. 180.
13. Collier, *Brasshat*, p. 1.
14. Brigadier-General J.E. Edmonds: 'An Instructor's Forecast', in British Legion *Journal,* Memorial Issue, p. 259.
15. Terraine, *Douglas Haig*, pp. 87–8.
16. Terraine, *Douglas Haig*, p. 87.
17. Charteris, *At GHQ*, p. 17.
18. Quoted Spears, *Liaison,* pp. 263–4.
19. Charteris, *Field-Marshal Earl Haig*, p. 100.
20. Hankey, *Supreme Command* p. 117.
21. See *Tour of the Aisne*, HMSO 1934.
22. Lady Haig, *The Man I Knew*, pp. 114, 120–1.
23. Lady Haig, *The Man I Knew*, pp. 114–15.
24. *The Inner Truth of October 31st 1914 at Ypres (as told to me by General*

Edmonds):17.2.31 in Liddell Hart papers 11/1931/4, LHCMA, quoted by John Hussey, 'A Hard Day at First Ypres. The Allied Generals and their Problems: 31 October 1914' in *British Army Review* 107, August 1994.

25. Hussey, 'A Hard Day at First Ypres'.
26. Holmes, *The Little Field-Marshal*, p. 251.
27. Holmes, *The Little Field-Marshal*, p. 251.
28. Charteris, *Field-Marshal Earl Haig*, p. 118–19.
29. Charteris, *At GHQ*, p. 60.
30. See Haig's letter to Sir Evelyn Wood 6 November 1914, quoted in Wood, *Winnowed Memories*.

Chapter 12

1. Charteris, *At GHQ*, p. 65.
2. Collier, *Brasshat*, p. 205.
3. Collier, *Brasshat*, p. 206.
4. Letter to Sir James Edmonds quoted by Terraine, *Douglas Haig*, p. 131.
5. Charteris, *At GHQ*, p. 74.
6. Lady Haig, *The Man I Knew*, p. 126.
7. Terraine, *Douglas Haig*, p. 177.
8. Rawlinson to Kitchener 15 March 1915, quoted Robin Prior and Trevor Wilson *The Command on the Western Front: The Military Career of Sir Henry Rawlinson 1914–18*, p. 77.
9. Quoted Terraine, *Douglas Haig*, p. 180.
10. Rawlinson to Wigram 25 March 1915, quoted Prior & Wilson, *Command on the Western Front*, p. 78.
11. Rawlinson to Kitchener 1 April 1915 quoted Prior & Wilson, *Command on the Western Front*, p. 79.
12. LHCMA, French to War Office 17 05 1915 – Robertson 3/1/1.
13. Rawlinson to Kitchener 1 April 1915, quoted Prior & Wilson, *Command on the Western Front*, p. 72.
14. Quoted Terraine, *Douglas Haig*, p. 182.
15. Haig to Rothschild 13 March 1915, NLS acc. 3155/214(a).
16. See Gary Sheffield, *Forgotten Victory*, and Jonathan Bailey, 'British Artillery in the Great War' in Griffith (ed.), *British Fighting Methods*, p. 28.
17. Warner, *Field Marshal Earl Haig*, p. 151.
18. Lady Haig, *The Man I Knew*, p. 127.
19. NLS, acc. 3155/213d.

Chapter 13

1. Terraine, *Douglas Haig*, p. 135.
2. Laffin, *Butchers and Bunglers*, p. 30.
3. Harington, *Plumer of Messines*, p. 72, quoted Powell, *Plumer, The Soldiers' General*, p. 121.

4. Quoted Terraine, *Douglas Haig*, p. 148.

5. Quoted Holmes, *The Little Field-Marshal*, p. 277.

6. Holmes, *The Little Field-Marshal*, pp. 278, 279.

7. Quoted Holmes, *The Little Field-Marshal*, p. 277.

8. Quoted Holmes, *The Little Field-Marshal*, p. 279.

9. Charteris, *At GHQ*, p. 87.

10. Terraine, *Douglas Haig*, p. 150, and see Repington, *The First World War*, pp. 35–41.

11. Holmes, *The Little Field-Marshal*, p. 299.

12. Terraine, *Douglas Haig*, p. 153.

13. Quoted Warner, *Field Marshal Earl Haig*, p. 160.

14. See, respectively, *The Press and the General Staff* and *Prelude to Victory*.

15. Charteris, *Field Marshal Earl Haig*, p. 152.

16. Quoted Charteris, *Field Marshal Earl Haig*, p. 152.

17. Churchill, *The World Crisis* p. 463.

18. Quoted Terraine, *Douglas Haig*, p. 153.

19. LHCMA, Robertson 4/3/23.

20. Quoted, Philip Magnus, *Kitchener: Portait of an Imperialist,* p. 302.

21. Quoted Holmes, *The Little Field-Marshal*, p. 296.

22. Lady Haig, *The Man I Knew*, p. 30.

23. Holmes, *The Little Field-Marshal*, p. 297.

24. Terraine, *Douglas Haig*, p. 155.

25. Rawlinson's Diary, quoted Prior & Wilson, *Command on the Western Front*, p. 107.

Chapter 14

1. Churchill, *Great Contemporaries* (1941 edition), p. 75.

2. Lady Haig, *The Man I Knew*, p. 133.

3. Quoted Alan Clark, *The Donkeys.*

4. Quoted Terraine, *Douglas Haig*, p. 158.

5. Haig's emphasis.

6. Charteris, *Field Marshal Earl Haig*, p. 90.

7. Charteris, *At GHQ*, p. 114.

8. Charteris, *Field Marshal Earl Haig*, p. 157.

9. See Prior & Wilson, *Command on the Western Front*, pp. 111–12.

10. Quoted Warner, *Field Marshal Earl Haig*, p. 174.

11. Charteris, *Field Marshal Earl Haig*, p. 165.

12. Haig's emphasis.

13. Quoted Terraine, *Douglas Haig*, p. 157.

14. Author's emphasis.

15. Charteris, *At GHQ*, p. 113.

16. Walter Reid, *To Arras 1917. A Volunteer's Odyssey,* pp. 110–11.

17. Laffin, *Butchers and Bunglers.*

18. Duff Cooper, *Haig*, p. 273.

19. Charteris, *At GHQ*, p. 118.

20. Churchill & Gilbert, *Churchill*, Companion Volume III, p. 1196.

21. Alan Clark, *The Donkeys,* p. 180 in paperback edition.
22. Harold Nicholson, *George V*, p. 353 in paperback edition.
23. Rawlinson to Derby 12 November 1915, quoted Prior & Wilson, *Command on the Western Front*, p. 133.
24. See also Churchill, *The World Crisis II*, p. 1213.
25. Lady Haig, *The Man I Knew*, pp. 137–8.
26. Esher to Asquith 27 November 1915, quoted James Lees-Milne, *The Life of Reginald Second Viscount Esher, The Enigmatic Edwardian,* p. 278.
27. Quoted Holmes, *The Little Field-Marshal*, p. 128.
28. General Sir Thomas Bridges, *Alarms & Excursions*, p. 138, quoted Powell, *Plumer*, p. 141.
29. Repington, *The First World War*, Vol.2, pp. 297, 341.
30. Churchill & Gilbert, *Churchill,* Companion Volume III, p. 1334.
31. Quoted Sommer, *Haldane*, pp. 331–2.
32. NLS acc. 3155/23d.
33. Quoted Holmes, *The Little Field-Marshal*, p. 2.
34. Robertson, *From Private to Field-Marshal*, p. 36.
35. Robertson, *Private to Field-Marshal*, p. 42.
36. Robertson, *Private to Field-Marshal*, pp. 89–90.
37. Warner, *Field Marshal Earl Haig*, p. 154.
38. Hankey, *Supreme Command*, p. 446.
39. David R. Woodward, 'Sir William Robertson and Sir Douglas Haig', in Bond & Cave, *Haig: Reappraisal*, p. 75.
40. Robertson, *Private to Field-Marshal*, p. 238.
41. Robertson, *Private to Field-Marshal*, p. 253.
42. Churchill, *The Second World War,* Vol. 1, pp. 526–7.
43. DHF *Records*, December 2002, p. 20.

Chapter 15

1. See Gary Sheffield's Haig Fellow's address, DHF *Records*, December 2001, p. 3.
2. LHCMA, Robertson 3/2/1.
3. See John Terraine, DHF *Records*, pp. 4–8.
4. Stephen Badsey, *Oxford DNB*.
5. Keegan, *The First World War*, p. 298.
6. Charteris, *Field Marshal Earl Haig*, p. 190.
7. British Legion *Journal,* Memorial Edition, p. 271.
8. Duncan, *Douglas Haig As I Knew Him*, pp. 20–1.
9. Keegan, *The First World War*, p. 311.
10. Duncan, *Douglas Haig As I Knew Him*, p. 22.
11. Duncan, *Douglas Haig As I Knew Him*, p. 22.
12. Duncan, *Douglas Haig As I Knew Him*, p. 126.
13. Duncan, *Douglas Haig As I Knew Him*, pp. 136–7.
14. Charteris *At GHQ*, p. 133.
15. Riddell, *War Diary*, Volume 1, p. 146.

16. Quoted Duff Cooper, *Haig*, p. 291.
17. Terraine, *Douglas Haig*, p. 176.
18. Major-General J.F.C. Fuller, *Memoirs of an Unconventional Soldier*, pp. 140–2.
19. LHCMA, Kiggell to Major-General Hickie 19.3.16, Kiggell 4/14.
20. Raymond Wable, *Le Maréchal Haig à Montreuil-sur-Mer*, paper presented 24 August 1968 to la Société Académique du Touquet.
21. Kenneth Clark, *Another Part of the Wood*.
22. Sassoon to Esher, 6 May 1917 quoted Lees-Milne, *Life of Esher*, p. 281.
24. Charteris, *At GHQ*, p. 129.
25. Quoted Warner, *Field Marshal Earl Haig*, p. 194–5.
26. See Terraine, *Douglas Haig*, p. 181.
27. NLS acc. 3155/213d.
28. Charteris, *At GHQ*, p. 143.
29. Duncan, *Douglas Haig As I Knew Him*, p. 41.
30. Charteris, *Field Marshal Earl Haig*, p. 218.

Chapter 16

1. P. Simkins, 'Every Man At War' in B. Bond (ed.), *The First World War and Military History*, pp. 304–5. See Sheffield, *The Somme*, p. 73.
2. Duff Cooper, *Haig*, p. 305.
3. Quoted Sixsmith, *Douglas Haig*, p. 166.
4. Charteris, *At GHQ*, p. 168.
5. See Griffith, *British Fighting Methods*, pp. 117, 118.
6. LHCMA, Robertson 4/4/44.
7. Duff Cooper, *Haig*, p. 331.
8. Terraine, *Douglas Haig*, p. 156.
9. See Prior & Wilson, *Command on the Western Front*, p. 112.
10. Gary Sheffield, *Forgotten Victory*, p. 139.
11. See Sheffield, *The Somme*, p. 72–3.
12. Robertson, *Private to Field-Marshal*, p. 225.
13. Max Egremont, *Under Two Flags*, pp. 47–8.
14. Charteris, *At GHQ*, p. 155.
15. See Prior & Wilson, *Command on the Western Front*, p. 202ff for interesting analysis of 'The Forgotten Battles 15th July to 14th September'.
16. Quoted Prior & Wilson, *Command on the Western Front*, p. 157.
17. See Prior & Wilson, *Command on the Western Front*, p. 157ff.
18. See Sheffield, *Forgotten Victory*, p. 177.
19. Prior & Wilson, *Command on the Western Front*, p. 301.
20. Duncan, *Douglas Haig As I Knew Him*, p. 48.
21. See Sheffield, *Forgotten Victory*, and also Sheffield, *The Somme*, p. 69.
22. See *Psychologische Strategie des Grossen Krieges*, quoted Warner, *Field Marshal Earl Haig*, p. 212.
23. Sheffield, *The Somme*, p. 112.
24. Sheffield, *The Somme*, pp. 160, 168.

25. Woodward, 'Robertson and Haig', p. 67.
26. Quoted Woodward, 'Robertson and Haig', p. 68.
27. The strange underlining is original.
28. LHCMA, Robertson 7/6/51.
29. Holmes, *The Little Field-Marshal*, p. 327.
30. Esher, Journal 29 July 1916, quoted Lees-Milne, *Life of Esher*, p. 292.
31. Robertson, *Private to Field-Marshal*, pp. 281, 283.
32. LHCMA, Robertson 3/3.
33. Joffre, *Memoirs*, ii, 477, quoted Sheffield *The Somme.*

Chapter 17

1. Duff Cooper, *Haig*, Vol. 2, p. 8.
2. Quoted Duff Cooper, *Haig*, Vol. 2, p. 9.
3. Duff Cooper, *Haig*, Vol. 2, p. 2.
4. Quoted Duff Cooper, *Haig*, Vol.2, p. 20.
5. Quoted Duff Cooper, *Haig*, Vol. 2, p. 23.
6. Charteris, *Field-Marshal Earl Haig*, pp. 152–3.
7. See a good study of Northcliffe in Piers Brendon, *Eminent Edwardians*.
8. Churchill, *The World Crisis*, II, p. 1136.
9. Beaverbrook, *Politicians and the War,* p. 95.
10. See Reid, *To Arras 1917.*
11. LHCMA, Kiggell 5/2.
12. Berthier, quoted Spears, *Prelude to Victory*, Appendix IX.
13. Memorandum of conversation between Curzon and Stamfordam, 4th March 1917 (Royal Archives), quoted Grigg, *Lloyd George, War Leader 1916–1918*, p. 41.
14. Arthur, *Lord Haig*, p. 114.
15. Hankey, *The Supreme Command*, p. 616.
16. Hankey, *The Supreme Command*, p. 616.
17. Sir Edward Spears, *Prelude to Victory*, Appendices.
18. Quoted Nicolson, *King George V* (paperback edition), p. 400.
19. LHCMA Robertson 7/7/10.
20. LHCMA, Robertson 7/7/11.
21. British Legion *Journal*, Memorial Issue, p. 236.
22. Quoted Duff Cooper, *Haig*, Vol. 2, p. 57.
23. LHCMA, Robertson to Haig 6 March 1917 – Robertson 7/7/11.
24. Quoted Sixsmith, *Douglas Haig*, p. 127.
25. Hankey, *The Supreme Command*, p. 618.
26. LHCMA, Liddell Hart 11/1935/107.
27. R. Storrs, *The Memoirs of Sir Ronald Storrs* (1937 reprinted (New York) 1972), p. 270.
28. See Charles Williams, *Pétain*, (London, Little, Brown, 2005)
29. Diary 12 May 1917, quoted John Grigg, *Lloyd George, War Leader,* p. 97.
30. Egremont, *Under Two Flags,* pp. 57–8.

Chapter 18

1. LHCMA, Kiggell 1/46.
2. Hankey, *The Supreme Command*, p. 677.
3. Gibbs, *The Realities of War* pp. 389–90, quoted Powell, *Plumer*, p. 155.
4. Royal Archives W38/83, quoted Powell, *Plumer*, p. 89.
5. Anthony Eden, *Another World 1897–1907*, p. 124, quoted Powell, *Plumer*, p. 137.
6. Gibbs, *Realities of War*, p. 47.
7. Quoted Collier, *Brasshat*, p. 283.
8. Quoted Peter Simkins, 'Haig & the Army Commanders', in Bond & Cave, *Haig: Reappraisal*, p. 81.
9. Terraine, *Douglas Haig*, p. 336.
10. See Ian Malcolm Brown, *Logistics on the Western Front*.
11. Hankey, *The Supreme Command*, p. 684.
12. LHCMA, Robertson Note 26/3/17 – Robertson 4/6/2.
13. *War Memoirs*, pp. 2157–8.
14. Charteris, *At GHQ*, p. 234.
15. LHCMA, Kiggell 2/4.

Chapter 19

1. Churchill, *The World Crisis*, II, pp. 1211–12.
2. Terraine, *Douglas Haig*, p. 337.
3. Lady Haig, *The Man I Knew*, p. 293.
4. Charteris, *Field-Marshal Earl Haig*, p. 273.
5. See Sheffield, *Forgotten Victory*.
6. Charteris, *At GHQ*, p. 241.
7. *Spectator* 17 January 1958.
8. See John Hussey, 'The Flanders Battleground and the Weather' in P.H. Liddle (ed.), *Passchendaele in Perspective, The Third Battle of Ypres*, p. 140ff.
9. Hankey, *Diary*, 8 August 1917.
10. LHCMA, Kiggell/3/9.
11. See Gary Sheffield, *Forgotten Victory*.
12. Grigg, *Lloyd George, War Leader*, p. 260.
13. Churchill, *The World Crisis*, II, pp. 1212–13.
14. LHCMA, K/2/5.
15. See Terraine, *Douglas Haig*, note to p. 363.
16. See Robin Prior and Trevor Wilson, *Passchendaele, The Untold Story*, Yale *Nota Bene* edition, p. 202.
17. Duncan, *Douglas Haig As I Knew Him*, p. 65.
18. See Geoffrey Till, 'Passchendaele: the Maritime Dimension' in Liddle, *Passchendaele in Perspective*, p. 73ff.
19. Egremont, *Under Two Flags*, p. 69.
20. Quoted Collier, *Brasshat*, pp. 285–6.
21. Terraine, *Douglas Haig*, footnote pp. 363–4.

22. Esher, *Journals & Letters of Reginald Viscount Esher*.

23. Robertson, *Private to Field-Marshal*, p. 329.

24. See Griffith, *British Fighting Methods*, p. 37.

25. See David Jordan and Gary Sheffield, 'Douglas Haig: Military Luddite or Airpower Advocate?', DHF *Records*, 2003, p. 22ff.

26. Charteris, *At GHQ*, p. 273.

27. Charteris, *Field-Marshal Earl Haig*, note pp. 287–8.

28. Charteris, *At GHQ*, p. 94.

29. Lady Haig, *The Man I Knew*, p. 221.

30. Churchill, *Great Contemporaries* (1941 edition), p. 190.

Chapter 20

1. Charteris, *Field-Marshal Earl Haig*, p. 294.

2. Hankey, *The Supreme Command*, p. 705.

3. Hankey, *The Supreme Command*, p. 739.

4. Quoted in David R. Woodward, *Lloyd George and the Generals*, pp. 174–5.

5. See John Hussey, 'The British Divisional Reorganisation in February 1918', in *Stand To!* No. 45, January 1996, p. 12ff.

6. See Duff Cooper, *Haig*, pp. 208–9.

7. Churchill, *Great Contemporaries* (1941 edition), p. 192.

8. Churchill, *Great Contemporaries* (1941 edition), p. 191.

9. Grigg, *Lloyd George, War Leader*, p. 221.

10. See Robin Prior and Trevor Wilson, *The Somme*, p. 12ff.

11. Prior & Wilson, *The Somme*, p. 285ff.

12. Robert Blake (ed.), *The Private Papers of Douglas Haig 1914–1919*, introduction p. 39.

13. Hankey, *The Supreme Command*, p. 575

14. Harold Nicolson, *King George V*, paperback edition, pp. 422–3.

15. Beaverbrook, *Men and Power*, p. 324.

16. Quoted Terraine, *Douglas Haig*, pp. 386–7.

17. LHCMA, K 1/59.

18. Esher, *Journals & Letters*, IV, p. 179.

19. Robertson, *Private to Field-Marshal*, p. 255.

20. Beaverbrook, *Men and Power*, p. 53.

21. It is difficult to imagine George VI having such a conversation with his ministers.

22. Beaverbrook, *Men and Power*, p. 211.

23. Churchill, *The World Crisis*, II, p. 1261.

24. Hankey, *The Supreme Command*, pp. 775–6.

25. See Robertson, *Private to Field-Marshal*, p. 330ff.

Chapter 21

1. Churchill, *The World Crisis*, II, p. 1279ff.

2. 'Record of a Conference held at the Commander-in-Chief's House at 7 p.m. on 23 March 1918', WO.158/72.

3. To Clive on 18 April 1918, PRO, and in a *Discours* to l'Académie Française in 1931; there is mistake in his speech in relation to the date, but not the time of the meeting at which the hand was stretched out. He may have confused the two meetings, in which case his history of these events is seriously flawed. I do not think that is the case. But I am indebted to John Hussey for allowing me to study a fascinating unpublished note by him, in which he narrates and meticulously analyses the intricate record of the historic meetings and which is supportive of the account contained in the amended Haig diaries. I agree that many aspects of the episode are not free from doubt.

4. See, in relation to this whole issue, Elizabeth Greenhalgh's very full article, 'Myth & Memory: Sir Douglas Haig and the Imposition of Unified command in March 1918', *Journal of Military History*, 68 (July 2004), p. 771ff.

5. WO.33/920. No. 7734, p. 411.

6. Tim Travers, *How the War was Won*, p. 54.

7. Travers, *How the War was Won*, pp. 66–70, but see Sheffield & Bourne (eds), *Douglas Haig*, p. 9.

8. See Greenhalgh, 'Myth & Memory', fn. p. 800.

9. Quoted Greenhalgh, 'Myth & Memory', p. 810.

10. Greenhalgh, 'Myth & Memory', p. 813.

11. Sixsmith, *Douglas Haig*, p. 157.

12. Keegan, *The First World War*, p. 424.

13. Churchill & Gilbert, *Churchill,* Companion Volume IV, p. 301.

14. Egremont, *Under Two Flags*, p. 77.

15. Duncan, *Douglas Haig As I Knew Him*, p. 120.

16. Churchill, *The World Crisis*, II, p. 1290

17. Churchill, *The World Crisis*, II, p. 1305.

18. Esher, Diary, 30 May 1918, quoted Sommer, *Haldane*, p. 358.

19. Rawlinson, 'Increase in our Offensive Power by additions of machine and Lewis guns', Rawlinson Papers 5201/33/77, NAM, quoted Prior & Wilson, *The Somme*, p. 291.

Chapter 22

1. Paddy Griffith, 'The Extent of Tactical Reform in the British Army', in Griffith (ed.), *British Fighting Methods*, p. 2.

2. Griffith, 'Extent of Tactical Reform', p. 18.

3. See Peter Simkins, 'Co-Stars or Supporting Cast? British Divisions in the "Hundred Days", 1918', in Griffith, (ed.), *British Fighting Methods*, p. 52.

4. In writing this section I have benefited greatly from Gordon Corrigan, *Mud Blood & Poppycock*.

5. Correlli Barnett, Haig Fellow's Address, DHF *Records*, December 2004.

6. The role of British artillery is well reviewed by Jonathan Bailey, 'British Artillery in the Great War,' in Griffith, *British Fighting Methods*, p. 93ff.

7. See Bailey, 'British Artillery in the Great War', p. 41.

8. See Michael Crawshaw, 'The Impact of Technology on the BEF and its Commander', in Bond & Cave, *Haig: Reappraisal*, p. 169.
9. J.M. Bourne, 'Haig and the Historians', Bond & Cave, *Haig: Reappraisal*, p. 6.
10. See Terraine, *To Win a War*, p. 131.
11. Quoted Terraine, *Douglas Haig*, p. 461.
12. See Gary Sheffield and Dan Todman, *Command and Control*.
13. Stephen Badsey, 'Cavalry and the Development of Breakthrough Doctrine', p. 155.
14. Sheffield, *Forgotten Victory*, p. 259, quoting from appendix G to September 1918, W.O. 95/1775, PRO.
15. Terraine, *White Heat*, p. 230.
16. Terraine, *White Heat*, p. 328.
17. General Lawrence wanted to send the cavalry division to exploit successes by the Australians and III Corps.
18. Diary 1 September 1918.
19. NLS acc. 3145/98.
20. Carl Bridge, *Oxford DNB*.
21. Monash, *The Australian Victories in France in 1918*, p. 96.
22. Monash, *Australian Victories*, p. 87.
23. Monash Papers Vol. 2, 4th April 1918, quoted Simkins, 'Co-Stars or Supporting Cast?', p. 54.
24. Peter Simkins, 'Co-Stars or Supporting Cast?', p. 57.
25. Diary 25 October 1918.
26. Christopher Pugsley, Haig Fellow's Address, DHF *Records*, 2003, p. 6, and see John A. English and Bruce I. Gudmundsson, *On Infantry* (Westport: Praeger, 1994), pp. 18–31.
27. Wilson, *Life & Diaries*, II, p. 126.
28. Hankey, *The Supreme Command*, p. 849.
29. Churchill, *Great Contemporaries* (1941 edition), p. 190.
30. For an excellent detailed account of the fighting at this stage, see Terraine, *To Win a War*, p. 161ff.
31. Diary, 30 September 1918.
32. Hankey, *The Supreme Command*, p. 849.

Chapter 23

1. Churchill, *Great Contemporaries* (1941 edition), p. 185.
2. Esher to Haig, 10 November 1918 (Sassoon papers), quoted Lees-Milne, *Life of Esher*, p. 320.
3. See Sommer, *Haldane*, pp. 367–70.
4. Lady Haig, *The Man I Knew*, p. 250.
5. Haig, *My Father's Son*, p. 14.
6. Haig, *My Father's Son*, p. 15.
7. Haig, *My Father's Son*, p. 107.
8. Haig, *My Father's Son*, pp. 29–30.
9. Beaverbrook, *Men and Power*, p. xviii.

10. Quoted Holmes, *The Little Field-Marshal,* p. 359.
11. Haig, *My Father's Son,* p. 19.
12. Quoted Robin Prior, *Churchill's World Crisis as History,* p. 261.
13. Quoted Robin Prior, *Churchill's World Crisis,* p. 263.
14. Denis Winter, 'Haig's Fictions,' in *Haig's Command: A Reassessment* (London: Viking, 1991).
15. See John Hussey, 'A Contemporary Record or Post-War Fabrication? The Authenticity of the Haig Diaries for 1914', *Stand To! The Journal of the Western Front Association,* 42 (1995), pp. 29–31 and 'Sir Douglas Haig's Diary and Despatches – Dating and Censorship', *Stand To!,* 47 (1996), pp. 19–20. See also Sheffield & Bourne, *Douglas Haig,* pp. 2–10.
16. LHCMA, Edmonds I/4/39a-b.
17. LHCMA, Edmonds 2/4/39b-c.
18. LHCMA, Lady Haig to Edmonds 17/1/30, Edmonds 2/4/62.
19. LHCMA, Edmonds 2/4/65a-b.
20. LHCMA, Edmonds 2/4/67b.
21. LHCMA, Charteris 5/30/32.
22. Charteris, *Field-Marshal Earl Haig,* pp. 373–4.
23. Norman F. Dixon, *On the Psychology of Military Incompetence* p. 387.
24. Niall Barr and Gary Sheffield, 'Douglas Haig, The Common Soldier and The British Legion', in Bond & Cave, *Haig: Reappraisal,* p. 229ff.
25. British Legion *Journal,* Memorial p. 256.
26. *John Bull,* 11 November 1922.
27. British Legion *Journal,* Memorial Issue.
28. NLS acc. 3155/248a.
29. NLS acc. 3155/248a.
30. Duncan, *Douglas Haig As I Knew Him,* p. 98.

SELECT BIBLIOGRAPHY

Arthur, G., *Lord Haig* (London, Heinemann, 1933)

Barnett, C., *The Swordbearers: Studies in Supreme Command in the First World War* (London, Eyre & Spottiswoode, 1963)

———, *Britain and Her Army* (London, Allen Lane, 1970)

Baynes, J., *Far From a Donkey. The Life of General Ivor Maxse* (London, Brassey's, 1995)

Beaverbrook W.M.A., (Lord Beaverbrook), *Politicians and the War 1914-16* (London, Thornton Butterworth, 1928)

——— *Men And Power* (London, Hutchinson, 1956)

Beckett, I.F.W., *Johnnie Gough VC* (London, Tom Donovan, 1989)

——— *The Judgement of History: Sir Horace Smith-Dorrien, Lord French and 1914* (London, Tom Donovan, 1993)

——— *The Great War 1914–18* (Harlow, Longman 2001)

——— & K. Simpson (eds), *A Nation in Arms* (Manchester, Manchester University Press, 1985)

Bidwell, S. & D. Graham, *Fire-Power: British Army Weapons and Theories of War 1904-1945* (London, Allen & Unwin, 1982)

Blake, R., (ed), *The Private Papers of Douglas Haig, 1914–1919* (London, Eyre & Spottiswoode, 1952)

Bond, B., *Victorian Military Campaigns* (London, Hutchinson, 1967)

——— *The Victorian Army and The Staff College, 1854–1914* (London, Eyre Methuen, 1972)

——— (ed.), *The First World War and British Military History* (Oxford, Clarendon Press, 1991)

——— & N. Cave (eds), *Haig: A Reappraisal 70 Years On* (London, Leo Cooper, 1999)

——— and others *Look To Your Front: Studies in the First World War* (Staplehurst, Spellmount, 1999)

——— *The Unquiet Western Front: Britain's Role in Literature and History* (Cambridge, Cambridge University Press, 2002)

Boraston, J.H., *Sir Douglas Haig's Despatches* (London, Dent, 1919)

Bourne, J.M., *Britain and the Great War* (London, Edward Arnold, 1989)
———— P. Liddle & I. Whitehead (eds), *The Great World War 1914–45* (2v. London, HarperCollins, 2000)
British Legion *Journal*, Earl Haig Memorial Issue (London, 1926)
Brown, Ian Malcolm, *British Logistics on the Western Front* (Westport, CT, Praeger, 1998)
Callwell, C.E., *Field-Marshal Sir Henry Wilson. His Life and Diaries* (London, Cassell, 1927)
Carrington, C.E., *Soldier from the Wars Returning* (London, Hutchinson, 1965)
Charteris, J., *Field-Marshal Earl Haig* (London, Cassell, 1929)
———— *At GHQ* (London, Cassell, 1931)
———— *Haig* (London, Duckworth, 1933)
Childers, E., *The War and the Arme Blanche* (London, Edward Arnold, 1910)
Churchill, W.S., *The River War* (London, Longmans, Green & Co, 1899)
———— *The World Crisis, 1911–18* (London, Thornton Butterworth, 1931)
———— *Great Contemporaries* (London, Thornton Butterworth, 1937)
Clark, A., *The Donkeys* (London, Hutchinson, 1961)
Collier, B., *Brasshat, A Biography of Field-Marshal Sir Henry Wilson, 1864–1922* (London, Secker & Warburg, 1961)
Cruttwell, C.R.M.F., *A History of the Great War* (Oxford, Clarendon Press, 1934)
Davidson, J., *Haig: Master of the Field* (London, Peter Nevill, 1953)
De Groot, G.J., *Douglas Haig 1861–1928* (London, Unwin-Hyman, 1988)
Dewar, G.A.B., & J.H. Boraston, *Sir Douglas Haig's Command 1915–1918* (2v. London, Constable, 1922)
Duff Cooper, A., *Haig* (2v. London, Faber and Faber, 1935–6)
Duncan, G.S., *Douglas Haig As I Knew Him* (London, Allen and Unwin, 1966)
Edmonds, J.E., (ed. and comp.), *Military Operations, France and Belgium* (14v. London, HMSO/Macmillan, 1922-47)
Egremont, M., *Under Two Flags, the Life of Major-General Sir Edward Spears* (London, Weidenfeld & Nicolson, 1997)
Esher, R.B.B., (Viscount Esher), *Journals and Letters* (London, Nicholson & Watson, 1934–8)
Falls, C.B., *The First World War* (London, Longmans, 1960)
Farrar-Hockley, A., *Goughie: The Life of General Sir Hubert Gough* (London, Hart-Davis, MacGibbon, 1975)
Foch, F., *Memoirs* (London, Heinemann, 1931)
Fraser, P., *Lord Esher* (London, Hart-Davis, MacGibbon, 1973)
French, D., *British Strategy and War Aims, 1914–1916* (London, Allen & Unwin 1986)
———— *The Strategy of the Lloyd George Coalition, 1916-18* (Oxford, Clarendon Press, 1995)
———— & B. Holden Reid (eds), *The British General Staff: Reform and Innovation* (London, F. Cass, 2002)
French, J.D.P., (Viscount French), *1914* (London, Constable, 1919)
Fuller, J.G., *Troop Morale and Popular Culture in the British and Dominion Armies 1914-1918* (Oxford, Clarendon Press, 1991)
Gilbert, M., *First World War* (London, Weidenfeld & Nicolson, 1994)

Gough, H., *Fifth Army* (London, Hodder & Stoughton, 1931)

Grieves, K., *Sir Eric Geddes* (Manchester, Manchester University Press, 1989)

Griffith, P., *Battle Tactics of the Western Front* (London, Yale University Press, 1994)

————— (ed.), *British Fighting Methods in the Great War* (London, F. Cass, 1996)

Grigg, J., *Lloyd George: From Peace to War 1912–16* (London, Methuen, 1985)

Grigg, J., *Lloyd George: War Leader 1916–1918* (London, Allen Lane, 2002)

Haig, D., *Cavalry Studies* (London, Hugh Rees, 1907)

Haig, The Countess, *Douglas Haig: His Letters And Diaries* (Unpublished, Moray Press, 1934)

Haig, The Countess, *The Man I Knew* (Edinburgh & London, The Moray Press, 1936)

Haig, The Earl, *My Father's Son* (London, Leo Cooper, 2000)

Hankey, M.P.A., (Lord Hankey), *The Supreme Command 1914–1918* (London, George Allen & Unwin, 1961)

Harington, C., *Plumer of Messines* (London, John Murray, 1935)

Harris, J.P. & N. Barr, *Amiens to the Armistice* (London, Brassey's, 1998)

Henderson, G.F.R., *Stonewall Jackson and The American Civil War* (London, Longmans, Green & Co, 1898)

Hindenburg, P. von, *Out of My Life* (London, Cassell, 1920)

Holmes, R., *The Little Field-Marshal: Sir John French* (London, Cape, 1981)

Hyatt, A.M.J., *General Sir Arthur Currie* (Toronto, University of Toronto Press, 1987)

Jeffrey, K., *The Military Correspondence of Field-Marshal Sir Henry Wilson 1918–1922* (London, Bodley Head for Army Records Society, 1985)

Judd, D. & K. Surridge, *The Boer War* (London, John Murray, 2002)

Keegan, J., *The First World War* (London, Hutchinson, 1998)

Kennedy, P. M., *The War Plans of the Great Powers, 1880–1914* (London, Allen & Unwin, 1979)

Kitchen, M., *The German Offensives of 1918* (Stroud, Tempus, 2001)

Laffin, J., *British Butchers and Bunglers of World War One* (Gloucester, Sutton, 1988)

Lees-Milne, J., *The Enigmatic Edwardian: The Life of Reginald, Second Viscount Esher* (London, Sidgwick & Jackson, 1986)

Liddell Hart, B.H., *History of the First World War* (London, Cassell, 1934)

Liddle, P.H., (ed.), *Passchendaele in Perspective, The Third Battle of Ypres* (London, Pen & Sword, 1997)

Lloyd George, D., (Earl Lloyd George): *War Memoirs* (London, Ivor Nicholson & Watson, 1933–6)

Ludendorff, E. von, *My War Memories, 1914–1918* (London, Hutchinson, 1919)

Magnus, P.M., *Kitchener, Portrait of an Imperialist* (London, John Murray, 1958)

————— *King Edward VII* (London, John Murray, 1964)

Marshall-Cornwall, J., *Haig as Military Commander* (London, Batsford, 1973)

Maurice, F.B., *Rawlinson of Trent* (London, Cassell, 1928)

Middlebrook, M., *The First Day on the Somme* (London, Allen Lane, 1971)

————— *The Kaiser's Battle* (London, Allen Lane, 1978)

Nicolls, J., *Cheerful Sacrifice: The Battle of Arras 1917* (London, Leo Cooper, 1990)

Nicolson, H.G., *King George V: His Life and Reign* (London, Constable, 1952)

Pakenham, T., *The Boer War* (London, Macdonald, 1982)

Pedersen, P.A., *Monash as Military Commander* (Melbourne, Melbourne University Press, 1992)

Philpott, W.J., *Anglo-French Relations and Strategy on the Western Front, 1914–18* (London, Macmillan, 1996)

Pitt, B.W., *1918, The Last Act* (London, Cassell, 1962)

Pollock, J., *Kitchener* (comprising *The Road to Omdurman* and *Saviour of the Nation*) (London, Constable, 2001)

Powell, G., *Plumer: The Soldiers' General* (London, Leo Cooper, 1990)

Prior, R. & T. Wilson, *Command on the Western Front: The Military Career of Sir Henry Rawlinson* (Oxford, Blackwell, 1992)

———— *Passchendaele, The Untold Story* (New Haven, Yale University Press, 1996)

———— *The Somme* (New Haven/London, Yale University Press, 2005)

Reid, W., *To Arras 1917, A Volunteer's Odyssey* (East Linton, Tuckwell Press, 2003)

Repington, C. à C., *The First World War 1914–1918: A Personal Experience* (London, Constable, 1920)

Robertson, W.R., *From Private to Field-Marshal* (London, Constable, 1921)

———— *Soldiers and Statesmen 1914–1918* (London, Cassell, 1926)

Russell, J., *The Haigs of Bemersyde: A Family History* (Edinburgh, Blackwood, 1881)

Secrett, T., *Twenty-Five years with Earl Haig* (London, Jarrolds, 1929)

Sheffield, G., *Leadership in the Trenches: Officer-Man Relations, Morale and Discipline in the British Army in the Era of the Great War* (London, Macmillan, 2000)

———— *Forgotten Victory: The First World War – Myths and Realities* (London, Headline, 2001)

———— *The Somme* (London, Cassell, 2003)

———— (ed.), *Leadership and Command: The Anglo-American Military Experience since 1861* (London, Brassey's, 1997)

———— & J. Bourne (eds), *Douglas Haig: War Diaries And Letters, 1914–1918* (London, Weidenfeld & Nicolson, 2005)

———— & D. Todman (eds), *Command and Control on the Western Front 1914–1918: The British Experience* (Staplehurst, Spellmount, 2004)

Simkins, P., *Kitchener's Army* (Manchester, Manchester University Press, 1988)

Simpson, A., *The Evolution of Victory* (London, Tom Donovan, 1995)

Sixsmith, E.K.G., *Douglas Haig* (London, Weidenfeld & Nicolson, 1976)

Sommer, D., *Haldane of Cloan, His Life And Times, 1856–1928* (London, George Allen & Unwin, 1960)

Spears, E.L., *Prelude to Victory* (London, Jonathan Cape, 1939)

Strachan, H., *The Politics of the British Army* (Oxford, Clarendon Press, 1997)

———— (ed.), *The Oxford Illustrated History of the First World War* (Oxford, Oxford University Press, 1998)

Terraine, J., *Douglas Haig, The Educated Soldier* (London, Hutchinson, 1963)

———— *The Western Front 1914–1918* (London, Hutchinson, 1964)

———— *To Win a War: 1918* (London, Sidgwick & Jackson, 1978)

———— *The Smoke and the Fire. Myths and Anti-Myths of War 1861-1945* (London, Sidgwick & Jackson, 1980)

Travers, T., *The Killing Ground* (London, Allen & Unwin, 1987)

———— *How The War Was Won* (London, Routledge, 1992)

Tschuppik, K., *Ludendorff: The Tragedy of a Specialist* (London, Allen & Unwin, 1932)

Turner J., (ed.), *Britain and the First World War* (London, Unwin-Hyman, 1988)

Warner, P., *Kitchener: The Man behind the Legend* (London, Hamilton, 1985)

———— *Field-Marshal Earl Haig* (London, Bodley Head, 1991)

Der Weltkrieg, 1914 Bis 1918 (2v. Berlin, Mitler and Sohn, 1929–36)

Williams, J., *Byng of Vimy* (London, Leo Cooper, 1983)

Wilson, T., *The Myriad Faces of War* (Cambridge, Polity Press, 1988)

Winter, D., *Haig's Command: A Reassessment* (London, Viking, 1991)

Winterbottom, D., *Henry Newbolt and the Spirit of Clifton* (Bristol, Redcliffe, 1986)

John Percival, The Great Educator (Bristol, Bristol Branch of the Historical Association, 1993)

Wolff, L., *In Flanders Fields: The 1917 Campaign* (New York, Viking, 1958)

Woodward, D.R., *Lloyd George and the Generals* (Newark, NJ, University of Delaware Press, 1983)

———— *Field-Marshal Sir William Robertson* (Westport, CT, & London, Praeger, 1998)

———— (ed.), *The Military Correspondence of Field-Marshal Sir William Robertson, Chief Imperial General Staff, December 1915-February 1918* (London, Bodley Head for Army Records Society, 1989)

INDEX

Index note: *passim* after an entry indicates scattered references through a page range. Where a relationship, such as 'sister' is given after a person's entry, this is their relationship to Douglas Haig.

BIRLINN LTD (incorporating John Donald and Polygon) is
one of Scotland's leading publishers with over four hundred
titles in print. Should you wish to be put on our catalogue
mailing list **contact**:

Catalogue Request
Birlinn Ltd
West Newington House
10 Newington Road
Edinburgh EH9 1QS
Scotland, UK

Tel: + 44 (0) 131 668 4371
Fax: + 44 (0) 131 668 4466
e-mail: info@birlinn.co.uk

Postage and packing is free within the UK. For overseas orders,
postage and packing (airmail) will be charged at 30% of the
total order value.

For more information, or to order online, visit our website at
www.birlinn.co.uk

Birlinn *Limited*
IMPRINTS: JOHN DONALD · POLYGON